The Islamic Enlightenment

Also by Christopher de Bellaigue

Patriot of Persia

Rebel Land

In the Rose Garden of the Martyrs

The Struggle for Iran

The Islamic Enlightenment

*The modern struggle between
faith and reason*

CHRISTOPHER DE
BELLAIGUE

THE BODLEY HEAD
LONDON

3 5 7 9 10 8 6 4

The Bodley Head, an imprint of Vintage,
20 Vauxhall Bridge Road,
London SW1V 2SA

The Bodley Head is part of the Penguin Random House group of companies whose
addresses can be found at global.penguinrandomhouse.com.

Penguin
Random House
UK

First published by The Bodley Head in 2017

www.penguin.co.uk/vintage

A CIP catalogue record for this book is available from the British Library

ISBN 9781847922410 (hardback)
ISBN 9781847922427 (trade paperback)

Printed and bound by Clays Ltd, St Ives plc

Penguin Random House is committed to a sustainable future for our business,
our readers and our planet. This book is made from Forest Stewardship
Council® certified paper.

For Diana Rodney

Contents

Introduction

At Lowood School for girls, in the reign of King George III of England, an ill-used, orphaned teacher called Jane Eyre lies abed thinking about her future.

'I have served here eight years; now all I want is to serve elsewhere. Can I not get so much of my own will? Is not the thing feasible? Yes – yes – the end is not so difficult; if only I had brain active enough to ferret out the means of attaining it.'

I sat up in bed by way of arousing this sad brain: it was a chilly night; I covered my shoulders with a shawl, and then I proceeded to think again with all my might.

'What do I want? A new place, in a new house, amongst new faces, under new circumstances ... How do people do to get a new place? They apply to friends, I suppose: I have no friends. There are many others who have no friends, who must look for themselves and be their own helpers; and what is their resource?'

I could not tell: nothing answered me; I then ordered my brain to find a response, and quickly ... as I lay down it came quietly and naturally to my mind:– 'Those who want situations advertise; you must advertise in the —shire Herald.'

'How? I know nothing about advertising.'

Replies rose smooth and prompt now:–

'You must inclose the advertisement and the money to pay for it under a cover directed to the Editor of the Herald; you must put it, the first opportunity you have, into the post at Lowton; answers must be addressed to J. E. at the post-office there: you can go and inquire in about a week after you send the letter, if any are come, and act accordingly.'

This sleepless hour is the corner that Jane Eyre turns in order to fall into the arms of Mr Rochester, for her decision to place an advertisement in the county newspaper will lead to her moving many miles from Lowood and taking up a new position, as governess of Mr Rochester's ward at Thornfield Hall. The passage here determines the path that a much loved novel will follow, and yet it is possible to think of it in a bigger, socially more significant way: as an avenue into a new world.

Jane's urges need no introduction: variety and movement are what she seeks, and the education she has received is her means of achieving it, for the instruction she has received at one of a burgeoning number of English girls' schools has not only lent purpose to an excellent mind, but also raised her above any sense of inadequacy. Jane is independent of spirit and this will allow her to be independent of means. Jane Eyre is modern.

Her modernity extends to the rational way she sees the world and her place in it. Jane is a Christian but in her hour of indecision she does not finger a wooden cross or leverage the Gospels – far less seek signs in the stars. Faith guides and gives her strength in the moral and emotional crises of her life; however, in times of functional dilemma – when she is in search of the 'clear practical form' that will set her fluttering brain to rest – Jane interrogates not God but Jane.

And yet, for Jane to see her scheme to its conclusion, she needs the help of certain features of modern England. Without the provincial newspaper, the post office and finally, when it comes to making the journey to Thornfield Hall, a wheeled conveyance trundling along one of the turnpike roads, safe enough for a woman to take on her own, she will be able to do nothing.

Perhaps more important than any of these things, Jane will need society to agree that she is sovereign over her own destiny – an unmarried woman free to climb aboard a post-chaise and go wherever she pleases, at no risk to her reputation.

Now I want to take up this picture of Georgian England and put it into a quite different setting. Imagine that the Jane Eyre of Charlotte Brontë's novel has been transposed to a non-European situation. By the standards of nineteenth-century globalisation this new environment is not very distant – to get there merely involves crossing the Mediterranean. There one meets the close sibling of the Judaeo-

Christian world inhabited by Jane, a civilisation built on the third and most recent of the Hebraic monotheisms and influenced by Greek patterns of thought.

This is the civilisation of Islam. How would this civilisation have dealt with Jane Eyre and the vistas of personal fulfilment preventing her from closing her eyes at night? Would it approve or wrinkle its nose? Would Islam 'get' Jane Eyre?

Were I able to answer this question in the affirmative, it is likely that you would not be holding this book, or you would be holding a very different book. Islamic civilisation in the first decades of the nineteenth century would neither have appreciated nor understood Jane Eyre, because it hadn't the wherewithal to do so.

First consider the vehicle by which Muslim audiences would have met her: the printed book. This would have been a non-starter at the time in which Jane Eyre is set, because almost four centuries after Gutenberg revolutionised intellectual and religious life in Europe with the invention of movable type, the printing press continued to be regarded by Islam as an unwelcome and alien innovation, and had not been admitted to general use. Then there was the matter of translating Brontë's prose into the local languages. The number of Turkish, Arabic and Persian speakers who knew good English was minuscule and there was no market in the Middle East for translated works from abroad.

Even if these constraints had been somehow overcome, and the trusty copyists were induced to inscribe large quantities of a translated Jane Eyre, audiences would have remained tiny for another reason. The latest scholarship puts the literacy rate in Turkey, Egypt and Iran – the three most important intellectual and political points in the region – at roughly 3 per cent at the turn of the nineteenth century, compared to more than 68 per cent for men and 43 per cent for women in England. In Amsterdam, the world's capital of literacy at the time, the figures were 85 per cent and 64 per cent respectively. There can be no reading public when no one can read.

Still, ploughing doggedly on, supposing we could wave aside these considerations and imagine that through public storytellers large numbers of Muslims were exposed to the life and times of Jane Eyre, what would their reaction have been? The notion of newspapers and a postal service would have caused bemusement in lands where neither existed, no less than the fantasy of wheeled traffic between towns. Then there was the moral Pandora's box opened by Jane's behaviour. It was scandalous that a heroine should gad about the country without a chaperone, fall in love with one man, attract the attentions of another – and after this wanton display be presented by the author as a model of virtue.

The very systems of society were completely different in Jane's England: where was the harem, the protected, female-only sanctum within the family, and why did Mr Rochester not have slaves? And don't even mention Mr Rochester's dissipated female guests at Thornfield Hall, playing airs on the fortepiano and riding horses and showing off their bosom and long flowing hair.

Perhaps the kindest thing that could have been said about the plot of *Jane Eyre* is that it illustrated the superiority of Muslim doctrine. Under Muslim law Mr Rochester would have been able to take Jane as his second wife (being permitted a maximum of four) and he would have been able to save what remained of her virtue without all that nonsense about the madwoman in the attic.

In short, from the perspective of a Muslim at the beginning of the nineteenth century, the character of Jane Eyre was a rank impossibility accessible to almost no one and the story of her life so preposterous as to approach derangement.

★

> With the invention of the steamship, possible destinations multiplied in number. Getting around became easier. Following that, with railways, travel became easier still. In the same way that travel was accelerated through this means, so was communication, by means of the telegraph. News that would have taken a year to arrive from a distant land now took an hour. The world was poured into a different mould.

In this paragraph from 1891, the Turkish woman of letters Fatma Aliye conveyed the immensity of the technological changes that had been agitating and inspiring the Ottoman Empire over the preceding decades. Her last sentence is deliciously unresolved: the meaning of life and the onus of interpreting it trickle from the certain past to a future that is soft and impressionable. It's all so different from Aliye's rigid and compartmentalised childhood in the 1860s, with the secluded and rarefied world inhabited by Aliye – daughter of a renowned Ottoman grandee – seemingly designed to maintain distinctions.

Aliye went into purdah aged fifteen, was married off four years later and learned French in secret in order not to outrage her mother, for whom the infidel tongue was a flag of apostasy. But no one – not even the frowning and despotic sultan, Abdulhamid II – could stop modernity, and the effect of the inventions that were seeping into the empire was to increase the sovereignty and autonomy of the individual. What Aliye wrote in seclusion the newly embraced institution of the press enabled her to diffuse among a rapidly expanding audience of literate Ottomans that was coming into existence thanks to the spread of education. Fatma Aliye's was a distinctive voice in the young universe of newspapers in Turkish; she wrote on girls' education and kicked against the stock male denigration of women. Her early literary output appeared under pseudonyms such as 'a woman', and when she eventually summoned the courage to publish novels under her own name, cynics of both sexes attributed them to her father or her brother.

The Brontë sisters had also published under pseudonyms – male-sounding ones in their case – because they had doubted whether anyone would want to read the work of unknown young women from Yorkshire. Strange to say, similar questions concerning the capacity of women would shortly be raised half a world away in Istanbul, where as early as 1869 a contributor to one of the new women's magazines, the weekly *Terakki-i-Muhadderat* ('Muslim Women's Progress'), declared irately, 'men were not made to serve women any more than women were made to be kept by men … are we not capable of gaining knowledge and dexterity? What is the difference between our legs, eyes and brains – and theirs? Are we not humans? Is it only our different sex that has condemned us to this condition? No one possessed of common sense accepts this.' As the Ottoman Empire modernised over the nineteenth century the world view of a growing number of assertive Turkish women grew substantially closer to that of their Western counterparts – to the point where the story of a young woman like Jane Eyre, taking decisions for herself, falling in love, making her living, making her way, wasn't so outlandish after all.

One of the things that make the life of Fatma Aliye so poignant is the productive relationship she had with the changing world around her. She was a true modern, formed by modernisation and forming it back again; and she advanced without fear into the new and dangerous fields of women's rights and public opinion.

Among her best-known works is a novel comprising letters by upper-class women speaking of their lives and their loves, a storyline that would have been nonsensical without an Ottoman postal service to draw on – this had been established in 1840. Aliye wrote about women who discussed philosophy with strange men aboard the steamships that plied the Bosporus dividing historic Istanbul from Asia; this service that had been introduced to great acclaim in 1854.

Fatma Aliye assumed the same philanthropic functions as many prominent women in the West, setting up a charity to help the families of soldiers who had fallen in the 1897 war between Turkey and Greece. Her works were translated into French and Arabic, and she was honoured with inclusion in the Women's Library of the World's Fair, in Chicago, in 1893. She spent her declining years pursuing her errant younger daughter Zubeyda, who had to her mother's chagrin converted to Catholicism and taken holy orders at Notre-Dame de Paris. In this lugubrious quest Aliye travelled around Europe – a Muslim woman alone (or with another of her daughters) in an infidel land. For a woman of her background to exercise this degree of autonomy would have been unthinkable in her youth. To travel to France and there hold intercourse with the natives would have been considered defiling of her morals, and she would have been shunned on her return. No longer.

What are we to make of the statement by Zubeyda that her mother had been 'haunted' by the question of the 'equality of the sexes in society and the struggle to achieve it'? In the Turkey of Fatma Aliye's childhood there had been no question of 'equality of the sexes'. There had been no 'struggle'. Now there were both.

We do not have to rely on a novel like *Jane Eyre* to have an idea of the strides that were made by women in the Western world in the early decades of the nineteenth century. Many history books and biographies have been written about women educating themselves and entering the workplace while a constellation of laws and attitudes changed around them. On the other hand, the story of their later Muslim counterparts – the story of Fatma Aliye, so to speak – is much less known in the West, and this cannot simply be ascribed to the natural inclination of people to interest themselves in stories close to home. Nor does this blind spot in the Western historical understanding relate solely to Muslim women; the West has traditionally refused to see in any aspect of Muslim culture and life the possibility – indeed, the inevitability – of regeneration and modernity. This black spot has existed for hundreds of years, but recently it has got bigger and darker. It dissuades us from trying to understand the past, encouraging us, instead, to go off on tangents, enter blind alleys and credit the claims of demagogues and simplifiers. It is an impediment to a balanced and coherent vision of world history.

In an era when a great many atrocities have been committed in the name of Islam, our ability to appraise Muslim civilisation has been impaired by a historical fallacy propagated by triumphalist Western historians, politicians and commentators, as well as some renegade Muslims who have turned on the religion of their births. These people are united in demanding that the religion of Muhammad re-examine its place and conscience in the modern world. Islam, they say, should subject itself to the same intellectual and social transformations that the West experienced from the fifteenth to the nineteenth centuries, and which laid the foundation for contemporary society. Islam needs its Enlightenment. Islam needs a Reformation, a Renaissance and a sense of humour. Muslims should learn to take insults to their prophet in good part and stop looking at their holy book as the literal word of God – just as many adherents of Christianity and Judaism have done.

The idea behind these counsels is a simple one. Internal deficiencies have barred Islamic civilisation from a number of indispensable rites of passage, without which it will never emerge from its state of backwardness. But these commentaries say more about the people who make them than they do about Islam.

If you think that modern Islamic civilisation has been untouched by reform, it stands to reason that a whole range of characters familiar from your own history will be absent from the pages of the Islamic past: that the world of Islam continues to await its secular philosophers, its feminists, its scientists, its democrats and its revolutionaries. Equally, who can dispute that an Islamic history bereft of intellectual and political reform will inevitably miss out on social and cultural modernity? Politics, education, science, medicine, sex – for more than 1.5 billion Muslims on the earth today (almost a quarter of the world's population) the list of areas that have yet to be smiled on by modernity is literally endless.

It is not necessary to be a specialist of Islamic societies to grasp that this line of thinking leads to a cul-de-sac. It does not escape the attention of inquisitive Westerners who travel to Muslim countries that for the people there the challenge of modernity is the overwhelming fact of their lives. The double imperative of being modern and universal, on the one hand, and adhering to traditional identities of religion, culture and nation, on the other, complicates and enriches everything they do. There is something wonderfully earnest and yet wholly irrelevant about Westerners demanding modernity from people whose lives are drenched in it.

Closer to home it suffices to open our eyes to see millions of people of Muslim faith or origin in the Western world who lead lives that have successfully incorporated the modern values of tolerance, empiricism and the internalisation or dilution of faith. They are not being paid much attention – and why should they be? They do not behead, rampage or try to convert their non-Muslim neighbours. But they are all around us, inhabiting the modern world and regarding themselves as Muslim.

How they arrived at this accommodation is the story I am going to tell, through the lives and adventures of the Muslim pioneers we never thought existed. My intention is to demonstrate that non-Muslims and even some Muslims who urge an Enlightenment on Islam are opening the door on a horse that bolted long ago. Through the characters in this book we will see that for the past two centuries Islam has been going through a pained yet exhilarating transformation – a Reformation, an Enlightenment and an Industrial Revolution all at once. The experience of these places has been one of relentless yet vitalising alteration – of reforms, reactions, innovations, discoveries and betrayals.

But how did we in the West miss all the changes taking place in the Middle East at a time when the region was becoming a more popular destination for travellers, from Herman Melville, who visited Jerusalem in 1857 – finding 'arid rocks' fixing on him 'a cold grey eye' – to Queen Victoria's twenty-year-old son Bertie (the future Edward VII), who toured the Holy Land in 1862 and came alive only when shooting quail on Mount Carmel? The answer is that few Westerners came to the East with very open minds, whoever they were. It is amazing how seldom one comes across a convincing nineteenth-century acknowledgement of the tense, volatile and ultimately highly breakable societies that were forming across the Middle East, or the possibility that their inhabitants constituted a dynamic, even revolutionary force. For those whose idea of progress was so narrow as to consist only of what they themselves had experienced, and who were disposed to see repose and decay in unfamiliar societies, repose and decay was indeed what they saw. Whether viewing the East through the speeding train window of their own countries' progress, or in the hope, as in the case of the Victorian commercial photographer Francis Bedford (who accompanied Bertie in 1862), of monetising the timeless Mount of Olives, it was the default position of Western visitors to deplore, deride or capture – at any rate, to notice – the torpor of the East.

The influence of this prejudice on Western views of history has been remarkable. The tendency to reduce Eastern populations to the status of infants has entrenched the idea that they were passive observers as events unfolded before their uncomprehending eyes. These lesser places were condemned for being soporific, passive and tenacious only in defence of the status quo. Languor and sensuality served as a point of departure for nineteenth-century writers from whom we have inherited the view of the Muslim world as an atoll untouched by the streams of history.

'The old Orient,' Flaubert wrote to a friend from Cairo in 1850 (seven years before publishing *Madame Bovary*, for which he would be arraigned on charges of immorality), in between vivid anatomical descriptions of Egyptian prostitutes, 'is always young because nothing changes. Here the Bible is a picture of life today.' His speculations about Egypt's future revolved not around what the country would do but what others would do to Egypt: 'England will take Egypt, Russia will take Constantinople,' he predicted. In the meantime Flaubert took anyone going.

The orientalist and future colonial administrator Gertrude Bell should have known better – at least she knew the languages of the places she was visiting – but in the 1890s she described Persia as having 'slipped out of the vivid world ... the simplicity of her landscape is the fine simplicity of death'. Recalling the experience of standing outside the gates of Tehran, she wrote, 'you realize what a gulf lies between you. The East looks to itself; it knows nothing of the greater world, of which you are a citizen, asks nothing of you and of your civilization.' Travel writers are different from journalists or historians. It is not so much the facts that interest them as their own pollination of them, and this makes them less than reliable contributors to the record. This is particularly true of the young Italian author and journalist Edmondo De Amicis, who visited Istanbul in the autumn of 1874. De Amicis was already known for the power of his descriptions, and his working method was to take notes prolifically before returning home to work up his written sketches, in the process 'improving' perspectives and compositional details for the final canvas, as it were. His travelogue *Constantinople* features scintillating descriptions of crowds on the Galata Bridge over the Golden Horn, the seraglio ('full of secrets and enticements ... this monstrous palace') and the city's European quarter, where Flaubert's *Madame Bovary* – its scenes of adultery presumably missed by the Turkish censor – is for sale.

In the case of De Amicis, the problems inherent in travel writing were compounded by the fact that he stayed in Istanbul barely a week and was in denial of the superficial nature of his engagement. Yet he was so sure of himself that he wrote *Constantinople* in the present tense, the tense of timelessness, as if all he witnessed had endured beyond his visit – and is carrying on right now, as we read.

De Amicis displayed his romantic sensibility to the fullest extent in his description of the city's dogs. This is a finely wrought Gothic vignette, all grotesque couplings, snarling battle royals and meatballs steeped in poison (distributed by a local doctor so he could get some sleep at night). For all its literary qualities, however, it leaves us in the dark as to the dogs' importance to the story of Istanbul's modernisation.

Not so a discussion of the same question by a Turk, Ibrahim Sinasi, a few years earlier. Born in Istanbul in 1826, Sinasi had received a wide-ranging education and gone on to father modern Turkish journalism, and his approach to the city's flee-ridden curs, rummaging through rubbish, barking, snarling and holding people up with their frenzied turf wars or contests over a scrap of bone, was defiantly unpicturesque. It was utilitarian. Was it right, he asked in his newspaper column, that an 'upright person' be exposed to 'this kind of irrational beast' while going about his business in the city? He recommended that the dogs be removed, if necessary to rural areas where they could be used as guard dogs, before concluding with an aphorism of which Victorian health campaigners would have approved, and which translates loosely as 'cleanliness is next to godliness'. The difference between De Amicis' and Sinasi's treatment of the same issue – the resident who uses Istanbul versus the visitor peering through his opera glasses – is an eloquent warning against taking orientalist writing on trust.

In fact, the East of which these European visitors wrote was, in important ways, very different from the way they depicted it. Their received wisdom and assumptions, which they passed on to their readers in the West, were at best incomplete. The lands of which these and other writers wrote in terms of petrified strata were in fact shaking violently.

That earthquake had been caused by the very same West from which the travel writers came – Frenchmen, Englishmen, Iberians, Italians, who over the course of the eighteenth and nineteenth centuries sensed that the Ottoman Empire was weakening and fanned out to take advantage. Onto North Africa, the Levant, Turkey and Greece stepped these merchants, ambassadors, soldiers of fortune, poets, missionaries and, ultimately, occupiers. For symbolic reasons their first impact is often dated to Napoleon's invasion of Egypt in 1798, when one of the world's most modern societies collided with one of the most backward.

The mass arrival of Westerners in the Muslim world for the first time since the Crusades forced the region's elites – rulers and clerics, administrators and military commanders – to concede that only by adopting Western practices and technologies could they avoid political and economic oblivion. The extraordinarily rapid changes that followed have been neatly summarised by the historian Juan Cole.

In the space of decades intellectuals forsook Ptolemaic for Copernican astronomy ... businessmen formed joint-stock companies (not originally allowed in Islamic law), generals had their armies retrained in new drills and established munitions factories, regional patriotism intensified and prepared the way for nationalism, the population began growing exponentially under the impact of cash cropping and the new medicine, steamboats suddenly plied the Red Sea and the Persian Gulf, and agrarian capitalism and the advent of factories led to new kinds of class conflict.[1]

Change accelerated throughout the nineteenth century. It recognised no boundaries, no red lines. In the middle of the century the Ottoman Sultan declared equality between his Muslim and non-Muslim subjects, the slave trade was outlawed and the segregation of the sexes, symbolised by the harem, went into decline. The sheikhs and mullahs saw their old prerogatives in the law and public morality taken over by an expanding government bureaucracy. Clerical opposition to medical dissection was overcome and theatres of anatomy opened. Culture, too, was transformed, with a surge in non-religious education, and the reform of the Arabic, Turkish and Persian languages – the better to present modern poetry, novels and newspaper articles before the potent new audience of 'public opinion'.

One of the features of innovation in the nineteenth century was its telescoped quality. This compression of events was illustrated by the fact that the movable-type printing press, dating back to the fifteenth century, was introduced almost at the same time as the telegraph, invented in 1844.

For all his unwillingness to recognise change when he saw it, Edmondo De Amicis did in the pages of *Constantinople* proffer one description of violent transformation. The city was, he wrote in this exceptional passage, 'in the process of transformation, composed of ancient cities that are in decay, new cities which emerged yesterday, and other cities now being born; everything is in confusion; on every side can be seen the vestiges of gigantic works, mountains bored through, hills cut down, entire districts levelled to the ground'.

The story of Muslim modernisation has sometimes been depicted as the efforts of a few potentates to enforce alien precepts on resistant populations. Muhammad Ali, Egypt's viceroy for most of the first half of the nineteenth century, and his near contemporary (and nominal sovereign), Turkey's Sultan Mahmud II, were indeed both modernisers and martinets, and there were many instances of popular opposition to what were depicted as godless innovations.

That reforms as fundamental as these gave rise to controversy and opposition is no cause for astonishment. Modernity is even at the best of times a tension, dislocation and agitation, and (in a phrase by Nietzsche that expresses a kaleidoscopic weirdness of perspective) 'a fateful simultaneity of spring and autumn'. But the idea that modernisation had no natural constituency in the Middle East is inconsistent with the very nature of progress, which is generally articulated by a minority, meets with opposition or mirth, and finally overcomes obstacles before taking root. And although the principles of modernity and progress were introduced to the Middle East from the West, the fact that they had originated elsewhere was not in itself an obstacle to their adoption in this new environment. Contradicting assumptions of wilful Muslim backwardness, Islam did not show any more opposition to modernisation than Judaeo-Christian culture had done to its earlier iteration in the West.

As the authentic thrill felt by many of the characters in this book shows, ideas transfer best when they are perceived to be universal and not the business end of a hostile ideology. The sovereignty of the individual, the usefulness of hygiene and the fallibility of a crowned head (to name but three) carry no brand of exclusivity but can be understood by all. In fact, the Muslim world adapted itself to these values and many others much more rapidly than the West had devised them, albeit with changes of emphasis.

Indeed, when they fought back against the new ideas and practices, Muslim conservatives and reactionaries found that they could not stop change, only hope to tame and subdue it. From this came the seductive idea that modernity could be reduced to a limited series of propositions (and gadgets) that would invigorate the body of Islam without changing it. Islam would borrow some of the advances that the Westerners had devised in their off-hours from being disagreeable and impious. These ideas would be grafted onto the surface of things to make them work better, while underneath good old Islam went on, superior to anything the West had to offer. But this cherry-picking approach did not really work. When people bend themselves to thinking of new ways of doing things it becomes hard for them to give up this progressive way of looking at the world. Every practical effort in this direction seems to be handsomely repaid in the form of new conveniences, expanded horizons and a sense of exaltation and self-worth. Progress is its own propaganda.

For an idea of just how much Islamic society changed over the nineteenth century it suffices to look at the evolution that was experienced by Egypt's clerical establishment. In 1798, when Napoleon invaded Egypt, the sheikhs responded to the values and knowledge of the French with revulsion, and the main Egyptian chronicler of the invasion, Abdulrahman al-Jabarti, entreated God to 'strike their tongues with dumbness ... confound their intelligence, and cause their breath to cease'.

A century later on, Jabarti's benighted country had changed to such an extent that its senior judicial authority, the cleric Muhammad Abduh, was an admirer of Darwin, corresponded with Tolstoy (who had been excommunicated from the Russian Orthodox Church) and used his knowledge of European languages to absorb as much as he could of infidel learning.

By the First World War, under the influence of Abduh and others like him, a liberal modernising tendency had emerged strongly in the three intellectual and political centres of the Middle East, Egypt, Turkey and Iran, attracting ideas that in turn spun off into the adjacent regions. Political consciousness had taken flight and political and national aspirations were increasingly aimed at securing that universal symbol of political liberalism, the democratically elected legislature, without which no regime could enjoy legitimacy.

Yet the onset of war and its devastating consequences emboldened opponents of liberalism and progressive thought who began to strike back vigorously. In 1919 the Treaty of Versailles, under which the victorious allies divided the spoils and imposed punitive reparations on Germany, also formalised the end of the Ottoman Empire. The Muslim lands were scattered and many entered the imperialist inventory of Western powers, while following the Second World War, despite a strong current of anti-colonialism, they became a Cold War battleground where the two blocs competed for influence. In the light of this mass subjugation and manipulation, it is not surprising that many Muslims sought political means to express their hatred of the West.

The First World War was a watershed in the history of the Islamic Enlightenment. Before the conflict the region had been moving towards modernity and the adoption of liberal, secular values. Now this movement was arrested and the revulsion of Muslims for colonial exploitation found expression in ideologies of resistance.

The rise of such ideologies and their mutation into violence begs an important question which bears directly on the Islamic Enlightenment. If Islam engaged so successfully with modernity until the First World War, why since then has reactionary revivalism been able to impose itself on ever larger swathes of the Muslim world?

Political Islam – Islamism, properly known – is an ideology that started as an anti-imperialist, and later also an anti-Communist, response to the carve-up of the Middle East, providing an outlet for a common fear among Muslims that the region would fall irrevocably to one or other of these all-absorbing ideologies. Radical Islam grew out of this, an unappetising millennialism that the vast majority of Muslims recognise but dimly. The violence and ignorance that we often see today being glorified by a minority of Muslims should in fact be seen as blowback from the Islamic Enlightenment – a facet, however detestable, of modernity itself.

When dealing with terms that have arisen and acquired currency in the West, such as 'modernity' and 'progress', one should exercise caution. The word 'Enlightenment' is perhaps the trickiest benchmark of all because it comes with its own baggage of self-congratulation. The Enlightenment of Sir Isaac Newton; the *Lumières* of France; the *Aufklärung* of Leibniz; in whatever European language you say it, this word evokes daring and challenge to the status quo on every front, from the Cartesian affirmation of individuality to the majestic opening chords of Mozart's *Magic Flute*, Enlightenment opera par excellence. These brilliant events happened amid more general ferment and change: the rise of education (from which Jane Eyre would benefit), mass printing and public opinion, refinements to hygiene and domestic life (it was during the eighteenth century that the modern nuclear family began to form), worlds discovered (in the heavens; under the microscope), museums going up, feudalism coming down, and preparations being made for the modern apotheosis of the French Revolution.

The Muslims were not the authors of the achievements that we now associate with the Enlightenment. No Istanbul blacksmith discovered movable type. No Muslim Voltaire sniped at the clerics by the Nile. But there is a great difference between accepting that Muslim civilisation did not initiate the Enlightenment and saying that it did not accept its findings or eat of its fruit. This is a big claim to make.

It means that Muslims are either congenitally barred or – even worse – have deliberately cut themselves off from experiences that many consider to be universal. It means that the lands of Islam have remained aloof from science, democracy and the principle of equality. It is a claim that is often heard in today's divided, rebarbative, edgy world, and it is nonsense.

This book argues that an Islamic Enlightenment did indeed take place, under the influence of the West, but finding its own form. The juxtaposition of the two words may look strange, but just as it's possible to speak about the Roman and British empires while understanding that they were different in terms of organisation, ethos and economy, so we can speak about a modern 'Islamic' Enlightenment and not expect it to follow the same path as its European or American equivalent. This term evokes the defeat of dogma by proven knowledge, the demotion of the clergy from their position as arbiters of society and the relegation of religion to the private sphere. It denotes the ascendancy of democratic principles and the emergence of the individual to challenge the collective to which he or she belongs. These ideas are transferable across all systems of belief, and they have also entered the Islamic one. They are at work right now – even if they have suffered rebuffs, as we shall see.

The Western awakening has been documented with great thoroughness, but this is the first book written in English, for the general reader, that documents Islam's transformation. I have drawn on the writings of scholars, journalists and memoirists. Writing in many cases with the poignancy that comes from describing their own experience, they have shown how from the eighteenth century the world of Islam was impelled towards change – not only by Western influences, but also by rumbling, internal needs. The world of Islam was convulsed into a new age.

'World of Islam' – and yet *The Islamic Enlightenment* concentrates on what happened in three places in the Middle East: Egypt, Turkey and Iran. Modernisation did also of course occur elsewhere. The first constitutional monarchy in the Muslim world was established in Tunis in 1861. In India, the Mohammedan Anglo-Oriental College, founded in 1875, became one of the first higher institutions of secular learning in the Muslim world. Yet the phenomena and characters we associate with the great shifts in thought and culture existed in their most influential form in the catalysing territories of Egypt, Turkey and Iran. Just as the heart of Islam looks to Mecca, for the nineteenth and most of the twentieth century the brain of Islam looked to Cairo, Istanbul and Tehran. It was in these three dynamic and turbulent loci that modernisation, social change and revolution took place – at first in lunges that happened concurrently but more or less independently, and then as a grand interlocked transformation that altered the Muslim world.

This gradual unification of different endeavours is reflected in the structure of this book, which begins with geographically delineated parts – Cairo, Istanbul and Tehran – before dovetailing in Chapter 4, 'Vortex', which deals with the furious social changes that took place over the nineteenth century, and Chapter 5, 'Nation', which addresses the rise of the modern state. The final chapter, 'Counter-Enlightenment', describes the challenge to these trends that was witnessed after World War I.

A new era opened in Islamic history in the 1980s when this book closes. Iran's revolution of 1979 twinned Islamic militancy with regime change and altered the terms of Islam's political engagement. When in 1981 Egypt's President Sadat was assassinated by his own soldiers, it was a triumph for *takfiri* Islamism, which declares impious or unjust Muslims to be deserving of death and is the basic precept behind many of today's militant groups. Turkey also embarked on a new path in 1980 when the military took over the country. The dictatorship of the military led indirectly – and inadvertently – to an electable Islamism that brought the AK Party of Recep Tayyip Erdogan to power in 2002.

These developments took place in the context of a strengthening internationalist jihad against the Soviets in Afghanistan, which in turn permitted Saudi Arabia, the jihad's sponsor, to muscle onto the world stage and challenge Iran, Turkey and Egypt as the motors of development in the Islamic world. Indeed, with the internationalisation of global Islamic causes, from the Afghan, Algerian and Bosnian wars to the emergence of transnational Islamic players such as al-Qaeda, established geographical centres of ideology and politics ceded ground to a global, virtual market of religious barter and exchange. No longer would Cairo, Istanbul and Tehran exercise leadership to the Islamic world, in thought, politics, and society. The very idea of a geographical physical centre exercising leadership over Islamic thought became outmoded and quaint. The relatively peaceful coexistence of Sunnis and Shias collapsed after the Western invasions of Afghanistan and Iraq in the 2000s, with Saudi Arabia and Iran squaring up against each other to divide a devastated landscape. In 2011 the Arab Spring briefly promised a revival of Enlightenment values before succumbing to further violence and totalitarianism, exacerbated by mass migration and environmental disaster.

This later chapter of Muslim history – since 1980 – has been much pored over and written about. The origins of its present-day predicament lie further back.

The modernisation of the Islamic world was sparked by the collision of Western and Islamic civilisations that accompanied Napoleon's invasion of Egypt in 1798. However, in order to understand how it came into being it is going to be necessary to return briefly to the more distant Islamic past, which provided fuel and inspiration for many of the arguments that came later on.

Roughly understood, the earlier history of Islam's heartlands can be divided into a period of glory, prosperity and achievement lasting over half a millennium following Islam's expansion out of its Arabian birthplace after Muhammad's death in 632, and a later period of insularity and strengthening conservatism that made the region acutely vulnerable to the West. The religion's medieval pomp proved its ability to generate ideas and lead the wider cause of human development; its later decline suggested the opposite. What should happen for Islam to rediscover its vital spirit? Would it need to open to the world or protect itself from it? These were the questions that nineteenth- and twentieth-century reformers asked again and again as they tried to find the right formula, and for guidance they reached back into their own past.

Central to the Muslims' ambivalent feelings towards Western innovation was the idea that they, not the Westerners, enjoyed God's favour. God had created Islam last of the Abrahamic faiths, not to complement Christianity, but to extinguish it, and it was naturally assumed that once Islam had been introduced there would be no further necessity for Christianity or Judaism.

For hundreds of years after Islam's foundation there seemed to be good reason for the *umma*, or community of believers, to consider themselves history's victors. Divine partiality fertilising human genius was the only way to explain Islam's miraculous expansion after 632, when it burst out of the Arabian peninsula, seized huge territories from Byzantium and ended Iran's 400-year-old Sassanian Empire. In the name of Islam arose new empires, first in Damascus under the Ummayad dynasty, then, from the middle of the eighth century, in Baghdad under the Abbasids. Expansion continued deep into Africa, Iberia and China. Islam went from being an embattled desert cult to the dominant force over the known world.

In 732 its troops came close to making Europe Muslim. Had the Battle of Poitiers been won by the Caliph, and not the Franks, as the Enlightenment historian Edward Gibbon later wrote, 'the interpretation of the Qoran would now be taught in the schools of Oxford, and her pulpits might demonstrate to a circumcised people the sanctity and truth of the revelation of Muhammad'. The German historian Hans Delbrück exulted that 'there was no more important battle in the history of the world'.

After Poitiers the Muslim and Christian polities were more or less established in their respective parts of Eurasia, and for much of the next millennium they pushed and yanked in the most prolonged clash of civilisations since the ancient Greeks and Romans grappled with the Persians. But there was no doubt that the political, military and moral balance was tipped in the Muslims' favour. Nowhere better illustrated Islam's refulgence than Abbasid Baghdad, which for some two hundred years had a claim to be the capital of the civilised world. Conceived in the mid-eighth century by the caliph Mansur, drawing in not only Arabs but also Persians and Aramaic-speaking Jews and Christians, the polis on the Tigris was the centre of an administration that united East and West for the first time since Alexander the Great. The Abbasid dominion was belted by writ, commerce and intellectual trade routes thousands of miles long. At the same time, willing to be marked by others, Islam under the Abbasids took on the taste and knowledge of others.

In the ninth century envoys sent out by the Abbasids traversed the known world and brought back Indian mathematical treatises, theories of Iranian statecraft and the models for that affable literary mongrel, the *Thousand and One Nights*. Most significantly, from Byzantium the caliph's men carried virtually the entire extant corpus of Greek written culture.

Informed by these cultural treasures, Muslims began to make their own contributions to human knowledge – not only in Abbasid territories, but also in a halo of principalities around. At the turn of the ninth century the astronomer al-Khwarizmi popularised the use of numerals and in time confounded Western scholars with his extraordinarily advanced star tables. One hundred years later the pinhole camera was first used in experiments by the Basran al-Haytham. In the early tenth century the physician al-Razi discovered the difference between measles and smallpox; the study of algebra – from the Arabic *al-jabr*, meaning 'restoration' – was advanced by his fellow Iranian Omar Khayyám, who also composed a manifesto for hedonists, the famous quatrains. At the other end of the Muslim world, Andalusia – a breakaway emirate that occupied much of today's Spain and Portugal – scored highly in agronomy, introducing the aubergine, watermelon, spinach and the hard wheat that is now regarded as indispensable for the best linguine. All the while, across its varied dominions, Islam fused with its environment to create an aesthetic culture of sophistication and beauty, excelling in architecture, textiles, ceramics and metallurgy.

So dynamic were some of the Muslim centres of learning in the golden age of Islam, so permitting of the unfettered exercise of the rational mind, that the Englishman Adelard of Bath, who spent the early decades of the twelfth century absorbing Arab knowledge while travelling in the Mediterranean, thumbed his nose at his benighted compatriots. 'I have learned one thing from my Arab masters,' he wrote, 'with reason as my guide, but you another: you follow a halter, being enthralled by a picture of authority. For what else can authority be called but a halter?'[2]

The achievements of classical Islamic civilisation – and the chasm between it and the generally retrograde Christian world, where learning had stagnated and knowledge was lost after the fall of the Roman Empire – would both haunt and inspire the modernisers who came to the fore in the nineteenth century. The process was further complicated by the fact that Islamic government, commerce and art had developed in tandem with the religious sciences and other, secular approaches to knowledge. A divide went up between the theological and the philosophical traditions – between faith and reason – and along this line the Islamic Enlightenment would be fought.

The Prophet had left behind a path for Muslims to follow – the sharia, whose raw materials were the Quran, the hadiths, or sayings of the Prophet, and the sunna, the record of his actions and example. The sharia provided rules that men and women should observe if they were to please God, but if it was to become a proper legal system, it would need to be elaborated by the religious authorities, the *ulema* (literally, 'those who know'), and schools of law were founded in order to achieve this.

The early Muslims had not given much thought to the philosophical question of their place in relation to the divinity, nor that of God to the cosmos. The Abbasids began to fix this. The translations they produced of classical Greek texts enabled literate Muslims to reflect with the ancients on the nature and mechanics of the universe and the methods of God.

In the eighth century a group called the Mutazilites argued for free will over fatalism and quoted Quranic verses showing God's displeasure at an inactive mind. According to one such verse, 'the worst of creatures for Allah are the deaf and dumb, those who will not reason'. The Mutazilites also came out against anthropomorphism – the idea that God has human attributes – and maintained that the Quran was not co-eternal with God, but had been created.

The arguments were speculative and provided an impetus to further speculation. Some learned *faylasufs* (a corruption of the Greek *philosophos*, meaning philosopher) went so far as to question the validity of specific religious truths – the miracle of prophethood, even the sharia itself. They saw divine laws as a useful if unrewarding means of sanding humanity's rough edges, yet inferior to the rounded conception of virtue to which they had access. Some of the most daring thinkers in the Islamic world now argued that these paths should be mapped by reason and experience. So it was with Ibn Sina, known in the West as Avicenna. Beautiful, captivating, peripatetic, he spent the first decades of the eleventh century being welcomed like a young Mozart into the courts of Persia, curing a king who thought he was a cow and writing his medical treatise, the *Canon*. He set down a famous 'proof' of the existence of God, which travelled into Europe where it survived until the Enlightenment. Convinced of the existence of God, he nonetheless exempted himself from the pettier divine restrictions, drinking a cup of wine every day on the grounds that it rallied him for further study and observing the five daily prayers not because it was the wish of the Almighty, but because it improved his concentration.

For all their elitism, the sages, artists and administrators of Islam's golden age created a culture that managed to be both one and many, with the centrifugal forces of tribe and ethnicity counteracted by the single, polar truth of God's last miracle. All human achievements were to the glory of God, but the industry, discernment and innovation that went into them were owned by man. Nor did classical Arab civilisation push the idea, beloved of later 'fundamentalists', that only things that had existed in the Prophet's time could be considered authentically Islamic. There had been no dome, no Sanskrit wisdom, no rose bower in the Prophet's Arabia, and mature Islamic civilisation made room for them all.

Unsurprisingly, not everyone was happy with this ecumenical, progressive approach to life, and a rival current, literalist and moralistic, argued that the speculation of the *faylasufs* was precisely what the Quran sought to prevent. Since humans could not understand God, the best way of approaching him was in the spirit of *bila kayf*, or 'without asking how'. This phrase was popularised in the tenth century by Ab'ul Hassan al-Ashari, a theologian from Basra, who, having started his career as a Mutazilite later became its opponent, arguing 'we believe that God has created everything by bidding it simply to be, as he says: "Indeed, when we will a thing, our only utterance is: be, and it comes to be."'

Although the Mutazilites were persecuted in the late ninth century, their legacy endured. They had encouraged speculation to an unprecedented degree and even their opponents were forced to recognise *kalam* – the discussion of religion on the basis of rational criteria – as a discipline in their schools. In the nineteenth and twentieth centuries Islam's reformers would often be accused of Mutazilism, just as their critics quoted a leading opponent of philosophy, the jurist Ahmad Ibn Hanbal, whose belief that God's will must be discovered through the hadiths led to him memorising as many as

25,000 of them. The division between fundamentalism and philosophy was being established in the ninth century.

From our twenty-first-century perspective it is evident that decline began even as Islamic civilisation bloomed. In the tenth century the Muslim world began to split, with Sunnis and Shias consolidating into rival states that fought each other. For a time it seemed as though the minority Shia might actually capture the Arab world, but the toppling of the Shia Fatimid caliphate in Cairo in 1171 by Saladdin established Sunnism as the dominant force. With the rise of the Safavid dynasty on the Persian plateau in the 1500s, Iranian Muslims disassociated themselves decisively from their Sunni co-religionists, and Iran became the Shia state it remains today.

External threats also slowed Muslim creativity. The Crusades beginning at the end of the eleventh century were interpreted as a sign of God's displeasure. The thirteenth century saw the *reconquista* of Muslim Spain at one end of the Islamic world and the Mongol invasions at the other. Unsurprisingly these cataclysms led to doubt, introspection and a desire to win back God's favour. It was this sense of acute danger, remediable only by replacing doubt with certainty, that led to the defeat of Islam's philosophical thinkers at the hands of their purist opponents.

Rationalism was the culprit. This was the contention of one irate refugee from the Mongols, Ahmad Ibn Taymiyya. He became the pre-eminent jurist of the age and slapped down reason in all its forms – even as a means of examining Islamic teaching. The *ulema* should refer only to the Quran, the hadiths and the sunna of the 'ancestors', by which he meant not only the Prophet but also his companions and their immediate successors. The goal of the believer was not to know God but to obey him. With regard to man's capacities, Ibn Taymiyya's vision was notably defensive and pessimistic.

By the time the Renaissance reached its apogee in Western Europe, the speculative tradition in Islam had been downgraded in the colleges and the triumphant strains were centred either on the literal meaning of the word of God, or on esoteric paths to knowing him. The literalist *ulema* and the mystics worked differently. The first sought to narrow the world and the second to escape it. They had a catastrophic cumulative effect on Islamic civilisation, which had been the product of a joyful engagement with the mechanics of the world and the channelling of curiosity into edifices of thought, art and administration. The result was that Islamic civilisation in many of its most vibrant forms slowed before halting completely. The fragile balance between conservatism and innovation, open-mindedness and authenticity, that permits cultures to advance while remaining recognisably themselves, came to an end.

At first this deceleration was concealed by the grandeur of the Ottoman Empire. In 1453, Constantinople, the Byzantine capital, fell to Sultan Mehmed II and became Istanbul; Hagia Sophia, the greatest basilica in Christendom, was turned into a mosque. A century and a half later the empire encompassed the Balkans, the Mediterranean as well as the holy places of Mecca and Medina, besides the Ottoman heartlands of Anatolia and the Caucasus. Yet the Ottoman dynasty is now more associated than any other with the loss of that originality and finesse that the Abbasids and Fatimids had possessed, and it was after observing the Ottomans that Europe came to the conclusion that Islam was a system for throttling human potential. Indeed, the state of the religious sciences in the Ottoman Empire grew suggestive of rigor mortis. Generations of scholars had whittled down the old rival hadith collections to a few supposedly authoritative compendia; the major points of difference between Sunnism's four schools of law had also been thrashed out long ago. The principle of *taqlid*, or emulation of those in religious authority, suffused the religious schools, and the exercise of independent reasoning, *ijtihad*, was no longer considered an acceptable way to determine God's will. With the sharia so authoritatively and exhaustively laid down, to seek the truth in the frail human mind smacked of insolence and folly. The temper in the cloisters and mosques turned against speculation, reason and creativity.

Islam fell victim to the same superstition and defensiveness that had beset much of Europe in medieval times. It was now accepted that Muhammad was sinless and that he had performed various miracles, such as splitting the moon to reveal a star between the two halves. Preachers drew attention to the evils of tobacco, coffee and mathematics; the profane traditions of music, dancing and saint worship, all associated with mysticism, were also denounced from the pulpit. As if to accentuate the faith's isolation, Christians and Jews were forbidden from entering Medina and Mecca. Perhaps most notorious of all, in 1580 the only observatory remaining in the world of Islam, at Galata in Istanbul, was razed on the grounds that it encouraged astrology and had angered God into sending the plague.

Education outside the religious colleges was similarly limited by ignorance and blinkered horizons. The point of going to school in eighteenth-century Egypt was to memorise the Quran. The Quran gave everything that was needed for this life and the next, so the village teacher, while making good use of his palm stick, offered little or nothing in the way of history, geography or natural science. Maths lessons were farmed out to the public weigher in the marketplace, to whom the young men (almost never young women) were sent to learn the rudiments of weights and measures. By the populace at large, alchemy was trusted more fully than chemistry; surgery was performed by barbers between shaves; and the time calculators attached to the great mosques continued to resist the Copernican truth of a heliocentric universe.

In this insular world it was far from certain that curiosity was a virtue, for curiosity released one from the security of seventh-century Arabia. As a modern Cairene has put it, 'no one had ever heard of Burma. No one even knew, or found especially intriguing, where the source of their own Nile was, aside from the fact that it lay far off, deep in the lands where African slaves came from. Of what use would such knowledge be?[3] Although areas of the Middle East had become part of an interconnected world – Egyptian cotton, for instance, was exported through Alexandria to Europe – there was little appreciation that diplomacy, trade and warfare could have an effect beyond a tightly limited ambit. By and large, Ottoman Constantinople considered the French Revolution to be a distant cataclysm of remote interest, and the revolutionaries to be a 'pernicious crew' that destroyed religion and taught lies. It is not thought that the word 'America' appeared in the Persian language until the final years of the eighteenth century.

As Europeans debated furiously the new opinions and proposals that had been generated by the Renaissance, the Reformation and the Enlightenment, Muslims found false refuge in refusing to question the reigning order. There was to be no Turkish Gutenberg. In fact, the printing press had been banned as soon as it appeared on Ottoman shores in the 1490s on the grounds that making the Quran accessible would only enable the ignorant to misinterpret it; later on printing was made a capital crime. A much-used way of batting away doubts and scepticism was to glorify one's own ignorance, approaching the unknowable godhead in the spirit of *bila kayf.* Ab'ul Hassan al-Ashari's little formulation was now in serial overuse, a blissful doctrine of abnegation that was deployed by sheikhs and other figures of authority in response to all kinds of unwelcome questions.

So it was that the civilisation of Islam mouldered and decayed, just as Christendom had after the fall of the Roman Empire. With a few exceptions, by the eighteenth century mainstream Islam had retreated into scholasticism and literalism, with archipelagos of sometimes lunatic mysticism. Of the spirit of enquiry that had animated ninth-century Baghdad, the ecumenists of medieval Andalusia and the ground-breaking astronomy and mathematics of north-eastern Persia, there was little sign.

I

Cairo

The world of Islam was only ready to shed its superiority complex once its supports were revealed to be rotten, but even then these delusions were abandoned only with pain and regret. It came as a shock to a civilisation that had throughout its history retained a vivid sense of its own genius. Over the centuries for Islam the crucial – and reliably flattering – comparison had been with the lands of Christianity, so close geographically and culturally, flowing along the same Abrahamic course, and yet turned into a heinous nullity by such incomprehensible doctrines as the Trinity, transubstantiation and the divine nature of Christ.

To Muslims it seemed only logical, therefore, that so many Christians should find service and solace among them. From Adelard of Bath, extolling Islamic science at the turn of the twelfth century, to the Ottoman admiral Hayreddin Barbarossa, born to Greek parents on Lesbos, whose galleys ruled the Mediterranean in the Age of Discovery, and Robert Sherley, who in 1598 moved from the hop gardens of Kent to become a diplomat for the Persian Shah, the Middle East was full of Christians trying to piggyback on Islam's success.

In 1798 the fiction of Christian deference to Muslim superiority fell away. Napoleon's casual annexation of one of the jewels of the Ottoman Empire laid down more than a military and political challenge. It was an agonising, highly personal affront, presenting Muslims with a choice: should they welcome the new forms of knowledge and organisation represented by the French, or reject these foreign innovations?

The year 1798, wrote the major chronicler of the invasion, Sheikh Abdulrahman al-Jabarti, was the beginning of 'the fierce fights and important incidents; of the momentous mishaps and appalling afflictions, of the multiplication of malice and the acceleration of affairs;

of successive sufferings and turning times; of the inversion of the innate and the elimination of the established; of horrors upon horrors and contradicting conditions; of the perversion of all precepts and the onset of annihilation; of the dominance of destruction and the occurrence of occasions'.

The Egypt that was conquered by Napoleon's soldiers in July 1798 was far from the prosperous and humming powerhouse that had dominated North Africa in the Fatimid heyday in the eleventh century. Egypt was the breadbasket of the Ottoman Empire – to which Sultan Selim I had annexed it in 1517 – and a major supplier of grain and raw cotton to France. Its position on the overland trade route to India gave it much strategic value, even despite the popularity of the sea route round the Cape of Good Hope, But the country was fractured and unproductive. Its population had been in decline since the Middle Ages and at the end of the eighteenth century numbered just 4 million souls (compared to 28 million citizens of France's republic). The province groaned under the rule of the Mamluks, a caste of former slaves who paid tribute to the Ottoman government, known as the Sublime Porte, in return for a free hand to oppress and extort. Thanks to maladministration and huge tax burdens, Egyptians sometimes starved in spite of the country's agricultural riches. As for the fabled city of Cairo, wattle had replaced stone as the chief building material of this former wonder of the medieval world.

Learning was in a particularly dire state. There were just twenty schools in Cairo, compared to seventy-five at the turn of the fifteenth century, while the citadel of the Egyptian intellect, the squalid, arcaded school of al-Azhar, suspected science, despised philosophy, and hadn't produced an original thought in years. Of the world outside Islam – the world of discovery and the Americas, science and the Industrial Revolution – there was a virtual boycott.

This Mediterranean anachronism now collided with the most self-consciously modern society on earth – and its new dynamo, Napoleon. The ambitious Corsican had burnished his reputation by winning notable defeats of the Habsburgs in Italy and Austria, his military brilliance offset by a vast ego and the attention span of an adolescent. Napoleon was not only a general: he was also inspired by the intellectual vigour of the Enlightenment and the transformative potential of the French Revolution. Recently elected to the

Institut de France – then as now the cortex of France's big, fearless brain – he was an accomplished mathematician and keen debater on matters ranging from habitable planets to the interpretation of dreams. He also bought enthusiastically, and with characteristic self-interest, into France's post-revolutionary imperialist doctrine, which would – in the words of his future ally Charles Maurice de Talleyrand – 'set everything in order, within itself and without itself, in the interest of the human species'.

Setting things in order first of all meant teaching the Mamluks how to fight. After putting ashore at Alexandria on 1 July and brushing aside the troubles caused by a disorganised supply train and the soldiers' thirst while heading south, by 21 July Napoleon had led his 25,000 men as far as Embaba, situated opposite Cairo on the Nile's left bank. There they were confronted by a smaller but much fresher Mamluk force.

Tall and imperious in the saddle, gripping their reins between their teeth, a blossom of silken vests and kaftans, the Mamluks at full tilt were an amazing sight – but they were hardly a modern fighting force. Galloping across fields of clover towards the French, they discharged first their carbines, then their pistols – dropping the used weapons to be picked up by their servants – before finally hurling javelins and swinging scimitars at close quarters. In the event, their display was ineffective. The Mamluks' advance was stopped dead by a phenomenon beyond their experience: tightly packed military squares spitting out grapeshot and musket volleys.

'The soldiers fired with such coolness that not a single cartridge was wasted,' one French lieutenant reported, 'waiting until the very instant when the horsemen were about to break our square.'[1] After barely an hour the enemy was routed in an engagement which Napoleon christened the Battle of the Pyramids, whose mysterious forms could be made out through the haze, even if the majority of the French had no idea what they were. The casualty figures – around one thousand Mamluks dead to twenty-nine Frenchmen – spoke of a hideous imbalance of tactics, training and equipment, and Sheikh Jabarti contrasted the efficiency of the infidel with the woeful defenders, who were 'at odds with each other, envious, fearful for their lives and their comforts, immersed in ignorance and self-delusion, arrogant and haughty in their attire and presumptuousness'.[2] The result of the battle, furthermore, did not simply reflect the particular qualities of the two sides. A medieval Eastern army was annihilated by a modern Western one and a proud Islamic capital – *al-Qahira*, 'the victorious' – was lost to the infidel.

In the weeks that followed the Battle of the Pyramids, the French established an administration in Cairo and Napoleon used his usual combination of charm and ruthlessness to bring the city to heel. He invited the leading sheikhs and other notables to join a diwan, or council, to run Egypt under his supervision. Any opposition was quashed and in October he put down a citywide rebellion with exemplary severity. But Napoleon was not satisfied with being an administrator and a pacifier; he was conscious of being part of a great human adventure and cherished a notion that under France's benign tutelage Egypt could be restored to its past glory. Had the French not given liberty to the Americans by helping them in their war of independence? Had he himself not freed Italy from the tyranny of the Habsburgs?

To benefit both sides in the new relationship, Napoleon had brought with him a retinue of scholars who would act in the field of knowledge as his army had acted on the field of battle, pointing to the future and shaming the past. Napoleon saw his savants as the successors of the wise men who had accompanied Alexander the Great on his expeditions to the East; for him the conquest of Egypt was the first stage of an odyssey of colonisation that would end with the expulsion of the British from India. They included Etienne Geoffroy Saint-Hilaire, France's first teacher of zoology; Tancrède Gratet de Dolomieu, the mineralogist after whom the Dolomites are named; and Nicolas-Jacques Conté, a man sufficiently versatile to invent the graphite pencil and devise the first airborne invasion plan (of Britain, by balloon). Another scientist, Etienne-Louis Malus, contrived to catch the plague during his stay in Egypt and then cure himself of it. Malus also discovered the principle of the polarisation of light. They were the products of the French Revolution and they whirred with incredible speed.

Installed in Cairo's pleasure quarter of Azbakiya, in a complex of buildings and gardens centred on the expropriated palace of a local grandee, the Institute of Egypt was a pop-up brains trust in the wilderness. It boasted an aviary, a botanical garden, an observatory, various small museums, as well as workshops for the production of a wide range of scientific tools, from precision instruments to sword blades and microscopic lenses. The savants slept in other houses that had been seized in the vicinity – when they were not out in the field, classifying fish or measuring the Sphinx.

Over the next few months, between pursuing Mamluk rebels, administering Cairo and solacing his mistress Pauline Fourès (whom he had abstracted, David-like, from her soldier husband), Napoleon joined his savants in disputation and bombarded them with questions: on linking the Mediterranean and the Red Sea (he visited Suez and followed the traces of Ramses II's canal as far as was possible); on maximising agricultural yields; on finding a substitute for hops in the making of beer; on stopping contagions. At the same time plans were advanced for a modern infrastructure: hospitals, agricultural colleges, a school for the fine arts. But if Enlightenment innovations were to spread, the leading Egyptians needed to be convinced of their value. And so the institute became the stage for one of the most poignant cultural encounters of modern times.

Jabarti was among the delegation of prominent Egyptians who accepted an invitation to visit the institute shortly after its establishment in August 1798, and it was Jabarti who provided our main account of events. Born in 1753, the sheikh came from an influential family. His father had been grand mufti and one of the country's few scientists worthy of the name, and he himself knew the top *ulema* and government officials. Yet while Jabarti may have been one of his country's leading minds, he was – like the majority of his compatriots – ignorant of the advances that had taken place in Europe. For Jabarti the supreme causal factor in history was God himself, his constant agency arcing over the lesser volitions of men. Pre-Enlightenment Europe had taken a similar view, unifying divine and human history to make a single thread. (Sir Walter Raleigh's *History of the World*, for instance, starts with the biblical Creation and goes on to Philip of Macedon.) But the Enlightenment had severed the worldly from the divine, and to this Jabarti would have found himself as opposed as any *ancien régime* Catholic stick-in-the-mud. Of France's so-called 'Republic' he understood little, only that it had been founded on the presumption that all men are equal before God. 'How can this be,' he asked, 'when God has made some superior to others as is testified by the dwellers in Heavens and on the Earth?'[3]

We can't be sure what Jabarti looked like. He left behind no portrait so we can't tell if his nose was long or snub. This shows us something about the environment he came from. To draw someone's likeness was to approach blasphemy; even pen portraits were considered frivolous. We know that Jabarti was a man of taste and refinement who liked to sit in his garden and write poetry to his friends. But he was also a mainstream cleric who deplored popular departures from strict Islamic doctrine, such as the veneration of saints, and there is no reason to suppose that he rejected other superstitions that were common at the time. The existence of djinns, for example, living alongside human beings and partial to damp, dark places such as latrines and wells, was beyond debate. Dreams were omens and the motion of the stars affected human fortunes. Satan was all around: leaving a Quran lying open was an invitation for him to spit on its pages. When Jabarti described the death of a Sufi divine as removing a talisman that had protected Egyptians, he wrote not poetically, but literally.

Jabarti was one of the first Arabs to realise the significance of the wave of modernity now breaking onto the shore of Islam, and the descriptions he left behind reflect his confusion and wonder in the face of a mysterious force. When he arrived at the Institute of Egypt, the French, who had anticipated a certain competitive spirit on the part of their guests, were well prepared. The sheikh and his companions were shown into the library that had been set up in the confiscated palace – where each researcher observed a studious silence and 'no one disturbs his neighbour'. The savants were all smiles and by way of an ice-breaker they brought Jabarti and his companions 'all kinds of printed books in which there were all sorts of illustrations ... of the countries and regions, animals, birds, plants, histories of the ancients, campaigns of the nations, tales of the prophets including pictures of them, of their miracles and wondrous deeds, the events of their respective peoples'.

Jabarti was immediately captivated, for here were 'such things which baffle the mind', and he described in rapturous terms 'a large book containing the Biography of the Prophet, upon whom be mercy and peace. In this volume they draw his noble picture according to the extent of their knowledge and judgement about him. He is depicted standing upon his feet looking toward Heaven as if menacing all creation. In his right hand is the sword and in his left the Book and around him are his Companions.' There were other pictures, 'of the countries, the coasts, the seas', as well as the Pyramids and, most shocking of all, 'The glorious Quran is translated into their language!' A group of French artists introduced Jabarti to the principle of realism in art. One of them 'did portraits so skilfully that one might say they were in relief and about to speak'.

Every action of the savants seemed designed to impress the visitors, and Napoleon's scientists duly gave a performance in their chemical laboratory lined with bottles. As Jabarti recalled:

> One of the assistants took a flask containing a certain liquid. He poured some of it into an empty glass; then he took another flask and poured another liquid into the same glass; a coloured smoke was emitted, and when this smoke had disappeared, the liquid solidified and acquired a yellowish colour. I touched this solid and found it to be as hard as stone. The same experiment was repeated on other liquids and a blue stone obtained; the third time it was a red stone like a ruby.
>
> Then the assistant took a white powder and put it on an anvil; he struck it with a hammer and there was an immediate and very loud explosion, like a gun; we were startled, which made the assistants laugh ... he showed us an engine inside which there turned a glass, which upon the approach of a foreign body threw out sparks and crackled. If someone touched with one hand something touching the engine, even a wire, and with the other touched the revolving glass, he would receive an instantaneous jolt which crackled the bones of his shoulder and arm ... through this means of communication, a thousand people or more might instantaneously receive the shock.[4]

It wasn't only the sophistication of European knowledge that confounded Jabarti, but also its invasive nature, for the savants recognised no borders between different fields of enquiry; they embraced art and science, history and speculation. From the spinal curvature of a baby crocodile to the grammar of the Quran, the foreigners seemed to catch everything in their net.

No wonder the sheikh was glum when he and his friends left the institute. They had been introduced to phenomena beyond their ken. Electricity, anatomy and the printed word formed no part of Cairene life at the time, and between the lines of his account we sense Jabarti turning over the implications of what he had witnessed. Take, for instance, the French artists' depiction of the Prophet. It was blatant *shirk*, or associationism, which challenged God's monopoly over creation and as such was banned under the sharia. But Jabarti's pious disapproval of portraiture was tempered by his pleasure at seeing the Prophet's handsome features. As for the translation of the Quran into an infidel tongue, it was too astonishing even to process.

In Egypt knowledge had been considered finite and largely the gift of Islam. Now the country had fallen to foreigners whose behaviour and pronouncements confounded these assumptions and suggested they needed to be swept aside as a matter of urgency. In the French scheme of things humanity was promoted from being a grateful recipient of knowledge to an unflagging generator of profound truths. It all implied nothing less than a fundamental reordering of the hierarchy of the world.

Jabarti could not see the usefulness of the sundials that were constructed by the French astronomer Trot. Rather than show the times of the Muslim prayer – like sundials the sheikh's own father had produced and that were now affixed in various mosques – they showed the hour of the day and the sign of the zodiac; useless information, so far as the sheikh could see.[5] He also disapproved of the French naturalists' practice of preserving previously unknown species for further study. Had the Prophet not declared that there were 10,000 kinds of beast above the water and 20,000 kinds of fish below? What was the point of going to all that trouble simply to confirm what was already known, and on far better authority?

'They conducted more experiments as extraordinary as the first,' the sheikh ended his account ruefully, 'and which minds such as ours could neither conceive of nor explain.'

In Jabarti's view, Napoleon's invasion and the chaos it caused in Egypt could only have been the will of God, for as the Quran stated, 'thy lord would never destroy the cities unjustly'. But what exactly was the aberration that God was punishing? Had the Egyptians offended God through a moral lapse or an intellectual one? Why was it that the lands of Islam, which had been favoured with the most sublime secret in God's power to bestow – the revelation of God's will through the Quran – now found themselves benighted and abused?

The differences between Jabarti's approach to knowledge and that of the French come sharply into relief when one compares their respective masterpieces. The Egyptian's literary memorials are his *Marvels of Deeds in Annals and Lives*, a twenty-seven-volume history of Egyptian life between 1688 and 1821, along with two shorter separate accounts of the occupation, while Napoleon's wise men are remembered through their *Description of Egypt*, a vast and magisterial compendium of much that they found in their new colony, which was written up by some 160 scholars and published in Paris in twenty-three volumes between 1809 and 1828.

Jabarti's works and those of the French are unashamedly elite productions, written over the heads of most ordinary people, but that is where the resemblance ends. Between them lies a chasm as wide as any between two works that have been generated at the same moment and in the same place – and ostensibly with the same goal of advancing human knowledge.

The *Marvels of Deeds in Annals and Lives* contains the fullest answer we have to the approach of the savants; it is a hand-on-heart expression of the fear and distaste felt by a natural conservative to events that threaten everything he knows.

This work begins – as Sir Walter Raleigh's did – with God's creation of the world, and while Jabarti avers that history is a useful discipline that 'fixes and transmits knowledge of the condition of diverse peoples and their countries', it is clear that man is the sum only of the qualities that God has chosen to implant in him: the 'sense of justice and injustice'[6] that leads him to yearn for government by an educated and impartial caliph, and his meek submission to an unchanging human hierarchy consisting of the prophets, the *ulema*, the kings and governors, and various lower categories.[7] For a man in Jabarti's position a revolution of the kind that turned France upside down in 1789 is anathema.

Just as he does not understand much of the science he observed in the institute, so France's political language is puzzling to him. The occupiers are forever boasting of their 'liberty' – the Arabic equivalent is *hurriya* – but from this Jabarti grasps only that they aren't slaves. He finds it impossible to appreciate freedom of the political and social kind that the French claim to have established in their nation, while the idea of stretching *hurriya* to mean emancipation from God – atheism – is too horrendous even to consider.

There is much in Jabarti that looks forward to the Muslim puritan of our times, deprecating the corrosive effects of moral licence from abroad. He cannot understand the kind of people who step on carpets in boots that have been in the filth outside and whose other practices include 'spitting and blowing their noses upon the furnishings'.[8] The French do not shave their heads or their pubic hair. The coarser soldiery is not above defecating in the mosques, while Napoleon's quartermaster enjoys reclining on a divan, 'an amber pipe between his lips and a coffee cup on the tray'.[9] The foreigners mix their foods in objectionable compounds. 'Some might even put together in one dish coffee, sugar, arrack, raw eggs, limes, and so on,' Jabarti writes in disgust.'[10] And he entreats God to 'strike their tongues with dumbness ... confound their intelligence, and cause their breath to cease'.[11]

Jabarti condemns the slippage in morals precipitated by the *Armée d'Orient* and denounces the slatternly European women who arrived in its slipstream, the nadir of debauch coming during the annual flood of the Nile, when impressionable Egyptian girls, 'turning their back on all shame, abandoned themselves to their desires without restraint. They boarded boats with the Frenchmen, dressed suggestively and laden with jewels, and delivered themselves day and night to dancing, orgies and song. The local sailors, their heads full of hashish, made all sorts of grimaces and mimicked the French slang, and their unruly cries mixed with the song of the women and the music.'

Some of the hostility that Jabarti evinces towards the French stemmed from the opportunism and insincerity of Napoleon himself. The general's proclamation following the invasion contained encomia to Muhammad and Islam; he later claimed that the Prophet had come to him in a dream. Few of the Egyptian sheikhs were fooled, however, and the head of the diwan, Sheikh Abdullah al-Sharqawi, denounced the occupiers as 'materialist, libertine philosophers ... they deny the Resurrection, and the afterlife, and ... [the] prophets'.[12] The sheikhs were not impressed by those Frenchmen who changed their religion in order to take Muslim wives, among them one of Napoleon's successors as commander-in-chief, the stolid and otherwise unsurprising Jacques – later, Abdullah – Menou. It cost these men nothing to make the Muslim profession of faith, Jabarti sniffed, as they had no religion to forswear in the first place. (The converts were not in the event required to undergo circumcision.)

In stark contrast to Jabarti's accounts, the Frenchmen's *Description of Egypt* does not confess any limit to what humankind can know. On the contrary, it expresses the ambition of a group of people to reveal the entire range of material and social phenomena of a place without reference to divine mystery. The savants elevate curiosity to the noblest of human traits and implicit in their quest is the idea that all facts and phenomena are susceptible to discovery.

A century and a half after the *Description* was published, the Palestinian-American scholar Edward Said would portray it as the foundation document of the pernicious exercise in Western intellectual imperialism that he criticised in his book *Orientalism* (1978). 'To institute new areas of specialisation,' as Said put it, with heavy irony; 'to establish new disciplines; to divide, deploy, schematise, tabulate, index, and record everything in sight (and out of sight)' – this was the ambition of the valiant Frenchmen.

In his condemnation of the *Description*, Said wrote that it reduced Egypt to a department of French learning; and if that is the case, God is a department within a department. The deity appears in the various discussions of Egyptian religious beliefs, illustrations of amulets in the forms of scarab beetles, and insights into the pharaonic cults. Different articles record the practice of visiting tombs; the authors deplore Egyptian fatalism. But the writers of the *Description* neither invoke God nor praise him. They are in no need of his help as they make their contribution to the humanist goal of mortal perfection. God is in the *Description* only because the people that are its subject insist on believing in him.

Nowhere in the *Description* do the various contributors relax their condemnatory stare on Ottoman Egypt, the negligence of its government and the 'absolute obsolescence of science and the arts'.[13] In his preface to this monumental work the mathematician Jean-Baptiste Joseph Fourier regrets that 'the Muslim religion would on no account permit the development of the mind'.[14] On the contrary, the country is 'immersed in barbarism' – and a similar torpor seems to afflict the Egyptian curs, which spend all day lying around in the sun, rousing themselves annually to copulate sadly.[15]

In response to the cultural self-confidence of the Frenchmen, Muslim traditionalists like Jabarti convinced themselves that the West was doomed because of its refusal to accept Islam – the odd flash of ingenuity would certainly not be enough to redeem its essential barrenness. But the sheikh was party to a grossly unequal contest over face, prestige and longevity, and he was forced to concede that some aspects of the invaders were not in fact barbarous at all: they displayed wisdom, good sense, even moral soundness.

One of these surprisingly good aspects of the West was the principle of equality before the law. Its application was demonstrated following Napoleon's abrupt departure from Egypt in August 1799 in order to pursue his political ambitions (he would seize power in the Brumaire coup a few months later). In June 1800 Napoleon's replacement as commander-in chief, the imposing, lion-maned Jean-Baptiste Kléber, was knifed in the heart by a fanatic. 'A man without importance succeeds through perfidy in assassinating the commander of the French,' Jabarti wrote incredulously. 'This man still carries the weapon with which he committed the crime, streaming with the victim's blood. Under such conditions one would expect the French to punish the guilty man and his accomplices immediately after his confession. But no, things happened differently. A court was convened and there was a trial.' The judicial process turned out to be scrupulously fair, with no one disputing the legitimacy of the death sentence that was eventually handed down. Kléber's assassin was executed with a pike rammed up his rectum and his skull was sent to France and put to educational use; it displayed the 'bump of crime and fanaticism'. France, Jabarti remarked in amazement, was a country 'without religion but which obeys the judgement of reason.'[16]

The significance of other French innovations was less clear to Jabarti. Napoleon's simple and unadorned way of life in the field, for example, travelling without a large retinue and mixing easily with his men, suggested a less stratified relationship between the leader and the led than was common among many Muslim rulers. Pre-emption seemed to be a guiding principle of public health, as the French set up a quarantine area and isolated houses affected by the plague. Then there was the curious French insistence on putting important decisions to the vote in the diwan that Napoleon had set up to give his rule a veneer of legitimacy (and which Jabarti went on to join) – 'the majority', the sheikh reported neutrally, 'has the force of the whole'.[17]

For Jabarti, reason could never be an acceptable substitute for revelation as a guide for living. He was sympathetic to the Wahhabi uprising that broke out in 1798 against Ottoman rule in Arabia – a rebellion that looked back to that thirteenth-century scourge of reason, Ibn Taymiyya, in its desire to prune Islam of inauthentic outgrowths and return it to the purity of the Prophet's time. Jabarti's own reforming instincts also lay in what we would nowadays call a fundamentalist direction, but he was writing at a time when terms like 'reform' and 'fundamentalism' were not in currency, and the barriers we imagine to lie between them were far from clear. He called for a restoration of the 'might of Islam' but nowhere do his writings make clear what this meant – perhaps because his thoughts on the subject were confused now that he had witnessed the triumph of Western power and ideas in Egypt.

The troubled emotions that Jabarti harboured with regard to the French would be shared by many others as Western incursions into Muslim lands proliferated over the course of the nineteenth century. Muslims were faced with the pressing question of whether the West should be emulated – indeed, whether it *could* be. In truth, the choice between engaging with Western ideas or looking away turned out to be a false one. Europe never gave the world of Islam the option of looking away.

Disputes soon emerged between those who viewed progress as a universal impulse that had first surged through Europe but was at work elsewhere, and others who argued that Europe had embarked on a trajectory of development on the basis of conditions that were unavailable to Muslims, and that it would be folly to pursue the same goal using the same path. These debates were between progressivism and conservatism, between the embrace of the future and the fear of losing the past, and disputants naturally used Muslim tools, including the Quran and the sharia. Inevitably, in a country where knowledge was monopolised by a single, clerical class, it was this group that produced both the first moderns and the first reactionaries. And perhaps unsurprisingly, given the minuscule size of that Egyptian intelligentsia, the progressive to Jabarti's conservative was the sheikh's own pupil.

The name of this man was Hassan al-Attar, and in later life he would introduce Egypt to unfamiliar sciences and reacquaint it with others that had been lost from sight since medieval times. Attar's journey towards becoming his country's first modern thinker also began – just as Jabarti's had stopped – in the crucible of occupation.

He was born in Cairo in around 1766, and described as 'a good-looking youth ... broad-chested, clear-eyed, of North African origin but wearing Egyptian clothes and speaking with an Egyptian accent'.[18] Attar's father was a humble apothecary and the boy himself worked in the same trade before his brilliance in memorising the Quran without aid won him entry into al-Azhar.

Although he had been admitted to Egypt's stronghold of learning and orthodoxy, however, Attar remained something of an outsider because of his foreign origins and his penchant for louche coffee houses whose clientele recited homoerotic poems. His catholic tastes no doubt disposed him favourably to the Institute of Egypt but Attar was not among the senior sheikhs and other notables who were invited to visit the savants. If he wanted to enter the temple of modern learning, he would have to go and see for himself.

One morning, probably in 1799, Attar set out for the salubrious garden neighbourhood of al-Azbakiya, where the French were billeted. He was nervous because he had heard reports of drunken brawls in the area, yet he was drawn by a strange compulsion, walking 'in confusion ... not knowing what direction or what street to take; I was expecting my own destruction'.

Attar seems to have caught the young savants unawares but they made him feel welcome and the Muslim scholar was soon spellbound.

These youths stood out like suns, vibrating and swaying like bridegrooms; their faces were veiled with beauty and they were tall and handsome like arrows. Their hair was like a banner which an army of lovers would follow, an army vibrating passionately with love ... A youth from among them made me look at a book and we began talking, and I found his Arabic to be free from ungrammatical usages and from barren phraseology and other defects. – ... But what increased my astonishment even more was his love for literature ... he told me that he had translated from Arabic into his own language and that this piece [which he recited] he had decided to memorise ... A passion stirred in me which I had not felt for a long time. And a passion for literature which had once grown stronger, then weaker, was now revived.

The young savant Attar had met was probably R. Raige, who aroused a similar passion in another young sheikh, Ismail al-Khashab, complete with sulphurous verses and nocturnal visits. Raige was sufficiently versed in medieval Islamic learning to quote from the medieval astronomer Nasir al-Din Tusi, whose ingenious double-epicycle device had found its way into Copernicus, as well as from *al-Shifa*, or *The Healing*, the compendium of philosophic and prophetic knowledge that had been compiled by the peripatetic Iranian Avicenna in the first decades of the eleventh century. It was no wonder, therefore, that Attar felt dizzy. The French approach to knowledge was more exhilarating than anything he had known: Raige had not feared to learn the language of another civilisation and adore its books – with no further justification than his delight in learning.

Attar went back to see Raige and his colleagues another afternoon.

When I arrived, they were beginning to let flow the wine, but observing the intensity of my disapproval, they let me look at some books, large and small, some of which I had never seen before, some of which [I knew to be] famous – and all either in the physical sciences or in literature. They put me at my liberty with their astronomical and engineering equipment, then they discussed with me various matters in these fields, writing down what I said ... After that they showed me some verses of poetry ... and asked me to explain their obvious meaning and their hidden meanings.

In Attar's recollection, the verses he extemporised in response to the French,

transported them with joy, astonishing them no end. They began to praise me for it, praising me to excess. Then they urged me to live with them, making me realise this was a real request which they meant. But I kept putting off giving an answer and kept it a secret ... knowing that if I had gone ahead with this matter, rebukes and hostility

would have awaited me as well as the scorn of society. Thus I returned
to my senses and made my decision. May God forgive me for what I
have done.[19]

For Attar's friends and acquaintances, among whom this charged
description would have circulated, its erotic paragraphs were the least
of its shocks; love poetry between men was an established, if risqué,
literary form, and crushes in the cloisters a far from unknown devia-
tion from the crisp austerities of a religious education. Attar here
confessed to worse sins than those of the flesh: a cleric of al-Azhar,
the most venerable school in Islam, was trumpeting his infatuation
with the infidel – in all his parts: his philosophy, his character, and his
unexpected mastery of Arabic culture and literature.

The readiness of the French to immerse themselves in an alien culture
and religion bespoke a cosmopolitanism that Attar had probably never
witnessed. In Egypt at the turn of the nineteenth century, there was
little intellectual intercourse between the two dominant religious communities, those of the Muslims and the Coptic Christians, and society was
further fragmented into Arabic-speaking 'sons of the soil' – called fellahin,
from the Arabic word for 'tiller' – along with Turkish-speaking Mamluks
and other Ottoman minorities. The openness of the savants to outsiders
must have been a revelation to Attar during his relatively lengthy period
of contact with them (perhaps as long as eighteen months), during which
time he gave the Europeans lessons in Arabic and benefited in return
'from the sciences taught in their country'.[20]

The longevity of Attar's attachment to the Frenchmen made his
decision not to accept their invitation to live with them doubly
significant. Had he taken his infatuation to its conclusion, burning
his bridges with his fellow sheikhs and allowing himself to be
adopted by the foreigners as their trophy, he would have been
expelled from al-Azhar and quite possibly been forced into exile; or
his life may have been ended at the hands of some fanatic. In any
case, he would have been unable to take up the task of reconciling
Islam with secular knowledge for which he is remembered today.

Attar's contribution to the Islamic Enlightenment was heavily
dependent on bigger historical forces, however, not the least of which
was France's waning colonial aptitude. Intended to establish a permanent presence, Napoleon's Egyptian colony in fact lasted barely two

years, joining a list of French imperial failures that included India and North America. In August 1801 the *Armée d'Orient* surrendered to a British expeditionary force and under the terms of the capitulation was permitted to go home. The savants whom Jabarti and Attar had known left too, taking with them the raw materials that would eventually form the *Description of Egypt*. The British nabbed the Rosetta Stone, however, which the French had discovered – and went on to decipher, using copies – housing it in that quintessential Enlightenment institution, the British Museum.

The immediate consequence of the occupation was that the Mamluks, the caste of slave-soldiers who had administered Egypt under loose Ottoman suzerainty, were scattered and would never again exercise dominance. The French withdrawal was followed by disorder, with the Ottomans and Europeans continuing to manipulate local proxies in order to achieve comparative advantage. In 1802 the Treaty of Amiens signed by the European powers restored Egypt to Ottoman control and Britain withdrew, but this did not mean that the country reverted to the status quo ante. For all the brevity of the occupation, and the relatively small number of ordinary Egyptians it had affected, the country had been scored indelibly by the nation that most embodied the values of radical modernity.

Attar may have turned down the Frenchmen's invitation to come and live with them, but he was known for having mixed with them, and for Francophiles such as him the atmosphere after the withdrawal was full of recrimination; the former head of the diwan, Sheikh Abdullah al-Sharqawi, now became a vengeful critic of the regime he had served. Lacking patronage, Attar went abroad in 1802. He would spend most of the next thirteen years in Ottoman Syria and Turkey, returning only after Egypt had been set on a new path by a stepchild of the occupation and an advocate of European values.

It may not have seemed so when the *Armée d'Orient* limped out of the country in 1801 but a new Egypt would come into being barely a decade after the French evacuation, learning for itself to 'establish new disciplines; to divide, deploy, schematise, tabulate, index, and record'.

The classic image of the Muslim moderniser is of an irascible man in mess boots; a man impatient with his compatriots' old-fashioned

mode of dress, their fatalism and their backsliding, malingering attitude
to hard work; an impulsive friend of modern values who, while being
perhaps a little rough in his methods, answers with admirable clarity
to the summons of progress. That image took well over a century to
develop and was embodied by figures as diverse as Reza Shah of Iran,
King Amanullah of Afghanistan, and the founder of modern Turkey,
Mustafa Kemal Atatürk.

These coercive modernisers took the same shortcuts. They set up
new, modern institutions but the ethos inside them was not always
modern. Schools and universities; the press, parliament and the courts:
these must not be populated by stuffed animals being shuffled around
but by free creatures moving and behaving as their instincts and culture
decide. But the dictatorial powers of the strong men who ruled Turkey,
Iran or Afghanistan stood in the way of such human autonomy. The
law existed but the courts were 'loyal'. Parliament and the press
followed the ruler's lead. And never was he prepared to relax his grip
on his subjects, because at heart he distrusted them and was impelled
by his desire to hustle them into change with his iron will. Sprees of
purgative violence in the name of progress would achieve what
hundreds of years of slow history had attained in the West. So, modernisation didn't behave so much like an animal deprived of one limb,
and thus able to move forward, only more slowly, but like one lobot-
omised, so that externally everything seemed all right while inside
critical malfunctions were going on.

Several of these autocrats will make an appearance in this book; it
is a disconcerting fact that the story of modernisation in the Muslim
world would be incomplete without them. Competition and rivalry –
both between themselves and between them and the West – spurred
them on, for without the shameful gap that had opened up between
the West and the lands of Islam there would have been little incentive
for Muslim civilisation to put itself through the torture of self-interrogation and cultural disposal that is integral to fundamental renewal.

Reform is rarely undertaken in times of serenity. It's an emergency measure requiring a steady – even severe – hand to see it
through. Individual visionaries, institutions and sometimes entire
social classes may go through eureka moments of great consequence
but for these to add up to lasting change requires a programme:
dedication, planning, legislation. In the Middle East of the nine-

teenth century, furthermore, reform needed to happen rapidly to keep out the European powers that had already turned Egypt into a cockpit for their ambitions and continued to threaten to take over the region.

Egypt's moderniser Muhammad Ali Pasha was an Albanian, possibly of Kurdish origin – the Ottoman world attached less importance to ethnicity than it did to ruthlessness, pluck and piety. Muhammad Ali, it turned out, had the first two but not the last. As the Ottoman Sultan's viceroy in Egypt for almost half a century – from 1805 to 1849 – he packed into this period as many reforms as had been carried out in the country over the previous three hundred years, transforming everything he touched in his haste to establish a powerful, European-style state and thus avoid foreign subjugation.

Born in around 1770 in Ottoman Macedonia, Muhammad Ali started life as a yeoman soldier and tobacco trader. Having proved himself a resourceful banger of rebel heads, in the spring of 1801 he was dispatched across the Mediterranean with four hundred mercenaries to help the British expel the French. The subsequent departure of the *Armée d'Orient* created the kind of power vacuum that someone of Muhammad Ali's dynamism, charm and intuitive grasp of political advantage – he had received no education to speak of – was equipped to fill. Manoeuvring between the Mamluks, the Ottoman authorities and the Europeans, over the next few years this consummate networker made himself vital to everyone, repulsed a second British invasion, and in 1805 hoisted himself into a position of power which left the sultan no choice but to name him governor. He was invested with the ceremonial kaftan by the same Sheikh Abdullah al-Sharqawi who had headed Napoleon's diwan – evidence of the flexibility required of Egypt's senior clergy.

For all Muhammad Ali's nominal dominance of the province, the Mamluks continued to control much of rural Egypt. In March 1811 Muhammad Ali used the pretext of a ceremony of investiture to lure the top Mamluk chieftains into a winding, narrow passage that had been hewn from the rock of the Cairo Citadel, where they were cut down from above by volleys of musketry. Other Mamluks were hunted down in the city, decapitated and their properties looted. The following day Muhammad Ali descended from the citadel to restore order and accept the compliments of Sharqawi.

Control over the abundance of Egypt, with its lush harvests resulting from the perennial saturation of the soil by alluvial minerals carried by the Nile from Abyssinia – the finest of all vegetal manures – seemed to offer the viceroy possibilities both grander and more lucrative than thraldom to the Porte; remaining nominally a vassal of the Sultan, he soon openly defied his authority. With the earlier dominance of woollens and linens as a staple of world trade at an end, cotton was now king, and over his reign Muhammad Ali would turn the Nile Delta into a vast cotton field supplying the power looms of Lancashire. He began by expropriating Mamluk feudal farms and destroying title deeds so the parcels reverted to the state; in 1812 the entire grain crop of Upper Egypt went to Muhammad Ali, who now owned the country's agricultural output and had a monopoly over foreign trade. 'He may cause any one of his subjects to be put to death without the formality of a trial,' wrote the Englishman Edward Lane, who visited Egypt in the late 1820s; 'a simple horizontal motion of his hand is sufficient to imply the sentence of decapitation.'[21]

In order to consolidate and enjoy his domestic mastery, Egypt's new tyrant needed to be able to protect it: and for this – as the Battle of the Pyramids had so baldly demonstrated – he needed a modern military.

It's no coincidence that so many modernising leaders have directed their initial reforming zeal at the armed forces. Muhammad Ali was not the first Muslim leader to see the importance of European military doctrine and technology. In India, the rockets developed in the 1790s by Tipu Sultan of Mysore had inflicted much damage on his British foes, and Tipu had also built battleships with copper bottoms, an idea he had picked up from the French. Closer to home, the only military reverse that Napoleon had suffered in his Middle Eastern campaign had been a defeat at Acre in 1799 at the hands of an experimental modern force raised by Selim III. There was abundant evidence to suggest that Western military prowess could be imitated – even bested.

In 1815 Muhammad Ali used the looting of shops in Cairo by his undisciplined Albanian soldiery as an excuse to begin military reforms of his own. He was helped by a Frenchman called Sève, who was deputed to train the army upstream at Aswan. Sève's qualifications were slender: he called himself a colonel but in fact had not risen higher than corporal in Napoleon's army before being cashiered for insubordination. Nonetheless he distinguished himself early on by facing down his mutinous recruits when they aimed their muskets at him, in this way winning their respect.[22]

There were other challenges. Thousands of slave-soldiers imported from Sudan (an Egyptian province) died from illness. Linguistic havoc ensued, with Sève and his fellow instructors barking orders in French and the cadets refusing in Turkish and Arabic. Then there were the soldiers' families, who followed them from garrison to garrison, sharing their rations and living in filthy shanty towns. But the viceroy and his instructors persevered, forbidding family itinerancy and imposing severe penalties for breaches of discipline. The principles of modern warfare were gradually instilled in this new force, and over the next few years the number of military colleges gradually rose to teach its officers, and with it the range and sophistication of the courses on offer, from fortifications to geometry and mapmaking. Meanwhile Egyptian workshops produced copies of European weapons and a naval flotilla. From Colonel Sève to the English naval fitters who in 1807 equipped the first ship in Muhammad Ali's fleet, the frigate *Africa*, with thirty guns, military technology and expertise had to be imported from Europe. The viceroy came to appreciate the galling dependency of all modernisers on the very Europeans who were in many cases their adversaries.

Having inserted himself into the Ottoman power structure, Muhammad Ali went on to make himself even more indispensable to the sultan by sending armies led by his sons to put down the Wahhabi uprising in Arabia, and by joining Ottoman campaigns against Greek nationalists. Through the 1820s and 30s there were other expansionary campaigns, into Sudan and – treacherously – the sultan's own strongholds of Syria and Anatolia. Their importance was not simply military and economic: the viceroy's modernising army was both a symbol and a catalyst of the new Egypt.

At its apex in the 1830s, Muhammad Ali's army numbered 150,000 men supplied by a tolerably efficient commissariat, and abiding, more or less, by European rules of warfare. In 1832, while campaigning at Homs in Syria, it put an Ottoman force to flight using a Western textbook combination of infantry squares pouring out musketry and grapeshot, a marauding cavalry on the wings, and a final, devastating bayonet charge.[23] Thus, wrote the British traveller and diplomat

Andrew Archibald Paton, the imperial Ottoman army was routed 'by the simplest and most inartificial application of the rules of European warfare', befuddling Turkish commanders who had 'not the most distant idea of its rudiments'. Between the medieval tactics employed by the Mamluks at the Battle of the Pyramids and the integrated modern warfare of Homs, a mere thirty-four years had passed.

The Egypt of the pasha was as imperialistic as any of the European states he wished to emulate, and for a short time his dominions accommodated the Sudan, the Hejaz (including Mecca and Medina), Syria, Palestine and parts of Anatolia. In the 1830s, however, the Sublime Porte and Britain, under its foreign secretary, Lord Palmerston, combined forces and boxed him back to the Nile. Now the tightly centralised bureaucracy Muhammad Ali had set up to administer an empire began to trace the outline of a nation state. The process was helped by the make-up of the army, into which the viceroy had inducted large numbers of fellahin. Culturally an Ottoman and convinced of the superior qualities of the Turkish elite, the viceroy had nonetheless recognised that an army without Arabs would be puny and unrepresentative. Indeed, he adopted an ecumenical attitude towards all ethnic and religious groups in Egypt, placing non-Muslims in important positions (his factotum in matters of commerce and foreign affairs, Boghos Bey, was Armenian) and welcoming all nationalities into the upper tiers of his administrative and commercial apparatus – including Frenchmen who had accompanied Napoleon to Egypt and were out of work following the Battle of Waterloo.

Inevitably, in a system fitted around its founder, Muhammad Ali's Egypt reflected the likes and dislikes of Muhammad Ali. The Frenchman P. N. Hamont, whom the pasha appointed to head Egypt's first school of veterinary medicine, described him as an 'enemy of the foot-draggers ... he wants to see everything, judge everything, he works night and day'.[24] He seemed actuated by the Napoleonic mantra of 'activité, activité, vitesse!' and with similar, explosive results.

The pasha's view of the people was as beasts of burden. He press-ganged labourers for public works: canals which brought a million new acres under cultivation, breakwaters, telegraph lines and textile factories. As many as 20,000 men, women and children are thought to have died while building a single canal in 1819.[25]

If modernisation was to be a success its biggest opponents, the *ulema*, needed to be humbled, and Muhammad Ali did not hesitate to tackle this most vested of interests. Attacking the clerics' power base he confiscated some 600,000 prime acres of land held in religious endowment, or *waqf* – one-fifth of the total land under cultivation in Egypt. His assault marked the end of the alliance between political ruler and sheikhs that had underpinned Muslim government since Abbasid times. The people grumbled, calling him 'infidel', and several rebellions led by sheikhs were ferociously put down. But Muhammad Ali was a master at dividing his enemies, which he accomplished through bribery, flattery and banishment. And as the pious foundations were confiscated, and the fruits of extortion passed from a plethora of tax farmers to the (no less extortionate, but more centralised) national treasury, so the Egyptian government grew in size and wealth, and the prestige of the clergy shrunk correspondingly. The stock figure of the sleek and avaricious priest walking the streets in stately procession gave way to a brutally slimmer sort of divine, standing in rags and reciting the Quran for a few piastres. In the meantime the viceroy sold on his grain at considerable profit to British merchants.

Muhammad Ali's reforms transformed education and the economy, transportation and public health – but not always to the better. A printing press was set up at Bulaq, a suburb of Cairo, which, overriding the objections of *ulema* and scribes, brought out useful volumes including European translations and the classics of Ottoman Turkish. Moreover, for the first time in the Muslim world the Quran was also set in type, and the mufti of Cairo was persuaded to approve this innovation. The fellahin planted some two hundred new plant species on the viceroy's orders and Cairo gained spanking new frontages tracing straight lines down thoroughfares planted with acacia. Women were drafted in to spin yarn according to quotas in the new factories where they worked veiled, constituting probably the earliest industrialised female workforce in the Middle East. Their sisters in the fields were harnessed to turn water pumps and mills in place of oxen that had been requisitioned for military use.[26] Costly rice-separators powered by steam were imported from England, mounted by English workmen on English bricks (although they promptly went silent for lack of spare parts). All Egyptians suffered under the new tax burdens. 'Woe to the peasant or townsman who could not pay his poll-tax,' wrote Andrew Paton, in other respects an admirer of the pasha's 'revolution'; 'he was bastinadoed until it was all acquitted'.[27]

Ruthless and tyrannical though he may have been, the pasha was also an inquisitive, unpretentious man, and foreign visitors to his summer palace in Alexandria, cantilevered, flower-scented, zephyr-kissed Ras al-Tin (Cape of Figs), were liable, if looking in at lunchtime, to be pressed to stay. A traditional building, inspired by the Balkan dwellings of his youth, it rapidly filled with European features like gas lighting, a billiard table and family portraits lining the walls. Seated at table (itself a novelty), surrounded by officials and plied with French wine, the pasha's visitors might find themselves the object of pene-trating questions by their twinkling, impeccably attired host – on whose countenance 'the character of a firm but determined will was indelibly stamped' – about recent developments in European politics or some invention of which he had heard.[28]

Under Muhammad Ali, Alexandria was transformed from the shabby, pestiferous roadstead onto which Napoleon had come ashore in 1798 into a modern entrepôt capable of handling Egypt's burgeoning cotton exports, equipped with shipbuilding yard, naval base and two hundred ships at anchor at any one time, and linked by a new canal to the western branch of the Nile. Alexandria became one of the most mixed cities on the Mediterranean, where Arabs, Turks, Circassians, Mamluks, Copts, Armenians, Maltese, Greeks, Italians and European exiles ranging from Saint-Simonians to penniless Polish noblemen mixed on terms of easy – if occasionally testy – familiarity. Being in Alexandria allowed the pasha to keep an eye on his business affairs and to monitor the progress of his new arsenal, a veritable 'Levantine Tower of Babel' employing every kind of Mediterranean half-breed as well as conscripts, prisoners and imported navvies from Toulon. In the words of an admiring Russian consul, every day 'we see some fresh innovation in the European style destined for the improvement of the city or for public utility' – the introduction of European numerals in the local administration; a multinational tribunal of commerce; a public health office established in the French Consulate.[29]

Among the harassed inhabitants of a rapidly changing Egypt there was understandable perplexity at the pace and purpose of Muhammad Ali's attempts at modernisation. 'The majority of the inhabitants,' sighed the veterinarian Hamont, 'don't believe in the science of the doctors, or of the vets … barbers are still preferred by the mass of the local people, and the blacksmiths given more credence than vets.'[30]

A despairing resistance was mounted by those who found themselves on the receiving end of Muhammad Ali's improvements. Some of the fellahin put rat's bane in their eyes to avoid conscription (those caught were condemned to forced labour in perpetuity and their female accomplices were executed), while others fled the land to look for work in ever expanding Cairo and Alexandria. When vaccinations against smallpox were carried out by force (the fellahin hid their families to avoid the needle) unrest followed which was forcefully put down. In the 1820s Edward Lane was shocked to hear Egyptians speak of massacring all Europeans as a warning to Muhammad Ali to desist from further innovation.[31, 32]

Yet the pasha's reforms did not touch everyone and the majority of Egyptians continued to live as they had for millennia, tilling the land along the banks of the Nile and its delta, placating the same God, trusting in the same sheikhs, but conscious, however disagreeably, that the only ever-present feature of the new Egypt was change itself.

The dissonances were jarring and the people doubtful, but it would be wrong to regard the modernisation of Egypt as a potentate's folly that was doomed to fail. Such a notion, promoted by 'progressives' and 'reactionaries' alike, rides on the fallacy that modernity is a fixed value to which there are only two possible responses – acceptance or rejection in favour of the status quo. The common experience of people who discover new values and technologies – or who are, as in the case of the Egyptian fellahin, discovered by them – is a jolting disaggregation that nonetheless has an internal logic and compulsion. Modernity can no more be rejected than a call can be unheard, and once it is out and quivers in the air, people will inevitably take it up. It can be distorted, or muffled, or countered with a roar, but never is the world the same after the airing of a modern idea as it was before.

Muhammad Ali Pasha modernised Egypt in the limited, contradictory manner of the visionary autocrat. He made no attempt to diffuse a spirit of irreverence, scepticism and individual empowerment that was – no less than howitzers and injections – essential to any Enlightenment project. He was the kind of man who went to the trouble of educating young mandarins and then snapped at them when they dared make a suggestion. 'It is I who govern,' the viceroy rebuked one such forward individual, and he ordered him to go away and translate foreign military manuals.

The country he aimed to create was strong, dynamic and forward-looking – but not particularly reflective or inventive. This is not to say that no development of ideas took place during his reign, or that the world view of the country's elite was stagnant and hidebound as it had been in the time of the Mamluks; on the contrary, in a pattern that we will encounter repeatedly in our review of the Middle East's reforming dictators, much intellectual activity took place beneath the surface, and new attitudes were discovered towards knowledge, the individual and God.

Few people contributed more to Egypt's process of intellectual liberation during Muhammad Ali's rule than the peripatetic scholar Hassan al-Attar. Having quit Cairo for fear that his Francophilia would get him into trouble, Attar spent the first decade of the viceroy's reign on the other side of the Mediterranean, where anonymity allowed him to pursue the interests that were close to his heart. It was in the libraries of Istanbul and Damascus – like Cairo, cities redolent of past Islamic glory – that Attar built on the secular revelations he had received in the Institute of Egypt. In the process he not only added to his store of knowledge but also drew important lessons about the universality of knowledge itself, both of which would be useful after his return home in 1813.

If the Istanbul that became Attar's temporary home in 1802 appeared more favourable than Mamluk Cairo to such an endeavour, this was largely thanks to the intellectual curiosity of Sultan Selim III. Here, making friends among scholars who threw their libraries open to him, Attar began studying a wider range of disciplines than would have been respectable in Egypt, including astronomy, logic and mysticism.[33] At the same time he acquainted himself with those strands of classical Islamic learning that al-Azhar had rejected as poisoned by philosophy and speculation. From the astronomy of Nasir al-Din Tusi to Avicenna's metaphysics and the sociological observations of the innovative four-teenth-century Tunisian scholar Ibn Khaldun Attar found among his intellectual forebears the same unprejudiced love of learning that had excited him about the French. For a man who would make the revitalisation of knowledge his life's work, these examples of Muslim brilliance also negated the superior ruminations of Westerners such as the savant Jean-Baptiste Joseph Fourier, who considered Islam inimical to the 'development of the mind'.

Attar was delighted to find that the great Muslim thinkers had not only been versed in theology and the law, but at the same time had 'an extended knowledge of other sciences'. Furthermore, these medieval scholars had seen nothing odd in consulting the works of non-Muslims, and Attar cited the example of a sheikh who, in order to answer Jewish criticism of Islam, quoted the Torah back at them.[34]

While in Turkey Attar was deeply disturbed by his inability to save a servant boy who had fallen ill with smallpox. The boy had died despite his master's application of henna, a traditional remedy thought to close the pores. (This was a few years after Jenner's pioneering first vaccination, of which Attar may have been ignorant.) The mishap inspired the Egyptian to deepen his medical expertise, and, living in Scutari on the Asian shore of the Bosporus, in the house of the Ottoman chief doctor, he was able to study further while enjoying the company of foreign physicians whom he quizzed about medical matters.[35]

The more Attar learned, the more he found himself rejecting the philosophically conceived and theoretical approach to the human body that Avicenna had enshrined in his *Canon of Medicine* of 1025. In its Latin translations this had been a set text for European medical students for five centuries, before it was superseded in Paris and Padua by the principles of experiment and observation. Attar came down on the side of the Europeans. 'According to Avicenna,' he wrote, 'the most conclusive approach to anatomy is through reading the well-established findings of a skilled man with precise knowledge … it is known, however, that dissection … is a science that cannot seriously be pursued except with one's two eyes.'

In the thirteenth century, the Syrian Ibn al-Nafis had postulated a circular motion of blood through the heart and lungs, disposing of the fallacy that the blood vessels contain both blood and air and anticipating the English physician William Harvey (to whom the discovery of 'pulmonary' circulation is usually attributed) by almost four hundred years. If Avicenna was medicine's great theorist, Attar concluded, Ibn al-Nafis had been its great practitioner. But the Syrian had willingly submitted to extraneous constraints: he had avoided human dissection because it was proscribed by Islamic law. Dissection remained taboo even at the beginning of the nineteenth century, for, as Attar noted sombrely, 'we have been dissuaded from the pursuit [of the empirical approach] because it has been considered an obstacle to God's law and to faith'.[36]

Here was another of those embarrassing gaps that had opened up between Europe and the lands of Islam, which Attar realised was a substantial obstacle to Muslim progress. Anatomy had been integrated into the Western medical tradition in the fifteenth century and it was indispensable to the world view of humanists such as Leonardo da Vinci. But dissection, without which anatomy was simply educated groping, scorned the Muslim belief that the dead feel every incision inflicted upon them. The Prophet had forbidden the cutting open of a dead body, 'though it may have swallowed the most precious pearl belonging to another'. Moreover, in its very pursuit of accuracy, anatomical drawing was also an unusually brazen violation of the ban on reproducing the human form.

Yet dissection was indispensable to modern medicine – and wasn't it the responsibility of Muslims to alleviate human suffering? Attar had no doubt seen the room of veterinary dissection that had been set up at the Institute of Egypt.[37] Now he needed no persuading; for him, the fields of empirical anatomy and astronomy were the most productive in modern science, yet they were 'almost non-existent now, except among a very small number of people, who save us from ignorance'.

Attar is thought to have left Istanbul in 1806 – the year before the modernising Selim was replaced by his reactionary cousin Mustafa – and he spent the next nine years continuing his studies in Alexandretta (today's Iskenderun, on Turkey's Mediterranean coast), Izmir and Damascus. But as the Ottoman heartlands were again in the grip of reaction, in 1815 Attar returned to the country which, in his absence, had become the centre of reform in the Islamic world.

Sparkling with a combination of knowledge and experience that perhaps no other Egyptian possessed, Attar was eager to contribute to the process of renewal initiated by Muhammad Ali Pasha in Egypt. Yet he soon discovered that Cairo had remained largely medieval and the country at large had not changed as profoundly or quickly as he had hoped. The group of progressives that Muhammad Ali had gathered around him was very small, and Attar himself would soon share their sense of isolation. He quickly struck up a rapport with the viceroy but was denied the support of the *ulema*, who well remembered his Francophile past. And as he was obliged to cling to Muhammad Ali and other friends he made in senior government circles, he became ever more suspect in the eyes of his fellow clerics.

His brilliance could not be denied, however. Upon arriving back at al-Azhar in 1815, Attar distinguished himself with a series of theological lectures that were so well conceived and delivered that even the conservative sheikhs left their classes to listen. But the great Cairene college remained far from congenial for someone of Attar's progressive, cosmopolitan disposition; squalid and unruly, it had the less endearing characteristics of an isthmus of city states, with violent rivalries between the different boarding houses, which were divided along ethnic and geographical lines, and further divisions arising between supporters of the various lecturers over control of the best teaching spots. The school was run by an inefficient despotism. An unpopular rector might be seized and flogged by a bunch of blind students; and troops were on hand to suppress any rioting. Needless to say, no Azharite rector to date had shown much appetite for the modernising reforms the college so badly needed.

By the end of the 1820s, when Muhammad Ali's reforms in areas like agriculture and military affairs were reaching fruition, the situation at al-Azhar had become so parlous that Attar was doing most of his teaching at home to select groups of students. The subjects he favoured – rational theology, logic, history, science, medicine and geography – conveyed an understanding of education that was notably eclectic. It was here, away from prying eyes, that he gave shape to his most important legacy: a generation of Egyptian modernisers who were formed by his conception of learning. Perhaps the closest of these acolytes was Rifaa al-Tahtawi, whose modernising influence was such that he would be called 'the father of Egyptian identity'. Rifaa received from the older man what may have been the most complete education available to any Egyptian at the time, and he would take many of Attar's ideas to their conclusion.

In between the teaching, Attar wrote prolifically in defence of logic and modern astronomy. He also produced a history of the Prophet's tribe, the Quraysh, which adduced historical, sociological and environmental reasons for key events in the Muslim foundation story. The framework of his analysis owed much to Ibn Khaldun, whose innovative depiction of history in cyclical terms had been largely disregarded in scholarly circles by the time Attar was writing.

The teaching behind closed doors and the careful defences of modern ideas couched amid longer and more conventional treatises speak of a chastened Attar – a long way from the rebellious aesthete who had visited the Frenchmen of the Institute of Egypt. To meet the mature divine was not to feel oneself in the presence of an iconoclast like Rousseau, for example, casting aside convention and the Church before going off to amass genii in the Alps. Attar had returned from his travels a cautious metropolitan, a North African parvenu with a social position to protect and a slave wife as cover for his homosexuality. (It was not very effective cover, as his 'condition' was well known, and he did not hide his disapproval of women in general, citing the Prophet's opinion that 'no people will succeed if their affairs are ruled over by women'.) He remained an innovator at heart, devouring any European book that came into his possession – reading much in Turkish translation – but to the public he maintained a bland and inoffensive front and received foreign visitors in secret – 'otherwise', as he confided to a French diplomat, 'I would do myself down in the eyes of the ulema'.[38] His experience had taught him that there was no alternative 'but for the country to change and renew itself through the new learning', and yet, in a career characterised by disappointment and frustration, only rarely did he find himself in a position to help the process along.[39]

In the 1820s one such opportunity arose, and happily it concerned anatomy, the importance of which had long ago impressed itself on Attar. Muhammad Ali had deputed a French surgeon, Antoine Barthélemy Clot, to whom he later awarded the honorific 'Bey', to set up Egypt's first medical college. There was a major obstacle to his work, however: in Clot Bey's words, this was the 'insurmountable religious opposition to the science of human anatomy'.[40] The authorities, he reported, were adamant; yet 'on this sole point rode the whole success of the project'.

Without clerical support there could be no dissection. Egypt's first batch of medical students had all studied at al-Azhar and could hardly be expected to defy the sheikhs who had taught them. Attar now stepped in, declaring his approval of anatomy classes and also expressing his support for hygiene, or preventive medicine. Attar was not alone in his progressive attitude, but he was, as Clot Bey's colleague P. N. Hamont put it, 'head of the faith in Cairo', and for all his controversial association with innovation and reform his was a voice that people listened to.[41] History does not record whose corpse was the subject of the first official dissection undertaken in Egypt, in February 1827, but an account left by Clot Bey gives a fascinating sense of the wiles and elisions that were used to get past Islamic law.

> To begin with we carried out the autopsies without the knowledge of the public, and surrounding the amphitheatre with guards who would perhaps have been the first to attack us if they had known what was going on. Little by little, the students got over all their prejudice and abhorrence and were convinced of the indispensible necessity of the study of anatomy. They took this conviction to their parents, sharing it with them, and nowadays the public is completely at ease with the idea of the dissection of corpses.

In another account he gave, this one to foreign acquaintances, Clot Bey described a gradual breakdown of popular prejudice.

> 'First of all,' said [Clot], 'let us get a dog and dissect him – not even a Moslem's dog, but a Jew's dog, or a Christian's dog,' and after a little grumbling they consented. Then at a cemetery outside of the town some skeletons and skulls were scattered about. 'Really,' said Clot, to his pupils ... 'what harm if we get a few of these skulls and bones for the sake of explanation to you; they may as well lie upon my table, as to lay bleaching in the sun.' This point was acceded to, but when he proposed to come to the dissection of bodies, there were some murmurs. 'Well!' said he, 'we will not take a free white man, but a black slave.' Again, at length, the point was given up; and thus, by one step after another, the educated Egyptians have arrived at a knowledge of anatomy.[42]

By the time anatomy became acceptable in Egypt, Attar had risen to become one of the country's top divines, but he was associated both with the despised government and ideas of foreign origin. The tension between these contradictory positions only increased after Muhammad Ali had him installed as rector of al-Azhar, arguably the most prestigious clerical position in Sunni Islam, in 1831. This crowning appointment, far from marking the start of reform inside Islam's most decrepit institution, turned out to be poison.

Four years later Attar was dead, his energy sapped by the vendettas waged against him, for while the sheikhs did not dare challenge the viceroy, the viceroy's chief priest was fair game. They sabotaged Attar's appointments and disparaged in farcical terms the editors and correctors he had assigned to a new government press; rather than put in a productive day's work, one of them explained, these men 'exploited their talents in reading and writing'.[43] There was of course no chance to update the old-fashioned curriculum and teaching arrangements. His enemies even went so far as to steal his shoes when he was in a meeting, reducing the rector of al-Azhar, by some reckonings the most important man in Islam, to walking home in his stockings.

Shortly before his death Attar confided to his follower Rifaa the fullness of his misery, writing of his desire to 'sit alone in my chair away from these voracious monsters ... I do not see anything but enemies wearing the clothes of friends. [I see] only arrogant, wily, malicious tricksters who are laying traps for me ... and my destruction stares me in the eye.'[44] He contrasted the mental athleticism shown by medieval thinkers with the sterility and loneliness of the present age, when he had 'no brother with whom to talk ... for the wise and the stupid have been put on the same level'.[45]

The author of fifty works on a variety of disciplines, and, more importantly, an intellectual explorer who would be recognised as a forerunner of Egypt's national revival, Attar had suffered greatly for his beliefs. If the environment in which he found himself had been less hostile, no doubt he would have been much more radical in pushing ideas which challenged the orthodoxy that eventually crushed him. The example of the French, the exertions of Muhammad Ali and his own had not yet brought about lasting changes for Egypt and its people. There remained a wide gap between the country that was being imagined by the viceroy and the real one on the ground.

Attar's painful sense of failure and Muhammad Ali's inability to protect him raise poignant questions about the nature of relations between Islam's progressive autocrats and the innovators and media-tors who threaded the values of modernity through society. Was their alliance heartfelt or expedient, and, if the latter, then who exploited whom? One is tempted to reproach the intellectuals for going along with the tyrants, but at the same time it is hard to see how such a pitifully small minority, struggling against a resistance to change that bordered on the pathological, could have done differently. In some cases it was only the protection afforded by a prince enjoying untram-melled powers that permitted the modernising thinkers and mediators to expound their avant-garde ideas in the first place – otherwise they would have faced a lynching from the mob. Moreover, in the early nineteenth century the choice wasn't between cooperating with a tyrant and cooperating with a more liberal ruler. Autocrats, of one kind or another, were the only game in town.

A continuum runs between Abdul Rahman al-Jabarti, Hassan al-Attar and Rifaa al-Tahtawi. It is not simply a line of pedagogical transmis-sion, but a trellis along which the climbing plant of knowledge is trained, thickens and matures. Jabarti was perhaps the first to appre-ciate the gulf that existed between Western and Islamic knowledge, which shocked him profoundly, while the same appreciation acted on Attar in a different way, pushing him to embrace the new. Having sat at Attar's feet at the turn of the 1820s (while the latter was teaching privately in defiance of Azharite orthodoxy), it was Rifaa al-Tahtawi (generally known today simply as 'Rifaa') who commandeered this modern knowledge most effectively and put it at the service not only of Egypt, a country whose modern meaning he can be said to have invented, but of Islam itself: he made it his life's work to show that the Muslim faith was compatible with progressive ideas.

Born in 1801 to a well-to-do family on the Nile south of Cairo, Rifaa's father belonged to the class of tax farmers that was ruined by Muhammad Ali's land expropriations; he died impoverished when the boy was about fourteen. Poor but able, Rifaa entered al-Azhar in 1817 where he met Attar, who took a shine to this intelligent young scholar with the almond eyes and thick, sensuous features. In 1824 Attar gave his new protégé a leg up by arranging for him to serve as an imam, or chaplain, in the viceroy's new army. This experience brought him into close contact with French military instructors, and Rifaa agreed readily when shortly afterwards Attar put him forward for a chaplaincy that promised opportunities of a quite different magnitude: accompanying Egypt's first educational mission to France.

The modern tradition of Muslim students heading west to study had started in 1815 with the dispatch of a handful of young Iranians to spend a few months in England; we will return to their story later. But the Egyptian mission just over a decade later, part of Muhammad Ali's campaign to absorb European learning, was the first to envisage a protracted stay for a large group of Middle Eastern Muslims in the land of the Franks – long enough for each student to master an expertise that would be useful on his return home. Rifaa would come back to Egypt an accomplished translator; others were to specialise in the law, in engineering and diplomacy.[46]

On the afternoon of 13 April 1826, the 25-year-old sheikh stepped gingerly onto the sloop *La Truite*, bound for France, where he would spend the next five years of his life. Rifaa was suffering from a slight fever, possibly compounded by the cups of seawater he had forced down as a prophylactic against seasickness – this on the advice of Attar himself, who of course had travelled extensively. He was delighted by the vessel on which he found himself: the logic of its specifications, the cleanliness of its crew. For the first few days of the passage across the Mediterranean, which Egyptians called the Byzantine Sea, *La Truite* was followed by a kindly breeze and Rifaa's fever passed 'as a result of the voyage and the movement of the ship'. After this plain sailing, however, a storm arose that threw the landlubbers down onto the decks, their faces ashen and their turbans askew, clawing at the timbers and beseeching help from 'Him who mediates on the Day of Judgement'. In his abject misery Rifaa recalled the poet's words: 'I swore on my life that I would no longer board a ship, only on the backs of animals would I travel for evermore.'

The forty-three men whom Muhammad Ali had selected for the mission were mostly well-born Cairenes, including Arabic and Turkish speakers and some Armenians. The purpose was to expand the horizons of these future members of the Egyptian administrative elite, but perhaps the most significant product of the mission was the memoir that Rifaa wrote during his stay abroad, and which he published after his return home in 1831. The *Travelogue of Rifaa Bey* was the first comprehensive description of modern France to be published in Arabic, and at the behest of Muhammad Ali it was translated into Turkish.It would soon achieve renown across the Ottoman Empire.

In some ways, the timing of the Egyptian mission was unfortunate. Inspired by Lord Byron's heroicised death while aiding Greek nationalism against the 'terrible Turk', public opinion in Europe was supportive of the insurgents who had spent the past four years rebelling against their Ottoman suzerain, and who were now being stamped on by Muhammad Ali's efficient (and French-trained) forces. The press regaled their readers with tales of Egyptian barbarism: the bag of rebel ears sent as a gift to the sultan; the Greek women and children on sale in the Cairo slave market. And yet even French philhellenism could not spoil an encounter that appealed, above all, to France's sense of self-worth. Some French newspaper editors were able to distinguish between the pasha's despised foreign policy and his wisdom in choosing France as the place to educate his elite, and in 1827 Muhammad Ali sent a token of his reciprocal regard in the form of a giraffe which Parisians thronged to visit at the Jardin des Plantes.[47] Modern Egypt's interest in France was, of course, a neat involution of France's interest in ancient Egypt. The French philologist Jean-François Champollion had by now deciphered the ancient Egyptian hieroglyphs that had been found on the Rosetta Stone, and the finishing touches were being put to the Louvre's Egyptian galleries, providing the grandest of settings for the country's loot from the land of the pharaohs.

It was entirely fitting that the Egyptian educational mission was organised by a veteran of Napoleon's celebrated Commission of Arts and Sciences, the geographer Edme-François Jomard (nicknamed 'the Egyptian'), editor of the *Description of Egypt* and promoter of African exploration; it was he who took charge of the students' curriculum and living arrangements once they reached Paris, in July 1826, also planning their visits to theatres, museums and the like. In the course of one such visit, among the embalmed cadavers at the Museum of Natural History, Rifaa and his companions came face-to-face with Sulayman al-Halabi, the zealot who had been executed for assassinating General Kléber back in 1801, and whose cranium, the visitors learned, exhibited all the features of a criminal fanatic.[48]

To that gruesome sight Rifaa had no response but to exclaim, 'there is no power and no strength save in the Great Almighty God!', and it is this sense of a meeting with the unexpected that carries his memoir so freshly down the years. It is hard to conceive of the sense of exposure the Egyptian students must have felt when confronted by what was at the time arguably the most agile and self-confident nation on earth. Into the France of scientific and medical advances, where the novel was being perfected by Balzac and group theory elaborated (by the twenty-year-old Evariste Galois, who went out with Gallic panache and lost his life in a duel), stepped the Egyptians, escorted in pairs from classes to museums and back to their digs.

There was a strict regimen to prevent necessary contact with the French spilling into unhealthier realms. To begin with the students lodged together in a mission house ruled with a rod of iron to ensure no unauthorised comings and goings, with strict instructions to each student not to do 'anything that may detract from his dignity'. Feted in banquets by Napoleon's surviving sages, lampooned in the satirical journals – La Pandore evoked in romantic detail their efforts to induct French ladies into the harem – they were all the while urged to even greater efforts by their unappeasable prince, who fired off unjustified denunciations of their idleness and lack of zeal.

There is no note of cynicism or dejection in Rifaa's travelogue, for although the intellectual relationship between France and Egypt had been established on unequal terms, the assumptions of European colonisation and its effects had not yet taken hold. (Rifaa entirely missed the significance of France's colonisation of Algeria, which took place when he was in Paris, and would, more than any other event, establish the character of French imperialism.) Written for a Muslim audience with only the sketchiest idea of Western lifestyles and attitudes, the travelogue takes the form of an uninterrupted, if implicit, comparison between what Rifaa has seen back home and what he sees now. To the reader in Cairo, Istanbul or the Levant, The Travelogue of Rifaa Bey comes as a bombardment of facts and suggestions, confirming or refuting earlier hearsay, or adding something completely new.

The land of the Franks offered fascinating and quite often contradictory clues to the new arrival. The country had adopted many of the egalitarian values of the revolution; centralisation and an intrusive state were the legacy of Napoleon. The Bourbon monarchy had been restored in 1814, and proponents of the divine right of kings once more asserted the values of church and throne, but liberals and revolutionaries would not easily be suppressed and would soon take to the barricades.

Rifaa's travelogue reveals to the Muslim reader that in France everything – but everything! – is being done differently. There are chairs to sit on, not a carpet, and when dining 'each person received something on his plate which he was supposed to cut with the knife that was before him, and then to bring to his mouth with the fork – not the hand'. From the coffee houses, with their enormous mirrors which transform a few people into a multitude, to the women, who reveal 'their face, head, the throat as well as what lies beneath it, the nape of the neck and what lies beneath it, and their arms almost up to the shoulders' – everything becomes the object of the imam's fascinated gaze.[49] He notes the salient features of Parisian life: the excellent drains, the different types of carriage – *roulages, diligences, coucous* and *fiacres* – the precocity of the children, the sheer number of institutions devoted to the pursuit of knowledge, and the fact that dancing with members of the opposite sex – indeed, with as many and in as short a time as possible – is considered not slatternly but becoming. The postal system, distributing the mail with uncanny accuracy (all the houses have a number), while enshrining a code of privacy which stops the letter from being opened by anyone save the addressee, is 'one of the most magnificent things imaginable'.[50]

The French regard for hygiene marks them out as the 'wisest among nations', even if in everyday social intercourse they are tight-fisted and insincere.[51] The imam skims over Catholicism, portraying it as a tissue of logical impossibilities presided over by a sexually repressed priesthood that has unaccountably given itself the right to forgive sins. But Catholicism doesn't seem to count for much, Rifaa claims; the French are Christians in name only, and if they value religion as having taught morality to an earlier, more credulous age, humankind is now refined enough not to need it. There are so few genuinely religious people in France, Rifaa concludes, that 'they are of no consequence'.[52] He takes particular pains to distinguish his French hosts from their Egyptian co-religionists the Copts, who 'display a natural tendency towards ignorance and stupidity'. Not so the French, who are no prisoners of tradition but wish to 'know the origin of things'.

Though Rifaa erred in some of his assessments – Catholicism would in fact show considerable vigour over the course of the nineteenth century – his words were an important signpost to Muslim reformist thought. According to Rifaa it was hardly surprising that Christianity was being swept away by secular knowledge; it was so shot through with irrationalities that it could not defend itself. Islam, on the other hand, that most logical of religions – rejecting sainthood, celibacy and the barely concealed cannibalism of the Eucharist – was ideally equipped to absorb the new knowledge without losing its essence.

The English scholar Edward Lane happened to be in a Cairo bookshop in the early 1830s, after the publication of *An Imam in Paris*, when he was joined by 'a man of a very respectable and intelligent appearance, applying for a copy ... asking what were the general contents of this book, a person present answered him, that the author relates his voyage from Alexandria to Marseilles; how he got drunk on board the ship, and was tied to the mast, and flogged; that he ate pork in the land of infidelity and obstinacy, and that it is a most excellent meat; how he was delighted with the French girls, and how superior they are in charms to the women of Egypt; and, having qualified himself, in every accomplishment, for an eminent place in Hell, returned to his native country'.[53]

The defamation overheard by Lane is of a kind that would become all too familiar as the number of Muslims travelling abroad to study rose during the nineteenth century. It was based on the idea that contact with other cultures is necessarily polluting, and that the Muslim who travels abroad will return home having lost his moral compass and cultural authenticity. In the case of Rifaa it was quite untrue, for he returned home a devout Muslim, still in his robes and turban – Muhammad Ali took a dim view of Egyptians who went native while abroad – and his trust in the divine revelation intact.

It was above all their lack of faith that Rifaa pitied in the French, even as he admired their other accomplishments:

> Is there another place like Paris,
> Where the suns of knowledge never set,
> Where the night of unbelief has no mornings?
> Forsooth, is this not the strangest of things?[54]

His translation work had introduced him to some of the most progressive and dangerous texts in the Enlightenment canon. Yet Rifaa apparently did not feel threatened by Voltaire's ill-concealed atheism, Rousseau's celebration of the nature of man or the philosopher Etienne Bonnot de Condillac's paramountcy of the senses; and his reasoning was not dissimilar to that of Avicenna, who had argued, some eight hundred years earlier, that philosophic speculation does no harm provided one has a solid grounding in the Islamic sciences.

He had translated and 'understood very well' the *Principles of Natural Law*, by the eighteenth-century Swiss thinker Jean-Jacques Burlamaqui, in which man is described as subject to a natural law whose author is God, and yet is endowed with will and reason. It is through reason that man is equipped to think, 'and is capable of forming just ideas of the different objects that occur to him ... of passing a solid judgment on the mutual fitness and agreement of things'.[55] Burlamaqui's attribution of divine origins to a system of natural law that Rousseau had drained of holiness would be useful to Rifaa later on, and the Egyptian's ideas about national identity were undoubtedly influenced by his reading of Montesquieu, who had identified geography and the environment as helping to delineate the different countries of the world, and who regarded a love of one's homeland as the basis of political morality. Scholars Rifaa had met in Paris had compared Montesquieu to the Arabs' own father of sociology Ibn Khaldun, whom his patron and teacher, Hassan al-Attar, had helped rescue from obscurity.

Rifaa's five years in France convinced him of the need for European sciences and technologies to be introduced into the Islamic world, but he chose not to enquire about the link between a free intellect and a free spirit, or whether the inquisitiveness he admired in the French people might be in some way connected to their quest for political liberty. The acquiescent attitude adopted by many Muslims to their temporal rulers was ingrained in the famous Quranic verse, 'Oh you who believe! Obey God and obey the Messenger and those among you who are in authority.' In Muslim eyes, the detonations of recent French history, from the violence of the revolution through Napoleon's ruinous expansionism to the restoration of the Bourbons, seemed dissuasively anarchic. While he was in Paris, Rifaa witnessed the revolution of July 1830, when the autocratic Bourbon Charles X was overthrown and replaced by Louis-Philippe of Orléans. Though the Egyptian's account of these events betrayed sympathy for the French liberals who established a constitutional monarchy with Louis-Philippe at its head, neither now nor later did he hint that similar arrangements might be desirable at home.

Instead, as with Jabarti following the murder of Kléber thirty years before, it was the integrity of the French justice system which won his admiration, for the trial of Charles X's prime minister, Charles de Polignac, was 'one of the most impressive that a person is ever likely to hear and constituted clear proof of the civilisation of the French and the justice of their state'.[56] (The word 'civilisation' was in fact of relatively recent origin, only entering the French lexicon in the 1760s; in England Dr Johnson refused to include it in his famous dictionary.) Rifaa found it remarkable that 'Polignac wanted only one legal scholar to defend him, and chose Martignac ... despite the fact that there was no friendship between them'. The lawyer, furthermore, 'fulfilled his task with the utmost faithfulness, applying all his expertise in order to defend his client', even if the former prime minister was eventually jailed for life.[57]

Rifaa had owed his place on the mission to France to Attar and it was the latter – having become rector of al-Azhar in 1831, the year of Rifaa's return home – who recommended the travelogue to Muhammad Ali's attention. For all the mutual affection between the two sheikhs, however, Rifaa would not repeat the older man's mistakes. Soon after arriving back in Egypt he contracted a sensible marriage (to the daughter of Attar's deputy at al-Azhar). Then he got on with his career during which he never faltered in his respect for the senior *ulema*. A generation earlier, Rifaa would have found it difficult to make a name for himself outside al-Azhar, but secular schools set up by Muhammad Ali had drained the college of its central importance in public affairs and distributed it between members of the civil service. Indeed, over the next forty years Rifaa built up something that Jabarti, who had died in 1825, would barely have recognised: a modern, bureaucratic CV.

Inevitably Rifaa spent much of his public career, which would last until his death in 1873, at the mercy of viceregal whim. He enjoyed favour under Muhammad Ali but not under the pasha's successor Abbas I (1848–54), who exiled him to the Sudanese capital, Khartoum, before he himself was murdered by his eunuchs. Rifaa was back in favour under two subsequent rulers, Said (1854–63) and Ismail I (1863–79), all the time exemplifying the progressive, forward-thinking mandarin. He was employed both as a civil and a military administrator and was a guiding light behind the country's expansive education policy, founding and running several schools – notably Cairo's School of Languages, to which was attached a famous translation bureau under his supervision. Through the doors of these institutions passed a future generation of Egyptian modernisers, from authors to ministers and architects of judicial reform.[58] In the course of his long career Rifaa also wrote the first Arabic grammar for schools, rose to the rank of colonel in the army and edited Egypt's first national newspaper.

Whether he was occupied as a writer, a teacher or a civil servant, the barest list of Rifaa's activities over forty years shows that he pursued the goal of progress with zeal and success, and in this too he represents a step change from Attar. Rifaa had made it his life's work to incorporate into Egypt the achievements of civilisation – a word whose Arabic equivalent, *tamadun*, from the word meaning 'city', he did much to popularise. In doing so his aim was not to supplant Islamic society, but to enrich and revitalise it.

The sheikh's love of the new was heartfelt and unapologetic. He was moved to poetry by the sight of a steamer plying the Nile, and went into ecstasies when he heard about the first transcontinental railroad that linked one American seaboard to the other in the 1860s. The extraordinary favour God had shown by bringing humankind into the world was in itself cause for optimism, and Rifaa lambasted those pitiable reactionaries who dismissed the modern era as 'without value and on the path to ruin'. On the contrary, he countered, 'the inventions of our era, welcomed with favour by nations and kings, are the noblest fruits of the mind; successive generations transmit them and show them under forms still more perfect and beautiful'.[59] To prove that God looked favourably on human progress he quoted from the Quran: 'It is God who has presented you the earth. Go out and eat of the daily bread that it gives you.'

Rifaa's sense of hope was partly a function of the glad moment he inhabited, for he was too young to have seen anything of the Napoleonic occupation of his country and would die before it went under an English heel in 1882: he could believe the civilisation of foreigners to be essentially benign. Having seen this civilisation in action, furthermore, he had a shrewd idea of its mobility. Appropriately enough, it is as a translator, in the broad sense of someone who fetches ideas from one home and makes them comfortable in another, that he is most remembered today.

Rifaa had been struck in France by the usefulness of an unadorned language conveying sense with the minimum of fuss. 'What in Arabic is seen as embellishment,' he wrote, 'the French sometimes perceive as weakness;' and he cast doubt upon those lexical ornaments which are the glory of Arabic, and which contribute nothing to ease of understanding.[60] Parisian French was constantly renewing, fitting itself for the purpose of narrating modern life. This, alas, could not be said for Cairene Arabic. In al-Azhar, of all places, the students glorified in their ignorance of syntax and were unable to compose even a simple treatise on some subject of general interest outside their area of expertise.[61] Then there was the sheer promiscuity of the European languages – every day seeding new words for which Arabic had no equivalent.

Rifaa undertook to close the distance between modern ideas and the capacity of Arabic to express them. He was the first Arab to use the word *jumhuriyya*, meaning republic, which is now incorporated into the official name of a score of Muslim countries around the world; he also sent *hurriya* down the track towards its present meaning of political and personal emancipation.[62] Rifaa discovered that some concepts were so foreign they resisted translation entirely, in which case the choice was between borrowing the French word and inventing a new one. His travelogue contains *duks* strolling down tree-lined *bulwars* while their poorer compatriots labour in *fabrikas* where everything is measured to the last *santimitr*.[63] All these transliterations of the French survive in the Arabic today.[64]

Translation is one of the great expressions of the universality of the intellect – the metamorphosis of an idea, with its shades of meaning more or less protected, into a new form. New and unfamiliar ideas rushed into Egypt over the nine years of the life of Rifaa's translation bureau, as he and his colleagues rendered an astonishing two thousand European and Turkish works into Arabic, ranging from histories of the ancient world to books about the Greek philosophers and Voltaire's influential life of the Russian moderniser Peter the

Great.[65] Montesquieu's *Considerations on the Causes of the Greatness of the Romans and their Decline* showed Rifaa's interest in the fortunes of great powers – and the lessons they might hold for those on the rise[66] – and he himself translated works on geography and geometry, as well as Fénelon's *Adventures of Telemachus*, which describes the education in princely wisdom that Ulysses' son (the Telemachus of the title) receives at the hands of his tutor, Mentor. Rifaa carried out this work after being exiled by Abbas to 'Egypt's Gulag'– Khartoum.

Rifaa's translation movement brought about arguably the biggest and most meaningful importation of foreign thought into Arabic since Abbasid times. These translations made a huge impact on the engineers, doctors, teachers and military officers who were beginning to form the elite of the country; they were the forerunners of the secular-minded middle classes that would dominate public life for much of the next two centuries. To them ancient history expanded the meaning of the instructive past, which had hitherto been confined to the Islamic period. Reading about the feats of the infidel suggested an alternative story of talent and achievement, disregarding conventional faith-based partitions. In the case of the *Code Napoléon* and France's commercial codex, both of which he rendered into Arabic, Rifaa also showed his receptivity to Western law.

Rifaa was instinctively an intellectual unifier of humanity – in contrast to his predecessor Jabarti, who sorted knowledge into what was comprehensible by 'minds such as ours'. Rifaa coined the word for nation, *watan* – another new word to get one's head around, which would spread to Turkish and Persian and be used to elicit nationalist emotions in opposition to their European equivalents. He pioneered a new literary form, the patriotic poem, and translated the Marseillaise. He realised the value of the past to this new, national sensibility, daring to criticise Muhammad Ali for letting the Europeans cart away huge amounts of ancient loot and prevailing on the viceroy to ban the export of antiquities. Rifaa stored much excavated treasure in his language school until a museum of antiquities was built, in 1835.[67] The collection forms the core of today's Egyptian Museum in Tahrir Square.

Some of his ideas were too radical, however, or would come to fruition much later. He proposed that the rabbis and the Coptic priests be integrated into the *ulema*, which no one has suggested

since. He was decades ahead of his time on advocating girls' education. In a famous treatise he issued a call for both sexes to be educated
equally, and rather than deploy Western arguments in support of
this view he quoted hadiths showing that the Prophet's wives had
been literate.[68] But girls' education was opposed by most Egyptian
Muslims, for it was regarded as a first step towards desegregation
of the sexes. Decades would pass before an Egyptian government
adopted equality in education as a political goal – it remains
unachieved even now.

For all the daring of some of his proposals, Rifaa's main ideas have
travelled well down the years. Egypt's leading mind had internalised
the eclecticism of the French savants in so natural and unforced a
manner as to defy all theories of congenital 'Muslim' deficiencies.
'Knowledge', he wrote, 'advances today in the theoretical disciplines
of science and in the branches of industry ... a zeal no less unceasing
is also being deployed in the science of holy law, the literary disciplines, the acquisition of foreign languages and the study of the
culture of all countries and all cities. All of that should furnish Egypt,
besides the satisfaction of her needs, beauties that will endow her
with splendour.'[69]

This passage was written in the late 1860s, during the modernising
reign of Ismail, a grandson of Muhammad Ali, which was the most
productive period in literary terms of Rifaa's life. It was during those
years that he produced works on education and Egyptian society and
the first two volumes of what he intended to be a complete history
of Egypt, before and after the arrival of Islam. Cumulatively these
writings show the hopeful world view of the early Muslim reformer,
in which civilisation has no nationality, religion or political colour.
And from this came Rifaa's ingenious answer to anyone who wondered
how it was that peoples who were closed to the truth of revelation –
the contemporary French, the ancient Egyptians – had achieved so
much. Even those who were ignorant of the word of God were not
entirely deprived of divine light, Rifaa maintained, and insofar as there
was a natural law affecting all God's creatures, it was written by the
Creator himself. Human beings had possessed reason before they
received the truths of the prophets, and it was this faculty that had
allowed them, even those unacquainted with Islam, to scale the intellectual heights.[70]

In his late works Rifaa addressed questions, such as the opposition of reason and revelation and that of predestination and free will, which had occupied Islamic thinkers almost since the time of Muhammad. As we have seen, the eighth-century Mutazilites, who had argued for man's autonomy of action and the createdness of the Quran, had been eliminated and the Asharite principle of *bila kayf* had smothered philosophy with a bleak and unthinking determinism. But Asharism had also introduced the doctrine of *kasb*, or 'acquisition', whereby seemingly voluntary actions, such as those flowing from moral dilemmas, are in fact 'acquired' from God by humans, becoming provisionally theirs – to be punished or rewarded as appropriate.

Rifaa's rewriting of *kasb* was typically sunny. It was through striving that human beings came closest to purity and perfection, he argued, and God let them roam across the various fields of enquiry in order to improve their knowledge and performance. Of course, if reason was found to contradict revelation, reason must be in error, for reason could not overrule what was known from a higher authority.

Rifaa's cast of mind was probing, questioning and open, but he was also capable of the kind of discretionary trust that some medieval jurists had placed in God's incomprehensible truth. Rifaa's last book was a biography of Muhammad, and there was no question of inter-preting allegorically the story of the purification of the Prophet's heart before his ascension, when angels cleaved open his chest, withdrew the black lump that Satan had placed there, purified it and put it back. Here was not an allegory but simply a truth that could not be squared with reason. The only proper response was to surrender before it.[71]

In his audit of nineteenth-century Europe, Rifaa came to the conclusion that its most attractive features – the peaks of *tamadun*, or civilisation – had actually been anticipated by Islam. The French notion of 'liberty', for example, was identical to Islamic 'justice', while 'equality' showed affinity to Muslim 'charity'.[72] 'Patriotism' was even related to religious zeal. Rifaa was one of the first to express what is now a familiar idea in the Muslim world: that prin-ciples we consider to be modern, such as pluralism, freedom and rights, existed in embryonic form in early Islam. One can understand why Rifaa and others followed this path, seeking consoling evidence both for the unity of humankind and the genius of Islam (in its uncorrupted form) as a precursor of modern values. But despite their good intentions the logic that lies behind such equivalences seems contrived and unconvincing.

Take, for instance, the Quranic idea of justice. This subjects all believers, from prince to pauper, to a uniform application of the holy writ – a laudable ideal that all cultures can applaud. But Rifaa went further and claimed that it denoted the emancipation of the individual, free to fulfil and perfect herself – it is the same as 'liberty'. But the two concepts are in fact incompatible – the first is about equality of restriction, the second about equality of opportunity. Moreover, equality as it is understood in the West defines social relations between human beings, from which God has been deliberately excluded. In Rifaa's system, on the other hand, where God places people at an equal distance from him, they bear equal obligations and enjoy equal privileges among themselves.

Later Muslim reformists have claimed that the Quranic statement 'the affairs of state of the believers are run by consultation' anticipates parliamentary democracy. But consultation by a ruler does not necessarily commit him to abide by the will of his people – and history has shown that he rarely does so if their will is to depose or restrict him or make him poorer. Moreover, consultation is one element of electoral democracy, but not the only one.

Today, Rifaa's unwillingness to consider the indispensability of political choice seems naive. At various points during his lifetime he had seen the royal houses of Europe fall under the weight of popular dissatisfaction, and his foreign contacts had given him the opportunity to learn about socialism, which many working-class Europeans increasingly regarded as the solution to their problems. Still, he felt no envy. Doubtless as the beneficiary of despots he could see the value of despotism, but his attitude to power wasn't only self-interested. It was rigorous in its opposition to disorder and in favour of maintaining the place of things. And there was a certain *de haut en bas* scepticism of the ability of the masses to make the right choices. He was an Azharite sheikh, after all.

Rifaa died in 1873, a decade into Ismail's disastrous reign. Between them, he and his forebears in a chain of instruction and experience, the sheikhs Attar and Jabarti, had observed and propelled Egypt's transition from a medieval society to one on the edge of modernity. It had taken barely fifty years.

Rifaa would not witness the full extent of the country's slide to destitution as a result of the ruler's profligacy, or the nationalist fervour and rise in anti-Christian feeling that followed. Rifaa had not anticipated the prickly, defensive form it took after the British invasion of 1882, which would morph half a century later into the Arab chauvinism of General Gamal Abdel Nasser and the jagged revivalism of the Muslim Brotherhood. Rifaa's idea of *watan*, or 'homeland', had been predicated on cooperation, not confrontation, with foreigners. But the idea of cooperation would become a sour joke, as the insatiable demand for credit evinced by Ismail Pasha and the bottomless indulgence shown him by European lenders brought Egypt to its knees economically and politically – prone, as it turned out, to the perils of colonisation.

When in 1956 Nasser shocked the world by nationalising the Suez Canal, he would say that Egypt had become the property of the canal, not the canal the property of Egypt. It is the perverse fate of 'national' projects dependent on finance and expertise from the West that they end up being anything but national; they are hostages in the hands of foreigners who defend them as if they were their own. This was certainly true of the Suez Canal, which the French devised, the Egyptians built (between 1859 and 1869) and the British took over as another piece in their jigsaw of world domination. Tens of thousands of press-ganged workers died during the canal's construction and Egypt spent at least one and a half times more than any other country to complete it. But under the terms of the agreement governing the project the host nation would only take control ninety-nine years after the canal came into operation – and then only if it could reimburse the foreign investors. So it seemed entirely natural that when in 1875 the country's approaching insolvency permitted the British government to snap up Ismail's 44 per cent share of the operating company for a paltry £4 million, making Britain the canal's largest single shareholder, the *Birmingham Weekly Post* averred that 'an Englishman feels proud now that he can "paddle his canoe" on his own canal', while the prime minister, Benjamin Disraeli, assured Queen Victoria of the absolute necessity that the canal should 'belong to England'.[73]

This wasn't what Ismail's uncle and predecessor Said had intended when in 1854 he decreed the bisection of the isthmus of Suez, a

75-mile-long plug of gypsum and limestone separating the waters of the Mediterranean from those of the Red Sea and preventing Egypt from taking over the trade that currently went all the way down the coast of Africa and round the Cape. Based on plans that were devised during the Napoleonic occupation and dusted down by Ferdinand de Lesseps, France's energetic former consul, the canal cost around £19 million, approximately £6 million of which had to be paid to Napoleon III (who, spurred by his wife the Empress Eugénie, had a big interest in the project) as compensation for contractual amendments that made it a little less disadvantageous to the Egyptians. The new viceroy, Ismail, had identified the canal as a suitable monument to his ambition to make Egypt modern in as short a time as possible, and he spared no expense in its realisation.

Sleepy-eyed, plutocratic, gallant and fat, Ismail was the second of Egypt's impatient transformers, and during the early part of his rule, which happened to coincide with a boom in cotton revenues caused by the American Civil War of the early 1860s, he was favoured with the means to modernise the country. Under Ismail, roads and railways were laid and the towns lit by gaslight; the number of Egyptian schoolchildren receiving a public education soared (albeit from a low base) to 90,000 in 1873.[74] Telegraph lines were laid between all major towns in the north of the country and Alexandria grew further as a European mart and exchange. (It was the first city in Egypt to boast the street numbers that Rifaa had so admired in Paris.) The railway constructed by British engineers at Said's behest in 1858 had cut journey times from Cairo to Alexandria from four days to eight hours; Ismail now extended the tracks all way into Sudan.

Like his grandfather Muhammad Ali, Ismail's ambitions did not stop at Egypt's borders. Frustrated in his aim of gaining independence from the Porte, he settled for the title of khedive, or master, which he acquired by paying a handsome bribe to the sultan. He threw himself into military campaigns of doubtful utility – deep into sub-Saharan Africa; to Crete where he fought insurgents on behalf of the sultan; and even to Mexico, to assist Napoleon III in his pursuit of American silver.[75]

Ismail was less arbitrary and bloodthirsty than Muhammad Ali, but the Chamber of Delegates he convoked in 1866 was in no way intended to limit the power of the khedival government – important tax reforms went through without any consultation and elections to the chamber had to be approved by the ruler. As Egypt's foreign minister told his French counterpart, the purpose of the chamber would be to act as a 'school through which the government, more advanced than the general populace, teaches and civilises that populace'.

It was the Suez Canal that would be the supreme civilising instrument, and at the same time an advertisement that Egypt belonged in the modern world. Towards the end of the 1860s the great waterway approached completion. No matter that the bottom had fallen out of the cotton market with the end of the American Civil War in 1865: Ismail borrowed more from the Oppenheims and the Société Générale in order to finish the job. As the inauguration approached he built a new Cairo, pointedly indifferent to the adjacent medieval capital with its bleached gateways and the mouldering al-Azhar. It was a new capital to rival the boulevards, mansard roofs and *rond-points* of Napoleon III's master builder Georges-Eugène 'Baron' Haussmann, whose renovation of Paris the khedive had admired during the universal exposition of 1867. An opera house was built in six months, a little more than it took to construct the khedival palace at Ismailia, a new settlement to serve canal traffic.[76] The people were of course not consulted on these measures; the new Boulevard Muhammad Ali, for instance, required the demolition of seven hundred houses as well as many shops and even mosques. Ismail paid for all of this out of his own pocket (his official salary was double that of Queen Victoria).

In the run-up to the grand opening of the canal the Prince of Wales made his excuses, as did US President Ulysses S. Grant, but in spite of these disappointments a clutch of genuine A-listers made it across the Mediterranean – Empress Eugénie and the Habsburg Emperor Franz Joseph among them. As if in recognition of the role played by France in exposing Egyptians' eyes to their own past, the guests included the son of a companion of Champollion on the great Egyptologist's expedition to Egypt in 1828 – when, thanks to his recent decipherment of hieroglyphics, he was able to understand inscriptions that had been incomprehensible for millennia.

The opening of the Suez Canal was the occasion for a month-long celebration of Egypt and its ruler, during which the guests enjoyed cruises to the cataracts and audiences with Ismail – visible throughout, at a safe distance, were the tents of the Bedouin and the sun-blacked faces of the curious fellahin, hinting at the old, untouched Egypt that he was furiously doing away with. On 16 November the focus of formalities switched from Cairo to Port Said, the canal's new Mediterranean roadstead, whither warships and pleasure vessels from a dozen countries converged amid cannon salvos and cheers. It was, observed Empress Eugénie, watching from her yacht, a 'magnificent reception; I never saw anything like it in my life'. The empress was flanked by her host and the emperor of Austria for the ensuing cere- monies, which began with prayers according to both Muslim and Christian rites and ended with a magnificent fireworks display. The self-congratulatory tenor of the French speeches suggested that France and Egypt shared the credit for the canal, but it was a British vessel, the *Newport*, which was first in when the inaugural flotilla set off to sail though the canal the following morning – an act of lese-majesty for which her captain received an official reprimand from the Admiralty and an unofficial vote of thanks.

However much the canal was – in the words of one of the French speakers at the inauguration – a 'grand and eminently civilising fact', it was also a bone with one end in France's maw and the other in Britain's.

After passing rose-scented Ismailia and going on to Suez, the bigwigs headed for Cairo, but sadly Giuseppe Verdi, whom the khedive had commissioned to write an opera to mark the occasion, was behind schedule with *Aida*. Ismail and his party made do with *Rigoletto*. Over the next couple of weeks the guests were entertained by vaudeville, trifles by Offenbach, racing, balls, illuminations, and dinners hosted by Ismail, with the Château d'Yquem flowing and the khedival plate, porcelain and crystal judged to be in excellent taste. Royal palaces had been turned over for the use of Ismail's fellow royals; the un-royal were billeted at Shepheard's Hotel, a rambling pile famed for its long bar. Finally, on 13 December, with a balloon flight over the pyramids, the peacocking came to an end.

Not, however, the worries over Ismail's ability to keep his credi- tors at bay – which rose steeply over the 1870s and led to his abdica- tion in 1879. Under Ismail the modernisation that Muhammad Ali began sixty years earlier had become a pauperising mania. The country was on a trajectory that nowadays looks pathetically predict- able, whereby an oriental leader possessed of unlimited powers incurs enormous foreign debts he cannot possibly repay, leading to increasingly close attention from his foreign creditors and, eventually, direct intervention.

'My country is no longer in Africa,' Ismail declared in 1878; 'we are now part of Europe.' But Egypt's foreign debt had soared from £3 million to £91 million in thirteen years, and the khedive was addressing these words to an international bankruptcy commission.[77] Taxes had been hiked, causing much pain throughout the population, and Egypt's share of the canal offloaded to Disraeli; and while the army was paid in arrears, if at all, the foreign banks insisted on being paid their interest on time and in full.

In February 1879 a defiant Ismail dismissed the European officials that Britain and France had foisted on his government, but it was an ill-judged act of defiance and four months later a blunt telegram from the Porte, drafted under European pressure and addressed to the 'ex-Khedive Ismail of Egypt', signalled that his reign was at an end. He was replaced by his 27-year-old son Towfiq.

Sailing off to Naples on his yacht, the ex-khedive may have reflected on the ruins of his design to liberate Egypt from the Ottomans and raise it to parity with Britain and France. He had been unrestrained by accountability and his flights of fantasy had opened the way to foreign involvement in the government, which would, with the British occupation of 1882, expand into full-blown colonial control. The effects of this puncturing of national sovereignty would have serious repercussions on the modernisation movement that had developed quite promisingly over the past three-quarters of a century.

If the fate of Ismail might not have surprised Sheikh Jabarti, that sceptic of Western influence who in later life had deplored the venality of Muhammad Ali, it would have profoundly dismayed Rifaa al-Tahtawi, whose faith in the West and in the ability of the lands of Islam to learn from Europe while retaining their authenticity now seemed misplaced.[78] From being a process of voluntary importation, the Islamic Enlightenment as envisaged by such subtle minds as Rifaa and Hassan al-Attar was in danger of becoming a costly and superficial imitation. In order for Egypt to prosper once more it would need a guarantee against monarchical whim and foreign intervention: it was a guarantee, some would come to believe, that only constitutional government could provide.

2

Istanbul

If the spur for reform among the Egyptians was Napoleon's invasion, it was military defeats at the hands of the Russians that goaded their Ottoman overlords to a similar self-interrogation. In 1768 the Ottoman Sultan Mustafa III went to war with Catherine the Great and his forces were humiliated. The Russian imperial fleet smashed the Turks in the Aegean and the Ottoman monopoly over the Black Sea was also brought to an end when in 1783 the Russians annexed the Crimea. Hard on the heels of these reverses came the global event of the French Revolution and Napoleon's seizure of Egypt, a stinging aspersion on the durability of Ottoman sovereignty by the nation that the Turks had considered their most reliable European ally.

Trying to keep its balance between a crazily revolving Europe that would slow down only after the conclusion of the Napoleonic Wars, in 1815, and Arab territories in varying states of recalcitrance (the Arabian Wahhabi revolt had broken out in 1798), the empire needed to modernise if it was to escape destruction at the hands of a combination of imperious northern neighbours and uppity southern subjects. Again, as was the case among the *ulema* in Cairo, questions over modernisation were queered by troubles in the application of Western ideas. In 1797, vainly trying to take back the Crimea, the Ottomans employed a big Western-style gun that, contrary to expectations, sent a shell into the air that blew up and destroyed the gun. This led to controversy back home, particularly in the offices of the Sublime Porte. Was the technology cursed because it was foreign, or did the Turks in fact need more of it and to use it better? Defeat against the 'Moskofs' convinced conservatives that God would abandon the Ottomans if they gave up the tried and tested ways, and the following year a government report compared the French

Revolution – with a vehemence that even Jabarti tended to avoid – to a nasty case of syphilis. The source of the sedition was well known, the report went on, for 'the ultimate basis of the order and cohesion of every state is a firm grasp of the roots and branches of holy law'.[1]

Questions of change and conservation were harder to answer in Istanbul than they were in Cairo, where Napoleon left a blank slate for Muhammad Ali and the gradual emergence of a centralised nation state greatly simplified reform. Things were more complicated on the shores of the Bosporus, where the sultan-caliph ruled over religious and linguistic communities so varied that Egypt looked positively monochromatic. The Ottoman sultans that ruled during the second half of the eighteenth century needed to balance their caliphal responsibilities to the *umma* (as custodian of Mecca and Medina) with commitments to a Europe in the process of abandoning the 'balance of power' principle that had governed power relations since the 1600s. Particularly galling to the Ottomans, who prided themselves on their deft handling of minorities ranging from the Sephardic Jews to Kurdish Yazidis and Lebanese Druze, was that imperial Russia had since the 1770s considered itself protector of its fellow Orthodox across the empire, and under this high-minded altruism the tsarina and her ministers fomented no end of trouble across the (partly Orthodox) Balkans. From being a European heavyweight, feared by the Pope but trading with all, Turkey had over the course of the eighteenth century been reduced to a chancellery riddle. The 'Eastern question' ran something like this: what should come after the empire expired, and were the interests of the powers served by hastening its demise? Tsar Nicholas would remark in 1844 that the Ottoman Empire resembled a dying bear – 'you may give him musk but even musk will not long keep him alive'.[2] His view was that Russia and Britain should partition the empire, freezing out the French, but the British knew that to empower Russia would be to imperil India, and the Crimean War – in which Britain ganged up successfully with Turkey and France against the tsar – would be the result.

The French had forced modernity on Cairo – dispersing the Mamluks, demoralising al-Azhar, and showing off their rational values for Jabarti and Attar. Istanbul, by contrast, experienced no invigorating collision; ghosts of old glory roamed as flesh and blood. For all the fires that would race along the wooden streets, the undimmed ravages of the plague, and the sultan's abasement at the hands of a tyrannical harem and disobedient regional magnates – for all these signs of dysfunction, when the morning sun struck the finials of the imperial minarets and stole down their granite flutes to warm the waters of the Golden Horn, who could doubt that this 500-year-old imperium enjoyed the favour of God?

This, at any rate, was the conviction of many in the Ottoman hierarchy, while the religious schools regarded the empire's problems as remediable only through the crispest interpretation of the sharia. These views were at first opposed by a small minority of soldiers, diplomats and scholars who were supported by Sultan Mustafa III (1757–74) and who oversaw a few military reforms, the first tortoise-like steps of Turkish publishing (the average yield was less than one title per year), and some experimentation with modern medicine. Progress was tortuous. It would be Mustafa's son Selim III, who came to the throne in that inauspicious year for monarchs, 1789 (succeeding his uncle Abdulhamid I), who would guide Turkey to its first experience of full-blooded reform.

Selim was born in 1762 and grew up cultured, inquisitive and deeply interested in the problems of the age. Having corresponded with Louis XVI he was naturally horrified at the execution of his brother monarch, though his admiration for the French survived even the tumbrils and the terror. In the 1790s, in concert with a small coterie of reformers and helped by French advisers, Selim pressed ahead with policies that were aimed at opening up the empire – developing military schools and establishing permanent embassies in foreign capitals. He taught incognito at his own school of engineering; and he wanted his sister, Hadice Sultan, to bring Turkish women out of servitude.

Among the evidence we have for an opening of Ottoman minds during Selim's reign – apart, of course, from the experiences of Hassan al-Attar, who found medical learning more developed in Istanbul than in post-occupation, pre-Muhammad Ali Cairo – is a slip of a treatise with a long name by a man about whom we know little. 'Diatribe on the Current State of the Military Arts, the Genius and the Sciences at Constantinople' was signed by a certain Sayyid Mustafa in 1803 (the year after Attar's arrival), and displays the same hunger for knowledge as that of the Egyptian. When he was young, the sayyid (his title indicates that he was a descendant of the Prophet) had felt 'an insatiable ardour to come to know an infinite number of unknowns whose value I appreciated, despite my ignorance'. Having learned French he became a teacher at Selim's new engineering school, which was, in common with all such institutions, aimed at perfecting the science of war.

'We started working in public,' he writes; 'it was the first time that the ignorant people at Constantinople had heard public mathematics lessons, or watched geometricians assemble together; inept and ignorant voices rose on all sides; we were molested, we were almost persecuted, and upbraided in shouts: "why are they drawing these lines on the paper? What advantage can it bring? War isn't waged with a compass" … and they bore down on us with a thousand other, similar phrases.'

Like Attar, navigating easily between Eastern and Western knowledge, Sayyid Mustafa had an instinctive feel for the mobility of these transferable ideas. Had not the Abbasid caliph Harun al-Rashid (766–809), the sayyid asks in his treatise, opened the eyes of medieval Europe when he presented Charlemagne with a clepsydra, or 'water clock'? 'The nations of Europe,' he goes on, 'famous and glorious for possessing so many works of art, and for culture and all the sciences, were taught by the Romans, and they by the Greeks, but none could dispute the primacy of the Persians, Egyptians and Indians, nor deny that these countries had been the home of the enlightened.' In his own time, however, 'through continuous modification and renewal in the state of all things, the masters are surprised by the brilliant career of their disciples and, unfortunately, are in sore need of them'.

In his pamphlet Sayyid Mustafa also speaks of his joy at the success that the sultan's new army has enjoyed in suppressing a vicious band of brigands, holed up in a supposedly impregnable redoubt. 'One would no longer doubt for an instant', he chortles, 'that this was a new order of things – a new world, so to speak – in which it was necessary to divest oneself completely of all ancient prejudices. As for myself, drunk for joy at seeing my country in the state I had so ardently desired, lit ever more each day by the lamp of science and the arts, I was no longer able to remain quiet.'³

The sayyid's pleasure at what appears to be a scientific solution to the country's turbulence echoes the triumphalism of Europe's intellectual frontiersmen – the exalting sense that what is right is useful. What, if not better equipment and training, superior nourishment and a knowledge of the arts of war, could explain the victory of the smaller force against heavy odds? The sayyid's account gives no sense of the hand of God at work, but that of his beloved sultan who has shown he is 'above the petty considerations of mediocrity, and thus he shut the mouth of ignorance'.[4]

Much of what Selim essayed at the turn of the nineteenth century Muhammad Ali would achieve in Egypt two decades later, and comparisons between the two rulers are inevitable. Portraits of Selim show a placid, heavy-lidded countenance, in line with his reputation for pleasure and indulgence; he certainly lacked the pasha's single-minded ruthlessness. Selim was to the seraglio born, and although he had the advantage of an education he was milder and more biddable than the self-made Albanian who hurdled the Mediterranean to make his fortune. Furthermore, the sultan faced opposition more formidable than anything Egypt could offer. He did not have the luxury of building his new realm over the ruins of the old, but had the far harder task of adapting an aged, brittle but seemingly imperishable superstructure to a new age.

The core of this structure was the Janissary Corps, Turkey's equivalent of the Streltsy which Peter the Great had had to crush before he could push through his reforms in the early eighteenth century – or, in imperial Rome, the Praetorian Guard of whom Juvenal asked, 'Who is to guard the guards themselves?' The Janissaries had been built up during the empire's late-medieval expansion using captured slaves who doted on their master the sultan. Replenished after each Ottoman military victory, ruled by no single ethnic group, for a time they were the most feared military force in Europe. Along with glory came perks – the seventeenth unit, for instance, had the privilege of encamping opposite the royal tent in time of war, while certain other units were permitted to bear arms during religious ceremonies. The Janissaries were confirmed foodies; the sultan regaled them with the finest mutton and their commanders hung soup ladles from their belts.

But the Janissaries had – like the Ottoman coinage in this age of soaring imperial deficits – become debased. They were a seedy criminal fraternity in hock to a mystical order, the Bektashis, whose sheikhs gave a quasi-religious legitimacy to any plot or insurrection they cared to launch. The Janissary response to any sultan who displeased them was to overturn their cauldrons (a traditional gesture of rebellion) and set fire to the city's wooden houses.

No sultan had succeeded in suppressing the Janissaries. They were recognised as the most formidable obstacle to reform. But Selim was heartened by his successful repulse of Napoleon from Acre in 1799 (even though he had been helped by the British and the plague), and he set about remoulding his victorious force into a big modern infantry called the New Order.

By 1807 the New Order comprised 27,000 troops trained in European drill and tactics. In theory it was to supplement the Janissaries, but it was clear that there could be no coexistence between two bodies whose ethos and philosophy were so opposed. Frenchmen – infidel Frenchmen! – had played a prominent role in the repulse of a British naval assault on Istanbul the previous year, and France's ambassador had the sultan's ear. All this truckling with foreigners and adopting their habits was too much for the old order. In May 1807, it struck back.

The trigger for rioting was the murder of a royal adviser who had ordered some auxiliaries to put on European-style uniforms. Affray turned to rebellion blessed by senior clerics and even government ministers. Selim realised the danger and backtracked desperately but he could not save his throne and he was deposed in favour of his reactionary cousin, Mustafa. In the event, the Janissary dictatorship with Mustafa as its figurehead lasted barely a year.

Then, in July 1808, after more military reverses and as food in the capital ran short, the new sultan was murdered in a counter-coup that did not, however, succeed in its aim of restoring Selim to the throne. Selim was disturbed while performing the midday prayer, lost consciousness from intense pressure applied to his testicles, and was hanged. And so, from the carnage (and from under a pile of carpets, where he had been hiding) emerged another of Selim's cousins, a 27-year-old moderniser who now found himself raised to the throne as Mahmud II, if only by default, for he was the last surviving descendant of the House of Osman.

It wasn't without significance that Mahmud II's accession to the throne coincided with Muhammad Ali's rise to absolute dominance over the water. Turkey's first great moderniser would spend his entire reign trying to muzzle Egypt's first great moderniser, who, when he wasn't making himself indispensable to the Porte by fighting rebellions in Greece, Arabia and elsewhere, did all he could to acquire territory of his own. It was a desperate realisation of his own military weakness that obliged Mahmud, in 1824, to enlist the help of his subject's enviably updated army and navy against the Greeks, but the pasha didn't bother to hide his ambition to inherit the riches of the Ottoman Empire. For all their strained relations, the sultan derived both inspiration and lessons from the Macedonian on the Nile.

Mahmud and Selim had shared a gilded incarceration and their conversations had convinced the former of the necessity of change if the empire was to survive. In 1822, the proclamation of a Greek Republic animated by the values of the French Revolution confirmed the wisdom of this prognosis. But Selim's murder had made Mahmud aware of the risks inherent in any reform effort that targeted strong vested interests, and the younger cousin would only wield supreme power unrestrainedly when he was sure it would not fail him. It wasn't until 1826, when Muhammad Ali was again demonstrating the success of his military reforms with a string of successes against the Greeks, that the sultan made his move.

In May of that year, Mahmud established a new force, transparently a revival of Selim's New Order, and the Janissaries rose rather than accept a modern drill. In what reads like an unwitting admission to their own obsolescence, their leaders declared, 'our ancient practice and drill for war is to hit earthenware jugs with rifle shot, and to hack at felt matting with the sabre. We want [to lay our hands on] those responsible for this innovation.'[5] The innovator was none other than the sultan, of course, but Mahmud had taken the precaution of winning support from influential religious officials, and public sentiment was now against the Janissaries' thuggery.

'The knife has reached the bone at last,' Mahmud declared on the morning of 14 June, before he set off from his palace to direct the massacre. And massacre it was, with some six thousand Janissaries killed under the sultan's heavy artillery, aided even by some religious students – after which the corpses were left for the dogs and some 15,000 survivors were exiled to various points of the empire.[6] 'Thirty minutes of grape-shot destroyed an institution which had lasted five centuries.'[7]

The way to reforming the Ottoman mind was open, and the man who bent himself to that purpose over the next twelve years decided the fate of an empire. Perhaps because he felt he was avenging his martyred cousin, Mahmud's sense of destiny was expressed in a firmness of intent that the panegyrists elevated into an imperious, terrifying anger, capable of stopping 100,000 giants in their tracks. He dispensed violence without compunction, murdering as many as two hundred women from his predecessor's harem, and hanging the leader of the Greek Orthodox Church (suspected of supporting Greek irredentism) from the gates of the patriarchate. Representative government and accountability were not for him, as they were not for Muhammad Ali – and understandably so, for in this delicate stage of the empire's infirmity only a despot could keep things on a straight path.

Eleven years later, in late 1837, the man who had destroyed the Janissaries rode across the bridge linking old Istanbul with Pera, the city's European quarter. Mahmud II was firm and erect in the saddle, grave of mien, and possessed of large coal-black eyes that conveyed both subtlety and a determination bordering on ferocity; to these regal attributes he allied the sartorial accessories of modernity. Instead of the robes and slippers of his forefathers, Mahmud sported a long coat buttoned at the neck, the Stambouline, and fitted trousers which he kept over boots of black velvet (somewhat in the manner of the Duke of Wellington); rejecting the broad, shell-like saddles and short stirrups of the Ottoman tradition, which had the effect of cramping the knees into the groin, he favoured long stirrups and a European saddle, which showed his elegant seat to best effect. To those who saw him that day, whether they were curious, hostile or indifferent, his appearance must have been little short of revolutionary.

The new bridge – wide, floating, wooden – had been thrown across the Golden Horn only a few months before. Following the ceremonies, which had been attended by various members of the sultan's harem, seated in magnificent carriages from whose grilled apertures they peered out, drawn by richly caparisoned oxen, the sultan had gone off to the easternmost finger of the Sea of Marmara, there to inspect new barracks for his beloved army and inaugurate a mosque done in the European idiom. He had been generous to the non-Muslims he had come into contact with, building houses and schools in Christian areas and returning enslaved Greek prisoners of war to their homes in the Peloponnese. The sultan returned to the capital aboard an Austrian steamer, which caused consternation, for 'never had one seen a king borrow a ship from the infidel for the transportation of his sacred person – the shadow of God on earth'.[8] Mahmud's clothes, his easy mixing with infidels and his disregard for the proper way of doing things were the outward signs of a deeply troubling mission to modernise the empire by adopting the culture of those – the Europeans – with whom it seemed to have least in common.

And now, as he crossed his new bridge, the sultan suffered an intolerable affront to his dignity, which sent a frisson throughout the city. The 'hairy sheikh', as Mahmud's assailant was known, must have been a dervish attached to one of Istanbul's mystical lodges. His name calls up images of matted, straggly tresses and a wooden, arced begging bowl, or *keskul* – indeed, the hairy sheikh is known to have enjoyed popular veneration as a saint. Throwing himself into the sultan's path as the royal party passed, he shouted, 'Infidel King! Haven't you had your fill of abominations? You will answer for your impiety before God. You destroy the institutions of your brother, you ruin Islam, and you bring down the Prophet's vengeance on yourself and us!' One of the sultan's guards called out that the man was mad, to which he replied, 'No, no, I am not in least mad. It's the faithless king and his ignoble counsellors who have lost their reason!' The hairy sheikh was immediately put to death and his body handed over to his fellow dervishes. The following day it was all over town that a celestial light had hovered over his body like the aureole of the saints.[9]

Ever since the obliteration of the Janissaries, Mahmud had been engaged in reform, alarming many, like the hairy dervish, who feared he intended to turn his back on religion. As it had been for Muhammad Ali, army reorganisation was naturally Mahmud's priority – and in his case it was accomplished with the help of a Prussian whose surname would evoke martial competence for almost a century, Lieutenant – later Field Marshal – Helmuth von Moltke (the German military would be led by Moltkes until the First World War).

In significant ways daily life grew more tolerable under the reformer sultan. Some efforts were made to reduce corruption in the courts and execution without due process was outlawed. Fires grew rarer with the pyromaniac Janissaries out of the way. The inhabitants of Istanbul gained their first newspaper in Turkish, as well as a small industrial base (armaments factories and weaving looms), an opera season (organised by Giuseppe Donizetti, brother of the Lombard composer Gaetano), and a revolutionary new headgear. The fez, originally a red or mauve beret of European inspiration – it later became a cylinder with a tassel – and unobjectionable from a Muslim point of view because it did not impede prostration, met its first prayer mat.

For all the anger that Mahmud's reforms excited in reactionaries such as the hairy sheikh, in truth the sanction of at least some of the Muslim *ulema* had always been necessary for any kind of reform – from the establishment of the first Muslim-run printing press, in 1727, to the introduction of the bayonet. Mahmud II played on the insecurities of clerics who had in any case fallen in the public's estimation (they'd proven themselves to be venal and corrupt), and wielded banishment as a stick to keep them supportive. Sophistry was employed to get around obstacles to change. Thus it was said that the adoption of European military drill did not constitute an illicit innovation, but was following on from the Prophet himself, who had borrowed the tactic of trench building from his Zoroastrian foes.[10]

'Men's exertions uproot mountains' ran an Arabic proverb which seemed to legitimise free will and reject the determinism that had hobbled the Muslims for so long. 'Who imitates another people becomes one of them' came the response, implying that an erosion of practice leads to an erosion of identity, for what is identity but an agglutination of practices and what remains of identity if they are allowed to degrade?

One of the sheikhs that took the lead in moving away from pietism under the protection of their reformist prince was Sanizadeh Ataullah. Born in 1771, educated at a famous religious college in Istanbul, his outlook had broadened as a result of contact with doctors who had been in Padua. Sanizadeh became one of the foremost Turkish polymaths; he knew Latin, French and Italian, and wrote on mathematics, history and the natural sciences, as well as the discipline for which he is remembered today, medicine.

In 1815 – a full eleven years before he declared his hand as a reformer – the sultan closeted himself away for several days in order to read Sanizadeh's manuscript on modern anatomy, physiology and pathology, *Mirror of the Body*. There was no originality to *Mirror of the Body*, nothing to surprise the Viennese professor from whom much of it had been lifted; for the lands of Islam, however, it was a revelation (nothing like it had been produced by the Muslims in Cairo) and the sultan ordered it to be reprinted at the royal press. Issued in three handsome volumes in red morocco, *Mirror of the Body* has been described by a Turkish scientific historian as 'the link between ancient and modern medicine'.[11] Its author was pleased that no foreign expertise had been needed for the illustrations accompanying the text; 'we succeeded, with God's aid, and by convening the numerous artisans who inhabit this capital of Constantinople, in having the necessary illustrations engraved on fifty-six copper plates'.[12]

The anatomists of Europe would have sniffed at these crude copies of European originals; in Istanbul their value was their absolute novelty. Here, disregarding Islam's prejudice against human depictions, were graphic drawings of bone, artery and sinew, scratched out by Istanbul artists and accompanied by three hundred pages of explanation (musculature; veins, nerves and glands; ailments ranging from pleurisy to haemorrhoids). Sanizadeh paid no deference to the archaic '*Yunani*' ('Greek') medicine of Galen and Avicenna, and while the significance of *Mirror of the Body* was lost on the illiterate majority, other groundbreaking works (on vaccination, for example, and treating syphilis, a malady known as 'the ailment of the Franks') were being added to the library of modern medical translations into Turkish – a thin but spreading wedge, stabbing at the moribund *Yunani* corpus.

As with the quadrants of Sayyid Mustafa and the books of Muhammad Ali's press at Bulaq, the effects of these innovations would be felt cumulatively, over time, and the sum of their influence was far greater than their sporadic, incomplete, almost random appearance might suggest. With each novelty a little fear was dispelled and the appetite whetted, and if the heavens did not fall in as a result of Sanizadeh's illustrations of the human form – if, on the contrary, pain and death were averted through enhanced knowledge of the bodily functions – who was to say that a scheme of gradual amelioration of the human condition was not God's wish?

In this way, through innumerable small measures and advances, fudges and elisions, the modern principles of empiricism, observation and analysis began to spread. The new thinking had shown itself first in military mechanics, before leaping to medicine and education; now there was general contagion. Statistics, modern sociology, agricultural innovation and political theory – these would all be guided by utility and progress.

During his twelve years of reform Mahmud set up and revitalised schools to diffuse this spirit, and none was more controversial than the medical school, where the spirit of enquiry fostered by Sanizadeh would be propagated. During Mahmud's inauguration speech in 1838 (he was the first ribbon-cutting sultan), he made the controversial announcement that all instruction would be in French – Ottoman Turkish wasn't rich enough in medical terminology. The sultan reminded his audience that the Europeans had derived much of their knowledge from translating the medieval Arab savants, although, as he went on (in terms that recalled the mathematician Sayyid Mustafa), 'the Europeans have been busy improving on them for more than a hundred years'. Mahmud realised full well that Turkish would not be a fit language for instruction until it had incorporated the full range of European terms and meanings, a task that, while it had begun (there was now a translation school on the lines of Cairo), still had a long way to go.

Also in 1838 Mahmud issued an imperial decree permitting human dissection at the medical school – eleven years after Clot Bey introduced the practice on the Nile – and the bodies of dead convicts were sent along for this purpose.[13] The old qualms were not immediately dispelled, however, with students refusing to dissect the corpse of anyone they knew to be their co-religionist, but their concerns were allayed by the chief medical officer, himself a very senior cleric, and 'in spite, therefore, of the Prophet's injunction – "though shalt not open a dead body, although it may have swallowed the most precious pearl belonging to another" – the students seized their instruments'.[14]

The sward and sediment of society was starting to loosen, as the American physician James DeKay observed in 1831 while strolling along a footpath above the Bosporus.

We suddenly came upon an old Turk, sitting in the ordinary posture on the ground, near a rustic marble fountain, and poring over the pages of a book with so much intentness that our presence was unheeded until we were close by his side ... he informed us that it was a treatise on cholera, drawn up by the medical board of Constantinople, published by the sultan, and distributed gratuitously throughout the empire. The doctrines of fatalism are generally represented to be carried so far by the Turks that it is thought impious to endeavour, by human means, to avert any impending danger ... to counteract this self-abandonment is one of the objects of the treatise, and it is shown that this pernicious belief is in no way connected with or dependent on their religion ... when it is recalled that only a few years ago such a measure would have endangered the throne, and the life of its author, the enlightened views and singular firmness of the present sultan may be justly appreciated.[15]

Perhaps it took an American, with his generous vision of self-improvement, and political disinterest – Turkey was not yet a strategic prize for the young United States – to discern the contours of Turkish achievement. After surveying the reservoirs, water courses and cannibalised Byzantine aqueducts that supplied Istanbul with fresh water, DeKay declared himself at a loss as to know which to admire most: the 'native good sense which pointed out the necessity and importance of furnishing the capital and its suburbs with pure and wholesome water, the ingenuity displayed in conquering almost invincible obstacles, or that wise and liberal economy which considered no expense too enormous, no sacrifices too great, in comparison with the health and comfort of the people'. If only the same could be said, he sighed, of his native New York City.[16]

DeKay's observations suggested a growing trend in favour of preventive health measures, but the ultimate public health disgrace – the plague – romped on unchecked and was familiar across the empire. Two centuries after the last big outbreak in Europe, malnourished Ottomans were all too acquainted with the delirium, buboes, bowel spasms and blackening of the skin, accompanied by a fever of up to 40 degrees, that marked the onset of the affliction; the rapidly putrefying victims were often abandoned to die alone, or, recognising the terminal nature of their afflictions, took their own lives.

Starting in 1812, a six-year pandemic wrought devastation along the empire's Mediterranean coastline. Perhaps as many as 250,000 Istanbullus were carried off in 1812 alone, and 45,000 in Izmir. No wonder the Ottomans were renowned for their contempt for death; it was born of familiarity.

'*Die Pest wird bestehen, so lange es Ulemas giebt.*' ('For as long there is an *ulema*, the pestilence will go on.') So wrote Lieutenant Helmuth von Moltke in frustration at the traditionalist clergy; they insisted that God's will may not be hindered, however gruesome it appeared. Millions believed the plague was spread by djinns (to which there are numerous references in the Quran); a hadith from the Prophet suggested that contagion was fallacy.[17] Some doctors of religion blamed these outbreaks on the sins of the people, with neighbourhoods inhabited by party-loving bachelors liable to be destroyed for their direct role in awakening God's wrath.[18]

In 1814 a French consul, A. M. Pouqueville, was urging notables in the Muslim quarter of Piraeus to set up a quarantine station when a dervish, 'one of those lunatics who lean on celestial authority in order to afflict the people', interrupted him to dissuade those present from 'listening to this Christian ... leave the French their customs and let us conserve those of our ancestors, and the principles of our religion!' And he went on to recommend a fatalistic attitude to what was, after all, 'one of the three hundred and sixty doors of paradise'. The dervish was applauded but a month later the pestilence arrived.[19]

However, the consul's experience was not indicative of the future – extreme fatalism was dwindling among the new men who filled the reformed ministries of Istanbul and Cairo. They saw that the plague had been defeated in Europe through quarantine, disinfection and the isolation and destruction of affected houses, and they resolved to enact similar measures at home. As with many other reform initiatives, Cairo was ahead of Istanbul. Muhammad Ali set up quarantine stations as early as 1813 and promoted hygiene by ordering the people to sprinkle the streets with water and air their clothes, as well as having letters fumigated before delivery. That reliable stick-in-the-mud Jabarti wrote of the measures without enthusiasm, noting the disruption they caused to the harvest, and there was much opposition to quarantine and the burning of victims' bodies, with the dead being buried in the old way (often in secret) and a consensus that impious precautions were driving Muslim businesses to the wall.[20] But the viceroy's mind was made up, his quarantine stations were like fortresses, and in 1831 he threw over ad hoc measures in favour of a coordinated approach in harness with the European consuls. There was a campaign to deprive the bacillus of its breeding grounds; stagnant pools were filled over, festering garbage heaps burned and foodstuffs monitored for freshness and quality.[21]

One of the tensions that one meets repeatedly in the story of the Islamic Enlightenment is that between a progressive despotism and a benighted popular will. In the case of the plague the benefits of the former become apparent. Without Muhammad Ali's absolutism the plague could not have been eradicated in Egypt because the majority deplored the methods he employed and did much to obstruct them. In the event, his system bore fruit in barely a dozen years, as the figures showed (reliable body counts were a crucial part of the struggle against the plague). In 1841 the number of deaths in Alexandria from the plague was down to 5,848; four years later the figure was zero.[22] With the suppression of the plague, of course, the obscurantists fell silent. Islam came onto the side of prevention, and the selfsame sanitation measures that had been denounced as heretical entered the routines of life.

Across the Mediterranean in Istanbul, Sultan Mahmud had long meditated a campaign against the 'angel of death', but it wasn't until the outbreak of 1836, which caused around 125,000 deaths in the empire's European provinces alone, that he acted decisively. Remarkably, he enjoyed the support of several members of the *ulema*, including his own former doctor and the head of the imperial printing press, who had published arguments, religious and logical, in favour of quarantine. An even more decisive clerical intervention came in 1838, when the empire's highest-ranking cleric, the sheikh ul-Islam, declared that 'when a town has the plague, it is permitted to avert it from the wrath of God and take refuge in the bosom of his mercy'.[23] With this fatwa, one of the most significant of Mahmud's reign, and coming just a year before his death, the bubo of fatalism was well and truly lanced. Measures derived from Europe – quarantine stations, plague hospitals and fumigation – were immediately put into action, with dramatic effects on mortality rates after 1844.

The plague had been a feature of Ottoman life for five hundred years. By around 1850, with a suddenness that must have been stunning, transforming attitudes to life and longevity, the Ottoman Empire became a plague-free zone. The end of the plague was bound up with the modernisation of medicine more broadly, fed in turn by the growing currency of secular views of mundane knowledge. In the words of a government report from the end of Mahmud's reign:

> All arts and trades are products of science. Religious knowledge serves salvation in the world to come, but science serves perfection of man in this world. Astronomy, for example, serves the progress of navigation and the development of commerce. The mathematical sciences lead to the orderly conduct of warfare as well as military administration. Innumerable new and useful inventions, like the use of steam, came into existence in this manner ... through science one man can now do the work of a hundred. Trade and profit have become difficult in countries where the people are ignorant of these sciences. Without science, the people cannot know the meaning of love for the state and fatherland. It is evident that the acquisition of science and skill comes above all other aims and aspirations of a state ... nothing can be done without the acquisition of science.[24]

This remarkable statement of faith in the aims of the Industrial Revolution, allied to a very Anglo-Saxon mercantilism, would not have been out of place in a speech at London's Royal Society. But the principles of the Victorian age had taken two hundred years to form; for the Ottomans, old assumptions had tumbled in decades. Who would have thought that science would in so short a time divest itself of its ancient function as an aid to faith, and come to justify itself? Astronomy, for instance, had served the needs of prayer and the Ramadan fast – when not lurching into the dangerous territory of astrology. For a growing number of the sultan's subjects the seven heavens were no longer a literal truth; they had become a figure of speech.

Alongside the new attitudes to knowledge and God's will, Mahmud introduced a radical solution to the tension that was inevitable in an empire that had both an Islamic mission and a non-Muslim majority – a solution strenuously encouraged by the powers (Britain in particular), but which he realised was essential to the empire's survival. Until Mahmud's reign the Ottomans had dealt with this contradiction by granting minorities separate legal status. A hierarchy, with the ruling Muslim elite on top and non-Muslims underneath, had protected the minorities from the fatal uncertainties that in Europe overshadowed any group that was not in power, and as a consequence the empire had been mostly free of pogroms, ghettos and inquisitions (indeed, an estimated 150,000 Jews fleeing the Spanish Inquisition in 1492 were welcomed to Turkey). But benevolent subjugation was now running up against two precepts that were intrinsic to modernity. The Ottoman system of dividing subjects according to their religious affiliation offended both against equality *and* national sovereignty. And the European powers, who viewed arrangements in the Ottoman Empire through the prism of self-interest, had become cheerleaders for both.

Under Islam, the Jews and the various Christian groups (the Greek Orthodox and Gregorian Armenians, for example) were protected subservient minorities called *dhimmis*. From this principle the Ottoman state had developed its concept of religious groups, or *millets*: commercially active, enjoying access to schools, hospitals and so on, but discriminated against by the sharia. Non-Muslims paid more taxes than Muslims. The testimony of a non-Muslim was worth half that of a Muslim. Few public positions were open to non-Muslims, and they were not permitted to bear arms. On the other hand, the *millets* enjoyed legal autonomy; they had separate tribunals and were judged by their own ecclesiastics who ran little theocracies inside the empire. The Greek patriarch, for instance, was within his rights to send an Ottoman citizen from his community into exile. There was also no standard procedure for dealing with crimes such as theft or adultery, and each *millet* handled infractions according to its own statutes. It was relatively straightforward for a Muslim Ottoman man to divorce his wife; for a Catholic Ottoman man it was impossible. If an Ottoman Muslim stole an egg his hand was in the balance. A Catholic might get away with a few Hail Marys.

Over the course of the nineteenth century, the esurient powers seized on the *millet* system as a means of keeping the Ottoman Empire in a weakened state. Essentially, the powers and the minorities paired off in strategic romances while the Porte looked on in impotent fury. With the Greek Orthodox already accounted for by the tsar, France got together with the empire's Catholics. Britain's ambassador to Constantinople, the pious, irascible Sir Stratford Canning (later Lord

Stratford de Redcliffe), offered his protection to the Protestant mission-aries. There weren't many Ottoman Protestants, though the ambas-sador had high hopes. On Mount Lebanon, the Druze and the Maronites were courted by Britain and France respectively. No one wanted the Jews.

The *millet* system was useful to the powers as a means of carving out micro-colonies on Ottoman territory called Capitulations. As Christians, British, French, Russian and other European citizens enjoyed *millet* status in the empire, and Capitulations constituted a kind of blanket immunity, freely surrendered by the Ottomans. The Capitulations were exploited to the utmost by the powers. In the 1840s, for instance, Canning gave a dressing-down to a senior Turkish official after a British subject was imprisoned – Canning's was the act of a proconsul, not an ambassador. As he and his fellow envoys knew, and their Ottoman hosts were generally forced to concede, such cases resided with the visitor nation's consular authorities, which even had their own prisons on Turkish territory. Some of the legations – the Italians were the worst – went so far as to peddle certificates of legal immunity. With the help of these 'protections', deep-pocketed Ottomans were able to immunise themselves from the laws of their own country.

To the pious Ottoman Muslim there was something perverse about this state of affairs. The sharia had been founded on the Prophet's words and example; how could it not work to the advantage of the faithful? The solution could only be found outside the traditional Islamic understanding of identity. Back in its formative years Islam had owed its survival in part to the Prophet's distinction between Muslims and *dhimmis*. The dominance of a Muslim elite and a lighter tax burden on Muslims had encouraged conversion and a blurring of racial lines; even now the various Ottoman communities – Turkish-speaking Muslims included – defined themselves according to their *millet*, not any newfangled notion of national identity. As the Victorian Ottomanist E. J. W. Gibb would go on to write, 'the Turk would no more have thought of dying for his country than for his meridian of longitude'.[25]

In order for the Ottoman Empire to achieve cohesion it needed to embrace a new and modern form of citizenship that was not based on religion. The empire's fractured and multifarious minorities must be brought back into the ambit of the state. A shared, secular identity – an Ottoman *patria* – would have to be invented.

A new definition of citizenship – an incipient Ottoman *e pluribus unum* – had begun to evolve following Mahmud's decree abolishing the Janissaries in 1826. In that document Mahmud had addressed an appeal for unity not to his Muslim subjects, as would have been customary, but to all Ottomans regardless of religious affiliation. In 1830 he took this sentiment even further, announcing that while he continued to distinguish between his subjects in the mosque, the church and the synagogue, outside these houses of worship 'there is no difference among them'. On the contrary, he went on, 'they are all indeed my children'.²⁶

The pretence was of Ottoman magnanimity from a position of strength. But it was obvious to the pious that reform had contributed to a disastrous shift in the hierarchy of communities – not only in the matter of the *millets*, but on wider questions of relations between the religions. The sharia forbids Muslims from ceding territory to non-Muslims, but this is what Selim III had done when he handed the Crimea to Russia after the defeat of 1792. Mahmud's recognition of independent Greece was also contrary to the sharia – as was his repatriation of Austrian citizens who had been captured and had converted to Islam. The Quranic get-out-of-jail card, 'necessity permits what is prohibited', was used in these and other cases. As with the recognition of full rights for non-Muslims, the new dispensations were an acknowledgement of a state of affairs in which the Muslims were no longer dominant.

For all the sultan's personal qualities, and the vigour with which he pursued reform, in territorial terms the reign of Mahmud II was a failure. In 1830 – the same year in which Greece won independence – Algeria was subjugated by France and became the first element in what would become a large North African empire (the significance of which eluded Rifaa al-Tahtawi in Paris). Ottoman control over the Balkans also loosened, with Russia establishing de facto protectorates in Moldova and Wallachia, and Serbia gaining near-independence, while the modernised army of Muhammad Ali probed Mahmud's Levantine domains in a widening arc.

The last of the humiliations that Muhammad Ali visited on his sovereign came in 1839, when an Egyptian force thrust its way deep into Asia Minor. That finished off the sultan, who had grown thin with worry, and was rumoured to be drinking pure alcohol and to be suffering from delirium tremens. He died on 29 June, five days after the Ottoman army was again routed by the Egyptians.[27] A favoured scholar lauded him as 'the Plato of the empire and the caliphate' and 'the sovereign to whom providence has revealed science and wisdom'.

Over the next three decades structural reforms known as the Tanzimat, or 'ordering', were implemented under Mahmud's sons Abdulmecid I (1839–61) and Abdulaziz (1861–76). The Tanzimat reforms were not democratic – the sultan kept his absolute powers – but they were conducive to a certain amount of delegation and secularisation, and brought about the expansion of a powerful lay bureaucracy and secular courts trying cases not covered by the sharia. In 1850 a code of commerce based on European practice was set up, and by 1868 education (a minority pursuit, it must be recognised: the vast majority of Ottoman citizens remained illiterate) had been almost completely secularised. Most significant from the minorities' point of view, they were promised equality under the law, as well as identical treatment to Muslims in education, government employment, taxation and military service. The last execution for apostasy (an Armenian who converted to Islam, while drunk, before reverting to Christianity, while sober) took place in 1843. After that, the Porte declared, 'the Musselman is now as free to become a Christian as the Christian is free to become a Musselman'.[28]

For many Christians and Jews in the empire, however, the new understanding of minority status promised by the Tanzimat rarely went beyond the rhetorical. Discrimination and brutality continued to be the norm, and Ottoman inclusiveness was often honoured in the breach. The armed forces remained fiercely sectarian; the Muslims were as reluctant to accept Christian brothers-in-arms as the latter were to serve, and in the event only a few Greek soldiers were taken into the navy, while a much larger number of Christians paid up the traditional exemption tax. In the medical school that Mahmud had founded at Galatasaray, in the European quarter of Istanbul (under the directorship of a young Viennese, Karl Ambroso Bernard), the historian and traveller Charles MacFarlane discovered that the Turkish students 'bullied all the [non-Muslims], ate and lived apart from them ... the Greeks hated the Armenians and the Armenians the Greeks, and both united in treating the very feeble minority of Jews with the greatest contumely'.[29] But the very fact that the school made room for these different groups on equal terms was a major innovation, and in the case of some of the minorities, in particular the Jews, it was *their* suspicious prelates that prevented more from joining.[30, 31]

Reform is always most vulnerable when it has yet to bear fruit, and while Sir Stratford Canning (who spent more than two decades as Britain's ambassador to the Porte) had a significant hand in formulating the Tanzimat, the cry that Turkey was exchanging the strongest of its own traditions for a potpourri of misunderstood foreign notions was widespread not only among the disapproving clergy but also among some Europeans. As the continent's most celebrated diplomat, Prince Klemens von Metternich (1773–1859), urged the grand vizier (and one of the architects of the Tanzimat) Mustafa Resid Pasha, 'do not destroy your ancient system in order to build a regime that would not fit your customs and way of life'.[32]

In the eyes of many, the Tanzimat seemed designed to do exactly that, and the contribution of the royal edicts to creating a new mindset was indeed considerable. The Tanzimat was the beginning of a journey that would conduct a small number of Armenians and Greeks to high office in the bureaucracy of a Muslim empire, and a larger number of their children through the doors of Muslim-dominated institutions of higher learning. Even more important, in the long term, were the traces left by the edicts on Islam itself. Expediency, the need to reinterpret Islamic law in the light of new conditions, all-trumping compulsion – under these and other pressures the sharia was beginning to write itself out of existence.

The prevailing currents were nothing if not favourable to the Tanzimat. The 1840s were a time of growing European scepticism. In England Darwin was elaborating the profoundly subversive evolutionary view that he would unveil in *The Origin of Species*, which amounted to a devastating assault on the biblical account of Creation. German popular materialists postulated that human 'consciousness' was merely a function of neural matter, while the nihilistic extravagances of the French Revolution showed they had legs in the 'springtime of the peoples' of 1848. After the suppression of the Hungarian uprising of that year,

Hungarian (as well as some Polish) revolutionaries took refuge in Istanbul, adding to the general atmosphere of irreverence.

By the time Charles MacFarlane visited Istanbul again, in 1848, students at the Galatasaray medical school who had been accustomed to learning from wax models were quite – even excessively – at ease with the new arrangements:

In the dissecting room we found a dozen young Turks by themselves, cutting up the body of a negress. On a 'side-board,' close at hand, lay the uncovered and horrible-looking corpse of a negro; and in an ante-room were slovenlily [sic] scattered the head, arms and legs, and all the *disjecta membra*, of another Nubian. As we entered, these Mussulman students were talking and laughing, were handling the black human flesh with as little scruple as if it had been mutton or lamb, and were working away with scalpels that were shorter than our silver fruit-knives. I asked one of them whether all this were not somewhat contrary to his religion. He laughed in my face, and said, '*Eh! Monsieur, ce n'est pas au Galata Serai qu'il faut venir chercher la religion!*' ['One shouldn't come looking for religion at Galatasaray!']³³

For a British Tory like Charles MacFarlane, the scepticism exhibited by the Turkish medical students was troubling. The medical college taught all its students 'one disbelief', he chaffed, while the artillery hospital at the Armoury employed a medical assistant who had put into Turkish 'some of the most spicy passages' of Voltaire, and who considered *Candide* to be 'very amusing and delightful'.³⁴ To these Turks, Panglossian optimism ('all is for the best in the best of all possible worlds') in the face of natural calamities like the Lisbon earthquake of 1755 must have been familiar, visible in the fatalist attitudes that were adopted towards the plague.

But for MacFarlane the nadir of degeneracy came at the military hospital at Scutari, where he found

an elegant saloon, set apart for the use of the doctors and the young Turks and their assistants. A book was lying open on the divan. I took it up. It was a copy of a recent Paris edition of the Atheist's manual,

Système de la Nature, with the name of the Baron d'Holbach on the title page as the author. The volume had evidently been much used; many of the striking passages had been marked, and especially those which mathematically demonstrated the absurdity of believing in the existence of a God and the impossibility of believing in the immortality of the soul. As I laid down the volume one of the Turks said to me, '*C'est un grand ouvrage! C'est un grand philosophe! Il a toujours raison.*' ['It is a great work! He is a big philosopher! He is always right!']

The fact that the language of the Armoury hospital visited by MacFarlane was French was as much a commentary on the inability of the Turkish language to convey modern ideas as it was on the dynamism of the language of the Enlightenment.

A language of administration, but rarely one of high art and never of orthodox religion, Turkish had not reached the excellence of its neighbours, Persian and Arabic. In its popular form it had flourished as a medium for orally transmitted folk poetry, but 'vulgar Turkish' was shunned by the mandarins of the Porte and the (Arabist) religious scholars alike. Then there were the lumbering manoeuvres of 'high' Ottoman poetry, so insular, artificial and estranged from the spoken language that towards the end of his six-volume *History of Ottoman Poetry* the Victorian scholar E. J. W. Gibb rounded on the literary form to which he had devoted his life (he died before completing his book), arguing that it captured no voice from 'outside the narrow school where it was reared ... baffled and helpless [in] the stagnant swamp of a dead culture'.[35]

The Ottoman idea of a literary language was that it should approach the subject in as ornamental and long-winded a fashion as possible, executing puns, ransacking the Persian anthologies and running together Arabic compounds like swags on an urn. Punctuation barely existed and there were no fewer than nine different calligraphic systems in use. Getting to the point was considered facile and functionality was ignorance. A later historian found he could condense a thirteen-page Ottoman document into two sentences and keep the gist.

The effects of an ill language on its literature were deadly. Originality was throttled so effectively that popular romances were forced into a single generic shape. So rare were instances of unconventional prose writing that if one came along (a well-known example was a letter by a prominent statesman describing a boat ride), it was acclaimed for its freshness.[36] Perhaps the most important purpose of language was to praise God and spread his word, while for many poets classic images such as the nightingale in love with the rose obviated the need for original thought.

For all its unwieldiness, poetry remained vital as a means of communication. Verses were the media, susceptible to improvement and modification before being passed on by word of mouth. If one bears in mind that memorising large amounts of words was a regular part of life in nineteenth-century society – not in the sense of rote learning at school, but as a means of retention – so its currency starts to make sense. To Ottoman Turks it would have been odd *not* to exploit the commodious, sophisticated and highly flexible memory bank we all possess, and they committed huge quantities of poetry to memory. Timely verses could provide pointed, satirical and (if necessary) anonymous comment on public affairs. They could skewer or flatter a statesman, or elicit replies, confirmations and subtle distortions wherever people gathered.

Beyond the faulty mechanics of the language there was another, social obstacle to the spread of skills and information. Knowledge was a means to social and economic success and was jealously guarded by those in possession of it. The book market outside Istanbul's Beyazit Mosque was run by a few score families operating a closed shop and protecting all information about their trade – 'to ask me for a catalogue is to laugh at my beard!' a visiting bibliophile was told. Another group with a unique skill, the dragomans translating documents in Turkish for the foreign missions, 'made a mystery of all matters related to that language, and endeavoured to persuade their employers and the public that, to acquire Turkish, it was requisite to … have studied from infancy'.[37] Similar thickets entwined parts of civil administration such as land ownership, which was guarded by a jargon so impenetrable that the simplest transaction was impossible without the help of a sage on commission.

The model for all these monopolies was, of course, religious, for knowledge of the deity has always been guarded, even in 'churchless' Islam, and the religious schools operated on the principle of delayed gratification. The lengthy and ill-defined nature of the period of instruction in school; the unquestionable authority exerted by age and experience; the 'protection' of a precocious scholar from challenging texts (especially philosophical ones) for which he was not 'ready' – all this acted as gauze through which it took years, even decades, for true erudition to strain through. And when the scholars finally reached the level of scholarship for which they had laboured, was it any wonder that they in turn applied the same restrictions on their juniors?

This dismal state of affairs was to change, however, over the course of the final decades of the nineteenth century. It is possible to date the arrival of the new medium that would transform the Turkish language to 22 October 1860, when a hand-operated printing press in one of the lean-to shacks and masonry cells that had attached themselves like barnacles to Istanbul's disintegrating city walls, whipped by the spray and wind off the Bosporus, brought out the first number of the newspaper *Tercuman-i Ahval*, or 'Interpreter of Conditions'.

The Ottoman Empire was already home to dozens of newspapers produced by non-Muslims – even if Muslims were among their audiences – and in many languages. Back in the 1820s the Istanbul resident Robert Walsh had noted the popularity of 'news-rooms' where 'a stool is placed in the centre, on which the man who can read sits, and others form a circle round him and listen ... with profound attention, interrupted only sometimes by a grave ejaculation of *"Inshallah"* (God willing) or *"Allah Keerim"* (God is merciful)'. Newspapers had also made their way into the coffee houses, 'and the same Turk I had noticed before dozing, half stupefied with coffee and tobacco, I now saw actually awake, with the paper in his hand, eagerly spelling out the news'.[38]

What Walsh had witnessed some forty years before was a single, government newspaper expatiating on the sultan's wisdom; the *Tercuman-i Ahval* was quite different in character. It was the first independent newspaper to be owned and operated by Muslim Turks. The important word here is 'independent' – its predecessors had been government ciphers. What was more, the *Tercuman-i Ahval* was a slick and innovative product. Column headings unknown to Turkish readers ('Internal Events', 'External Events,' 'Serialisation') were scratched out by the city's best calligraphers, and the blocks of type were expertly set (probably by moonlighting employees of the royal mint).

The *Tercuman-i Ahval* was founded by a Paris-educated translator and scion of an aristocratic family, Capanzade Agah, but it was Agah's first editorialist, the same Ibrahim Sinasi we met in the introduction, who would be Istanbul's Rifaa al-Tahtawi and have a lasting effect on Turkish letters. Born in 1826, the orphan son of an artillery captain who had been killed fighting the Russians, Sinasi was a terse, with-drawn and rather begrudging polymath who had learned Arabic, Persian and French – the last through his friendship with a French émigré and Muslim convert, Comte Charles de Châteauneuf – after entering the administrative division of the Istanbul Arsenal.[39] Sinasi's talents won him the attention of the grand vizier Mustafa Resid Pasha, whose name was closely associated with the Tanzimat reforms, and so it was that in early 1849 Sinasi found himself dispatched to Paris on government scholarship. While there he met his future collaborator Capanzade Agah, perfected his French and observed the battle of ideas, classes and words on a European stage.

The five years Sinasi spent in Paris were a time of reaction. In February 1848 the 'citizen king' Louis-Philippe of Orléans, whose trium-phant installation amid a blaze of pluralist optimism Rifaa al-Tahtawi had witnessed eighteen years earlier, was deposed after widespread disillusionment. But the egalitarian objectives of the Second Republic that replaced Louis-Philippe, including full employment and universal male suffrage, proved unachievable without further convulsions, and popular support grew for the capitalist autocracy promised by another pretender, Bonaparte's nephew Louis-Napoleon. The trend was consummated with Louis-Napoleon's proclamation as emperor in 1852, and the Second Empire began. Sinasi's sympathies in this period were with moderate republicans such as the poet Lamartine (briefly France's ruler under the Second Republic) and the newspaper editor Samuel Sylvestre de Sacy – son of the celebrated orientalist Sylvestre de Sacy – who secured the Turk's election to the Société Asiatique. But despite fabricated accounts by later admirers to the effect that Sinasi had hung the republican flag over the Pantheon, it was as an Ottoman that he observed events in Paris, not a Frenchman. In 1854 he went back to Istanbul in the midst of the Crimean War – his home town was full of invalids, some of them being tended by Florence Nightingale – with advanced thoughts about freedom, the nation and electoral democracy.

He also had a shrewd idea of the improving effects of the press on language. The inadequacies of the Ottoman Turkish language remained legion. It needed to be made pithier and more technical,

more concrete and less transcendental. At the same time, it needed
to surf the crests of modern aspiration: individualism, civilised living,
the rights of man. Sinasi's experiences in France had taught him that
the goals of human progress and linguistic development were linked.
He would apply himself to both.

More important for the advancement of these goals than Sinasi's
modest creative output was the example he set and the literary taste
he exhibited. Under Sinasi's influence Turkish literature was elevated
from the status of a joke, or a game of wits, and he delivered poetry
from those laboured symmetries and contrivances that corseted
meaning. For him words were for writing, not declaiming – a way of
conveying meaning, not decorating the void. Sinasi can be said to have
invented modern Turkish prose and drama, while in the case of poetry
he released it from its dungeon of precedent, shifting the poetic
imagination from the abstract to the concrete and experimenting with
rhyme and metre.

His version of the fable of the donkey and the fox is almost child-
like in its simplicity:

> Shall I not come to you, oh, my lion,
> So I can see and admire your beauty from close up?
> Let my master's noble and kind shadow be forever,
> Where your sacred paw treads a rose will bloom.

In the words of a much later literary giant, the twentieth-century
novelist Ahmet Hamdi Tanpinar, 'one of the notable things about
these lines is that they were all written in a language that was close
to the Turkish spoken in homes and the streets'.[40] It was nothing less
than a revolution, and before Sinasi was done the language had changed
from a 'plaything for the amusement of the learned' to an instrument
for the 'moral and intellectual education of the whole people'.[41]

For all the lingering importance of poetry, it was in the irresistible
and constantly mutating new medium of the independent press that
Sinasi set most store. Sinasi was Turkey's first modern playwright,
publishing across several editions of *Tercuman-i Ahval* a comedy of
manners, the *Wedding of a Poet*, which satirised arranged marriages in
a rumbustious and colloquial Turkish. His editorials in the same paper
read as a kind of induction course for Turks who needed to be weaned

off government propaganda sheets clogged by officialese, and who might yet be swayed by religious pedants. Among other charges that these bigots laid at the door of the press was that it was part of a European plot to destroy Islam and destabilise the country.

In his maiden editorial Sinasi argued that when people in a 'social body' submit to the law, they automatically acquire the 'right' to express themselves on the state of their country 'by word and by pen'. For proof of this he pointed to the 'political newspapers of the civilised nations whose minds have been opened by the power of knowledge'.[42] Sinasi was one of the first thinkers in the Middle East to define rights not as conferred from above, but as inseparable from the growth of a law-based society.

Sinasi's next editorial was more technical, explaining how newspapers worked and how they might contain 'instalments' which could later on be cut out and bound as a book, allowing voluminous items (such as his *Wedding of a Poet*) to be spread over several weeks. There was, he explained, a useful word denoting 'those who desire to be a customer for a specified period of time', a 'subscriber' (whose Turkish equivalent is borrowed from the French word, *abonnement*). In the same article he gave a short history of printing, from its presumed origins in China, and an account of the earliest examples of journalism, such as the Roman daily record, the *Acta Diurna*, which was carved on stone or metal and then copied by scribes.[43] In this way Sinasi subtly coupled modern universalism to Islam itself, for few Muslims are ignorant of the Prophet's injunction, 'Seek thou knowledge, even unto China.'

Sinasi left the *Tercuman-i Ahval* after just twenty-five issues to set up his own paper, *Tasvir-i Efkar*, ('Illustration of Opinion'). Twice a week this four-page production was a platform for a talented group of writers, some of them fellow members of the Board of Education, or former colleagues at the Arsenal, and they expressed themselves on such a wide range of domestic and foreign issues, and with such authority, that it soon became the country's journal of record. The subjects addressed by Sinasi in his own editorials ranged from municipal administration to literature and good manners – he showed the magpie instincts of the modern columnist. In one article he applauded a strain of opinion in Italy demanding that the Pope abandon his claims to worldly power (the 'Rome Question') and in another urged the keeping of proper customs inventories as an aid to determining the empire's external trade balance. Sinasi also introduced the Turkish reading public to the word *millet*, or nation, in its modern, multi-confessional sense.

Cosmopolitan, outward-looking, drawn to questions of human and economic development, Sinasi was described by subsequent Turkish literary historians as the pioneer of a new mode of thinking. In a sign that the Turkish language could, after all, be induced to change, he popularised imported political concepts like 'freedom of expression' and 'natural rights', but for all the universalism of his vision (he would later avow, echoing Victor Hugo, 'My nation is humanity and my fatherland is the earth'), his world view was shot through with national vigour. Ranging from Russia's systematic incitement of the Ottoman Christians – he singled out the St Petersburg press for particular criticism – to instability in neighbouring Greece (King Otto had recently been overthrown), Sinasi showed a steely approach to the national interest, and an enthusiasm for sending in the troops, for, as he put it, 'if you desire peace and improvement, prepare for war'.[44]

One of the most fascinating of Sinasi's editorials reveals his ability to draw philosophical significance from apparently quite workaday subjects. The government had announced a scheme to introduce street lighting to parts of central Istanbul, which was opposed by knee-jerk conservatives (it had been introduced in London almost two hundred years earlier, also to opposition). Sinasi, of course, was enthusiastic, not only for practical reasons of reduced criminality and enhanced commerce, but also because the illumination of the streets (initially through fixed lanterns lit by householders, subsequently through gaslight) seemed to presage the deeper and less extinguishable illumination of people's minds. 'Who opposes street lighting,' he demanded, 'if not those ruffians who profit from the darkness of the night?'[45] And then, in a barbed reference to the intellectual monopolists whose feeble glow depended on surrounding gloom and the ignorance of others: 'a firefly only glows at night'.[46]

Sinasi was too cautious to proclaim his radicalism but in general he regarded authority with distrust and in the viper's nest of Ottoman public life his truculence, hauteur and readiness for a quarrel in print made him enemies. His defence of rational values also brought him criticism from conservatives who considered him dangerously radical.

Here was a promising servant of the state who had accepted the Porte's patronage only to set up a soapbox to comment on issues that didn't concern him – and he had the temerity to turn down a compromising gift of five hundred gold coins that Sultan Abdulaziz offered him when the first issue of *Tasvir-i Efkar* came out. Sinasi also appeared in public shaven-cheeked, a sign of effeminacy and enchantment with the West that disturbed his hirsute compatriots. In fact, as he explained, supplying his Parisian doctor's notes as evidence, he had shaved for medical reasons after contracting ringworm. Sinasi's religious commitment was dubious (here he differed from Rifaa); he rarely mentioned God in his writings, stressing instead the agency of 'rational man' legislating in favour of 'rights and justice'. A eulogy he wrote for Mustafa Resid Pasha contained whispered republican sentiments and he praised the famous reformist for daring to 'inform the sultan of his limits'.[47]

There remained many who did not believe in such limits, not least Sultan Abdulmecid himself, who in 1855 had Sinasi removed from the Board of Education for 'continually writing in a critical vein of government affairs'.[48] This was a paranoid reading of Sinasi's generally measured editorials, but by now the climate had turned against even the principle of a free press, and Sinasi's old paper, *Tercuman-i Ahval*, had been served a closure order (lasting just twelve days, it is true, but setting a baleful precedent, as any more recent Turkish journalist can attest). His crime had been to describe the country's education system as 'broken' and the teachers as barely literate.[49]

In the same way that later governments around the world took their time to grasp the legal and political implications of the Internet, in Ottoman Istanbul there was a startled pause to take the measure of the independent press and compose a response. The irony was that, having accepted one Western import, the authorities then felt compelled to bring in another to suppress it. That was the motivation behind Turkey's first ever press law – closely modelled on the censorship measures of Napoleon III – which established a government commission to sit in judgement on the press, outlawed anonymous articles and promised imprisonment for journalists and closure for any newspaper acting 'against the government'. This new legislation arrogated to the Porte the right, 'whenever the general interest of the country may require it, to act ... against those newspapers which do not recognise the above-stated principles'.

The press law came into force on 1 January 1865, and before the month was out Sinasi had fled to France, the first in a wave of journalists who would take themselves, and in some cases their newspapers, to the more clement atmospheres of London, Paris or Geneva. For Sinasi it was the end of a remarkable journalistic career almost as soon as it had begun, and the resumption of his life as a linguist, for this second Parisian exile would be dominated by his efforts to compile a gargantuan Turkish–French dictionary – though he also made time for his evening coffee on the Quai Voltaire, and rarely missed a performance of Molière at the Théâtre Français (even his leisure time was stamped with the Enlightenment). In 1867 – having assured himself he would not be pursued legally – he made a flying visit of extreme bad-temperedness to divorce his wife, but it wasn't until 1869 that he came back for good, the great dictionary only half complete.[50] After his return, Sinasi seems to have been overwhelmed by depression, and cut himself off from society. His death in Istanbul in 1871, aged just forty-five, was barely noticed.

Although he was not celebrated in his lifetime, Sinasi is now recognised as having had an influence on Turkish literature that was out of proportion with his own modest production. 'In the name of simplicity and newness,' Ahmet Hamdi Tanpinar later wrote, 'in his rejection of the usual ornamentations, his preference for experimental rhyme and his use of the past tense, he changed the axis of literature in a matter of eight or ten poems and a few stray stanzas and couplets.' Coming up against a tradition 'that had in every respect been rooted and emplaced over five hundred years', Sinasi had shaken 'that old tree from its roots ... uprooting the system of values that lay behind it'.[51] What Tanpinar did not dwell on was the precedent-setting significance of Sinasi's great formal innovation: a Western-style newspaper without government ties. Despite the censorship law of 1865 the news continued to gush and the number of outlets to rise, and a fourth estate that had begun as a small and isolated extension of government grew into an independent creature with a mind of its own.

At the time of Sinasi's flight to Paris, in 1865, the number of newspapers published in Turkish was four – including the two he himself had started. Before the end of his life a further twenty-one titles had come into existence, even if some of these had later closed down, and by 1876 the number had soared to 130. Although there is some vagueness over circulation figures, sales of 10,000 per day were not uncommon and some issues of *Tasvir-i Efkar* seem to have sold as many as 24,000 copies, which compares favourably not only with the Japanese and Russian press of the time, but also with the more established markets of Germany and Britain. 'The shop owners and servants read newspapers in Istanbul now,' Sinasi's follower Namik Kemal commented in 1883. 'At any rate, they listen.'[52]

The effects of the Ottoman explosion in communications that took place in the 1850s, of which Ibrahim Sinasi was a catalyst, can scarcely be exaggerated. Genteel life in the capital – and, increasingly, in the provincial towns – was transformed. In Istanbul, scientific, literary and poetic clubs opened in public buildings and people's homes, and Freemasonry was all the rage. (Napoleon's invaders had brought Freemasonry to Egypt; it had an older history in Turkey because of its popularity among Levantine traders.) The high-ranking educationalist Mehmed Tahir Munif Pasha – who was a Mason, had a French wife, and kept open house when he was not serving as a diplomat abroad – dared to argue in favour of evolution (though like Darwin's contemporary Alfred Russel Wallace he exempted human beings from the theory), and for reform of the cumbersome and unphonetic Ottoman script. This was the first of a series of attempted reforms that would eventually lead to the adoption of the Latin alphabet.[53] Opinions were formed and hardened away from the traditional crucibles of the Palace and the Porte, with debates held in private libraries, assemblies springing to life, and innocuous-sounding organs like the 'Society of Poets' elaborating subversive views owing much to European socialism. By the 1860s the culture of unleashed expression was sufficiently big, diffuse and irreverent to affect the policies of the empire and fill the Porte with dread of a new and many-headed monster: 'public opinion'.

Along with the growth in communication, barriers between communities and classes also grew porous, perhaps most noticeably on board the steamships that had been sailing back and forth across the Bosporus since 1854, whose passengers – rich and poor, male and female – were thrown together on terms of unwonted familiarity.

It was little wonder that the authorities viewed with alarm the transformation of the public discourse that took place in the 1860s and 70s, and their diminishing ability to regulate it. Every occasion for the mingling of the people had become an opportunity for comment and complaint – in most cases following the lead of a stubbornly untrammelled press. In just a few years the mindset of Turkish journalism – and with it, that of educated society as a whole – had opened up, moving from 'report to comment, from comment to criticism, from criticism to opposition', and now, increasingly, 'from opposition to defiance'.[54]

Reform is often embarked upon with chilling premonitions of the price of failure. So it was with the Ottoman transformation of the nineteenth century, only with the additional, irksome sense that the objective of modernity had been defined in Europe and could not be redefined in Turkey. The Ottomans might hope to indigenise Europe's cult of the individual, its enthusiasm for nation states sustained by geography, education and patriotic myths, and its mantra of rights for all; what they could not do was reject modernisation bag and baggage, for that would throw Turkey back a century and smash it to smithereens under the pressure of minority irredentism – or even pitch it into the embrace of its neighbour Russia. Even more urgently than Egypt, Turkey had to adapt or die.

Geopolitics was an additional complication. The Ottoman statesmen who guided the empire could not afford to alienate the liberalising colossus of Britain, whose ambassadors to the Porte behaved as if they owned the place. (Canning was the worst in this respect; it was said that he was unwilling to share power with the sultan.) In this way a pattern began to emerge that has since become familiar across the Islamic world: coercion and opportunism on the part of the West, and a series of reforms, conceived of insecurity and ambivalently implemented, on the part of the Muslims. It is not coincidental that the two big spurts of Tanzimat reforms came at moments when the Ottomans were in especial need of Western diplomatic support. The first major reform package, in 1839, followed the rebellious Muhammad Ali's military incursion into Anatolia, while the second, in 1856, came at the end of the Crimean War, when the empire groaned under debts from its Western allies. The semi-coerced nature of the Tanzimat was of course noted by its critics, who denounced the reformists for encouraging Western economic penetration.

It was the beginning of a Muslim crisis of identity whose signs we see around us today. Turkey's reforming statesmen and the class they represented were Europeanised to the extent that they knew French, sat on chairs and regarded religion as a private affair, but their very hybridity was a source of grumbling and self-criticism, with one pasha remonstrating at the parade of shallow, shuffling proto-Europeans through the imperial chancery. 'I would rather see my son a really good Christian and an honest man,' he said, 'than a Constantinople Turk *alla Franca*.'[55] The wise reformist made haste slowly, for while change could save the empire, it could also break it. 'Our speed is limited by the fear of making the boilers burst,' remarked perhaps the most effective statesman of the era, Mehmed Emin Ali Pasha; 'our metamorphosis must be cautious, gradual, internal, and not accompanied by flashes of lightning.'[56]

Even with this measured approach, the empire's unity was under constant threat; from the European provinces demanding more and more autonomy, from an internal imbalance and power struggle between the monarch and uncooperative regional magnates, and from a decline in productivity under pressure from British imports. Christian missionaries also spread as a result of demands for religious freedom on the part of Canning and others; to Ottoman Syria these mostly American and British Protestants introduced such symbols of modernity as the potato, kerosene lamps, wire nails and sewing machines.[57] Istanbul was acquainted with whalebone, pianos and cameras.[58] This last was another blow to Islamic iconoclasm, as the more adventurous (and self-regarding) sort of Muslims rushed to have their portrait taken.

Even victory in the Crimea had brought strains to the empire, as the powers leveraged the war loans they had extended to the Porte in order to secure footholds for their railway companies, banks and shipping concerns. The Tanzimat reforms had tiptoed around the imperial purse, which in turn lulled Abdulmecid and his brother and successor, Abdulaziz (an eccentric and spendthrift sultan who recognised Ismail as Egypt's khedive before going on to sack him), into heroic overspend, with the latter splurging on miniature horses, music boxes and ironclads, and undertaking a ruinous trip to Europe. All this was financed by debt serviced by debt on the fantastically wasteful khedival model, which led to default in 1875 – with catastrophic effects on Ottoman credit-worthiness.

The sultans' heroic overspend fuelled a cultural confusion to rival that of Cairo under Ismail. The Ottomans' abandonment of the medieval Topkapi Palace, a labyrinth of pavilions with an Islamic (non-figurative) decorative scheme and an aversion to corridors, was a highly symbolic rejection of the old. The new was a neoclassical meringue with all the mod cons. The Dolmabahce Palace went up in the early 1850s, boasting the world's biggest throne room, a giant chandelier burning four hundred jets of gas, French parterres in the garden and passages filled with forgettable pastoral scenes. Here, and in a plethora of lesser palaces, Sultans Abdulmecid and Abdulaziz beguiled their hours amid crystal and porphyry bought on foreign credit, the former venturing to a Crimean victory ball at the British Embassy, where he observed quadrilles and partook of an ice, and Abdulaziz indulging his hobbies of ram-fighting and camel-wrestling.

Amid the lavish spending, the educational promise that was implicit in modernity was being forgotten. True, over the first half of the nineteenth century, the copyists and clerics had overcome their dislike of the printed word, but – as in Egypt – the virtuous circle of knowledge and consumption remained incomplete.[59] For all the brave plans set out by the Ottoman ministers, primary and secondary schools had increased very slowly in the cities and hardly at all in rural areas. As late as the 1860s the literacy rate for Ottoman adults was perhaps no more than 15 per cent, a low figure even for a modernising Eastern empire. (In the 1870s, by contrast, the rate in Japan was 40 per cent for men and 15 per cent for women).[60] In the words of a prominent Ottoman reformer, the unlettered majority were 'without pen and without tongue', and this vivid phrase tells of their inability to impress their demands on a society that had spurned the old medieval tolerance of illiteracy (in military leaders, for instance). In the formula-driven, theory-rich age of machines, the bifurcation between those who had received an education, and those who had not, was brutal.[61]

Was this, then, much-vaunted modernity? The question was asked by progressives and conservatives alike, and gradually dissatisfaction and unmet expectations gave rise to a new phase in the history of reform – enacted on new ground. No longer would the debate pivot on whether to accept or reject Westernising measures, a question that had already been answered, but on something more radical: limiting the autocratic power of the state.

The men associated with this new phase, which we would nowadays call democratisation, were not primarily ministers or bureaucrats, but were suspected by the state. They were poets, journalists and playwrights, members of a new class within the emerging, European-style bourgeoisie, and they, not Napoleon's savants, would bring true political change to the Middle East.

On an April night in 1873, several hundred Istanbullus exited the Gedik Pasha Theatre in a state of exhilaration. They had just witnessed the opening performance of a new play, *Homeland or Silistria*, an account of the successful Turkish defence of the fortress of Silistria against the Russians during the Crimean War. Since the end of the conflict in 1856 the Ottoman public had been starved of good news, with separatism unabated in the Balkans and a dizzying rotation of personnel in Istanbul (six grand viziers in just three years), famine ravaging the interior and the economy heading for the default that would come in 1875. Russia's influence was once more in the ascendant, while the increasingly unstable Sultan Abdulaziz preened absurdly; he was said to have awarded a medal to a victorious fighting cock, and could not bring himself to forgive a pasha who had dared to wear spectacles in his presence. At least for now, at one of the capital's popular new theatres – its red bills were everywhere on street corners and in the mosques – humiliation and failure could be forgotten, if only for a few hours.

Homeland or Silistria tells the story of Zekiyeh, an orphaned maiden (played by the celebrated Armenian actress Piranuh), and her handsome beau, Islam, who is off to defend the besieged castle of Silistria against the Russians. Taking in imposture, filial love, violence and romance, this pneumatic melodrama ends with Zekiyeh's death, her father Sitki and Islam united in grief and triumph, and the audience engulfed by sobs, songs and the fanfare of trumpets.

Homeland or Silistria was written by Namik Kemal, a 33-year-old newspaper editor and follower of Ibrahim Sinasi, and on the opening night he responded to the delirium of the crowd by appearing onstage before slipping discreetly away. His admirers were not satisfied, however, and sought out the offices of his newspaper, *Ibret* ('Admonition'), shouting 'Long live Kemal!' Their clamour was reportedly loud enough to interrupt the sleep of Abdulaziz himself, who was dismayed to hear a crowd hollering for someone other than himself. The people also yelled, 'May God grant our wish!', a pun on the name of the sultan's nephew and heir apparent, Murad, whom many believed would be an improvement on his uncle, and with whom Kemal had good relations. There was also much admiration for Piranuh as the embodiment of the patriotic Zekiyeh, and receipts from the next performance of the play – after which there was again disorder in the streets – were presented to her in their entirety.[62]

Homeland or Silistria had exposed sensitivities at the very top of the Ottoman state. But the play owes its enduring significance less to personal rivalries than to the novelty of its themes and the consuming public emotions they aroused. The feelings that Kemal had tapped – and that he would continue to tap over some five hundred more performances, some as far afield as Izmir and Salonica – indicated a transfer of fidelity among Middle Easterners from the traditional objects of God and sultan to a more abstract value that had been decorated with blood over the past century of European and American history, and which now, after a brief lag, had landed in the Gedik Pasha Theatre. It was patriotism that pulsed through *Homeland or Silistria* – or, less charitably, jingoism, a word that Londoners would coin during a spasm of Russophobia in 1878 – and it was of patriotism that the cast sang before the final curtain:

> Before us the enemy, ready with arms,
> March, heroes, to the aid of the fatherland!
> March, onward, march, salvation is ours;
> March, heroes, to the aid of the fatherland!

Just as Ibrahim Sinasi had alerted the reading public to the modern meaning of *millet*, so Namik Kemal gave a militant flavour to another Arabic word that the Egyptian sheikh Rifaa al-Tahtawi had popularised a few years before, and which Kemal now bathed in a quasi-religious light. The Romantic vision that Kemal had of the *vatan*, or fatherland, was more than earth, rivers and the coast of the sea; it was, he wrote in *Ibret*, not some 'imaginary line' scratched out by a clerk's pen, but a 'sacred concept born of a host of noble feelings such as nationhood, brotherhood, respect for one's ancestors, love of family and memories of youth'.[63]

Kemal's patriotic output situated him in the European tradition of the modern artist exerting himself to create the nation. This tradition was exemplified by Giuseppe Verdi, whose 1848 opera *La battaglia di Legnano* had drawn on an ancient military victory to inspire the foot soldiers of the modern Risorgimento.[64] The Risorgimento had concluded with the proclamation of Rome as capital of the new state in 1871 – the same year Bismarck founded modern Germany. Kemal wrote *Homeland or Silistria* shortly after these epochal events, and while it was true that the Ottomans governed not a new nation but an old empire, his idea of the homeland flowed from an appreciation of the European achievement in constituting nations from people of different beliefs, ethnicities and languages, instilling in each citizen a sense that the homeland was a part of his or her life, or – more elementally – that the citizen was part of the homeland. In this way Namik Kemal began to define Ottoman patriotism and in doing so opened the way for the Turkish nation of today.

Kemal was recognised as one of his country's most gifted writers, as well as a forthright critic of the government's despotism and lack of patriotic backbone, but his staid and conventional origins had given little indication of future controversy. He was born in 1840, the scion of a line of senior Ottoman officials, and as a young man he had seemed destined for a career as a courtly poet with a niche in the Ottoman Translation Bureau (he had translated Montesquieu) when an unexpected and much celebrated literary encounter pushed him in a more radical direction.

Kemal's epiphany took place during Ramadan, in 1862, as he idled away the fasting hours in wandering among the booksellers outside the Beyazit Mosque. One of the stallholders thrust into his hand a new lithographed poem on a scrap of paper, by someone who signed himself as 'Sacred'. Kemal gave up his twenty *paras* without much expectation, but 'Sacred' turned out to be none other than the newspaper editor Ibrahim Sinasi (who was fourteen years his senior) and his poem was spellbindingly different from anything Kemal had read before. Kemal instantly appreciated the revolutionary nature of the older man's simplicity and integrity of expression, and turning his back on his old literary friends he offered his services to the newspaper *Tasvir-i Efkar*, which Sinasi had opened a few months before.[65]

In the event, the ardent Kemal would show all the campaigning spirit that Sinasi lacked, and when he took over *Tasvir-i Efkar* on the latter's retreat into exile, in 1865, he gave it a new character: spiky, topical and deeply patriotic. Although he held with the usual multi-confessional Ottoman identity, Kemal urged no quarter for rebels on the island of Crete who had proclaimed union with Greece, and he embarrassed the Porte by pointing out that in Greek taverns in Istanbul shanties might be heard calling for Turkish throats to be cut. Popular subscriptions were being raised to defend Muslims on Crete, over which, Kemal said, the government should have no control. In this way he not only insinuated that officialdom was corrupt, but also questioned the assumed identity of interests between the government and the people. Here was the embryo of Turkish civil society.

The authorities suspected Kemal and his fellow members of the Society of Poets of founding a secret group inspired by revolutionary societies in Italy and Poland that aimed to topple the sultan. In the event, it would be a member of the khedival house of Egypt who went furthest – and fastest – in articulating the political objectives of the young subversives. Prince Mustafa Fazil was the younger brother of the authoritarian moderniser Ismail Pasha of Cairo. Round, red-haired and an opponent of the khedive, he had spent much of his life away from his Egyptian estates, holding ministerial office in Istanbul and assiduously promoting himself among Europe's crowned heads. In 1866 Ismail persuaded the Porte to strip his brother of the khedival succession, and in response, from his Parisian base, Mustafa Fazil addressed a dramatic open letter to the sultan that underlined the perils faced by the empire.

'Sire,' it began, 'that which enters the palaces of princes with the greatest difficulty is the truth,' and the prince went on to enumerate the empire's failings in administration and industry and the decline of its virility and moral sense. 'Your subjects of all sects,' the sultan was informed, 'are divided into two classes: those who oppress without restraint, and those who are oppressed without pity.' The cure he proposed was a reformed political system that would restore liberty and individual initiative, deny the powers grounds for further interventions in Ottoman affairs, and (in a tantalising nod towards secularism) keep religion to the sublime domain of 'eternal truths ... if it descends into interference with worldly affairs, it becomes a destroyer of all as well as of its own self'.[66] In short, the sultan must 'save the empire by transforming it! Save it by giving it a constitution.'[67]

Mustafa Fazil's letter is one of the most quoted documents in modern Turkish history, comparable to the missive of exhortation that the exiled Italian patriot Giuseppe Mazzini wrote to King Charles Albert of Piedmont in 1831, which is nowadays considered a milestone in the history of the Risorgimento. Like that letter, after which Mazzini founded his 'Young Italy' movement, the importance of Mustafa Fazil's animadversion was that it spoke with a directness that was deeply embarrassing to authority. His letter would act as a beacon to the young, hotheaded and partially Western-educated elite whose aspirations it expressed, particularly those, henceforth called the 'Young Ottomans', who embodied the country's movement towards liberty and renewal.

The now-disowned prince was able to write with such freedom because he was in Paris, but his manifesto was immediately adopted in Istanbul by the Young Ottomans, and some 50,000 lithographed copies were distributed in the capital and further afield. Now that the challenge to the spendthrift and imperious Abdulaziz was out in the open the sedition gathered pace, with Kemal and two other influential journalists, Abdulhamid Ziya and Ali Suavi, intensifying their criticisms of the government, mosque imams being tutored in modern political theory and a plot hatched to assassinate key ministers. By now, however, the authorities were properly alarmed and the arrests began, but not before several agitators – including Kemal, Ziya, Suavi and Sinasi's former confrère Agah – fled to join their royal benefactor in Paris. It was in Europe, and on Mustafa Fazil's tab, that the next battle would be fought for a Turkish constitution.

A constitution in a Muslim country cannot be the Quran. The Quran is, as it tells us, a 'guide' for believers, and for all its general injunctions as to piety and decorum, and a few precise ones concerning personal morality and punishment, it is silent on the vast majority of activities that make up the business of government.

This is what the very earliest successors of the Prophet Muhammad had discovered in the early seventh century, as Islam grew, expanded and had to confront a far wider range of conditions than was the case under its founder. The method the early Muslims found to control the sprawling and varied communities they ruled was to unify them under a temporal ruler called a caliph who was invested with some of the Prophet's functions and powers. While the caliph was sanctified by the *ulema* and his office burnished by time (the Ottoman sultans were proud to call themselves caliph) there is nothing specifically Islamic about the institution. Neither the Quran nor the Sunna, or example of the Prophet, makes mention of anything like a caliphate. Clearly, government in the Muslim world, even expressly 'Islamic' government, has from the very beginning required a good deal of human invention.

The caliphate and the smaller courts that submitted to caliphal rule were no less guilty of despotism and abuse than other monarchical regimes, and yet for all its faults the caliphate had sprung from Islamic society and could not be traduced as an infidel innovation. By contrast, the constitutions that were codified and put into use by the United States of America and the nation states of Europe derived from hundreds of years of Western thought – more than two thousand years, if you count the constitutions of Aristotle. To bring a code of this kind into the Islamic world would certainly excite major palpitations, accusations of heresy, and perhaps social disquiet. But some version of constitutional government was inescapable now that modern values were, in fits and bursts, taking over the Ottoman state. The question was how to embrace constitutionalism, with its accent on representation, religious equality and the separate spheres of authority, without destroying Islam.

Here was the conundrum that would occupy the architects of Ottoman constitutionalism, and which, through the ambushes of the twentieth century, vex Muslim political thinkers to this day.[68]

There had been democratic probing in the Islamic world even before the famous letter of Prince Mustafa Fazil. In 1861 the ruler of Tunis – himself an Ottoman vassal – was induced by the British and French consuls to accept a constitutional monarchy under which ministers answered to an appointed council. Five years later Egypt's Ismail Pasha set up his elected assembly. But in both cases the principle of representation was weak and the ruler reserved most powers for himself; neither amounted to anything like real constitutional rule and the new Tunisian system was swept away in a popular revolt in 1864.

For Turkish constitutionalists like Namik Kemal the Tunisian and Egyptian examples were of little value because they – much like the Tanzimat reforms – were products of foreign pressure. Kemal wrote of Ismail's assembly that it had been created to win European applause, its members elected 'to the crack of the gendarme's lash', and that when it was explained that the opposition sat on the left of the chamber, 'they trampled each other in a general rush to the right'.

Kemal envisaged something quite different for Istanbul, an autonomous, elected body – a real parliament. His vision would have a formative effect on Turkey's political evolution. Besides being his country's outstanding cultural innovator, Kemal also thought deeply about the mysteries of constitutionalism in an Islamic context.

Kemal was a fervent Muslim who went on to translate the Quran into Turkish, but he gloried in the achievements of the West – and between 1867 and 1871 he was able to observe these at first hand. Life as a maintained revolutionary was not easy; Paris was lonely and punitively expensive, and the Young Ottomans were fragmenting under clashing personalities as the ever-resourceful Mustafa Fazil rowed back into favour with Abdulaziz. But it was in Europe that Kemal had his first and only experience of liberty, and particularly in the course of two visits to London, when he started a new newspaper, *Hurriyet* ('Freedom'), that was read clandestinely in Istanbul, devoured politics and literature in the Reading Room of the British Museum, and mischievously positioned himself in Abdulaziz's line of vision when the sultan came to town on a state visit. 'Who are they?' Abdulaziz asked his entourage as he entered the Crystal Palace in Hyde Park and saw three men in fezzes, one of them sporting the luxuriant beard and unruly locks of the literary insurrectionist. The answer was that they were the Ottoman revolutionaries Ziya, Agah and hirsute Kemal, come to salute their sovereign.[69]

Kemal took a somewhat undiscerning view of the marvels of Britain, which was, even though it had colonised much of the world, also the principal source for Marx's theories of class conflict – of which Kemal seems to have been unaware. 'If London be called the model of the world,' he enthused, 'it would be no exaggeration.'[70] He loved almost everything he saw, from the dynamic political parties and Houses of Parliament, in which 'public opinion' found a majestic and very physical form, to the splendidly appointed observatories, libraries and theatres. The English seemed always to be reading – in the streets, in the shops, even while travelling by boat – and he warmed to the courteous schoolchildren, the upright and patriotic bureaucrats and the even-handed judges. He assured himself that such achievements could be replicated in Turkey, and that the empire could be saved, for 'it took Europe two centuries to achieve this condition, and while they were the inventors in the path of progress, we find all the means ready to hand ... is there any doubting that we too can reach a state where we are numbered among the most civilised of countries?'[71]

And what of the obstacles posed by Islam, the absolute rule of sultans, corruption, separatism and Russian meddling? Kemal addressed himself substantively to these questions after the amnesty that was declared by the Porte in September 1871, when he and most of his former Young Ottoman colleagues were allowed to return home. Fatalism and resignation must be abandoned, Kemal argued on the pages of the newspaper *Ibret*, and replaced by liberty. 'You may crush in a man's brain with stones,' ran one article, 'but is it possible to change those opinions of which he is persuaded? You may cut up a man's heart with daggers, but can you detach from his heart those beliefs that he has ratified with his conscience? Speech, poetry, politics, taste, opinion – these are free and natural and it is not through compulsion that they can be changed, but naturally.'[72]

Kemal's view of humanity as innately free overlapped with that of many Europeans, but for him the freedom of human beings was the gift of God and there was no reason to import Europe's secular basis for politics and social organisation. Modern laws must be based not only on the consent of the people, but also on an abstract and unchanging good, 'and in Islam the good and bad are determined by the Sharia, which is the expression of the abstract good and the ultimate criterion of the truth'. There was no reason why the sharia should impede material and social advance, for 'as we were commanded to receive all products of progress from any part of the world, there is no need to return to the past, or come to a halt in the present'.[73]

Kemal regarded the Tanzimat's sidelining of Islamic jurisprudence in favour of Western legal precepts as a typically blinkered rejection of one of the glories of Turkish life. His ambition to unearth Islamic versions of modern concepts associated with the West and exhibit them as proof of the compatibility of the two systems are reminiscent of the laboured equivalences of Rifaa al-Tahtawi, who at the same time was trying to convince Egyptians that Western 'rights' were the same as Islamic 'justice'. As with Rifaa, Kemal's efforts may have been useful in reassuring people that what he proposed, although it sounded radically new, did not contravene Islam. But his task was even harder than that of the Egyptian sheikh, for unlike Rifaa, who accepted the autocracy of Ismail Pasha, Kemal was a democrat.

In the 153rd verse of the third sura (or chapter) of the Quran the Prophet Muhammad is urged by God to take counsel with his followers. Kemal, Ziya and some of the other reformists quoted this verse to show Islam's compatibility with the principles of representation and consultation. They associated the *baya*, or oath of fealty, that the early Muslims gave the Prophet with the exercise of popular sovereignty – a form of election. Some Muslims had decried the institution of a parliament as an illegal 'innovation' of the kind that the Prophet had warned against, but Kemal disagreed; it was no more an illegal innovation than steamships, and 'should the Ottoman Empire then not buy steamships, and let the Greeks capture Crete with their little lemon boats?'[74] Kemal could find nothing in the sharia against republican government; however, in view of the traditions of the Ottoman Empire, a constitutional monarchy would be most appropriate. As to the precise model, Islamic history furnished no example and so Kemal was forced to look abroad. His exposure to Europe had come principally through France, but it was Britain's constitutional monarchy that appeared the most stable and conducive to individual achievement.

In Kemal it is possible to discern the first stirrings of modern pan-Islamism, mixed with Ottoman feeling. Again, his models were European. Pan-Slavism was the ground on which Russia and the Balkans came together; pan-Germanist lieder stirred emotive Teutons. 'We should know,' Kemal wrote, 'that we in this country are obliged to make a political and military union in response.'[75] That union, as the exuberant popular reaction to *Homeland or Silistria* made clear in 1873, was more likely to be built on a new interpretation of the nation than on the authority of the sultan. That, in turn, necessitated new relations between the Crown and the people, with legislative and executive authority separated from each other and the people perhaps even enjoying the right to choose the sultan and caliph. 'The Imamate is the right of the people,' Kemal had written elliptically, and following the play's opening performance the people were in the streets, yelling his name. This alarmed the authorities and a few nights later the playwright was arrested and banished. He wasn't alone; three other journalist colleagues also went into exile (though not Ziya, who was rowing back into official favour), and the Gedik Pasha Theatre was placed under censorship, all plays requiring prior police approval.

Kemal's 38-month-long exile raised him to become his nation's conscience, the Turkish Victor Hugo. Kemal was not exactly unaware of the heroic dimensions of his victimhood, and he belted out the Marseillaise, which he had translated into Turkish – as Rifaa had into Arabic – on the steamship that took him away from Istanbul. Like Hugo, Kemal produced some of his best-known works while in exile, but there the resemblance ends, for while *Les Misérables* emanated from a comfortable house on Guernsey, Kemal's island exile was a dungeon in dirt-poor, infernally hot Cyprus, whose main attractions, besides solitary confinement and malaria (which laid him low for several months), were rabies, cholera and scorpions.[76]

He coughed blood, drowned his sorrows (if he had learned to drink in Paris, he was not the last Muslim to do so), and dreamed nightly of his beloved daughter Ferideh. 'I got your letter and the slippers you made,' he wrote to her in one letter. 'I was so happy that it was as if you had come to my side. You know how the peacock in the story admired his splendid colours and then saw his black legs and cried out in dismay? I'm the opposite; I observe my decrepitude and am sad, then I look down at my shoes and laugh from joy like a child.'[77]

Extraordinarily, despite the psychological effects of his incarceration – a condition he referred to as 'castling' – Kemal succeeded in maintaining contact with the outside world, forming friendships with local officials, some of whom were his admirers, and even receiving royalties from under-the-counter sales of his works in Istanbul and Cairo. His character grew more pious under the influence of a religious scholar who was imprisoned alongside him. But the pardon he longed for, and which his friends in the cabinet gave him reason to believe might be forthcoming, would not materialise until politics in the capital were propelled forward by dramatic and sudden events, and the liberals' objective of a constitution came unexpectedly into view.

For many people who were living in Istanbul as the empire faced destruction in the spring of 1876, the word 'constitution' had reassuring connotations to do with limiting the caprice of the sultan. Following the defeat of France in the Franco-Prussian war of 1870–1, the authoritarian regimes of Russia, Austria–Hungary and a newly-unified Germany were now considered in the ascendant, and the first two meddled impenitently in Turkey's Balkan possessions (the Russians wanted to unite the Slavs behind them, while Austria tried to prevent Slavic sentiment from spreading inside its borders). In 1875 the governments of Tsar Alexander II and Emperor Franz Joseph intervened diplomatically after tax rises led to revolt in the Ottoman provinces of Herzegovina and Bosnia, and they foisted administrative reforms on a disobliging Porte, while Turkey's default of the same year raised anti-Ottoman feeling to an unprecedented height among European bondholders. In Istanbul, Abdulaziz and his chief vizier, Mahmud Nedim Pasha (nicknamed 'Nedimoff' for his Russophile feelings), struggled to dissipate heady, revolutionary sentiments among the people, but had nothing with which to do so – the treasury was bare. Salaries in Istanbul went unpaid while the peasantry dropped from famine, and the free-spending Abdulaziz (he had made the Ottoman navy the third largest in the world) was suspected of going to excessive lengths to accommodate the outrageous demands of the powers. It was a set of conditions not dissimilar to those emerging concurrently in Ismail's Egypt – and which led ultimately to the Anglo-French invasion of 1882. Public opinion was now sharply against the sultan.

From the religious students who complained about concessions that were being made to the Christian provinces (and were now arming themselves), to the intelligentsia drawing attention to the incarceration of heroes like Namik Kemal, there were, as ever, both liberal and conservative elements to the disquiet. But the liberals did not preponderate in the Porte. The earliest proponent of constitutional government, Prince Mustafa Fazil, had died in 1875, Ziya had gone over to the government side, and no one knew when Kemal would emerge from his Cypriot dungeon. The standard of constitutionalism had by now passed to a new man, one of action rather than thought, and arguably the most radical of all Turkish reformists: Ahmet Midhat Pasha.

Dapper, bespectacled (it was he who had offended Abdulaziz by not removing his glasses in the celestial presence), and fulsomely bearded, Midhat Pasha was synonymous with the decisive exercise of power in the face of bickering and drift. Born in 1822 to a judge who had served in the Balkans, he had memorised the Quran by the age of ten and entered his first government office in his teens. He soon gained a reputation for energy, patriotism and innovation along Western lines, and in 1864 was appointed to govern one of the empire's most intractable provinces, an area encompassing the Danube basin in its Bulgarian reaches. With its mix of Christians, Turks and Jews, and history of Russian interventions (Silistria lay within its borders), the Danube region would have taxed the capacities of any administrator, but over the next three years Midhat not only maintained peace between the various groups, but transformed the province's infrastructure. Roads were paved, hundreds of bridges were built and street lighting was introduced in the towns. A network of credit cooperatives freed farmers, Christian and Muslim alike, from the claw of the moneylender.[78]

The headstrong and self-motivated Midhat breathed easier when he was far from the pettifoggery of the capital, and his next great appointment, in 1869, as governor of the distant province of Baghdad was perhaps his crowning success. Among the novelties he introduced to this notably backward part of the empire were a tramline (operated by Baghdad's first joint stock company), a water supply system, an Arabic newspaper, quarantine, a savings bank and wool and cotton mills. Thanks to the (multi-confessional) schools he opened, literacy rates, which ran at just half a per cent in 1850, began to crawl upwards, while new port facilities on the Persian Gulf and regular steamships up and down the Euphrates hinted at the potentialities of maritime commerce. There was some opposition, not least from the nomadic tribes he forcibly settled, but by registering title deeds and allocating land on secure tenure Midhat incentivised agricultural investment with tangible effects on prosperity and security.

Midhat was a quintessential Ottoman in that he saw solidarity between the different peoples as essential to its survival – his was a broad, Austro-Hungarian-style conception of identity, encompassing various groups under the same rule, not a narrowly ethnic or linguistic one as prevailed in Germany or Greece. In office he promoted men of ability regardless of their background, and under his patronage talented Armenians, Jews, Arabs, Croats and Albanians all prospered. Religious dogma rarely detained him, and he predicted that 'in forty or fifty years people will not build churches or mosques any more, but only schools and humanitarian institutions'. Returning from Baghdad to the capital in 1872, he found life there vexing – including a brief, unhappy stint as chief vizier – while discontent and violence simmered. He compared the country to a ship without captain or rudder. But Midhat had a solution.

In the spring of 1876 the chief vizier, Mahmud Nedim Pasha, was considering handing over much of the economy to European interests as a way of consolidating the debt. His government seemed powerless to reject an international conference, insisted upon by Russia, which would impose internal reforms to be supervised by Europe and formalise the partial occupation of the Balkan provinces. But public opinion had different ideas and in early May theological students in Istanbul launched demonstrations that obliged the sultan to sack his chief vizier. The atmosphere in the capital was febrile; there was a brisk trade in arms and theological texts circulated which showed that absolutism was a violation of the sharia. The students were calling for Midhat, but their hero was a step ahead and had become part of a loose group of conspirators, including other reformist statesmen and top military officers, who were plotting the sultan's deposition.

In the early hours of 30 May 1876, warships directed by these conspirators came alongside the Ottoman-rococo frontage of the Dolmabahce Palace. Soldiers picketed the rear entrance; Abdulaziz was trapped. As dawn broke a cannonade announced the change in sultans to the delighted populace. Abdulaziz's nephew, the man whose name the theatregoers had yelled following the premiere of *Homeland or Silistria*, now took the oath as Murad V, and thousands gathered to watch him process through the old city, the 'cheers of Western Europeans' mingling with 'the *zitos* of the Greeks and the native acclamations of the Mussulmans'.[79] It was spring in Istanbul; the new sultan magnanimously attributed his enthronement to 'the will of my subjects', and the exiles, including Namik Kemal, were brought home to share in the glory. Midhat Pasha, Kemal and other supporters of the new sultan immediately plunged into discussions on a constitution, the first such document in the Muslim world.

However, the hopes that had been raised with Murad's accession were dashed almost immediately by the sultan's psychological infirmities. Murad had been known for his lively intelligence, wide reading and secret contacts with liberals like Kemal, but these qualities had turned his uncle Abdulaziz against him and the young prince had been forced into a miserable life of isolation alleviated by the bottle. Within days of coming to the throne two events impaired him further: the suicide of Abdulaziz, who slashed his wrists in captivity, and the massacre of several members of the cabinet by an unhinged infantry captain. The new sultan now became an embarrassment and a liability, crashing through windowpanes and clambering up balustrades rather than shouldering his public duties. Doctors were consulted and the sultan's condition pronounced incurable; all the while the fate of a great empire hung in the balance. Finally, with great reluctance, Midhat Pasha and the other constitutionalists reconciled themselves to a second change of monarch.

On 27 August Midhat visited Murad's younger brother Abdulhamid, and showed him a draft constitution which the latter approved. Namik Kemal begged Midhat to delay Murad's deposition, but the pasha was unmoved. On 31 August there were fresh cannonades, and Abdulhamid II became sultan.

Abdulhamid had assured Midhat that he would promulgate the constitution immediately and intervene in politics only on the advice of his ministers. It is hard to overstate the importance of this pledge and its logical consequences. An Ottoman constitution enshrining the representative principle would do more than keep the European wolves from the door. It would be a leap forward for an entire civilisation, spreading self-belief and a sense of vicarious achievement among educated Muslims around the world. Who could then argue that Islam and constitutionalism were incompatible?

In a little over one hundred years the most significant polity in the Muslim world had accommodated many of the elements of modernity.

For all the undeniable popularity of these new ways of thinking and behaving, however, it is little cause for surprise that the first attempt in the Muslim world to achieve a liberal constitution in fact failed ignominiously. The principles of popular participation and account-ability had been set in the West, and the West's own political develop-ment had been agonisingly slow. Britain, for example, had taken four centuries to move from James I lecturing Parliament on the divine right of kings to the constitutional rule whose benefits Namik Kemal observed, and all that via more disorder and outbreaks of regal and aristocratic despotism. The United States constitution of 1787 was the culmination of some of the best European political ideas back to Seneca and Cicero.

The Western experience of modern constitutions hinted strongly that Turkey's first text would not be its last, and that the country stood at the beginning of a long evolution. France had been through no fewer than twelve distinct constitutions before eventually it found some stability with the constitutional laws of 1875, and its various texts had oscillated between monarchical absolutism and, later on, electoral democracy as expressed in universal male suffrage. The Belgian consti-tution of 1831 was hailed as 'the charter of modern liberties *par excellence*' – with sovereignty vested in the people and the king denuded of divine right or prerogatives.[80] But unbridled liberalism of this kind would not be adopted by Turkey. The elements that the Turks borrowed from Belgium were not the democratic ones; a more apt comparison might be with the Prussian constitution of 1850, which gave the monarch extensive powers and provided for an appointed upper chamber. At least the Turks were ahead of Russia; Turkey's pre-emptor in other ways of progress would not gain a constitution and parliament for another thirty years.

For all the tardiness of the West's democratic evolution, the idea that the Ottoman Empire must in a matter of a few years emulate or even improve on that record was implicit in foreign criticisms of the Porte and its own, halting progress towards the same objective. Sir Stratford Canning had not bothered to hide his frustration at what he saw as the foot-dragging of the Tanzimatists in the 1850s and 60s – that these changes went slowly was no cause for wonder. In 1876, when there were inter-communal massacres in Bulgaria, and the Turks committed atrocities, Britain's prime minister, William Ewart

Gladstone, effectively discounted the idea of Turkish self-improvement when he said, 'from the first black day they entered Europe, they [have been] the one great anti-human specimen of humanity'.[81] Most damning of all, as a measure of the West's insincerity in seeking reform, the powers chose to dismember the empire rather than support an Ottoman constitution that could keep it alive and even bring it back to health.

The task of framing the Ottoman state on liberal lines would have been hard enough under Sultan Murad, a man who, alone among the crowned heads of Islam, might have given up a portion of his powers with good grace. But Abdulhamid's interest in constitutionalism was hostile from the beginning, and he hid his real feelings with vague appeals to different strains of opinion. No constituent assembly convened; negotiations happened behind closed doors and under the eye of the monarch. Midhat Pasha's reappointment as grand vizier at a crucial time in negotiations was misinterpreted as a victory for the liberals. All the while, it was in the palace that the crucial document took form.

The process of creating a Turkish constitution, difficult enough as it was, was further complicated by an ominous unanimity among the European powers on the need for devolutionary reforms in the Balkans – reforms that a constitution might be useful in forestalling. Abdulhamid was indeed resigned to a constitution, but it would be his own constitution, not the liberals'. Only after his opponents had been outmanoeuvred and traditionalists had shot down a draft daring to affirm the rights of the sultan (which must, of necessity, be limitless and therefore impossible to affirm) did he finally declare his hand.

The basic law that was proclaimed in driving rain on 23 December 1876 did not in fact uphold the rights of the people, but the infallibility of the sovereign; in it inhered not the principle of accountability, but that of servitude. The text's bright points – a bill of rights, an elected second chamber, an independent judiciary and provincial decentralisation – were overwhelmed by the looming effigy of the sultan-caliph. The constitution declared him sacred, and declined to put a ceiling on his powers. No bill could become law without his ratification and no law could originate but in the government – which he appointed. Perhaps most poisonous of all, the constitution's 113th article effectively allowed the sultan to banish anyone of his choosing.

In the event, Turkey's first constitution was undone by the monarch's bad faith (he believed that liberalism and constitutions would divide the empire), the ineptitude of his ministers, and the barely-concealed hostility of the European powers, who knew that successful reform would shut them out of Turkish affairs.

As his admirers point out even now, Abdulhamid did not violate the constitution over the remainder of his reign (which would end in 1909), but it was no hardship to keep within the confines of so vast a freedom. Certainly he wasted no time in exploring the possibilities of article 113, and his first target was the man with whom the flawed basic law was most closely identified: Midhat Pasha. A brilliant provincial governor but flat-footed as a national statesman, Midhat was disarmed and finally dismantled by his Machiavellian prince, who proved adept at pitting his officials against each other, and thus blunting radical proposals. While the pashas bandied drafts between them, the powers were deciding the future of Bosnia–Herzegovina and Bulgaria, and Midhat bargained away liberal principles in his desperation to promulgate a constitution – any constitution – as a means of forestalling Europe's demands.

In going back on his own principles, Midhat lost the support of liberals like Kemal, who was particularly disgusted by article 113, and it was an isolated and unappreciated grand vizier who was lured to the Dolmabahce Palace on the night of 5 February 1877. On arrival he was told to give up his seals of office, and was put aboard the imperial yacht for his journey into exile.

For the men that were most closely associated with the first modern political movement of the Middle East, the 1876 constitution was a disaster from which few recovered. Midhat Pasha was eventually permitted to return home, and even appointed to further governorships, before being brought back to Istanbul (again on the imperial yacht) to face trumped-up charges of murdering Abdulhamid's uncle Sultan Abdulaziz six years earlier. It was Abdulhamid who directed court proceedings from behind the scenes, while Midhat Pasha amused the court with his mordant wit – questioning the chief physician's apparent ability to know from the Asian side of the Bosporus what was happening on the European shore, and his inability to see an incision around Abdulaziz's heart. For all the amusement, a guilty verdict was never in doubt.[82] The pasha was saved from execution by foreign pressure, but exiled to Taif, in the southern Hejaz of Arabia, where he was strangled, presumably on Abdulhamid's orders, in April 1883.

Destiny was hardly kinder to the visionary who had invented and bellowed liberty for the Ottomans, who had taken Sinasi's new vehicle, an independent press, and turned it into a juggernaut for reform and self-improvement. Disgusted with the constitution, Namik Kemal was first imprisoned as a common criminal, and then exiled to the Aegean – where he spent the rest of his life filling a range of degradingly junior bureaucratic posts. He died on 2 December 1888, the day after he received an imperial instruction that he discontinue work on a history of the Ottomans he had been writing.

By that time the regime of Abdulhamid had grown into in a royal dictatorship, with the sultan at the top and a vast, tentacular bureaucracy spreading below him. Progress was redefined as the importation of modern technology and of modern ideas. One of the few exceptions to this rule was the telegraph, which became an indispensable tool in the sultan's armoury of repression. The parliament that was promised under the constitution duly convened, consisting of a chamber of 115 elected deputies, and including generous minority participation, but when its members dared summon three government ministers to answer charges that had been laid against them, the sultan lost patience and had it dissolved.

War broke out with Russia in April 1877, barely a month after the Ottoman parliament was inaugurated. The conflict ended in defeat for Turkey, and a humiliating peace, signed at Berlin, under which Bulgaria was broken up and Ottoman Serbia, Montenegro and Romania achieved independence. The sultan responded to these reverses with remorse. 'I made a mistake when I wished to imitate my father Abdulmecid,' he lamented, 'who sought reforms by permission and by liberal institutions.' And he pledged henceforth to follow his grandfather, Mahmud II, for 'like him I now understand that it is only by force that one can move the people with whose protection God has entrusted me'.[83]

Abdulhamid did not acknowledge that it was his grandfather's coercive modernisation that had led, through the gradual development of a literate, patriotic Ottoman elite, to a state of affairs in which a Namik Kemal or a Midhat Pasha could articulate a modern world view – which would not die in the absence of a constitution and the years of despotism that followed, but, on the contrary, would continue to smoulder till it exploded once again.

'Our country is no more,' Kemal wrote in a poem not long before his death, 'yet still it is, while you and I are there. In this condition we can have no greater enemy than ourselves. We are in the hands of the foe; for the sake of God, O countrymen, enough!'[84]

3

Tehran

Iran entered the modern era later and more sluggishly than its main competitors and neighbours, none of whom had suffered to the same degree from the immense geographical isolation and cultural backwardness of the Persian plateau. For centuries Turkey had been part of the European balance of power while Egypt's religious minorities and Mediterranean position ensured that even in the benighted eighteenth century the country had commercial interaction with Europe and the New World. On the eastern flank of Persia the Muslims of India were being pulled into new forms by British rule, while the Indonesian archipelago, home to a very large number of Muslims, was gradually colonised by the Dutch. Iran, on the other hand, was relatively untouched by the Western world.

That Iran began modernising from a direr position even than the Egypt of Jabarti and the javelin-toting Mamluks is perhaps surprising when one considers that barely two hundred years earlier the plateau had enjoyed a level of security, trade and prosperity that had brought it international respect. Under the Safavid dynasty, whose noontime lasted from the turn of the sixteenth century until the early 1700s, Persia was united after centuries of fragmentation, its shah a byword for splendour and its people busy trading with and chafing their regional rivals, the Ottomans. Enterprising Europeans entered the shah's service as his envoys. Caravansaries, or fortified inns, were built along the main trading routes, and silk – Iran's luxury product par excellence – was transported from the mulberry orchards of the northern provinces to Isfahan, in the centre of the country, and from there onwards to the Persian Gulf for export to Europe.

In 1722, however, Iran's serenity was broken by Afghan invaders, who destroyed the old order without creating a new one. The country entered a period of dissolution, violence and horror, as several Transcaucasian provinces were snatched by Russia and Turkey and first one warlord sought to impose his writ on the plateau through the sword and, failing, gave way to the next. The most efficient of these brutes, the tribal freebooter Nader Shah, ravaged the people with his campaigning and depredations, which depopulated huge areas. The country was brought so low that in the mid-1740s, an English merchant lamented that the 'variety of troubles that have lately happened in these parts has occasioned an entire stop to trade', and that 'there is a great appearance of everything going to confusion in Persia'.[1]

Of what this raggedy and sickly Persia consisted it was hard to say. In the eighteenth century, perhaps half of the population of between 5 and 10 million lived in communities of varying autonomy that were scattered among the valleys and mountain ranges from which they derived protection. They engaged in nomadism, followed tribal laws and customs, and nurtured beliefs (some chiliastic, others involving reincarnation, vegetarianism and the veneration of the sun) that in many cases had only a tenuous connection to Islam. Life here corresponded minimally with the norms of sedentary, not to say urban, life, and central authority was something to be feared and hated.

As for the main cities, Isfahan, Tabriz and Mashhad, and smaller provincial centres such as Ardebil and Kerman, here too life and wealth were at risk from famine, sackings and the abuse of power by whichever tribal chieftain happened to be in charge. No one contested the tyrant's privilege to seize land and kill on a whim, while the apparatus of religious justice merrily sentenced the worst kind of miscreants (murderers, highwaymen and apostates) to be crucified, blown from guns, buried alive, impaled, shod like horses, torn asunder, set alight and skinned alive. Jealous of the popularity of mystic divines who were distinguished from the mainstream clergy because they preached esoteric paths to God, the *ulema* declared campaigns against them, decreeing, for example, that the noses and ears of dervishes should be cut off.[2]

While Egypt and Turkey were making modernising reforms, Iran suffered from unchecked despotism and experienced messianic movements of volcanic intensity and violence, and the basic indices of human development – health, literacy and the empowerment of women – puttered along at pre-modern levels. Why was Iran so far behind?

There are two main factors to identify here. Firstly, again in comparison with Egypt, Turkey and the rest of the Mediterranean rim, Iran was doubly isolated from the countries that led the field in propounding new theories and technologies. This was a blessing from a political point of view, protecting the country from invasion, but a paucity of contact also meant a paucity of new ideas, retarding the growth of a bureaucratic elite interested in reform.

Religion was the second stay on progress. Iran was the major power espousing Shiism, Islam's biggest minority sect. Shiism had never rejected speculation in the way Sunnism had, nor had it closed the doors to *ijtihad* – the exercise of independent reasoning to interpret the sharia – as was the case in al-Azhar. There was, however, one aspect of the religious set-up that did act against modernisation, and that was the stubborn independence of the major *mujtahids*, or doctors of the law, from temporal authority.

Shiism's top clerics gravitated to the main shrine towns – Najaf and Karbala in Iraq, Isfahan and Mashhad in Iran – from where they maintained polite but distrustful relationships with the shah and the top princes. The religious foundations of the Shia world constituted almost a parallel state that was innately sceptical of the shah's claim to absolute authority – in Shiism this is reserved for the imams, specially anointed descendants of the Prophet, and in their absence, the most learned clerics. This clerical establishment was too diffuse and autonomous for the monarch to bend it to a modernising political will, as Muhammad Ali had done to al-Azhar.

Illiteracy was probably as widespread as it was in Egypt, and learning remained the monopoly of the neighbourhood mullah. At the end of the eighteenth century, Iranians were almost entirely ignorant of the changes that had been fashioned in Europe by the Renaissance and the Age of Discovery; their curiosity about other lands was – in the words of a modern Iranian historian – 'minimal'.[3]

And yet, despite the isolation and ignorance of many of its inhabitants, at the end of the eighteenth century Iran possessed a magic quality that was absent from the Ottoman lands, and which would eventually permit it to move in a new direction without jeopardising its survival. This was something that had rarely, if ever, been seen in the Muslim world: a national identity.

The very idea might seem outlandish, given that European definitions of nationhood had yet to be exported to the East, but the inhabitants of the Iranian plateau had coalesced in important respects over the course of their shared history, distinguishing them from their neighbours in the Turkish and Arab ambits.

The foundation of this national consciousness was the Persian language. Unlike, for instance, ancient Egyptian, which withered gradually after the Muslim Conquest of 640, surviving only as the liturgical language of the Coptic Church, Persian survived the roughly simultaneous Arab advance eastwards and Iran's incorporation into the caliphate. Much as English was enriched by French words and locutions following the Norman Conquest, Persian emerged from its collision with Arabic enhanced in suppleness and expanded in size, a fit tool for the works of beauty that Iranian poets would go on to compose. Similarly, Islamic beliefs and Iranian architectural forms spawned a new aesthetic, which manifested itself in fine cities such as Safavid Isfahan (largely built by Shah Abbas I in the early sixteenth century), and which spread as far as Central Asia and India – in stylistic terms the Taj Mahal is the most famous Iranian building in the world.

Another compounding factor in Iranian identity was religion. Shiism, having enjoyed much support and possibly a preponderance during the medieval period, was declared the country's official sect under Shah Ismail I, founder of the Safavid dynasty, in the early 1500s. This turned Iran into the sole Shia state in the world, eternally distinct from the Sunni Turkish Empire to the west and a source of solace for Shia minorities in Mesopotamia, Lebanon, India and the principalities of the Persian Gulf.

Finally, over Iran's distinct linguistic and religious identity lay a specifically Iranian view of culture and the past. Despite the vicissitudes of their history, including the wholesale destruction wrought by the Mongols in the thirteenth century, the Iranians retained a sense of their distinctness and superiority. Literature was important to this, in particular the epic national poem of history, myth and the princely virtues, the *Shahnameh*, or Book of Kings, which roots Iranian greatness deep in the pre-Islamic past. Topography was a friend to this

Iranian exceptionalism, with the plateau conveniently protected by seas to the north and south, and by mountain, marsh or desert to the east and west.

These three factors – linguistic, sectarian and cultural – would equip Iran to make the transition from medieval empire to modern nation state more easily than either Ottoman Turkey or Egypt. Eighteenth-century Iran might be said to have been a nation state in waiting.

Not that the few Western diplomats, soldiers, merchants and men of the cloth who bothered to visit the country around the time of the Napoleonic Wars noticed much movement in this direction. On the contrary, they were able to witness the construction of forts of straw and mud by press-ganged peasants whose condition of life – in the words of one such visitor, the diplomat and author James Morier – 'resembled that of the Israelites, who were no doubt employed in the same manner in building for Pharaoh, and with the very same sort of materials'. They chanced upon *chappar*s, or couriers, tightly bandaged with linen, as in Herodotus' time, and local governors attending to business on carpets spread out in the street.[4]

Despite appearances, though, the ground for change was in fact being readied from the 1790s with the rise of a new dominant group. The Qajars were a tribe of Turkish origin that had served the Safavids, but in 1779, taking advantage of the opportunity created by a rival's death, their fearsome chief Agha Muhammad Khan began to unify the plateau through relentless campaigning and consolidation, an endeavour that was crowned with success in 1796, when he was proclaimed shah, with his capital at Tehran. Two years later, Agha Muhammad Khan was dead, murdered by his servants. He had been castrated by a rival dynast while in captivity as a youth (no doubt contributing to his vengeful nature), and in the absence of children the throne passed to a nephew, the massively bearded, bejewelled, mega-fecund Fath-Ali Shah. Fath-Ali would go on to sire more than 260 children, making him one of the most procreant men in the historical record, and abundantly making up for his uncle's emasculation. More importantly for the story of Iranian modernisation, the West was getting interested in Fath-Ali Shah, and he in it.

The initial spur was defence on one side and grand strategy on the other. The French Revolution had passed Iran by. Few Iranians had heard of America. But Russia? Now that was different. A century of reform and modernisation under Tsar Peter and the adventurous German-born Tsarina Catherine the Great had brought Muscovy to the forefront of imperial nations, and, through successive encroachments into Iran's Caucasian provinces, to the fringes of Persia itself. It was this rejuvenated titan, whose army had shocked Europe in 1799 by vaulting the Alps and defeating the French in Italy (prompting Napoleon to abandon his Egyptian campaign), that presented Iran with an irrefutable case for change.

In 1804 Iran and Russia went to war over tracts of modern-day Georgia, Armenia and Azerbaijan, a conflict that would drag on until 1813 and end in Iranian defeat. In May 1807 Iran and France – the latter was engaged in a major war of its own against Russia in Europe – signed a treaty of alliance directed against St Petersburg. No sooner had that happened, however, than the Treaty of Tilsit, signed in July of the same year between Napoleon and Tsar Alexander I, unpicked the Franco-Iranian pact and Britain stepped in with proposals of its own. The British ambition was to prevent Napoleon from gaining influence on India's western border, and overseeing military reforms was the obvious way to achieve this. Within a decade of its reunification under the Qajars Iran found itself annexed – like Turkey and Egypt – to the European system of treaty and belligerence.

As with Turkey and Egypt, the initial impulse in Iran was contingent on the resolve of one man. Fath-Ali Shah had devolved the burden of foreign and military affairs to his son and heir apparent, Abbas Mirza, who held court in the north-western city of Tabriz, uncomfortably close to the Russian border. Because of his keen appreciation of the Russian threat, Abbas Mirza had a better idea of the need for reform than his father, and the signs indicated that he would be his country's Muhammad Ali or its Mahmud II – he was determined that Iran should advance by adopting the knowledge and expertise of the West. 'Provided Providence does not set itself against the *élan* of his noble character,' wrote a French soldier of fortune who had attached himself to the prince, he 'will be the reformer of his country'.[5]

Charming and intelligent, possessing dark and expressive eyes, an aquiline nose and a refulgent, jet-black beard, Abbas Mirza was as dignified as his father was vain and resplendent. He favoured sober dress (a diamond-hilted dagger his sole extravagance) and English boots,[6] and came a distant second to Fath-Ali Shah in reproductive matters, siring a paltry forty-seven children. Although he was scrupulous in his outward observance of Islam, in common with the modernisers of Turkey and Egypt, he was far from being a zealot. He was solicitous of minorities such as the Jews and the Armenians, and when he invoked Islam as a guide in public affairs it was usually with the aim of softening fanaticism and facilitating change.

The prince was as conversant with modern politics as it was possible to be in a semi-ruined bastion city on the fraught interstices of the Qajar, Russian and Ottoman Empires, and he was 'fond of reading' (in the words of one surprised British visitor), with a 'large collection of English books' and a collection of maps from the press at Istanbul.[7] If his feelings for neighbouring Russia were understandably mingled with apprehension, his admiration for Napoleon was heartfelt and survived both the Treaty of Tilsit and Napoleon's defeat at Waterloo. In 1817 – as Bonaparte whiled away his retirement on St Helena – another European visitor reported his surprise on entering Abbas Mirza's residence and being confronted by 'a portrait of the [Russian] Emperor Alexander, and one of Bonaparte, the last of which was a striking likeness'.[8]

Abbas Mirza was a valiant general who had taken part in his first campaign aged eight (alongside his great-uncle Agha Muhammad Khan), but in the course of the long, drawling and ultimately disastrous Russo-Persian War of 1804–13 there was no concealing the inability of his much larger forces to land a blow on his adversary. Iran could not even point to the enemy's fighting excellence as a mitigating factor; the Russian forces were composed of poorly trained men who were mutinously unhappy at being posted to pestilential wastes thousands of miles from home.

The reason for Abbas Mirza's failure was that the institution he commanded was medieval. Iranian forces were dominated by levies whose loyalty was to their tribe and who treated deployment as a vague call to migrate rather than a coordinated manoeuvre, with random groups carrying bows and arrows arriving at a chosen objective several weeks apart. There was no infantry to speak of and battle plans placed much reliance on horsemen, who, for all their deftness (like the Mamluk cavalry they could halt their steeds at high speed without being thrown, and fire accurately over their shoulders at a gallop) had been known to seize defeat from the jaws of victory by abruptly downing weapons in order to gather booty and carry off fair-skinned Georgian slaves.[9]

Then there was the matter of deficient Iranian armaments. The Iranian artillery did not extend beyond short-range pieces called *zamburaks*, or 'little wasps', which often exploded on firing, causing the camels that dragged them to run amok. The Iranians had no appreciation of the value of the element of surprise. Abbas Mirza's forces were not used to posting sentries at night, nor to military secrecy, and battle plans were bruited through the camp with no regard for the inevitable presence of enemy spies.

How to reform such a force so it could fulfil its primary function of defending the country? That was the question facing the Crown prince as bursts of fighting interrupted the truces and diplomacy, and the Russians were inhibited from using their full capabilities by Napoleon's invasion of July 1812. But Abbas Mirza did not waste the periods of inaction in this long, untidy war; his inability to defeat the numerically inferior Russians had a similar effect on him to that exercised by Muhammad Ali's new infantry squares when they defeated Sultan Mahmud's forces in 1832. It was a painfully instructive encounter with a modern fighting machine: a spur to reform.

To begin with, the military advisers who helped Abbas Mirza in his modernising endeavours had been mostly French, but after Tilsit France showed less interest and the British stepped in smartly with experts, arms and a cash subsidy aimed at keeping the Iranians in their camp. In time Britain's largesse would allow Abbas Mirza to purchase 16,000 muskets, 1,000 sabres and 10 cannons (cast in India, and engraved with Fath-Ali Shah's name and arms).[10] It was an early example of recycled aid and the subsidy was in effect a voucher for British arms – even the Iranians' serge uniforms were supplied from Lancashire.

By 1813 the number of British soldiers seconded to Abbas Mirza numbered around fifty, while a foundry established in the Tabriz citadel was turning out thirty cannons a year, as well as shot, cartridges and gun carriages.[11] The endeavours of Iran's British instructors might have yielded little, however, were it not for the example set by Abbas Mirza himself. It was none other than the heir presumptive, future 'Pivot of the Universe', as the Persian shah was known, who took the lead in unlearning hundreds of years of military tradition, attiring himself in a European uniform, handling that suspect foreign weapon, the musket, and drilling small groups of men in enclosed spaces so they would not be ridiculed by their friends and relations.

Harangued by their prince, squads of goatherds learned to march abreast and turn on command – manoeuvres that a few years earlier would not only have seemed undignified and possibly sacrilegious, but also perfectly irrelevant to all they knew of the arts of war. As Abbas Mirza related to Britain's first fully-fledged ambassador to the Qajar court, Sir Gore Ouseley, in 1811: 'I caused a passage in the Quran that is favourable to the improvement of the means of attack and defence in the case of religion to be … approved by the chief of the law in Persia, and disseminated throughout the country.'[12] It was the same tactic that progressives in Turkey and Egypt had used to show that their modernisation efforts were in full concordance with Islam – the common aim was to show that religion did not put up obstacles to reform.

It takes little effort to imagine the worry and perplexity that Iran's first modernising measures caused. The Iranians had built an order where power was modulated only by tribal custom and religious law, and the word of the monarch was a sentence over life and limb. 'The Shah rarely orders other than three kinds of punishment,' the British diplomat and author James Morier reported (in phrases that recall Edward Lane's similar appreciation of Muhammad Ali's absolute power); 'the belabouring of the soles with a stick, the amputation of the nose or the ears, and death. He is surrounded by ghulams [slave-soldiers] and farrashes [menial servants who specialised in administering corporal punishment] and, at the slightest sign, imperceptible to anyone else, the guilty party is seized and his punishment immediately discharged.'[13] In the military sphere there was no tradition of the reciprocal constraints on which modern armies depended – that is to say a mesh of highly regulated and interlocking hierarchies that neither officer nor man could disavow with impunity. For the Iranian horseman, acts of artistry and valour won battles (and paeans from the poets), not the sublimation of the individual to an intractable machine. And yet this is what Tabriz's British instructors now demanded, and which seemed to the nimble, somewhat iconoclastic Iranians to clog the workings of war, rather than facilitate them.

Even Abbas Mirza was unsettled, sighing deeply after listening to some especially arcane provisions contained in the British military regulations, and confessing that 'this discipline is a most difficult thing'. Nor could the prince, whose idea of *noblesse oblige* was to be accessible to his subjects, see why the lower ranks should be disbarred from addressing him directly.

Facial hair was another subject on which he initially found it impossible to concur with his favoured British officers. They insisted that the Iranian infantrymen be clean-shaven, but he himself boasted a long beard (if not as long as that of his father) and ferocious moustaches, and refused to countenance such encroachments into personal and religious territory. Abbas Mirza's mind was changed, however, after a mishap on the firing range. A powder horn exploded in the hand of a gunner, whose long beard was blown away from his chin. The prince was so affected by the woeful appearance of the scorched and mutilated soldier that he resolved instantly on the abolition of beards. So it was that when Sir Gore Ouseley and his suite approached Tabriz by the Tehran road in 1812, they were met by a strikingly modern 'troop of Persian horse-artillery, dressed like Europeans, with shaven chins, with English arms and accoutrements, booted and spurred, riding with long stirrups, who, headed by an English officer, had come to salute the Ambassador'. Further on, at the entrance to the town, 'disciplined troops lined the road to a considerable distance, and presented arms as we passed, whilst a numerous band of drummers and fifers headed our procession, playing country dances and reels in a manner truly astonishing … twenty guns were fired as a salute to the Ambassador upon reaching the house appointed for his habitation, in a style that would have done credit to any artillery'.[14]

In 1812 Abbas Mirza's European-trained army boasted more than 13,000 infantry, cavalry and gunners, and in that year there were signs of progress in the form of a victory against Russian forces in the densely forested region of Qarabagh, where the Russians lost three hundred men and the Persian guns blew up the Russian magazine.[15]

By this time, however, Abbas Mirza had lost many of his other British instructors as a consequence of a new Anglo-Russian alliance against Napoleon, and the modernisation of his army was only half done. The perils of falling between two stools were demonstrated in October of that year, at Aslanduz, a ford over the River Aras, where

Abbas Mirza blithely neglected to post guards around his camp, which led to his forces being decimated. The combined Persian dead from this engagement and a second rout inflicted by the Russians in the new year was around five thousand, and Fath-Ali Shah's hand was badly weakened as the British pressured him to end a war that no longer suited them by stopping his subsidy. The resulting Treaty of Golestan, signed with Russia in October 1813, was a disaster from the Iranian point of view. It formalised the loss of Iran's Caucasian territories, permitted no power other than Russia to deploy warships on the Caspian Sea, and, most ominous of all, allowed Russia a say in choosing the heir to the Persian throne.

It was little wonder that patriotic Persians regarded the Treaty of Golestan as the result of Christian collusion against the Iranian nation, and swore to reverse its provisions. The jeremiads claimed that defeat on the battlefield had stemmed from the adoption of infidel innovations – exactly the argument of conservative Ottomans following the self-destruction of their big modern gun when it was fired against the Russians in 1797 – and they pointed out that Iran's European friends had twice abandoned them after coming to their separate accommodations with Russia. Abbas Mirza was indeed furious at the withdrawal of Britain's military mission, but, despite this disastrous outcome, in his view there was no alternative but to modernise apace. Luckily, he perceived another field in which London could be made his accomplice: education.

In 1811, Abbas Mirza had sent two young Persians to England to study, but the experience had been unhappy. Having barely escaped with their lives after their ship foundered, they ran up big wine and tailoring bills in London before one of them, Muhammad Kazim (son of Abbas Mirza's portrait painter), succumbed to tuberculosis and was buried ('with all respect and ceremony due to the Mussoulman religion') in St Pancras churchyard.[16] Despite the failure of this first mission, the prince remained convinced that by immersing a number of receptive young Persians in England, progress could be made across a range of fields. Someone would be needed to watch over the next batch of students, however, and the prince's eye alighted on Colonel Joseph D'Arcy of the Royal Artillery, who, having led the Iranian army to victory in 1812 at Qarabagh, was preparing to go home. Once D'Arcy's consent was secured, it only remained for the prince to choose the members of the mission. We are fortunate that one of the five, Mirza Muhammad Saleh Shirazi, would leave behind a remarkable document of his experiences – as remarkable, in its way, as Rifaa al-Tahtawi's description of France a decade later. Mirza Saleh's travelogue was at once modern Persia's first affirmation of the mobility of ideas, a simultaneous translation of the opening of his own mind, and a blueprint for the Iranian Enlightenment.

Born in around 1790, Mirza Saleh (the title Mirza denotes a court official) was a polymath, bookworm and xenophile. His father hailed from the southern city of Shiraz and was both affluent and pious enough to have made the pilgrimage to Mecca. In 1811 Mirza Saleh showed his ability to rub along with Englishmen when he was deputed by the Iranian government to accompany Sir Gore Ouseley and his wife as they made serpentine progress (inhibited by Lady Ouseley's delivery of a baby, the first British child to be born on Persian soil) from the port of Bushehr on the Persian Gulf to the court of Fath-Ali Shah in Tehran. The journal that Mirza Saleh wrote of the journey would later prove useful to Sir Gore's elder brother Sir William, when the latter wrote an account of the trip. The senior Ouseley described Mirza Saleh as 'a young and ingenious man of letters', whose views on demography, history and architecture he trusted implicitly.[17] Unmarried and blessed with an enquiring, sceptical mind, the young Iranian was an obvious candidate for Abbas Mirza's mission of discovery.

D'Arcy's letter informing the Foreign Office of his commission stated the names and objectives of his five charges. Mirza Reza sought a 'knowledge of artillery'; Mirza Jafar, of chemistry; while Mirza Jafar Husseini would study engineering. A master craftsman called Muhammad Ali hoped to learn to make locks. As for Mirza Saleh, he would 'acquire knowledge of the English language to become translator to the Persian government'.[18] Laconic though they are, these summaries reveal the ambitions of Abbas Mirza: to take, through his envoys, a crash course in modernity.

The notion of travel to an infidel land – as we have seen in the case of Rifaa al-Tahtawi – was not a simple matter for the Muslims. Trade was acceptable, conquest laudable, but to go to the Christian countries in search of knowledge was an admission of Islam's backwardness, and courted cultural and moral contamination. The fate of the unfortunate Muhammad Kazim, buried in a Christian churchyard, contained a warning for anyone contemplating such a reckless course.

Mirza Saleh's friend Ismail tried strenuously to talk him out of leaving Tabriz for such uncertain ends. What, Ismail asked, could Mirza Saleh possibly gain from meeting 'ignorant' people (by which he meant people who are ignorant of Islam)? To this Mirza Saleh replied with a spirited defence of unprejudiced intellectual acquisition: 'Why', he demanded, 'should I not learn something new every day, and, if I can, shine a light into the eye of my heart?'[19] Mirza Saleh predicted that he would exert a favourable influence on those he met, exposing them to the 'jewel of religions' and a 'divine law that is the essence and soul of truth'. Remarkably, given what we know about the subsequent spread of Christian missionary activity across the Muslim world (an early exponent, Henry Martyn, had recently arrived in Persia from India), Mirza Saleh seemed to anticipate few obstacles to converting Britons to Shia Islam.

The exchange between Mirza Saleh and his friend is an illustration of how the call of the new affects different people, rousing one to optimism and anticipation and creating fear and resentment in another. From Mirza Saleh's comments it is clear that his outlook was coloured by mystical ideas about the diffuse, highly personalised nature of faith, while Ismail thought in terms of danger and cultural infection.

The first major educational mission from the Middle East to Europe set out northwards from Tabriz in April 1815, and in taking up his pen to record what happened Mirza Saleh did something startlingly new, for until then there had been little in the way of travel writing by Iranians about non-Muslim countries.[20] Mirza Saleh's journal blended statistics about the Caucasus with impressions of the landscape in a manner that would have been entirely familiar to European readers. He also exhibited a marked absence of xenophobia or cultural mockery. This was a contrast with the prickly, defensive travelogues that many earlier Muslims had written following visits to the West – and contrasted with the arch superiority of most Western travel literature about Iran. Sir William Ouseley, for instance, harped on relentlessly about what he regarded as the deficiencies of the Iranian character (incompetent rapscallions), traits that would be immortalised in the hugely popular picaresque novel *The Adventures of Hajji Baba of Ispahan* (1824), written by the diplomat-adventurer James Morier.

Mirza Saleh's account would be different. Whether he was riding through the Georgian mountains, forested with oak and walnut, or dining with the Armenian priests of Yerevan, his journal bears witness to an alert, highly receptive mind. This approach reflected the absence of available literature on any subject outside the limited world of Islam; he was forced to seek knowledge wherever he found it. From D'Arcy, for instance, he received a (misleadingly patriotic) account of the Protestant Reformation that left out Martin Luther and Henry VIII's peccadillos but highlighted William Tyndale's translation of the Bible into English.[21] Reaching Moscow in August 1815 – it was now being rebuilt after the great fire that had razed it during the Napoleonic occupation of 1812 – he persuaded a young Turkish speaker to translate extracts from a Russian book about the abortive French campaign, which he then incorporated into his journal. Thus one of the first modern biographical fragments in Persian arrived courtesy of a Turkish translation of a Russian book about a French emperor. It was in Moscow that the party heard the news of Napoleon's defeat at Waterloo, which signalled, as we now know, more than half a century of Anglo-Russian dominance of world affairs.

He wrote about Moscow's churches, nunneries and madhouses, and its trade in pelts and skins, but above all he directed his admiration at St Petersburg, his jumping-off point for the West. The new city that had been built by Peter the Great in the most taxing of circumstances – and at a cost of thousands of lives – astonished him with its multi-storey buildings, its huge towered bridges straddling the water, and the size and variety of its commerce. It was here that he saw his first opera and zoo (attractions included a sheep with six legs and another with two); he also noted Potemkin's crystal factory and Russia's famous cross-bred horses from Arabian mares.

The Iranian party then boarded ship at Kronstadt on the Finland Sea and set sail for Great Britain. At the end of September they put into Great Yarmouth, on the Norfolk coast, and a few days later, accompanied by Colonel D'Arcy, the party had their first experience of Georgian London, which would be their home for the next four years.

By the time Rifaa al-Tahtawi and his companions reached Paris in 1826, the tone of relations between France and Egypt had been established by the Napoleonic invasion and the subsequent removal of pharaonic loot for the Louvre. That France considered itself a natural master in the Islamic world would be emphasised further by the takeover of Algeria in 1830. The same could not be said of London in 1815. Britain as yet had no Middle Eastern possessions and its interests in India were managed not through the Crown but by a commercial joint stock company, the East India Company. Evangelical Protestantism and assumptions of racial superiority had not yet fully impressed themselves on relations between Indians and Britons on the subcontinent – indicated by the social acceptability of mixed households and excitement over the unifying philology of Sir William Jones (who in 1786 had suggested that Sanskrit, Latin and Greek had common roots). Echoing the relatively liberal atmosphere at Hyderabad and Calcutta, behind the neoclassical facades of Regency Britain there was much interest in Muslim and Persian culture, ascribable in part to the status of Persian as India's court language, and in part to the social success enjoyed by Fath-Ali Shah's recent ambassador-at-large (and eventual foreign minister), the handsome, leonine Mirza Abul Hassan Shirazi. In 1809 and again in 1819 he journeyed to Britain, where he learned English without much concern for the grammar, negotiated tenaciously over political and economic relations, and hurled lances in Hyde Park. He was regaled with Persian lyric poetry by Emily, the daughter of the co-director of the East India Company, Sir Thomas Metcalfe, and was invited to inspect fine orientalist libraries.[22] It was a brief return to the curiosity of Elizabethan times, when Shakespeare conjured an image of Eastern opulence by calling the shah the 'Great Sophy' (after the name of his Safavid dynasty), and the Kentish adventurer Sir Robert Sherley did not consider it beneath him to enter the service of the Persian government.

And yet, for all the intellectual inquisitiveness of its better-educated inhabitants, and the odd glimpse of future multiculturalism (the lexicographer Dr Johnson and the artist Sir Joshua Reynolds both had black freedmen as servants), the Persian party were definitely pioneers. They were among the very first Iranians to stay for an extended time in England in a private capacity, so could call on neither a permanent diplomatic legation (Mirza Abul Hassan Shirazi had been recalled) nor a friendly Iranian family for advice. An early trip to a bathhouse summed up their confusion; it ended in disarray, with the Iranians covering everything in henna, with which they had dyed their beards, the bath keeper apoplectic with fury, and Mirza Saleh handing over five shillings to pay for the mess. Shortly after that Colonel D'Arcy took them to report to the Foreign Office, where they were informed that under the provisions of the Aliens Act (an anti-immigrant law that had been promulgated to control the movements of French refugees from the revolution, in part through the suspension of habeas corpus), if they were caught approaching military installations or the sea they would be punished with six months in jail – hardly a message of welcome.[23] Then there was the shortfall in funds that had dogged the mission from its start, which neither the British government nor Prince Abbas Mirza seemed minded to make good, and which soured relations with D'Arcy (he held the purse strings). The master craftsman Muhammad Ali complained bitterly that, having enjoyed the perquisites of being an armoury apprentice in Tabriz, he had been brought to Britain under false pretences and was now reduced to spending his days wandering the streets in perplexity.

To none of these irritations did D'Arcy apply the balms of sympathy and tact. The colonel was a martinet and he was impatient to be married to his aristocratic fiancée; the last thing he wanted was responsibility for a bunch of bumptious incomers. Tension mounted after the students moved to a village outside London for reasons of economy, where Mirza Saleh engaged a clergyman to teach him Latin, and there were skirmishes over English teachers and the Iranians' demand for money for new clothes at the end of Ramadan. The Iranians even threatened to take D'Arcy to court over the money they suspected him of keeping from them.

The resentful dependency that queered relations between D'Arcy and the visitors would be replicated on a larger scale everywhere in the Muslim world, as nation after nation identified Western progress as the ideal to be followed but hated having to kowtow to Westerners in order to obtain it. D'Arcy's graceless, miserly attitude showed that he understood nothing of this; nor did he grasp that the five young men might, if they were generously educated before being returned home, go on to become lasting friends of Great Britain. The Persians were young, inexperienced and spoilt, and in truth their plight was not as desperate as they made out; they spent lavishly in a fashionable coffee house, went to the opera and enjoyed a social life that included teaching Persian without accepting a fee.

And then, with wondrous rapidity, the situation improved. It was 21 May 1817, when Mirza Saleh, somehow liberated from the provisions of the Aliens Act, took up a long-standing invitation from a West Countryman, Robert Abraham of Devonshire, an architect who was an acquaintance of one of Mirza Saleh's London friends, and at the same time began one of the most remarkable descriptions of Georgian England.[24]

The journal that Mirza Saleh wrote about his British stay – in which this trip to Devon features prominently – is emphatically not a private journal. The writer's aim is to put as much useful information as possible at the disposal of his Iranian readers. Evidently the most important reader will be his beloved prince, Abbas Mirza, and his intention is to describe Britain's 'talents and productivity' on the understanding that this will spur similar endeavours back home. At the same time, however, it is the unaffected record of the quickening effect that contact across cultures can have on a sensitive and optimistic soul – a repudiation of insularity, and a moving endorsement of the universality of the human experience.

A sense of diligent journalism permeates Mirza Saleh's journal after his coach quits London for the West Country on the turnpike west, and in comparison to the potholed and rutted roads of Iran, passable only on horseback or on foot, his detailed description of this speedy and efficient mode of transport would have struck his readers as a great novelty. To begin with he sits inside the coach, with a Spaniard and several farmers for company (all equally impossible to understand); after tea he takes his place on top, where he stays until Salisbury Cathedral comes ethereally into view the following morning. Bowling along to Exeter, he speaks at length to a woman and her daughter, and is delighted by the 'conversation and purity and insight' of the young girl.[25] For the folk back home, used to a strict segregation of the sexes, the outlandishness of forming a spontaneous acquaintance with female strangers did not need spelling out.

From his detailed description of Exeter Cathedral, with its twelve bells, enormous organ and two vast stained-glass windows containing the finest 'paintings' he has ever seen (like enamel), it is clear that this

Shia Muslim has wandered around its sacred precincts without hindrance. After supper with another acquaintance, who shows him a paper mill and an engine for producing coal gas, he sets off with Robert Abraham to the stannary town of Ashburton. There, among the tin mines, Mirza Saleh exchanges his European travelling clothes for Iranian robes, causing the daughters of his host amusement and consternation. Indeed, much of Mirza Saleh's stay in the West Country is spent in the company of these and other Devonshire girls, whom he describes as 'moon-faced' and 'sweet-natured', although he seems to have exercised some self-censorship, for in his descriptions of bucolic musical interludes and dancing parties on hillsides overlooking the River Dart, mention of cider is suspiciously absent – they drink only tea.[26] Never less than appreciative of the local maidens and their philanthropic work for the poor and old, he quite runs away with himself in his description of young Sarah Abraham, who displays 'the utmost excellence, perspicacity, sagacity and delicacy' while conversing with him on the road to Plymouth, not to mention a beguiling combination of 'greatness, pride and sobriety'.[27]

At Plymouth Dock, the premier naval base of the premier naval power of the world, Mirza Saleh stares in admiration at the vessels that the Aliens Act was designed to prevent him from seeing, lavishing his ever improving descriptive powers on 'the most secure port in England'. The anchorage is so extensive a thousand warships could park there, protected by ramparts bristling with cannons. He explains dry docks and breakwaters to people whose only experience of the sea is as poetic metaphor.

The aged King George III had been confined after supposedly going mad, his prerogatives carried out by his son, the Prince Regent, but the people still celebrated the monarch's birthday; amid the salutes and huzzahs, and while clutching the hand of Miss Sarah (again, a liberty he would not take with a girl back home), Mirza Saleh ventures out in his Iranian robes, gets mobbed by five hundred people for the outlandishness of his appearance, and flees.

Back in Tabriz, Mirza Saleh had promised his pious friend Ismail that he would spare no effort to expose the 'ignorant' people he met to the 'jewel of religions'. But his journal makes no mention of Muslim proselytisation during the visits he makes to churches and the conversations he has with affable curates. He evidently made a careful study of Christianity, finding Protestantism preferable to Catholicism. And when finally the time comes to leave Devon, perhaps with the memory of Miss Sarah's hand hot in his, he movingly sets aside all thought of religious difference, writing: ' Good God! Of what importance are differences of religion – these separations of sect on the one hand, and of nationality on the other? I wept for the members of this family, old and young, such that I have never been so affected.[28]

On his return to London in June 1818 Mirza Saleh began work on the long historical section of his book. His English was by then much improved and he was able to read extensively – exactly what we do not know, as he includes no bibliography.[29]

In London, his social life had expanded to include some Protestant Unitarians (he was drawn to them because they reject the divinity of Christ, a highly problematic idea for Muslims), as well as distinguished intellectuals such as the astronomer Sir William Herschel, who had discovered Uranus (his telescope was no less than forty feet long), besides being a composer of note. Thanks to introductions made by D'Arcy – with whom relations remained nonetheless tense – Mirza Saleh was a habitué of London's Freemasonry lodges, temples of Enlightenment thought. He no doubt derived many of his ideas from intercourse of this kind, besides using the library at the British Museum, which he describes as 'full of books in every language on the humanities and science' – and from which Namik Kemal would also draw inspiration half a century later.

There was little that was revolutionary in the several hundred pages of history and actuality that Mirza Saleh wrote; it traced British history from Julius Caesar through to Magna Carta, and from the Tudors and Stuarts to the Georgian monarchy. Written by a Muslim, thousands of miles from home, the most significant thing about this book is that it exists at all. It is as if Mirza Saleh is telling his Iranian readers, 'Everything we have heard about our homeland and religion being the centre of the world – it's false.'

He opens his history in a way that is pregnant with meaning for Iran and its prospects of improvement, writing that although the people of England used to be 'bloodthirsty and degenerate evil-doers', over the past four hundred years they have built 'the best of nations'. He marks out the reign of Elizabeth I as the starting pistol for stunning advances in knowledge and the arts, when the country went 'from a state of ignorance to one of perfection'.[30]

From the French invasion of Egypt (Napoleon's professed respect for Islam was a 'trick', he writes, echoing British views of the recently deposed emperor), he segues into an encyclopedic account of London. This takes in house design and domestic mores (he is surprised that when people enter houses, rather than take off their dirty shoes, they remove their hats), local administration, fire engines, docks, parks and schools. It is clear that Mirza Saleh took his commission to amass useful information very seriously.

Presenting Regency England in accordance with the dominant 'Whig history' of inexorable progress is one thing, but Mirza Saleh was also determined to convey a sense of the country's political balances, which, though far from fully democratic, would have offered a tantalising comparison with the despotism of Qajar Iran. Mirza Saleh describes in some detail the prerogatives of the king, the House of Lords and the House of Commons.[31] But he reserves his greatest astonishment for the ability of a single artisan, 'a poor man, with a shop', to hold up the building of grand Regent Street, running from Carlton House to Regent's Park, by refusing to sell his freehold to make way for the new thoroughfare.[32] 'And suppose', Mirza Saleh writes with pardonable hyperbole, 'that the whole army were to come down on his head, they cannot oblige him to give it up ... the prince himself cannot inflict the slightest financial or physical harm on him.'[33] Democracy and liberty formed no part of the agenda of Fath-Ali Shah or the heir apparent, and in his writing Mirza Saleh was careful not to argue in their favour, but the very airing of such possibilities is itself a kind of nudge, prompting the question, 'Why not us?'

In May 1819 Mirza Saleh and his travelling companions were recalled by Prince Abbas Mirza. They had all found vocations after the first few, somewhat directionless months of their stay in England. Two of the five had taken courses at the Royal Military Academy, at Woolwich, and a third had learned modern medicine. Apart from his labours as a historian, Mirza Saleh had been able to receive lessons in Latin, French and the 'natural sciences', as well as learning the art of lithograph printing. He had also discovered what he identified as the secret

'Enemy of the foot-draggers': by the time of his death in 1849 Muhammad Ali Pasha had transformed Egypt into a cash-crop economy criss-crossed with canals and studded with modern towns, and where a new national consciousness was coming into being.

No society could progress with a javelin-throwing military. This was the lesson of the Battle of the Pyramids, in 1798, when Napoleon's invasion force met the Egyptian Mamluks on the outskirts of Cairo. After barely an hour the defenders had been routed by an integrated modern force formed into squares and spitting out grapeshot.

The Egyptian chronicler Abdulrahman al-Jabarti denounced the Mamluks as 'immersed in ignorance and self-delusion', but he too felt profound ambivalence for the modern values that were being imported by the infidel.

The state of learning in Egypt at the time of the French occupation was dire, with the majority of astronomers refuting Copernican proofs of a heliocentric universe and printed books seen as an offence against God. The unidentified men in these engravings were probably sheikhs, or men of religion, affiliated to the school of al-Azhar.

'My country is no longer in Africa,' Muhammad-Ali's grandson Ismail I declared in 1878; 'we are now part of Europe.' In terms of attitudes and amenities, parts of Egypt were indeed unrecognisable from the medieval backwater of the beginning of the century. Ismail's credit-fuelled development was symbolised by the Suez Canal, a triumph of modern engineering that was opened to great acclaim in 1869.

False Start: Iran's Crown Prince Abbas Mirza was born in 1789 into the Persian imperial traditions of ornament and autocracy. But his hero was Napoleon, and he appreciated that reform was essential if Iran was to survive the depredations of London and St Petersburg. From his bailiwick near the Russian border, this cultivated man dispatched Persia's first educational missions to Europe, sponsored the translation of key European works, and imported metal casting techniques and the printing press. But Abbas Mirza predeceased his father, Fath Ali Shah, and never had a chance to spread reform across the country.

Whether it was putting on western uniforms, marching abreast or shaving their beards (the alternative was to be singed by gunpowder), soldiers in Iran's modernising military forces had to ditch much cultural baggage. This Russian-style military band was immortalised in an elaborate tiled depiction on one of Tehran's royal palaces.

Probably more eulogies have been composed for the humbly-born Amir Kabir, Iran's dominant statesman at the mid-point of the nineteenth century, than for any other Iranian political figure.

The assassination of Nasser al-Din Shah by Mirza Reza Kermani on 1 May 1896, was the opening act of the Middle East's turbulent twentieth century. Mirza Reza was publicly hanged, a scene captured here by the Iranian-born photographer Antoin Sevruguin, whose shadow, along with those of an assistant and a hooded camera, stamp the scene with modernity.

Throughout the nineteenth century schools of anatomy were part of developing education systems, first in Egypt, then Turkey. The rise of scepticism and irreverence is illustrated by this group photograph of medical students in Istanbul, with its ghoulish tableaux of human remains.

The Eastern Question: by the end of the nineteenth century the Ottoman Empire had been disturbed by separatism at the empire's edges and a suppressed experiment with representative government within. The placid waters of Istanbul, seat of the empire, would soon know revolution, invasion, and political collapse.

of Britain's prosperity: its being a 'country of freedom'.[34] As for the homesick Muhammad Ali, he had become one of the first Muslims in history to understand the workings of a steam engine, and found life in England so agreeable that he married his landlady's daughter – who accompanied him back home to Tabriz. The duties of the returnees in their homeland would be twofold: to apply the skills they had learned, and teach them to others.

Their return journey took them via the Mediterranean and Turkey. On arriving in Istanbul, entering the lands of Islam after a five-year absence, Mirza Saleh had to remember to 'comport myself in accordance with my own religion'. The Ottoman capital was in a state of phoney war between Sultan Mahmud II and the Janissaries, and Mirza Saleh lamented the failure of the Turks to institute a modernising regime, which he blamed on the sheikhs (or, as they are called in Iran, mullahs). 'As long as the mullahs interfere in the affairs of the Ottoman government,' he wrote, 'it shall make no progress. Sultan Selim made an attempt to introduce the European order in Istanbul but the mullahs stupidly called this order non-Islamic. The Sultan also wanted to introduce European science but the mullahs again through jealousy prevented him and thus kept the people from leaving the path of ignorance and darkness. In fact, it is obvious that whenever the mullahs interfere in the affairs of any government, that country and that administration shall never make progress.'[35]

He must have felt keenly the differences between still unreformed Istanbul and the England he had left behind. For example, despite being relatively narrow, the Golden Horn could still be crossed only by boat – this was also a contrast to the soaring bridges he had seen while travelling through St Petersburg. When Sultan Mahmud came out of a mosque he was protected not by a bodyguard composed of modern soldiers but hemmed in menacingly by the Janissaries in their obsolescent finery. The Persian visitor could not have foreseen that seven years later Mahmud would feel strong enough to crush his Praetorian Guard, setting in motion Turkey's modernising revolution.

Five years after Mirza Saleh's return to Iran, Prince Abbas Mirza's court chronicler wrote that 'master craftsmen who were sent from Persia to England at great cost have now returned ... and are making guns and other instruments of warfare better than those made in

England ... in addition to Latin, they know the languages of France, England, India, Poland and Russia. Among them are engineers and a physician whose competency has been approved by English masters. Now, by order of the Prince, some of the children of the nobility are studying technology and languages with them.'[36]

All in all, the effect of the returnees on their compatriots was indeed substantial – even if the gunsmith Muhammad Ali was not quite matching the foundries of Birmingham. Mirza Saleh's contribution was perhaps the most significant of all; the Crown prince made use of him as a secretary, translator and diplomat. Readership of his travelogue was probably confined to a small circle consisting of Abbas Mirza and his entourage; and its restricted circulation is little surprise, for its contents were dynamite that needed to be handled carefully. One of its effects was to show the way towards a more functional, observational Persian, while his use of translated extracts sparked a translation movement, albeit on a smaller scale, of the kind that Cairo and Istanbul were also experiencing. (One of the words he coined was *durbin*, literally 'see-far', for telescope.)

Mirza Saleh also made use of the skills he had picked up as a printer's apprentice in London, having brought back a small press. This wasn't the first attempt to print books in the national language; Sir John Chardin, an Anglo-Huguenot merchant, had been commissioned by the Safavid Shah to import a press in the seventeenth century. But costs had been high, and from then on (as in Egypt and Turkey), a combination of religious qualms, opposition by copyists and unfamiliarity with the technology meant that the country – with the exception of liturgical texts for the Christian minority – remained a print-free zone.

Now, with the help of Mirza Saleh's press, printing in Iran became an accepted tool of government. (For some time the mullahs would remain wedded to their manuscripts.) In 1829, while on a diplomatic trip to St Petersburg, he oversaw the acquisition of Iran's first lithographic press, a big technological leap as it would now be possible to print maps and scientific diagrams.[37] By 1847 the printer's art had progressed far enough for a British merchant to write, 'we have now in Tabriz no less than sixteen printing establishments, and more in Tehran; in fact books have become so cheap in Persia that it has done much injury to the trade of the copyists'.[38]

In due course Mirza Saleh was able to address another lacuna in Persian communications, for in May 1837 he brought out the country's first newspaper, the *Kaghaz-e Akhbar*, a literal translation of the English 'newspaper'. Among reports of comings and goings in the capital, a fire at the royal palace in Naples and a new steamship that was capable of crossing the Atlantic in less than two weeks, there was an unusual item about a dervish, 'petulant, naked, matted-haired, foul-tongued [and] impudent', who had accosted the Ottoman sultan, Mahmud II, while the latter crossed his brand-new bridge over the Golden Horn. This was the same 'hairy sheikh' whose execution had been followed by rumours of a celestial light over the corpse. For all the intrinsic curiosity of this event, its usefulness for Mirza Saleh seems to have been as a commentary on affairs inside Iran and the rankling feuds between the *ulema* and Sufi mystics.

Of Mirza Saleh's fellow students in London, almost all went on to achieve distinction. One became chief engineer to the army and translated a biography of Peter the Great, while another was appointed ambassador to Constantinople and returned to England on a diplomatic mission in 1860. The master-craftsman Muhammad Ali re-established himself in Tabriz before moving to Tehran, where he became head of the royal foundry; his English wife introduced some Western ways, such as the use of knives and forks, into their household.[39] After training as a physician, Hajji Baba, the surviving member of the educational mission of 1811 that had preceded Mirza Saleh, became first the Crown prince's doctor and then the shah's. He went on to design Iran's first European-style polytechnic.

All in all this could be considered a good return on Abbas Mirza's investment, boding well for future educational missions – indeed, for the success of his reform project in general. So why were the achievements of Iran's first comprehensive engagement with Western ideas not consolidated and built upon by the prince whose idea it had been in the first place? The bitter fact was that, of the Middle East's three concurrent thrusts towards modernity, it was Iran's that was most successfully parried by the exponents of obscurantism, zealotry and fear. In the Iran of the first half of the nineteenth century there would be nothing comparable to the hospitals, canals, ports and schools of Muhammad Ali, and no shining statements of scientific and secular ardour as emanated from the bureaucracy of Mahmud II. And it would be another generation before the values expressed by Mirza Saleh would be taken up by numbers big enough to change Iran.

The Crown prince himself was a major reason for the delay. Abbas Mirza was in a constant state of competitive rivalry with his innumerable brothers, and this sharpened his already keen desire to win back the Caucasian lands that Iran had lost at the Treaty of Golestan in 1813. Notwithstanding his desire to reform, and the efforts he expended in doing so, revanchism was uppermost in Abbas Mirza's mind for much of the period he spent waiting to be shah.

To this end he unwisely accepted the support of the Shia clergy, with whom he had little in common but whose help he needed to launch a campaign. The mullahs were upset by Russia's savage treatment of Muslims in the Caucasus. Russia's viceroy in the region, General Alexis Petrovich Yermolov, had made no secret of his detestation for the people under his rule, and was known for selling Chechen women at a rouble a head and slaughtering whole villages of Circassians. In 1826, armed with declarations of jihad from the top mullahs, the Crown prince led his country into another conflict with its neighbour to the north. But Iran's developing army was still no match for the Russians, and the results were again disastrous. Within two years Iran had lost yet more land in the Caucasus, and Tabriz itself was occupied.

The consequences of this defeat were even worse than Golestan. Under a peace treaty signed in February 1828 in another Iranian village that would suffer from its association, Turkomanchai, Iran formally ceded ownership of the lost lands, recognised Russia's exclusive right to trade and navigate on the Caspian Sea, and gave permission for Russia to build consulates across northern Iran – a footprint that would expand until it amounted to unofficial annexation. The shah also agreed to pay a bullion indemnity whose first instalment alone was delivered by a train of 1,600 mules. Finally the Iranians undertook to hand over the Russian subjects they had captured, including Georgians and Armenians who had converted – some of them under duress – to Islam.

Of all the provisions of Turkomanchai, this last was most odious to the Iranian people. The Russian diplomat who came to Tehran to implement the hateful new treaty, the celebrated poet and dramatist Alexander Griboyedov, sent his men into private homes in search of enslaved Christians, and rumours flew that inside the Russian legation Muslim women were being forced to abjure their religion. The tension climaxed when a Russian Cossack shot dead a Muslim youth and the mob threw off restraint. The mullahs again cried jihad, the legation's defences were overwhelmed, and everyone inside was butchered, including Griboyedov. After the carnage a dead body erroneously thought to be that of the poet was paraded through the streets, as people shouted, 'make way ... for the Russian ambassador on his way to visit the Shah! Stand up, out of respect: salute him in the foreign style, by taking off your hats!'[40]

Back in Tabriz the Crown prince heard what had happened and wept. Fearing another humiliation on the battlefield, he tried desperately to limit the damage by dispatching a delegation led by his son (and containing Mirza Saleh) to issue a grovelling apology to the tsar in St Petersburg. In the event more fighting didn't suit the Russians; the delegation was cordially received and Mirza Saleh took the opportunity to buy his lithograph presses. But the incident highlighted the challenges of reforming the system, and as the delegation admired Russia's citadel of modernity – peering through telescopes, visiting factories, universities and schools – the main feeling among the Iranians was not hope but frustration. 'It would be extremely easy to build such schools in Iran,' wrote a member of the delegation, with wistful longing. 'A few of the leading foreign savants could be brought to Iran and a school set aside for teaching the children of the nobility'.[41] And yet, which European power would extend such help when the lives of its citizens might be threatened at any time by the passions of the people? There was rarely a better demonstration of the incompatibility of modernising reform and holy war.

In the event, Abbas Mirza never became shah; he died in 1833, a year before his father Fath-Ali. But by then he had fatefully enmeshed the country in a burgeoning Anglo-Russian rivalry that would limit the freedom of whoever occupied the Persian throne. The British had begun to strengthen their grip on the Persian Gulf, while the rival empires disputed control of the routes to India that crossed Afghanistan, Baluchistan and the Hindu Kush. The destiny of Iran itself, adjacent to these barren but vital territories, was now of interest to the premier imperialists of the age. Iran had been thrust into what would later be named the 'Great Game'.

To blame Iran's sluggish pace of development mainly on the mach-inations of outsiders would be wrong, however. After all, Turkey and Egypt had tried gamely to deflect the hostile interest of the European powers, while harnessing their energy and capital. Could Iran not have done the same?

The answer to this question lies in the personal characteristics of the rulers themselves, and in this respect Iran was at a disadvantage in comparison with Egypt and Turkey. Fath-Ali Shah was succeeded by his grandson Muhammad, the eldest of Abbas Mirza's twenty-five sons. Well formed, courteous and restrained in his appetites (he contented himself with just three wives), the pious, mystically inclined Muhammad was less interested in progress than in prayer, and his fourteen-year reign was stagnant compared to the corresponding period of reform in neighbouring Turkey.

He came to the throne against a backdrop of revolts launched by jealous pretenders and interventions by Russia and Britain, who were strong enough to meddle directly in the Iranian succession. His reign was punctuated by further internal revolts, bureaucratic infighting and financial uncertainties, and much fruitless energy was expended trying to take back territory that had belonged to Iran in Safavid times. In 1837, with Russian support, Iran tried to annex Herat, in western Afghanistan – whose ruler Britain had taken firmly under its wing. The British responded with gunboat diplomacy in the Persian Gulf and the shah was forced to lift his siege of the city.

The fate of reform under Muhammad Shah was illustrated by the obscurity in which Mirza Saleh, that early and promising champion of modernity, ended his days. In any modernising state a man of his accomplishments would have ended up in a very high position; instead he found himself languishing in a minor government office and his newspaper was shut down. Such was Mirza Saleh's fall from promi-nence, the date of his death, and the place of his burial, have since been lost from view.

For all that, Mirza Saleh's journal is a valuable and poignant record. It is a tragedy that his words, at the time when they could have done most good, were available to be read only in manuscript form and were not propagated through the printing technology that he himself had tried strenuously to popularise. His journal would not be printed until the 1960s, by which time the ideas it put across had been mostly absorbed.

Mirza Saleh's fall, of course, did not prove the futility of trying to introduce reform in Iran. Rather it showed how important it was to any incipient movement that the state be controlled by a forthright, determined and durable moderniser. Fath-Ali Shah, Abbas Mirza and Muhammad Shah did not satisfy these criteria, and that left Iran in the middle of the nineteenth century – while Europe suffered its aborted springtime, the Tanzimat reforms advanced in Turkey, and Egypt looked forward to building a great modern canal – as a nation that had barely advanced from the medieval decrepitude in which the Qajars had found it in the 1790s.

Muhammad Shah died in September 1848 and was succeeded by his seventeen-year-old son Nasser al-Din. While a European education had become de rigueur for the scions of the Turkish and Egyptian ruling houses, in Iran the young Nasser al-Din's schooling was dominated by traditional advice on ethics and princely conduct, the so-called 'mirrors for kings', leavened by translated geographical treatises and access to the Western newspapers and magazines that were starting to become available. It is a measure of the insularity of the Iran he inherited that at a time when the sight of passenger ships pushing out smoke along the Bosporus had become quite normal for Istanbullus, in Tehran the steam engine remained so alien that it took all the ingenuity of Nasser al-Din's court to induce a toy steamer to chug from one side of an ornamental pool to the other.[42]

Intelligent and impressive in his make-up (an early account describes his woad-thickened eyebrows and lashes darkened with coal), Nasser al-Din would at least meet the physiological condition for success as a reformist. He ended up reigning for forty-eight years, longer than either Muhammad Ali or Mahmud. The salient features of the new shah, however, hidden behind a cloak of inscrutability, were vulnerability and inexperience. Nasser al-Din was without a constituency, kingly acumen or obvious buoyancy in the turbulent waters of the Anglo-Russian rivalry. To compensate for his own failings, he attached himself to a man some thirty years his senior; a man with the experience and guts to steer him through an apprenticeship on the job. It was the swarthy, heavily bearded Mirza Taki Khan Farahani, better known by the highest title he attained, Amir Kabir, or Great Commander, who took on this godfather role, and in doing so he became Iran's enduring emblem of reform.

Born in 1807 in the dry middle of the Persian plateau, Amir Kabir had a background that the grandees at court wouldn't let him forget. His father had been a cook in the household of Abbas Mirza's chief minister and as a boy the amir showed evidence of unusual alert-ness and was singled out to receive lessons with the minister's children. Official favour smoothed the way to preferment, and in the 1830s he rose as an administrator of the army that Abbas Mirza had modernised. To competence, determination and a distaste for courtly obsequiousness he allied the tenacity and wiles of a diplomat. He was in the mission (along with Mirza Saleh Shirazi) that was sent to St Petersburg to make amends after the murder of Griboyedov, and he distinguished himself during sensitive border negotiations with the Ottomans in the Turkish city of Erzurum, which lasted almost four years.

In 1848, to add to his other duties, he was appointed chief tutor to the Crown prince, Nasser al-Din, who had taken over the heir presump-tive's traditional bailiwick of Tabriz. Within months Muhammad Shah was dead, and such was Amir Kabir's success at smoothing his ward's path to absolute power that the new shah swiftly appointed him chief minister (he had already been made head of the army). He also soon became the shah's brother-in-law, by marrying Nasser al-Din's sister Malekzadeh.

Only it wasn't absolute power that Nasser al-Din wanted in the early years of his reign. He was a young man, hunting-mad, highly sexed and only intermittently interested in ruling Iran. He would disappear for weeks on end to the slopes north of the capital, and might return with thousands of carcasses and a new concubine. The minister's tone towards his liege may have remained deferential as custom exacted – 'may the soul of this slave be a sacrifice to the dust of His Majesty's feet' ran a typical line from their correspond-ence – but everyone knew it was he and not the monarch who was in charge.[43]

Unlike his predecessors, Amir Kabir prioritised reform. He began his tenure by establishing internal stability, which was essential for any kind of reform project. He employed exemplary severity while stamping out several revolts in the provinces, executing rebel leaders and massacring the followers of a messianic figure called the Bab. Thanks to the late Muhammad Shah's prodigality towards the clergy, and the reluctance of the regional magnates to pay taxes, the treasury was empty; Amir Kabir responded by cutting endowments and salaries, and he called in overdue taxes from truculent governors and chieftains.

As order was re-established, and finances improved, the amir started to make his way down the classic checklist of the nineteenth-century reformer. He founded Iran's first modern hospital and its first institution of higher learning (the polytechnic in Tehran, designed by Hajji Baba, which employed mostly Austrian professors). He implemented the most comprehensive programme of town planning and civil engineering since Safavid times, including frontier fortresses, the Tehran bazaar and a canal. From the establishment of a postal service to smallpox inoculation and factories for the manufacture of carriages, cannon and samovars (a Russian cultural import that thrives to this day), Amir Kabir showed his partiality for the most useful ideas of the age, wherever they came from. Like Muhammad Ali, whom he admired, he took an interest in cash crops, overseeing the planting of sugar cane and the strain of American cotton that had so speedily enriched Egypt.

The powers naturally favoured this disruptive newcomer with a close attention. The amir had to deal with the unwelcome after-shocks of Muhammad Shah's unsuccessful attempt to seize Herat in 1838. Rather than employ Britons or Russians, he employed military instructors from Italy and Austria, and with the same accent on self-sufficiency he built several armament factories around the country. He managed to prise the Caspian fisheries, an important source of revenue, away from a Russian monopoly, and contracted it to Iranians. But with the Russians in control of the Caspian Sea and British ships bossing the Persian Gulf, Iran's vulnerability was already painfully evident to the amir.

He baulked also at the powers' typically opportunistic sponsorship of Iran's religious minorities. 'I fail to see where the dictates of these Excellencies would end,' he jibed at a Russian intercession on behalf of the Armenians, 'nevertheless, so long as there are prospects, the struggle should continue.'[44] In his methods – in the mixture of national consolidation and calibrated globalisation, of the state and the private sector – it is possible to see the germination of a modern mixed economy and the nation state.

The newspaper he set up, the *Vaqayi-i Ittifaqiya*, picked up where Mirza Saleh's newspaper had left off, but with an official stamp of approval that the earlier publication had lacked. Announcements of progressive measures were made in its pages, such as a ban on the seizure of supplies by the army from the local population, and information was given out about the dangers of drinking brackish water, while inquisitive readers were introduced to subjects as varied as the struggle of the Italian nationalist Giuseppe Mazzini against the Habsburg Empire, Egypt's plans for the Suez Canal, the 1851 census of the United Kingdom, and the doings of cannibals in Borneo.[45]

While in Erzurum negotiating with the Ottomans, Amir Kabir had noted that the Porte only managed to carry out its reforms after relegating the *ulema* from the pinnacle of society. He endeavoured to replicate this highly sensitive reordering in Iran. The amir himself observed the conventions of Islam, fasting and praying as Islamic law required, but he had only suspicion and contempt for the overbearing mullahs. Such was their influence, however, that he was unable to institute major legal reforms to compare with the secularising measures of Turkey's Tanzimat, and he could no more than nibble at the clergy's judicial powers. Instead, he waged ad hoc battles of wills against individual mullahs and practices.

His attempts to restrict the displays of flagellation and self-mutilation witnessed during the mourning ceremonies that feature in the Shia calendar suggest that he felt embarrassment at these displays of religiosity. But the public did not share his shame, and he was forced to back down, though he had better luck in ending the clergy's practice of granting sanctuary to suspected criminals in the grounds of their mosques and shrines.

Arguments over the sanctity of holy spots reached a crescendo in Tabriz in 1849. There, a cow marked down for slaughter escaped death by entering a shrine, upon which its agitated owner dropped dead and the cow was hailed as a blessed augur. Encouraged by the *ulema* (and, it seems, by the British consul in the city, who endowed the shrine in question with a crystal candelabra) the populace anointed the favoured quadruped with ornate cloths and kisses, and illuminated the city as if preparing for a millennial prophet.[46] Each day brought news of fresh miracles and religious ecstasy shaded into outright insurrection, with the city's shopkeepers exempting themselves from taxation and other earthly irritants and the Friday-prayer leader ordering death for anyone caught drinking alcohol near the shrine.[47] Amir Kabir shut the sedition down by luring its leaders to Tehran, where they were detained while the fervour subsided. His sure assessment of the popular mood no doubt owed much to the efficient internal spy network he had set up, and which brought him reports from around the country.

By 1851 the amir's efforts to stabilise Iran were yielding results, but the financial burden of pacification had been shouldered by the nobles, and the shah's mother, Malek Jahan – who had been unceremoniously lowered from her former position of dominance over her son – found ready allies in a campaign to defame and undermine Amir Kabir. It was whispered that the amir wanted to depose Nasser al-Din and replace him with the shah's half-brother, and theories also circulated that he was in league with the British. The amir, it was true, had not helped himself, with his ability and arrogance, not to mention the indelible meanness of his origins.

The rumours about plotting with the foreigners were unpersuasive; in the words of Mary Sheil, wife of the British minister in Tehran, the amir had 'faced and resisted, perhaps injudiciously, the two lions, between which ... that meek lamb, Persia, was placed'. Nor, for all his day-to-day power, does Amir Kabir seem to have had designs on the throne. But he was undoubtedly grand and proud, and, as Mary Sheil wrote, he 'made the usual mistake of degrading the Shah into a cipher. He even spoke of him with contempt, often styling him ... this young fellow.'[48]

The charges of arrogance were amplified by Amir Kabir's enemies and in November 1851 the young, impressionable shah dismissed his illustrious premier – the man to whom in happier times he had made almost filial professions of love, and given his younger sister in marriage – and shortly after even exiled him to Kashan, on the fringes of the Iranian desert. While driving outside Tehran, Mary Sheil chanced upon the departing Amir and the shah's sister. 'They were both in a [horse-mounted palanquin], surrounded by guards. It seemed to me like a funeral procession, and I have seldom beheld a more melancholy sight. I longed to ... take the doomed Ameer and his poor young wife with their two infant children into the carriage, and to drive off with them to Mission-house ... I may as well antic-ipate his fate.'[49]

Mary Sheil's pessimism was not misplaced. The amir had been the object of competing overtures from her own husband and his Russian opposite number, both hoping to protect and thus earn the gratitude of a statesman who might yet return to power. But their actions only sharpened the shah's suspicions and his resentment at foreign interfer-ence in his realm. The amir and Malekzadeh were isolated at the royal palace at Fin, on the outskirts of Kashan, though they were permitted to wander between the cypress trees and watercourses of the refreshing garden there. The dutiful Malekzadeh did not abandon her husband in favour of her brother and mother, and, according to Mary Sheil, 'as a security against poison that exemplary lady made it a rule to partake first of all the food presented to the Ameer'.[50] All the while the shah's ear was being 'filled with the danger of leaving alive a man like him', and at length he issued an order to a senior retainer called Hajj Ali Khan, a man whom the amir had 'raised from the dust', to hasten to Fin and 'relieve Mirza Taghi Khan'.[51]

Amid the arrangements for his death, agents of the shah's mother had given Amir Kabir to understand that his release from captivity was imminent, so when Hajj Ali Khan and his accomplices reached Fin on 10 January 1852, they learned that their prospective victim was in the bathhouse, being washed in preparation to don his robe of honour. News of their arrival was withheld from Malekzadeh, who was in the adjacent palace (no doubt reflecting on her good fortune), and when Hajj Ali and his accomplices entered the bathhouse they found the amir's eunuchs gathering up his clothes. He met his fate coolly, asking only to see his wife – this was refused – before he ordered his own barber to open his veins on his wrists and stayed him from binding them afterwards. As he died, Amir Kabir vented his anguish by hurling a copper bowl at the wall and cursing the shah. Then he collapsed and as he writhed feebly in his own blood one of Hajj Ali's goons planted the heel of his boot between his shoulders, slipped a cloth around his neck, and pulled until he stirred no more.[52, 53]

There was little surprise in Iran at Amir Kabir's death, though many were shocked by the dastardly manner of its accomplishment. His period in office marked the first and final sustained attempt at modernising reform during the long reign of Nasser al-Din Shah, and the only time that this jealous, insecure and increasingly sybaritic monarch was constrained to share power with anyone.

Amir Kabir's record until then gives a tantalising glimpse of what he might have achieved. He was in power for just three and a half years and although his accomplishments were inevitably dwarfed by those of Muhammad Ali and Mahmud II (enjoying far greater prerogatives and longevity), they were nonetheless remarkable. Had he thrown his weight around a little less, and had he negotiated a little more delicately the sensitivities of the shah, the pique of the shah's mother, and the interests of Russia and Britain – if he had done all this, a place in the first rank of Middle Eastern modernisers might have been his. As it was, his career as a proponent of reform was barely under way before his veins were opened in the Iranian desert.

The cook's son had probably saved the Qajar Empire, but his efforts redounded to the advantage of Nasser al-Din Shah, and not his subjects. It was the beginning of a despotism that would last almost half a century, and which, while it was less puritanical and efficient than that of Turkey's Abdulhamid II, would have a similar effect of compounding resentment before the inevitable detonation.

The death of Amir Kabir came early in the shah's reign, but it could be argued that this was its defining event, forming the shah's attitude to modernity, which turned out to be narrow and monopolistic. For while Nasser al-Din was attracted by new ideas and gizmos – he developed a keen interest in photography and in the internal combustion engine – his plan was less to use technology and innovation to bring the state he had inherited up to speed with the modern world and more to protect its essential features, the most important being the pre-eminence of himself.

It is likely that more poems and epigrams have been composed in memory of the chief minister he murdered than for any other nineteenth century Persian, and the marble bathhouse in which the amir died is visited by sombre tourists even today. Mention is rarely made of Amir Kabir without a regretful sigh, and his death is presented as a martyrdom of far-reaching significance that held up Iran's development for a half-century or more. But it can also be argued that his defeat was unavoidable because of the arbitrary and absolutist political environment in which he found himself. In Iran, as in Egypt and Turkey, a movement of reform could only succeed if it was driven by a visionary and physically healthy monarch who could devote himself to a long and productive stream of reforms. That had been the case for both Muhammad Ali and Mahmud II, and it was no less true for Amir Kabir's ungrateful master, Nasser al-Din Shah.

Amid the story of thwarted progress represented by Amir Kabir, whose death inaugurated more than forty years of quixotic monarchical tyranny, it is easy to miss the significance of a minority religious movement that burst into life around this time, and whose claim to modernity might appear utterly negated by the medieval other-world-liness of its origins. The Babi movement, which began in the 1840s, went on to become an important catalyst of social progressiveness in mid-nineteenth-century Iran, promoting interreligious peace, social equality between the sexes and revolutionary anti-monarchism. Babism was a reflection of an older Iran that had been mass-producing messiahs in opposition to mainstream Islam since the seventh century – the kind of place that had produced the literally off-the-wall Rawandiyya, whose acts of worship had included jumping naked from town ramparts and other elevated positions (they thought they could fly). And yet the new current was also a product of Iran's grappling with novelty and change, and it went on to present a vision of moder-nity that was based on secularism, internationalism, and the rejection of war. It is this vision which has enabled it to survive to the present day – as Bahaism, which emerged from Babism in the late nineteenth century– in pockets and communities peopled by 5 five million souls, and which qualifies it for inclusion in any narrative about modernisa-tion in the Middle East.[54]

Babism's origins lie in the second quarter of the nineteenth century in Shiraz, in southern Iran (the home town of Mirza Saleh), where a pale, pensive boy called Sayyid Ali Muhammad grew up in a devout, well-to-do merchant family. The boy was poorly educated, which gave credence to his later miraculous acquisition of divine, or 'unlearned', knowledge – similar claims had been made about the Prophet

Muhammad. Again, like the founder of Islam, young Ali Muhammad had a background in commerce. He spent his late teens assisting his uncles in running a thriving import-export business out of Bushehr on the Persian Gulf Coast with India, Muscat and Bahrain, all the while burnishing a reputation for austerity, devotion and visions.

A seer without credibility is a crank, but Ali Muhammad's professional trustworthiness combined with an ability to conjure up Quranic commentaries and a propensity for seeing beyond the surface of things won him a growing reputation. In one almost Eucharistic dream he drank the blood of the martyred Imam Hussein, 'with greatest joy', to whose clairvoyant properties he ascribed his subsequent ability to bring forth verses and prayers. He was also known for self-mortification, which earned him criticism from the orthodox, for, as one critic reported, 'as I have heard, once in Bushehr, where hot winds are as burning as the breath of a furnace, at the peak of the heat, he ascended up to the roofs and stood in the sun bareheaded, reciting his incantations'.[55] Back home in Shiraz, between trips to the holy shrine cities of Iraq, Ali Muhammad was increasingly the object of admiration and puzzlement. 'He is no longer like us sinners,' the Shirazis told each other. 'He has become famous ... and can perform miracles.'[56]

By the early 1840s the reformist hopes raised by Abbas Mirza had died with their author, and public devotion was on the rise in the form of endowments of Sufi shrines and ceremonies to commemorate the martyred Shia imams. Ali Muhammad's elevated spiritual state had convinced him that he had been selected for a divine mission, and in 1847 – a year before the end of Muhammad Shah's undistinguished reign – he announced that 'the yearnings of the fifty thousand years are now fulfilled ... I am that divine fire which God kindles'. In the spirit of social and legal revolution that animates all millenarian movements, he also declared the abrogation of holy law and the ending of the established order of things, including Qajar feudalism, the Islamic prohibition of usury, and the pulpits, disquisitions and theological minutiae of the traditional clergy. He was part Martin Luther, part mystic saint, and by operating semi-clandestinely over the next few years was acclaimed by a widening group of followers as the Bab, or 'gate', to the twelfth imam. His appeal won him converts from the lower echelons of the bureaucracy to the remotest villages, where secretive communities arising in his name dissembled their beliefs in order to evade persecution, burst out in rebellions, and engendered fear and paranoia among the orthodox.

The authorities, both clerical and governmental, found themselves in a dilemma, for while the threat posed by the interloper was clear, persecuting or killing him might simply increase his popularity. In 1848, in the presence of the young Nasser al-Din (who was still Crown prince), the Bab was tried before the *ulema* of Tabriz with the aim of discrediting his claims. 'I am that person whom you have been expecting for more than a millennium,' he insisted, but he did not accede to the mullahs' demands that he produce proofs such as David's coat of mail, Moses' rod and the ring of Solomon. 'I am not permitted to bring such things,' he explained, before falling back into ungrammatical Arabic extemporising. Nasser al-Din, who had begun proceedings half convinced of the Bab's divinity, quickly lost his admiration.

A few months later the realm had a new shah, with Amir Kabir at his side, and as in other matters at this early stage in his reign Nasser al-Din allowed himself to be guided by his chief minister with regard to the Bab. Amir Kabir's vision differed from that of the Bab in that it was reformist, not revolutionary, and it regarded a trammelled Shia clergy as vital to the smooth functioning of society. But the burgeoning Babi movement had other ideas, the mood in many places on the Persian plateau was pregnant with menace and zealotry, and arms were hidden in anticipation of a general jihad against non-Babis.

There was a series of uprisings between 1848 and 1852, when government forces laid siege to Babi strongholds or pursued militants into the mountains; the country was in the grip of a millenarian madness that Amir Kabir saw as his duty to crush. The existence of a fast-spreading heresy contending that a new prophet had arrived to supersede Muhammad not only represented a mortal threat to Islam, but also to any monarch who ruled in its name; the mainstream mullahs and the shah were united in desiring to stamp it out. Several thousand Babis are thought to have died in the fighting and reprisals – possibly the bloodiest military actions conducted by Iran in the nineteenth century.

In July 1850, amid continuing unrest and the Bab's refusal to recant, the Tabriz clergy sentenced him to death for apostasy. The Bab was brought to the barracks square for execution by firing squad, but when the smoke cleared he was nowhere to be seen, and everyone assumed a miracle had taken place. In fact the first volley had severed the ropes that bound him, and the Bab had taken advantage of the smoke to hide in the barracks. He was brought out a second time, and this time the shots were true.

Even after the death of its founder, however, Babism refused to die. Any trace of ambivalent feelings by Nasser al-Din towards the movement was removed after some of its adherents reacted to the Bab's execution by trying to assassinate the monarch in 1852 – a botched attempt that pushed him into a frenzy of massacre and persecution and the movement into schism, with some Babis hewing to a doctrine of political abstinence and others continuing to plot the monarchy's overthrow. Hostility to Babism and its offshoots became a tenet of the Iranian state (as it is once more, under today's Islamic Republic), and a propaganda campaign stigmatised its adherents not only as renegades from the true path, but also as avaricious, egotistical and morally lax. Later the shah impressed on his son, the governor of Isfahan, that 'punishment, isolation and intimidation of this despicable sect is one [*sic*] of the necessities of kingship'.[57]

But persecution only galvanised the Babis, who continued to survive in large pockets around the country. Their resistance to horrendous tortures, which included the insertion of lighted candles into orifices gouged from their flesh (following which they might be halved with hatchets or blown from mortars), made them much feared. An Austrian officer in the shah's service gave an account of scenes that could have come from the imagination of the Marquis de Sade: 'They will skin the soles of the Babis' feet, soak the wounds in boiling oil, shoe the foot like the hoof of a horse, and compel the victim to run.' But still, 'no cry escaped from the victim's breast', until 'they hang the scorched and perforated bodies by their hands and feet to a tree head-downwards, and now every Persian may try his marksmanship to his heart's content . . . I saw corpses torn by nearly 150 bullets.' In many cases no information had been extracted from the victim except that he was a Babi.[58]

Bereft of its founder, smashed by the state, Babism splintered and the majority of the faithful ended up gathering around a former disciple of the Bab, Mirza Hussein Ali Nuri, who was known as Bahaullah, or 'Glory of God', and whose teachings are the foundations of Bahaism. It is now, with Bahaullah, that the story of a contagious madness gradually turns into a surprising fable of modernity, and the reason for this is that Iran at the time of Bahaullah possessed no secular arena in which to articulate desires for change. As a result this desire found expression in the only arena that did exist: the religious one. Bahaism was revolutionary because it declared the necessity of squaring reform with Islamic law to be null and void; Islamic law itself was no longer in force. From this emerged a movement of social and political transformation that was among the most progressive in the Middle East.

Bahaullah was a political moderate with good connections (Amir Kabir had tried to co-opt him with a government post), which enabled him to escape execution following the assassination attempt on the shah. He was imprisoned in a festering and filthy jail where he saw several of his fellow Babis put to death. The experience was of great importance, and by 1853, when he emerged from prison and into exile in the Ottoman Empire – the first period of which he spent in one of the sultan's salubrious European territories, before being transferred under Iranian pressure to Lebanon – he had resolved to regenerate the Babi community.

In 1863 Bahaullah declared that he was the 'manifestation of God' that the Bab had prophesied would come in his place, and over the next twenty years his movement set down roots not only in Iran and the Ottoman Empire but also, through evangelism, in the United States, Europe, India and Central Asia. Unsurprisingly, Bahaullah had little joy co-opting the temporal leaders of the age, to whom he addressed letters, or 'tablets', calling on them to throw their kingdoms at his feet. Queen Victoria replied equivocally; the tsar promised to investigate further. Napoleon III tore up his tablet and said that if Bahaullah was God, he was too.[59] Nasser al-Din Shah had Bahaullah's messenger executed.[60]

Yet even if the theology of Bahaism was a little whacky, the social vision was anything but. The manifesto that Bahaullah laid out during his long exile was in part a reflection of the progressive bits of the Tanzimat agenda. But it went far beyond the Turkish reforms in its vision of consultative democracy, the distinction it made between religion and politics, and its promotion of a world civilisation united by a common language and eschewing nationalism and war.

Bahaullah was in favour of a constitutional monarchy and equality for all subjects, regardless of religion, which put him in the ranks of Ottoman constitutionalists like Namik Kemal. But Kemal was a devout Muslim, while Bahaullah was the founder of a new religion; and Bahaullah went much further than other reformists like the Egyptian Rifaa al-Tahtawi in rejecting the principle of authoritarian monarchy on which Iranian patterns of government had been based. 'We affirm the appearance of reason among all human beings,' he wrote to a follower; 'therefore you will see absolutism discarded upon the dust.'[61] And in a passage that implied a division of human potential into the secular and profane, and with no special role for the clergy, he wrote that God had invested kings with the 'rulership of the earth', but had assigned 'the hearts of men as His own domain'.[62]

While reformists like Kemal and Rifaa al-Tahtawi were trying to reconcile Islamic and modern values, for Bahaullah and his followers the old axioms were now irrelevant and had been replaced by the assumption of his own divinity, which of course rendered the office of shah irrelevant. With the exception of this startling (and, to most, indigestible) bit of dogma – indeed, *because* of it – the principles governing virtually every human activity were once more open to interpretation. Having declared the redundancy of the Muslim clergy, Bahaullah and his son and successor, Abdul-Baha, proposed one of the most enlightened social systems of the time.

Bahaullah believed that the introduction of parliamentary rule was linked to the advent of his divine ministry, and he married messianic and democratic themes in his writing. His book of laws, completed in 1873, decreed that in every town where there was a community of Bahais they should set up a council, enjoying legislative powers and responsible for the welfare of the poor, called a 'House of Justice'. Tehran's first House of Justice was established in secret in 1878 – almost thirty years before Iran's first parliament opened – though its members were later imprisoned. He wrote that 'among the signs of the maturity of the world is that no one will agree to bear the burdens of autocratic rule'.[63] In a letter he wrote to Queen Victoria, he praised her for abolishing the slave trade (also forbidden under Bahaism) and for entrusting 'the reins of counsel into the hands of the people' – a reference to the Reform Act of 1867, which had enfranchised much of the British working class. Almost alone among a tiny group of public figures advocating women's education (Rifaa was another), he decreed that parents should educate their male and their female children, and although he echoed the Bab's tolerance of bigamy (two wives as opposed to the Quranic four), he made clear his preference for monogamy.

Perhaps surprising for a doctrine fired by persecution and revolt, Bahaullah declared the abolition of religious war and forbad Bahais from denigrating other religions. He allowed his followers to wear foreign clothes (considered defiling not only by many Muslim authorities, but also by Hindus and Buddhists), make friends with the members of other religions, and read their holy books. While deploring the ravages of European imperialism in Africa and elsewhere, and the expense and destructive capacities of modern armaments, he approved of Britain's constitutional monarchy; it seems likely that Queen Victoria's proclamation of religious toleration of 1857, in which she decreed that none of her Indian subjects should be 'favoured ... molested or disquieted, by reason of their religious faith or observances', influenced his son Abdul-Baha's insistence on complete religious freedom for all groups – which took him well beyond the *millet* system in operation under the Ottoman Empire.[64]

The monarchs themselves may not have paid much attention to the tablets that Bahaullah sent them, but these documents were circulated widely – if clandestinely – among the Bahais of Iran, and more openly elsewhere. When one examines the features of the new faith – the shredding of Islamic law, its anticlericalism, the democratic leanings and above all the annulment of the Prophet Muhammad's status as bookend of revelation – it is not surprising that a doctrine containing so many elements that were noxious to Islamic belief was cantoned, isolated and (in Iran, at least) driven out of public view. The religion continues today, its efforts to live in peace with Islam largely rejected, and its followers considered apostates in its Iranian birthplace.

The Bab, Bahaullah and their followers were outriders and the causes and controversies they espoused would occupy Islam, the cavalcade they spurned, for decades to come. Perhaps most surprising of

all, the Bab's most celebrated follower became – though she may not
have recognised herself as such – Iran's first feminist.

Gifted, pious and endowed with an irresistible combination of beauty
and charisma, Fatemeh Zarrin Taj Baraghani (whom the Bab renamed
Qurrat al-Ayn, 'solace of the eye') is one of the most remarkable
characters in nineteenth-century Iranian history. She is both feminist
icon and medieval saint – Simone de Beauvoir meets Joan of Arc –
and now that she is gone and her place in history is secure it is possible
to see in the events of her life a chain of clairvoyant images, snapshots
of a society that, while riddled with superstition, also teetered on the
edge of modernity.

   She was born in 1814, in Qazvin, the daughter of Muhammad Saleh,
a leading local divine. Despite being puritanical in his observance of
Islamic law, in matters of female learning Muhammad Saleh was a
progressive, and he gave Fatemeh an education of the kind that was
barred to almost all girls at the time. She soon surpassed many of
her father's students, and such were her accomplishments in memorising the hadiths and esoteric interpretations of the Quranic verses,
he was moved to declare that 'if she were a boy she would have
illuminated my house and come to be my successor'.[65] Married off at
fourteen to her cousin Mullah Muhammad, another cleric, she and
her husband went to live in the shrine city of Karbala, in Ottoman
Iraq, where she gave birth to two children but did not relax her
cerebral pursuits. Mullah Muhammad, it soon became clear, was
perplexed and not a little discomforted by this headstrong spouse
whose interests ran dangerously beyond the generally accepted limits
of womanly enquiry.

   Qurrat al-Ayn was not at peace with the legalistic mood in the
cloisters – to which her husband fully subscribed. This laid emphasis
on the role of the clergy, almost invariably men, as arbiters of temporal
affairs, but did little to prepare people for the revolutions in society
that, according to the doctrines of millennial Islam, will prefigure the
end of the world. Qurrat al-Ayn's Islam was of an ecstatic nature, and
she directed her prayers and fantasies towards this liberating end time,
when the sharia would be abandoned and replaced with perfect
freedom under God.

The writings of the then unknown Bab came as a blessing on her spiritual quest. 'As soon as I heard of this cause,' she wrote, 'I recognised it,' and she abandoned Mullah Muhammad and their children (with whom she had returned to Qazvin) to devote herself to its prosecution.[66] Back in Karbala she built up a following of acolytes, using her talents in oratory to captivate audiences of both men and women whom she addressed from behind a curtain, or smaller classes admitting women only, when she would not have to be veiled. An eyewitness wrote that 'a large number of people attended her teaching circles and prayed behind her. As she spoke, they listened with great astonishment in their hearts and were moved by her speeches.' To be a prayer leader as a woman and to be an acknowledged theologian was remarkable for the time. In the words of a Babi hagiographer, 'none could resist her charm; few could escape the contagion of her belief. All testified to the extraordinary traits of her character, marvelled at her amazing personality, and were convinced of the sincerity of her convictions.'[67]

In a poem that expresses the sense of ecstatic anarchy that is contained in the concept of the end time, she wrote:

> Cast off the garments of old laws,
> Of outworn traditions!
> Immerse yourself in the sea
> Of my bounteousness!

Another expresses (with prophetic poignancy, as it would turn out) her impatience at God's concealment and her desire for a naked truth:

> How long must your lovers endure
> This anguish from behind the curtain?
> At least bestow upon them
> A glimpse of your unveiled beauty …

The clergy reacted to Qurrat al-Ayn's growing fame and following by complaining about her to the Ottoman governor, while the more circumspect Babis charged that she had 'abrogated the Sharia that we inherited from our fathers and grandfathers without the mandate of [the Bab]'. The truth was obscured by the deliberate ambiguity

of the Bab's pronouncements, which used the established Shia practice of *taqiyya*, or the expedient white lie, to evade accusations of
apostasy. Imprisoned and then released, Qurrat al-Ayn was expelled
from Ottoman territory in March 1847. She went back to Iran, where
her progress from town to town met with the same mix of fawning
and suspicion – such were the polarising powers of the new faith.
Meetings were violently broken up and she began to advocate direct
action against the movement's enemies. Even though the Bab also
called her Tahereh, 'the pure', she was denounced as unchaste and
the official Qajar chronicler accused her of conducting sermons like
an orgy.

The Qazvin to which she returned later that year was sharply
polarised between the Babis and their opponents – of which her
uncle and father-in-law, Muhammad Taki, was a leading example.
In the summer of 1847 Muhammad Taki was assassinated while
saying the dawn prayer in his own mosque. Qurrat al-Ayn was
suspected of involvement, and she fled to Tehran where she sought
refuge in the household of Bahaullah (this was before his exile and
declaration of his own prophetic mission). Muhammad Taki's assassination and the government's repression of anyone suspected of
involvement marked a shift towards open warfare between the Babis
and conventional Shias.

The rising tides of persecution and a quickening spirit of Babi
defiance led to a sensational meeting in the summer of 1848. Under
conditions of unprecedented tension, angst and secrecy, eighty-one
leading Babis convened in the orchards of Badasht, on the
Mazandaran–Khurasan road in north-eastern Iran. They were bereft
of the Bab himself, who had been imprisoned in a remote castle on
the Kurdish borders; in his absence the movement's leaders had to
decide once and for all whether Babism constituted an entirely new
religion or simply a new coat for an old one. The aim of the radicals
among them was also to hoist the black standard that in the Shia
tradition signifies the advent of the Mahdi, divine herald of the end
of time.

For the Babi religion the debate amid the almond and pomegranate
trees was primarily doctrinal, but Badasht is also recognised as a
milestone in the history of women's political consciousness in Iran.
Qurrat al-Ayn was among the delegates. She, Bahaullah and their

followers were joining forces with another leading Babi, known by
the moniker Quddus, meaning 'holiness', whom the anti-Babis had
driven out of the shrine city of Mashhad. Qurrat al-Ayn's sacred
mission turned out to be of acute social significance because it
involved overturning one of the most symbolic restrictions that
Islamic orthodoxy places on women.

The council at Badasht started as a power struggle, with the radical
Qurrat al-Ayn standing against the conservative Quddus, who
denounced her as 'the author of heresy', and the conciliatory Bahaullah
trying to arrange compromise between the two. The factions were
divided into the three camps, each established in a different orchard
in the village, where the principals and their supporters had pitched
their tents. At a crucial stage in proceedings Quddus was in Bahaullah's
garden when he received a pressing invitation from Qurrat al-Ayn to
visit her. He refused, saying, 'I have severed myself entirely from her,'
so Qurrat al-Ayn came to him – and she did so in a state of undress
that constituted open rebellion against religious law.

According to one eyewitness:

> Suddenly the figure of Tahereh, adorned and unveiled, appeared before
> the eyes of the assembled companions. Consternation immediately
> seized the entire gathering. All stood before this sudden and most
> unexpected apparition. To behold her face unveiled was to them incon-
> ceivable. Even to gaze at her shadow was ... improper ... that sudden
> revelation seemed to have stunned their faculties. [One of the partici-
> pants] was so gravely shaken that he cut his throat with his own hands.
> Covered with blood and shrieking with excitement, he fled away from
> the face of Tahereh. A few, following his example, abandoned their
> companions and forsook their faith.

The same informant leaves no doubt of the religious importance of
Tahereh's sensational entrance.

> Undeterred by the tumult that she had raised in the hearts of her
> companions [she] began to address the remnant of the assembly.
> Without the least premeditation, and in language that bore striking
> resemblance to that of the Quran, she delivered her appeal with
> eloquence and fervour. She concluded her address with a verse from

the Quran: 'Verily, amid gardens and rivers shall the pious dwell in the seat of truth, in the presence of the potent King.' Immediately after, she declared, 'I am … the Word which shall put to flight the chiefs and nobles of the earth.'[68]

Qurrat al-Ayn's removal of the veil was a blatant rejection of the Prophet Muhammad's command to his followers, set down in a famous hadith, that 'when ye ask of them [the wives of the Prophet] anything, ask it of them from behind a curtain. This is purer for your hearts and for their hearts.'[69] 'Curtain' and 'veil' are the same word in Arabic, and this ambiguous hadith is the basis on which the practice of veiling women has been sanctified – and its observance often presented as a litmus test for faith. In the Persia of the mid-nineteenth century unveiling in the presence of any male other than a member of the immediate family was akin to prostitution in its sinfulness. By removing her veil, Qurrat al-Ayn was showing her companions that the old laws no longer held true, and through this gesture she impressed on them that the Bab's revelation of his miraculous status and the dawn of a new prophetic cycle were at hand.[70]

After the Badasht meeting broke up, with the principal delegates reconciled and marching north to establish a Babi enclave, the sight of an unveiled Qurrat al-Ayn chanting prayers alongside Quddus prompted a group of villagers to attack them. Several Babis were killed; the rest fled. Persecution of the Babis, orchestrated by Amir Kabir, was now reaching its bloody climax, and it culminated with the Bab's execution in July 1850.

After her revolutionary removal of the veil, Qurrat al-Ayn became a hunted fugitive, slipping from village to village before eventually being captured. She was brought before Nasser al-Din Shah in Tehran, who liked her looks and ruled that her life should be spared, but still she refused to recant and the house of the Kalantar, or chief of police, where she was confined, was besieged by admirers. Finally, in September 1852, following the unsuccessful assassination attempt on the shah, she was sentenced to death.

According to a Babi account of events:

one night, aware that the hour of her death was at hand, she put on the attire of a bride, and anointed herself with perfume, and, sending for the wife of the Kalantar ... confided to her her last wishes. Then, closeting herself in her chambers, she awaited, in prayer and meditation, the hour which was to witness her reunion with her Beloved. She was pacing the floor of her room, chanting a litany expressive of both grief and triumph, when the guards ... arrived, in the dead of night, to conduct her to the Ilkhani garden, which lay beyond the city gates, and which was to be the site of her martyrdom. When she arrived [the military officer overseeing her execution] was in the midst of a drunken debauch with his lieutenants, and was roaring with laughter; he ordered offhand that she be strangled at once and thrown into a pit. With that same silken kerchief which she had intuitively reserved for that purpose ... the death of this immortal heroine was accomplished. Her body was lowered into a well, which was then filled with earth and stones, in the manner she herself had desired.[71]

At the time her fame was so widespread that *The Times* of London reported on the execution of the 'fair prophetess of Qazvin'. In the decades that followed, her renown continued to grow, despite the unrelenting efforts of the Qajar authorities to suppress Babism and Bahaism.[72] 'Oh Tahereh!' mourned the Turkish poet Suleyman Nazif, in 1919, 'you are worth a thousand Nasser al-Din Shahs!'[73]

The execution of Qurrat al-Ayn ranks with that of the Babis' tormentor, Amir Kabir, as an illustration of the tortuous relationship that mid-nineteenth-century Iran had with movements of reform. The fact that these two important figures were on opposite sides shows too that modernity can have many faces, from the Western-inspired, utilitarian state-building of the amir, for whom orthodox Shia Islam was a restraint on disorder, to the intuitive individualism and spiritual anarchy of Qurrat al-Ayn. Of course her values belong to the enchanted age, of magic and divine grace, but the way she chose to express them, by casting off first her husband, then her religion, and finally her veil, prove to us, down the years, that aspirations we complacently associate with the West need not have a Western origin at all.

For all the diffuse strivings of Qurrat al-Ayn, Amir Kabir and Abbas Mirza, and for all the optimism and industry of Mirza Saleh, the fact remained that well into the second half of the nineteenth century Iran was a distant third in the race towards modernity that had engaged the heartlands of Muslim civilisation. The hand of Nasser al-Din Shah would get heavier as the century advanced, and his aversion to sharing power more untenable, but the unfinished efforts of its early modernisers added up to a compelling heritage that later innovators would adopt, unify and take forward. When that happened, and their efforts were allied to wider demands for freedom, even this most medieval of modern tyrants would be unable to resist.

4

Vortex

Whether it was through schools, armies or canals, by the last quarter of the nineteenth century the rulers of the most productive intellectual and political economies of the Middle East were striving either to manipulate modernity or to delay it. But no longer was it possible to control the movement of ideas, and self-generating forces arising from the people – Bahaism was one – affected the direction and pace of change. Contrary to the wishes of conservatives, despairingly attached to the warming ice packs of tradition, it was impossible to be unaffected. Who could resist the power of autonomous judgement encouraged by the printed newspaper, or fail to hear in the tick of a modern watch the reordering of time itself?

Notwithstanding the revulsion that many felt for the notion that the lands of Islam had no alternative but to adapt to new methods and ideas, the main centres of the Middle East were caught up in a vortex of change. Quite apart from the accelerated pace of social upheaval, the other novelty was its shared and diffuse nature. Through travel, the spread of journals, and the increasing likelihood that educated Muslims would see each other while on the Hajj, a sustained intellectual and social correspondence was getting under way between Tehran, Cairo and Istanbul – and of course between them all and the outside world – as they received ideas, mulled them over, and more often than not reacted to them in similar ways.

It seems appropriate that the all-embracing nature of the evolution that took place in the Middle East should be mirrored in the structure of this book. With the integration of their respective experiences into one broad course of emancipation and demand, albeit following slightly different timescales, it is no longer necessary to disaggregate Tehran, Cairo and Istanbul at a narrative level, and from now their stories will merge. Integration would last until the late twentieth century, when sectarian enmity began pulling the lands of Islam apart once more.

Whatever the West could throw up in the form of overarching ideologies, whether it was secularism, national identity or new kinds of relationships of class and kinship, a plethora of competing world views entered the region in profusion and disorder. The Middle East was reconstituted thanks to the anti-slavery effort, democratic openings, the emancipation of women and the decline of polygamy. No new idea, no matter how radical, could be rejected in its entirety because to utter it was to raise the possibility of its enactment. With each innovation a strain was placed on the existing civilisation, even if it was the strain of saying no.

The seeds of social and intellectual change were to a large degree carried by economic winds, for by the end of the nineteenth century, Egypt, the Ottoman Empire, French and Italian North Africa and, to a lesser extent, Iran, had been annexed to global mechanisms of trade, finance and consumption. Across vast areas subsistence farming had been replaced by the cultivation of cash crops for export, while tenure was moving from the old system of tax farmers holding land on behalf of the state to one of private estates tilled by sharecroppers, alongside a large number of small peasant proprietors and a landless proletariat. Cotton was the regional cash crop par excellence (along with tobacco, wheat, barley, figs, raw silk, raw wool and opium), and Egypt was a case study in the perils of overspecialisation, with a single commodity accounting for more than 90 per cent of the country's total exports in 1865. Even after the later fall in cotton prices Egypt remained a cash-crop economy – albeit a more diversified one – and, as such, at the mercy of the Western consumer.

Thanks to innovations in transport, the regional nodes were now growing closer to each other and to the rest of the world. The southern and eastern Mediterranean boasted several world-class ports receiving goods and passengers (P&O had started plying these waters in 1853, catering in part to European pilgrims to the Holy Land), the Suez Canal yielded its shareholders 8 or 9 per cent per annum, and rivers like the Tigris and Euphrates were opened for commercial navigation by steamship. For millennia the main vehicle for internal trade had been the camel, plodding along at four to five kilometres per hour.

With the new railways that were now being laid (except in Iran, where Britain and Russia exercised an unofficial Great Power veto on this strategically valued form of infrastructure), not only did commerce get faster, but everything else: investment, migration, unrest, infection.

By 1913 Egypt boasted some 4,300 kilometres of track, and Turkey 3,500, with regional lines such as that from Izmir to Aydin along the Aegean coast helping form new trading clusters. Different parts of the empire turned away from Istanbul and towards Manchester, Hamburg and Marseilles. In fact, so stretched was the skein of imperial trade that by the 1910s, according to one Turkish historian, it had become 'difficult to talk about the Ottoman economy ... as a meaningful unit of analysis'.[1]

The region's rulers were naturally unhappy at their inability to compete in the global market for finished goods, but advantages of productivity, scale and capital formation lay unassailably with the West, which, exacerbated by the exceptionally low import duties that the Europeans insisted on for their merchants, turned the Middle East into one of the least protected markets in the world. Most local handicrafts were beaten by European factory-made goods on price and quality, with a disastrous impact on production. In 1862, for instance, the British consul in Aleppo reported that the number of looms in the city had fallen from 10,000 to 2,800, while in Morocco in the 1870s the makers of fezzes, pots, hardware and glass were suffering the effects of foreign competition. Meanwhile the price of a yard of British cotton cloth fell inexorably – from 7 francs in 1800, to 3 francs in 1830, and 60 centimes in 1860.[2] Industrial manufacturing in the Middle East fared even worse – after vigorous early promotion, spearheaded by Egypt's Muhammad Ali, had ended in failure. By the third quarter of the nineteenth century, more than fifty years after the region had taken its first steps towards modernisation, there was hardly any industry to speak of.

The impact of the economic imbalance was aggravated by European finance, though this was temporarily staunched by the 'Long Depression' of 1873–9. Private investment hastened the development of public utilities like railways, streetcars, water, gas and electricity, while gushing credit – the better for Sultan Abdulhamid II, Nasser al-Din Shah and the khedives to pay for arms, palaces and foreign trips – heavily indebted the region. In the case of Turkey and Egypt the credit famine that manifested itself during the Long Depression led to default and the seizure of the economy by foreign officials, who imposed painful austerity measures and revenue raids in the name of loan recovery. In Iran the mania for foreign finance had reached a climax in the notorious Reuter concession of 1872, under which Nasser al-Din Shah effectively sold his country's resources and infrastructure to a British businessman, Baron Julius de Reuter – a decision so vulgarly self-interested that it eventually had to be taken back under pressure at home and abroad.

Middle Eastern society naturally changed in reflection of these economic and political developments. The region was producing more, importing more, and, despite high inflation and spectacular pockets of destitution, getting richer. Better security and public health were showing results, and for the first time in centuries the populations of Egypt, Turkey and Iran began posting consistent annual increases – around 0.8 per cent per annum for Turkey and Iran after 1830, and 1.5 per cent per annum over the second half of the century in the case of Egypt.[3] Conurbations were growing, in Istanbul's case from 400,000 in 1800 to well over a million on the eve of the First World War – as more people survived childhood, fewer died of disease, and the cities started to take on their modern status of magnets for the rural poor. Much migration took place as a result of political upheaval, and Ottoman Anatolia gained around 2 million Muslim inhabitants following the Treaty of Berlin of 1878, which stripped away much of the empire's Balkan lands and led to a Muslim exodus to Anatolia. Egypt's population grew by 30 per cent between 1850 and 1880; some of the cotton towns by as much as 170 per cent over the same period. With the cotton boom, Alexandria had taken its place among the great Mediterranean port towns, along with Istanbul, Marseilles and Genoa; its population rose from around 8,000 at the time of the French invasion to 220,000 in 1882, while the number of passengers alighting there went from 10,000 in 1837 to over 50,000 in 1871.[4] The number arriving at the new Port Said, at the head of the Suez Canal, grew even faster, reaching 59,000 in 1871.

As the most cosmopolitan and Westernised city in the Muslim world, Istanbul acted as a kind of pilot neighbourhood for the evolution of family structure; the mean age of women at marriage rose from nineteen in 1885 to twenty-one in 1907 (it was just a year older in the United States), and people had fewer children thanks to efficient use of that venerable form of birth control, coitus interruptus. By 1907 almost half Istanbul's Muslim households had fewer than four members, while statistics gathered in the same year showed that only 2 per cent of married men in the city had more than one wife.[5, 6]

Migration, technology and, for the economically vibrant areas of the region, an almost unmanageable intermingling of different communities – these were the features of the Middle East as the century wore on, and unsurprisingly the fabric of society grew stressed in consequence.

There were numerous reports of brawls and disputes in the highly charged atmosphere of Egypt's boom towns, including one, in 1865, which involved some Italian marines and some Arab boys, was exacerbated by the police (either Turks or Albanians), and led to a mob besieging the house of the Italian consul. In another, six years later, the Delta railway town of Tanta was the scene of sectarian violence between Greeks and Arabs who were defending the honour of a long-deceased mystic whose memory had been defiled. Tensions in Tanta seem to have been exacerbated by the privileged position that the Greeks – along with the Greek Orthodox Syrians – occupied as money-lenders and gin owners, and the propensity of the Greeks to get drunk and insult Islam only made matters worse.[7]

Disputes of this kind had taken place in the past, but the numbers involved, the participation of foreign powers in the form of their representative consuls, many of them with business interests of their own, and the accelerated nature of communications, which meant that a local fracas could spread miles away, placed a new burden of consequentiality on what might once have been shrugged off as a petty local affair. The new world, brought to the Middle East, was faster, more integrated and more concurrent than the old.

This new world – the Western world – was also showing its real intentions, which early modernisers like Rifaa al-Tahtawi had considered essentially benign, but which increasingly centred on acquisition. At different speeds, and with different emphases, the various parts of the Middle East were moving towards shared political and economic servitude to the West, and one can read in the humiliations of the last quarter of the nineteenth century an augury of the nationalist eruptions that would follow.

The worst humiliation befell Egypt – the only one of the region's three dominant territories to be formally colonised. In 1879, Britain and France, leveraging their creditor status, unseated the insufficiently pliant Khedive Ismail and replaced him with his son Towfiq. Three years after that, Britain invaded the country in response to a burgeoning patriotic movement there – the beginning of an occupation that would last three-quarters of a century.

Unsurprisingly, a rising popular sense of grievance was observed – not only in Egypt, but also in Turkey and Iran, where Europe's meddling was less overt – both against the foreigners and those rulers whose cupidity had let them in. The emergence of patriotic feeling in Egypt; the protests that were staged against the Reuter concessions in Iran; Turkish denunciations of the Ottoman Debt Administration and its medicine of austerity – these reactions showed that Middle Easterners were fast shedding any residual faith they had in the political intentions of the West. And yet, distrust of Westerners had not morphed into a coherent and energetic counter-movement against their ideas. Wahabbism, that austere revivalist creed that had sprouted as a protest against the first steps of Ottoman Westernisation in the eighteenth century, had still to spread much beyond its Arabian homeland; while Salafism, which we nowadays understand as the pursuit of the pristine Islamic society that existed under the Prophet, didn't exist as a social programme. For all the sinister characteristics of the Western administrator, banker and missionary, Europe (and increasingly the United States) was bearing gifts of great complexity and attractiveness, and a growing number of Muslims regarded them as the shape of the future – not just of the West, but of all humanity.

Whether it was in the salons, the universities, or the Masonic lodges – Freemasonry had taken off in the Middle East in the 1870s, with everyone from the royal ruler to respected clerics flaunting his membership of this quintessential Enlightenment institution – by the end of the nineteenth century Western ideas were in the ascendant. A steadily growing elite of professionals and administrators perceived that the terms of human existence were being drafted anew and it is a remarkable fact that in Cairo in particular it was easier then to put forward radical and irreligious views than it is now. Thanks to the explosion of printing and the steady (if slow) rise in literacy, books, articles and speeches were now being translated into Arabic, Turkish and Persian almost as soon as they appeared in the West.

Rather than go over classics such as Montesquieu's *Considerations on the Romans* and Fénelon's *Telemachus*, the new Middle Eastern intellectuals preferred to immerse themselves in the atheistic philosophy of Arthur Schopenhauer, the evolutionary polygenism of the biologist Ernst Haeckel and the precursor of chaos theory as laid out by the mathematician Henri Poincaré.

Further impetus for change came from Protestant missionary schools that were being set up in Lebanon and elsewhere, which, while generally taking in the children of religious minorities, had a wider effect on the Muslim society as well. Inspired by debates that bubbled up in these schools, leaning on Darwin (whose *Origin of Species* had come out in 1859) and other broad-shouldered evolutionists such as Alfred Russel Wallace and Ludwig Büchner, publications like *al-Muqtataf* ('The Digest') in Egypt and *Akhtar* (' Star') in Iran disseminated ideas that were at variance with the Quranic account of Creation, while from the philosopher Herbert Spencer they derived novel, organic ideas about society, and from Italian and French sociologists the concept of the 'crowd'.

The Ottoman press thrived in spite of the penchant for censorship displayed by Sultan Abdulhamid, and there was a vogue for scientific articles with titles like 'Origin of the Species of Vertebrates', and descriptions of the Lapps and Eskimos. From the provincial city of Bursa, in western Anatolia, a clerk wrote a letter to a popular journal in which he posed the question, 'What are the sciences good for?' before answering with a materialist flourish: 'What is there in the world besides sciences?'[8]

In Egypt the Roman Catholic intellectual Shibli Shumayyil revelled in the pious odium he received after he described the soul as the result of material operations, for, as he wrote, 'all this fuss made me want to slap people awake from their deep slumber ... housed in stasis, and on the margins of life'.[9] Shumayyil remained at liberty and he was not killed for his audacity; it is hard to imagine a similarly bloodless outcome today.

In an attempt to reduce the potential for scandal, the editors of *al-Muqtataf*, the Lebanese Christians Yaqub Sarruf and Faris Nimr (both of whom had attended the Syrian Protestant College, which

later became the American University of Beirut), presented
Darwinism as a less subversive doctrine than it actually was. In their
synthesis of *The Origin of Species*, which was only translated in its
entirety in 1918, they leavened Darwin's beliefs with those of his
contemporary Wallace – in particular Wallace's belief that 'all
animals evolve one from the other except humans'. Sarruf and Nimr
agreed with Wallace that human consciousness and qualities such
as wit or artistic aptitude could not be ascribed to natural selection,
but rather an 'unseen universe of the spirit', a formula that allowed
them to accept much of what Darwin proposed, but without
toppling man from his pedestal next to God. *Tatawwur*, a neologism
meaning 'evolution', was increasingly in currency among Arabic-
speaking Muslims, as was *Darwiniya*, or Darwinism, while *al-Muqtataf*
treated its readers to articles, many of them lifted without attribution from Western journals like *Popular Science Monthly*, on subjects
as diverse as glassmaking, microscopes and maintaining a thick head
of hair.

Even this apparently neutral information was far from innocuous.
From the output of journals like *al-Muqtataf*, it was clear that the
world contained more diversity than most Muslims had been prepared
for by traditional education, and that it was possible to tell its natural
history without reference to divine Creation. Reams of writing now
existed in Arabic, Turkish and Persian, reasonable, self-contained and
entertaining, which made no mention of God, not even to thank him
for giving us the push that set us off; the human intellect was elbowing
the divine Creator aside. The secular intellectual sphere was expanding
with incredible speed. Between 1880 and 1908 more than six hundred
newspapers and periodicals came into existence in Egypt, and it was
a similar picture elsewhere in the region.[10]

Just as Darwinism had been implicated in political controversies in
Britain – grist for Malthusians, white supremacists and slave abolitionists alike – so *Darwiniya* bore on Egypt's tortured situation. The
country's colonisation by Britain in 1882 had prompted a 'scramble
for Africa' in which some 80 per cent of the continent had come under
European rule. The horrendous Battle of Omdurman, in 1898, in
which the British lost just forty-seven lives while annihilating 10,000
of their Sudanese foes, was an excruciating demonstration of the
evolutionary nostrum of survival of the fittest.

'The law of natural selection,' observed a demoralised Egyptian intellectual, Qasim Amin, had impelled the Europeans, 'powered by steam and electricity,to seize the wealth of any country weaker than them.'[11] Even the great Turkish empire of Abdulhamid II, although draconian in its promotion of Islam and its loyalty to the sultan, and keen to block the entry of all 'non-essential' (that is, cultural) elements of the West, remained the economic plaything of its European creditors.

Al-Muqtataf was just one sluice gate in what became a three-way flow of ideas between Istanbul, Tehran and Cairo, as students, dissidents and traders moved with ease around a geography that was increasingly seen as single. Thanks to better technology and transport, banned newspapers continued to be published. Printed thousands of miles away from the censor, they were still able to reach their audience. Two of the most influential Persian newspapers of the period, *Qanun* ('The Law') and *Sour-i Esrafil* ('The Trumpet Blast'), had their editorial offices in London and Calcutta respectively, and *Qanun* was printed in Istanbul. The influence of these publications was utterly disproportionate to their tiny size; they caused debate and ructions wherever they were smuggled, and readership massively exceeded circulation. *Al-Muqtataf* sold a mere three thousand copies, but each of these might be read by dozens of people – a group of enthusiasts in Baghdad, for instance, clubbed together to buy a single subscription.[12]

Anticlericalism, the hallmark of the European Enlightenment, was rampant among the new intelligentsia formed of bureaucrats, journalists and progressive clerics, and one of the most extraordinary instances of the new irreverent cross-fertilisation came in Iran's north-west.

During the summer of 1910, a trainee mullah in Tabriz called Ahmad Kasravi was in the habit of going at night to the roof of his house to stare at a mysterious ball of fire streaking across the sky. Kasravi did not know what he was looking at, for the Ptolemaic astronomy he had been taught at the seminary was silent on such 'tailed stars'. It was only by reading *al-Muqtataf* – which had reached northern Iran all the way from North Africa – that he learned that he had been watching a comet, and that it had been named after an English astronomer royal, Edmund Halley, two centuries before.

Kasravi was already known in the seminary for his scornful, sceptical manner; his new discovery confirmed in his mind the idiocy of his teachers and the backwardness of their methods. 'It was this star', he would recall, 'that set me on the road of European learning.'

What he learned further entrenched his growing hatred of the clerical class from which he happily abstracted himself. Knowing excellent Arabic, as well as English, French and Turkish, the young schoolteacher and bureaucrat was well placed to puncture clerical boasting, and the pamphlets he wrote (many of them anonymous) popularised the picture of the greedy, ignorant mullah. He deplored the sheikhs' remunerative sideline of recounting the sufferings of the Shia imams with extreme theatricality for the benefit of sobbing parishioners, and came under suspicion for bringing a book in French to the mosque. 'What is to be done about him?' a seminarian asked. 'He needs a whipping!' came the mullah's response.

Kasravi was there when a simpering cleric bade farewell to a group of rich pilgrims, and his description might have been plucked from the pages of *Candide*. These men were merchants whose hoarding had led to the deaths of scores of poor people in a famine, but the cleric predicted celestial rewards for the pilgrims, 'in the deceitful manner that is the mullah's hallmark'. Kasravi was unable to contain himself, expostulating, 'These are the men who killed their own neighbours and families through hunger and who will be damned in the sight of God ... speak of yesterday, when widowed women pressed their half-dead babies to their breasts, and mother and child dropped dead from hunger!'

Kasravi in Iran and Shumayyil in Egypt were far from alone, and naturally the more pious of their contemporaries – Muslim or otherwise – were appalled by their adoption of the most barbarous and destructive ideas that Europe had to offer. Of all the acts of intellectual and physical licence to which these notions gave rise, perhaps none would equal in drama and intensity the final performance of a fleshy, multiple-chinned, positivist Turk called Besir Fuat.

Born in 1852, the son of an Ottoman civil servant, Fuat was an ardent Voltairian and one of the empire's more outspoken critics (the reason he disliked most of what was being written was that it was not scientific enough); among his many translations was an essay entitled 'Heart' which criticised poets for ascribing metaphysical functions to what was, after all, a muscle.

In the 1880s he suffered personal blows. His son, named after Namik Kemal, died tragically young. Fuat's own mother, who had been suffering from a persecution complex, was committed to an asylum on the advice of an Italian doctor called Mongeri. Fuat now found that the money he received for his translations and articles covered neither her hospital bills nor the maintenance of a second family which comprised a prostitute he had met on one of many excursions into debauch (these had been recommended by Mongeri as an antidote to his depression, and most effective in conjunction with leeches) and their daughter. In 1885 he began to contemplate suicide.[13]

Fuat did not act precipitately. He spent the next two years trying to sort out his affairs, including the division of his meagre assets, and wrote productively up to his death, besides going to the theatre almost every night. It has been suggested that these were not the actions of a suicidal desperado, and clearly what happened next was calculated to generate maximum effect.

One of the reasons why suicide is significant beyond the single life that is extinguished is that it entails a revolt against any divine rule over earthly existence; in planning his death, Fuat intended writing God out altogether. He left instructions that his body should be given to medical students for dissection (despite the tolerance of anatomy there was always a shortage of bodies) and he decided to write a real-time account of his death to the extent that this was physically possible – a materialist narrative as life drained away, unburdened by any religious or metaphysical feeling.

One evening in February 1887, Fuat entered the downstairs library in his house, shut the door and slit his wrist and his carotid artery. Beforehand he had injected himself with cocaine as a painkiller, and now took up his pen:

> I carried out the operation. I felt no pain. The more the blood flowed, it smarted a little. My sister-in-law came down as the blood flowed. I got rid of her by saying that I was writing an article and was keeping the door shut. Luckily she didn't come in. I don't imagine I shall have a sweet death. I lifted my arm furiously so the blood would flow. I began to lose consciousness.

How long Fuat was sentient for after this is unclear. Towards midnight he was strong enough to shout for a servant. The servant was confronted by his master, covered in blood, who ordered him to shake his arm in order to increase the flow. The servant's cries brought the women of the house running. A doctor was summoned, whose futile efforts to save Fuat's life brought forth the taunts of a man who believed he had cheated destiny. 'Doctor!' Fuat gloated as the life slowly ebbed away, 'why are you even trying? I won't live longer than five minutes.'[14]

The reason why Besir Fuat's demise caused a sensation in Istanbul was not because suicide was unheard of – on the contrary, it seems to have been quite common – but because his intention had been to serve science. One newspaper commentator wrote that whoever had provided Fuat with his painkiller should be punished, for if he had not taken cocaine he would have been unable to bear the pain and would have cried out. Another pointed out the effects that European godlessness had had on 'some young people', noting that suicide was repugnant to Islam, and speculated that Fuat would be punished in the next world. Yet more pundits identified a current of anti-religiosity in society, for which the solution was more Islamic studies in schools.

In the event, Fuat's family did not follow his instructions that his body be handed over to the royal medical school, and he was buried according to Islamic rites. But the press coverage that was given to his death ensured that his calculated rejection of God's writ over life and death received yet more publicity. The censor was roused, and a ban was served on any further mention of suicide in the press. This was observed for six months, after which one of the papers announced morosely: 'The suicide epidemic goes on!'[15]

The rise of an Arabic print and reading culture centred on Cairo was a part of what is now called the *nahda*, or 'reawakening', of Arab culture, which drew on Western exemplars as well as existing traditions. Rifaa al-Tahtawi is considered by many to be the founding father of the *nahda*, but there were many contributors, from the Aleppo polyglot and essayist Maryana Marrash (1848–1919), whose literary salon attracted musicians, authors and oenophiles, to the

Christian Maronite Ahmad Faris al-Shidyaq, one of the most naturally modern thinkers of his time.[16]

Born in Lebanon in 1805, Shidyaq's outlook and career were much
marked by his elder brother Asad's death at Maronite hands after
converting to Protestantism. Shidyaq himself took an ecumenical
approach to matters of faith, converting first to Protestantism and later
on to Islam. Feeling little loyalty to his native Lebanon, he spent long
periods in Cairo, Malta, Turkey and Western Europe. He translated the
Bible into Arabic, applied unsuccessfully for the chair of Arabic at
Oxford, and wrote to Queen Victoria and Napoleon III – which puts
him in the company of Bahaullah, founder of Bahaism. His importance
to the Islamic Enlightenment is as a literary pioneer, for in the middle
of the century he became the first Arab exponent of a prose genre
whose infinite perspectives, formal freedom and propensity for social
commentary made it the mirror of modern life: the novel.

Shidyaq was familiar with Laurence Sterne's lively and discursive
Tristram Shandy, as well as Voltaire's *Candide*, but when he composed
his immense, frequently obscene gallimaufry *Leg over Leg*, he was
also drawing on Arab traditions. (The *nahda* has frequently been
depicted as a response to Western innovation; in fact, as with so
much of the Muslim Enlightenment, it was less a wholesale importation than a blending of the alien and the familiar.) Shidyaq described
Leg over Leg as 'a repository for every idea that appealed to me,
relevant or irrelevant', and alongside its many themes, which range
from merciless anticlericalism to an approving depiction of a
woman's education –'there can be no *Nahda* in the East,' he is
reported to have said, 'without a *Nahda* of women'– for comic effect
he also drew on neglected Arabic words, including *buldah*, or
'freedom from hair of the space between the eyebrows', and *bahsala*,
to 'remove one's clothes and gamble with them'.[17]

Shidyaq's novel did not communicate with great numbers of people.
Leg over Leg (which was published in Paris in 1855) had few readers
during the lifetime of its creator. Today, however, it seems intensely
prophetic. In the first years of the twentieth century the Arabic novel,
or *riwaya*, encompassing a range of prose genres, from melodramas
to satires and romances, began to supplant poetry as the cutting-edge
literary form; the tradition went on to spawn such admired modern
novelists as Naguib Mahfouz and Albert Cossery.

The idea that the prism of the novel is for viewing life vividly, in all its beauty and ugliness, had of course been gestating in Europe for hundreds of years. Sir Walter Scott, an exceptionally successful exponent of the medium in the early decades of the nineteenth century, viewed the novel as a literary receptacle in which events follow 'the ordinary train of human events and the modern state of society'. The sentiments of Scott were universal, like the form itself; and they were echoed by Ahmet Midhat, Turkey's most popular author of the later decades of the nineteenth century, when he wrote of Beyoglu, Istanbul's louche, pretentious European quarter, 'wherever you look, you see a novel'.

For all the innovations of Shidyaq's *Leg over Leg*, it would be Turkish culture centred on Istanbul that witnessed the most rapid development of the novel in the Middle East – hardly surprisingly given that it was the region's most cosmopolitan and most Westernised city, where Gentile Bellini had produced portraits in the quattrocento, *Madame Bovary* was on sale and storytellers from Verdi to Scott himself (in his Byzantine melodrama *Count Robert of Paris*) set their exotic tales.

Over a career that spanned more than forty years and left behind almost two hundred novels, translations and works of popular science, the fulsomely bearded figure of Midhat, who is usually depicted wearing his red Ottoman fez, developed a style that combined verve, informality and didacticism. Writing allowed him to advance cautiously progressive ideas, and between descriptions of men about town and women with fashionably pale skin he took guardedly liberal positions on subjects like arranged marriages, extramarital affairs, prostitution and slavery. 'My goal', he wrote, 'was to speak with the majority, to try to illuminate them, to be an interpreter of their problems,' and although that 'majority' remained illusory in numerical terms (for all the new schools and expanded education, the literate percentage of the population had not yet climbed into double figures), the cultural momentum in favour of education had acquired irresistible moral authority.[18] The children of those who could not read Midhat today would assuredly read his successors tomorrow.

The social content of Midhat's work was startlingly new. In addition, he helped to distinguish prose from poetry in the minds of his readers, bringing the former closer to journalism. Indeed, many of the heroes described by Midhat and others in the first wave of Turkish novels were involved in the young sectors of journalism and the press.

The importance of Midhat, however, is not just as a milestone in the history of the Turkish novel. He has a documentary function as well. He and other novelists working at the time reflected the Middle East's split personality now that European cultural norms had entered and were jostling with indigenous ones. There was quintessentially modern idiosyncrasy in this society, bordering on schizophrenia – you only had to spend time in Istanbul, and see how it was coping with the new stresses and paradoxes, to appreciate that.

Islam said it was a sin for women to show themselves bareheaded, but good Muslim women were flocking to the studios to unveil for the portrait photographer. For an Ottoman dandy a chance meeting with a maiden in the street necessitated a split-second decision; if she was traditional in appearance – black and inaccessible in her yashmak – he must look away severely, but if she swayed towards him in a lacy, pale green skirt, short-sleeved blouse and brigantine hat he would behave in the opposite manner, touching his brim and oozing, 'Bonjour, mademoiselle!'

There was a widespread disquiet over what many saw as the essential shiftlessness of the emancipated, Westernised woman, as described by the Turkish poet Abdulhak Hamit:

> Her face is composed, her words are contrived,
> Her task is to inflame the soul, or break the heart;
> Her friendship can be bought for a thousand francs;
> Who knows what she costs her lover!
> She looks at you in a flirting way:
> Her attention is always on clothes;
> If you're out of fashion, you might as well be gored, one
>   might say,
> There's no chance for friendship, she immediately turns
>   away.[19]

It had always been the custom for Middle Eastern men to walk in front of their wives and barely acknowledge them in public, but in the Istanbul of the belle époque people learned that the French wafted their womenfolk through doorways using exquisite gestures, and conversed with them on the streets. Such behaviour now started to creep onto the pavements (another innovation) of Istanbul. There was much confusion around the dining tables that had been installed in many homes. Before, eating had been a serious business directed at one's belly; one sat cross-legged, there was much belching and smacking of chops, by both sexes, and conversation was for before or after. Now, talking between mouthfuls became de rigueur. Knives and forks were rife and there was something vaguely menacing called table manners.

The mania for newness extended to words. Perfectly good ones were being thrown over. Turks no longer belonged to an *aile* (from the Arabic), meaning family, but a *familiya*. And there was no escaping the foreign name-dropping: have you heard Waldteufel's latest waltz?

Most symbolic of all the modern confusions was that concerning time. People lived in different times – different eras – in the same city. The modern Istanbullu wore a wristwatch, observed a fixed, 24-hour day, and kept appointments with European promptness at a certain prearranged location – the Luxemburg Cafe in Beyoglu, for instance, where the girls wore monocles in a style anticipating 1920s Germany. For another, less Europeanised inhabitant, a variable 24-hour day would begin each evening at sunset, requiring him to adjust his watch. This was referred to by foreign travellers as 'Turkish time', or 'Arab time', and it drove them mad.[20] A third Istanbullu, the most traditional, judged the progress of the day by that of the sun across the sky – arranging his appointments by the five prayers, to which, of course, the muezzin must alert him.

However one chose to measure it, time was starting to gather speed, a sure sign of incipient modernity. In one of his best-known novels, *Observations*, Midhat writes of 'gaining time' by taking a Bosporus ferry that makes fewer stops as it chugs along the straits: 'As the English put it, our time is money!' And so it is, for Midhat is a journalist and his aim is to provide the very latest news. 'The last telegraphs come at evening time,' he explains, and 'the later you write the political synopses, the fresher and more important they are'.

These and other ambiguities clouded perspectives in the late nineteenth century, and many Turks saw in them a conflict between what was *alafranga* and *alaturka* – Frankish or European vs Turkish style. According to this view of the world, everyone was suspended somewhere between the extremes of abject surrender to European mores and adhesion to the old ways – with tragic or comic consequences.

Another of Ahmet Midhat's characters, Mustafa, is so obsessed with novelty that he gives up his traditional wooden mansion on the Asian side of the Bosporus in order to build a European-style brick house on the edge of Beyoglu. 'Now in such a house in that kind of neighbourhood,' the author tells us, 'there was no question of an *alafranga* gentleman's filling up his house with Arabs and their like. It was obvious that there was need of Greek and Armenian servants to be in the midst of things when his friends came.' In keeping with *alafranga* practice Mustafa's spoilt daughter has her hair 'combed by a private female hairdresser. Her father obtained a piano instructor for her, but since she lacked ability, she was unable to learn a thing.'

Midhat's approach to modernity was to see it as a series of challenges and dilemmas that could usually be solved using good sense and an allegiance to the culture – if not the practice – of Islam. But other writers viewed the phenomenon as an internal disorder experienced by the men and women it was supposed to emancipate. This psychological interest in the repercussions of modernity was also new, and it reflected the interest that such writers showed in the complex and contradictory characters that populated European novels, such as Julien Sorel, Stendhal's protagonist in *Le Rouge et le Noir* – with the 'black' in the title representing the clergy, and the 'red', the vital life force of youth. Modernity seeded anguish and self-loss – 'the truth, the bitter truth', as Stendhal's epigraph runs – of which the Turkey of Abdulhamid II had its share.

Just as the nature of the ills was new, so too were the artistic sentiments that rose to meet them. The new literature was both modern and a critique of the modern. It was doubled up with pain – which religion, banished to the sidelines, could not dispel. An imperial bureaucrat and scion of a prominent trading family, Halid Ziya Uşakligil (1866–1945), became the most successful exponent of this disturbing genre, and his early masterpiece evokes another clash of colours within a man's breast: the blue of optimism and the black of despair.

Published in 1897, Uşakligil's *The Blue and the Black* – the title was not in fact inspired by Stendhal, but by the poet Sully Prudhomme – describes the turbulent life of a vulnerable, solitary 22-year-old called Ahmed Cemil. Ahmed Cemil's ambition is to become a famous avant-garde poet (of course), and he hungers for a new kind of language clever enough to think for itself; but the death of his father has forced him to take odd jobs in order to support his mother and sister.

Ahmed Cemil writes articles and contributes translations for an Istanbul paper, besides tutoring a little boy three nights a week. He disappears shivering into the darkness in winter, dodging the curs, sloping through the mud, and when he passes one of Istanbul's tumble-down ruins his heart trembles 'as if a hand would suddenly stretch out and grab his collar'. His mother worries that he will collapse under the workload and lack of sleep, to which he replies, looking at his sister Ikbal, 'we need the extra money, don't we, Mother? We've a bride to marry off.'

Marriage is indeed the secure harbour that might eventually receive both Ikbal and her brother, but a rapacious hedonism prowls the new Istanbul. It has already swallowed Raci, Ahmed Cemil's work colleague and literary rival, who is usually to be found blind drunk in one of the brothels of Beyoglu.

One rainswept evening Ahmed Cemil's editor, Ahmet Sevki, adjusts his cravat, straightens his fez and moistens his moustache before the two men leave the office in search of the errant Raci. They pass crowds of people crossing the Galata Bridge under a carapace of umbrellas and watch the lights from the restaurants glance over the passing trams and the shoes of the pedestrians. The funicular railway brings them to Beyoglu's pulsing, sparkling, mile-long main street. Raci is temporarily forgotten; Ahmet promises to show his boss the Couronne, the Cambrinus and the Central, famous cafe bars where electric lights are fixed to the walls, the tables are marble-topped and splinters of music escape along with jets of cigarette smoke whenever the doors swing open. They end up climbing a narrow, dirty, scuffed staircase to an *établissement* where a black-nailed stoker overnighting in Istanbul is drying himself in front of the fire while two milliners' apprentices take liberties with an overweight serving girl.

This is the Palais de Crystal, where Raci was last seen, and the two men find seats near the stage as the club fills with clerks, appren-tices, barbers and seamen. Eventually a troupe of European girls, their complexions rinsed yellow from the interminable nights and cigarette smoke, each one the daughter of a dirt-poor father from somewhere along the Danube who has found no answer to his destitution other than to sell his kin into bondage, drag their unwilling bodies onstage to sing, dance and play various instruments. Raci arrives as the club is coming alive with roars and shouts from the clientele, and Ahmed Cemil and his boss pursue their quarry into a brothel annexe that features a Madame de Pompadour, a vaudeville soubrette, and a Balkan peasant girl who is sweating copiously under her Albanian waistcoat.

The Blue and the Black is full of humid, flickering images of this kind, and Uşakligil's technique of paying detailed attention to each frame has been compared to the (still relatively young) medium of photography. Uşakligil – unlike many conventional opponents of modernity – is not writing his critique from a vantage of piety. His character Ahmed Cemil is ambivalent about religion in the way that people often are in rapidly secularising societies, and the terror and dread he feels seems in part to be a terror at no longer having the secure mooring of belief. The appalled fascination with which the author describes the exploitation of the dancing girls at the Palais de Crystal, furthermore, shows a sensitivity to inequality and the moral aspects of enslavement that is independent of Islam and derives from a secular understanding of human rights. There is nothing contrived about these groundbreaking passages; just as modernity has burst into new territories, so has unease about the messages it brings.

By the time Uşakligil was writing there was no doubt that one of these messages concerned industrialisation. Across the Middle East this process had been retarded by the economy's defencelessness in the face of Western mass production. But after the government introduced incentives in the 1870s, the Ottoman Empire began building up some industrial capacity in private hands – and not only in Istanbul. There were iron foundries in Izmir and Salonica which produced basic machine tools, cigarettes and bricks; Adana on the Mediterranean boasted steam-powered silk and cotton mills. The biggest factories employed two hundred people and some had mixed workforces. Industrial relations would become a subject of debate as socialist ideas about workers' rights trickled in from Europe and advances in technology highlighted the complex, competitive interplay between machine and man.

The ability of technology not only to improve lives, but also to disrupt and impoverish them, is made graphically apparent in *The Blue and the Black.* Halfway through the book another of Uşakligil's young male characters, Vehbi, inherits ownership of the newspaper and leverages his new status to become Ikbal's husband and persuade Ahmed Cemil to mortgage his house for the purchase of a new press. Vehbi soon shows himself to be a thug and a scoundrel, beating Ikbal (who eventually dies in childbirth) and driving Ahmed Cemil towards bankruptcy.

In a fine passage towards the end of this lyrical, baffled book, Uşakligil shows his mixed feelings towards the new industrial world when he places Ahmed Cemil beside the lithograph press that now constitutes his only worldly good. The way Ahmed Cemil sees and describes this piece of machinery and the men who operate it is not the way of an industrialist, meditating on economies of scale, but that of a psychologist warning of the attritional effects of war.

> The chief typesetter ... leaned his body, which since the age of ten he had broken and exhausted by binding and unbinding the ideas at his fingertips, over the cold plate of the press; and in these unbearable conditions, in the dirty air and dim light afforded by the rancid-smelling lamp, tweezers in hand, began to do battle – removing a full stop here, inserting a comma there, his lungs constricting in his chest from impatience, regret, and tiredness ... widening the columns, sorting each wrong word or letter and replacing it with the right one, strolling with the tip of his tweezer among these thousands of small things ...

Ahmed Cemil is moved by the scene of physical and psychological depletion before him; so is the reader, and how new and puzzling it must have been for the literate classes of belle époque Istanbul to read in a book that modernity didn't simply threaten Islam but also threw a cloak over the human quest for happiness.

The quest was too pressing to be rejected, however, and its appeal was expanding unstoppably. While the first Middle Eastern novels were being written, and *Darwiniya* was propounded, and iconoclasts like Besir Fuat thumbed their noses at God and death, a segment of society with much to gain from the new spirit of personal autonomy was stirring. This was the monstrous regiment of Jane Eyre and Fatma Aliye.

★

In the beginning there was seclusion. It was the overwhelming fact of life for urban women in the Middle East, particularly those from the middle and upper classes. By and large the rural communities were less concerned with separating the sexes – for good economic reasons: women made a vital contribution to the family income – and travellers to the remoter areas of Turkey, Iran and Egypt alike found lightly veiled women out walking in the lanes, working the land, and present at marriages and religious ceremonies. Some Nubian communities, one upper-class Egyptian woman reported wonderingly in 1909, placed men in charge of sewing while their womenfolk tilled the fields; in the tribal areas of Iran women were integral to the success of the arduous seasonal migrations. There was no exclusive relationship between Islam and the practice of veiling. When the English traveller Lucie Duff-Gordon visited Upper Egypt in the 1860s, she found that some of the Christian women were more heavily veiled than their Muslim counterparts.

In poorer parts of the cities women could be found running shops and working in the small number of factories that existed in private hands. The American company Singer had a part in increasing female employment as it churned out sewing machines from its factory on the River Clyde (more than a million per annum by 1913), and in Istanbul and Cairo seamstresses selling their services door to door gradually supplanted women of the house sewing by hand.[21] Even Halid Ziya Uşakligil's otherwise technophobic novel *The Blue and the Black* recognises the value of the sewing machine as a passport to autonomy; it shows the neglected wife of the ne'er-do-well Raci begging money to buy one, for, as she puts it, 'is a small sewing machine not enough for a woman and her small son to get by on?' Indeed it was, and it was one of the reasons why by 1897 in Egypt alone some 64,000 women – 2 per cent of the total – were at work in a profession or trade.[22]

Higher up the social scale, however, society was walled off by paternalism and sloth. 'One only sees the working class woman in the street,' declared Elizabeth Cooper, an American traveller, when she visited Cairo in the early years of the twentieth century, and 'these women who wander about unveiled are neither envied by the secluded, nor are they themselves satisfied with their freedom, believing that it is only poverty and need that compel them to leave the seclusion of their homes'.[23] Much as in London, Paris and New York, it was the privilege of the affluent to maintain defences that were plush and impregnable.

The unit of seclusion was the harem – from the Arabic verb meaning 'to deprive' – that hived-off area of life where the patriarchs of the Middle East exercised their dominance over wives, concubines and slaves, and which Western artists and writers delighted in depicting as airless prisons where under-appreciated beauties (the junior wives of an absent provincial governor, for instance) ran to fat and conspired against each other while staring at the symbolically appropriate caged hoopoe. Like all successful caricatures, it was not without truth.

During her stay in Cairo shortly before the First World War, Elizabeth Cooper was invited to join a group of women in the snuggery of cushions and divans that had been fitted into a wooden lattice casement that protruded from a traditional house, from which they watched unobserved the arrival of a trousseau at the house of the newly-weds opposite. In a sentence that conveys the befuddlement of upper-class culture at the time, Cooper writes that the girl was 'wildly excited at the thought that she was going to the opera, where she would hear [Gounod's opera] Faust sung in Arabic'– again, from behind a lattice screen.

Some Middle Eastern women would remember the harem as a place of protection and solace, where women came together to create bonds of sorority, and mutual help between wives of the same man led to better conditions for all. For the senior wife in a large household, the harem was a satrapy over which she could establish a gorgeous despotism of her own. Generally, however, the life inside was associated with quaintness and eccentricity – there was much fancy dress and outlandish entertainments such as freak shows and menageries of animals – and its main features were in fact futility and boredom. Under-utilised, under-stimulated women were criticised for their shallowness, but as historians of the phenomenon have pointed out, such defects were hardly surprising from adults who were treated as children and whose social circle consisted solely of other harem women and servants. Not infrequently these wretched creatures suffered from the neglect or cruelty of their husbands, or were constantly giving birth, while what must have been an overwhelming sense of powerlessness caused 'nervous and illogical behaviour, and depression, which in turn led to plots, conspiracies and suicide'.[24]

The intrepid Englishwoman Ella Sykes, who accompanied her brother on a diplomatic mission to Iran in the 1890s – by which time Nasser al-Din was in the evening of his reign – descried only bitchiness, ostentation and a lack of intelligence in the imperial harem. The harem wasn't simply a complex of rooms. It was also a frame of mind, a terror of being seen by those who weren't allowed to see, and a state of complete unfamiliarity with ordinary life. It was the ultimate manifestation of the shah's tyranny because he was able to impose his every whim on the playthings within.

In one notorious example he decreed that the women of the harem should abandon their traditional attire of long, loose, embroidered trousers in favour of a kinky pastiche of the costume of the Paris ballet that had so entranced him during a European trip. This consisted of a loose-sleeved jacket of the richest brocades, and a species of knickerbocker, with the knees exposed and white socks rising halfway up the calf – an egregious combination that remained harem 'uniform' for the rest of his reign.

Nowhere were the coarsening effects of the shah's despotism displayed to grislier effect than in his preferred parlour game, 'lights out', as described by his daughter Taj al-Saltaneh.

'My father would sit on a chair near the light switch. As they [the women of the harem] were busy in their conversation, he would turn out the light. Suddenly all hell would break loose. Screams, cries for help, oaths, curses and wailing would be heard everywhere … amid this pandemonium of keening and wailing whose effect was heightened by the absolute darkness … the lights would suddenly come back on, catching everybody in some act. Usually the clothes would be ripped to shreds, the faces and cheeks bloody, the bodies obscenely exposed … the women's faces were grotesque, their hair dishevelled, their eyes bloodshot and filled with rage … the session concluded, the poor women would scatter to go home, where they attended to their appearance until morning. I was amazed when it was time to resume the game, they were eagerly prepared, and gleefully submitted to an orgy of punching and kicking.'[25]

In view of the freakishness of harem life, it was not surprising that Ella Sykes returned home with a gloomy perspective on Iranian women, who 'recognise that their fate is hard when they are brought into contact with European women'. Although Iranian women had property rights, they were often unable to exploit them because of their illiteracy and seclusion, and Ella, a spinster, recalled that 'it was pathetic to be urged never to marry a Persian'. '"Oh *Khanum* (Lady)," a woman would say, "my husband makes me 'eat' much sorrow. If his *pilau* (rice) or sherbet is not to his liking he may beat me, and I know that if I had an illness that made me ugly he would divorce me on the spot. And when I get old he will treat me worse than a servant."'

The depressed conditions of feminine life in the Middle East derived from a simple principle. For most families a woman constituted a moral asset whose value depended on her being passed undefiled from father to husband. No one was in doubt of her womanly allure while she remained young, but she must be protected from her own untameable sexuality.

The frustration, vapidity and hint of masculine menace that characterised the harems of the well-to-do bear down on the life of Huda Shaarawi, a beautiful and spirited Egyptian aristocrat whose autobiography describes Egyptian seclusion on the cusp of change in the 1880s and 90s – like making an ocean crossing in the company of fellow passengers it may be unwise to trust, being buffeted by forces outside one's control.

Huda experienced all the privileges and tribulations of being born female and upper class – living in a large house, enjoying a beautiful garden and wanting only the freedom to decide things for herself. From an early age she foresaw the superior position that her younger brother would assume in relation to herself. 'You are a girl and he is a boy,' her stepmother reasoned when she quibbled at the attention he received; 'when you marry you will leave the house and honour your husband's name but he will perpetuate the name of his father and take over his house.'

When Huda was around twelve years of age she overheard her female relations discussing a possible match between her and her guardian (and cousin), a man in his forties with children older than herself. Being a child she put such thoughts out of her mind and was not even alerted when she received jewels and the house was unexpectedly redecorated.

Other cousins called to formalise the engagement; still the girl was unable to appreciate the enormity of what was happening, and during the three-day wedding party she allowed herself to be transported by the elegance of the flower-strewn bridal throne, the tent with its carpets and hangings, and the magnificence of her own gown and tiara. 'I laughed and was merry along with my friends,' she recalled, 'so much so that the household interpreted my earlier behaviour as nothing more than the ordinary display of fears common to prospective brides. Suddenly,' Huda goes on, 'a commotion erupted outside the great hall.' The dancer rushed out amid *zaghrudas*, the shrill ululations that Arab women emit when they are festive. 'To the roll of drums the women hastened out of the room or slipped behind curtains, while the eunuch announced the approach of the bridegroom.'

A sense of what was about to happen struck Huda forcefully.

In an instant, the delicious dream vanished and stark reality appeared. Faint and crying, I clung to the gown of a relation ... who was trying to flee like the others and I pleaded, 'Don't abandon me here! Take me with you.' A woman came forwards and lowered a veil of silver thread over my head like a mask concealing the face of a condemned person approaching execution. At that moment, the bridegroom entered the room. After praying ... on a mat of red velvet embossed with silver he came to me and, lifting the veil from my face, kissed me on the forehead. He led me by the hand to the bridal throne and took his place beside me. All the while, I was trembling like a branch in a storm. The groom addressed a few words to me but I understood nothing. When the customary goblets of red sorbet were offered, I was unable to taste the ritual drink. Finally, my new husband took me by the hand. In my daze I knew not where I was being led.[26]

She was thirteen.

The first modern Middle Eastern government to offer women a chance of social and economic improvement was that of Muhammad

Ali. And like much else the Pasha did, it turns out to have been motivated by military concerns.

Syphilis had entered the Middle East from Europe in the seventeenth century, and never left. Some Europeans considered it worse than the plague and in Egypt it found a perfect carrier in the form of Muhammad Ali's mobile, campaigning army (before he put an end to this itinerancy), who also used local prostitutes. In the 1830s, Clot Bey, the French doctor whom Muhammad Ali had brought in to set up a modern health system (and the man who launched the country's first theatre of anatomy), proposed to address the problem within broader efforts to replace the traditional Egyptian midwife, or *daya*, with a modern system of women's health. Trained medical assistants would examine military spouses and educate them about syphilis; they would also vaccinate against smallpox, which in the early 1820s typically caused the deaths of some 50,000 infants annually. In this way, the *dayas*, with their charms and incantations, would be gradually supplanted in the affections of Egyptian mothers and mothers-to-be.[27] At least, this was the plan.

The school of midwifery that the civilising Frenchman Clot Bey proposed was inspired by existing institutions in France. There was an acute need for personnel but Egyptian mores got in the way. Respectable Muslim parents would not consent to their daughters going out to work, nor to their attending any kind of school that would enable them to do so. Clot's solution was to dispatch officials to the Cairo slave market and to a hospice for the poor, from where they scooped up a total of thirty girls. During their instruction as midwives and women's health advocates more generally, the girls received a government stipend in addition to free lodging and food; and upon starting work in one of the health clinics that were being established around the country they were given a monthly salary, a military rank like their male counterparts, and transport (a donkey).

All in all, it wouldn't have been a bad deal for the independence-seeking young women of Egypt – except that the country's young women did not yet answer to this description. Clot Bey's School of Midwifery was dogged from the start by a shortage of students and teachers alike, expecting mothers continued to patronise the old *dayas*, and in the end the new medical assistants became a kind of regulatory body supervising the *dayas* and making sure they were supplying regular data about births and deaths. The pasha had astutely recognised the value of data collection to the planning of his modern and highly controlled state.

When you consider that a century later a government job in teaching or medicine would be regarded as the acme of achievement for middle-class girls across the Middle East, it is surprising to learn that the first female civil servants in the region were not the daughters of officials or professionals, but Abyssinian and Sudanese slaves.

Nor did things improve much over the next half-century or so in the field of women's education – in spite of the advocacy of Rifaa al-Tahtawi and some of his followers. Islamic doctrine did not stand in the way of women's learning, but social attitudes did. The story of women's education in Egypt remained a tussle between coercive benevolence and an obstinately resistant society. It was one thing for an Egyptian woman to know the Quran, quite another for her to gain unfettered access to the world of books. As the twentieth-century writer Suhayr al-Qalamawi would recall her grandmother saying, 'this habit of reading is an ailment which women of my generation did not suffer from. Bless our good old times! I never allowed my daughters enough time a day to read.'[28]

Well into the 1870s there remained insurmountable opposition to the education of women and widespread scepticism over its benefits. The first free Muslim women to be educated – in the following decade – were apparently left unsatisfied by their marriages to uneducated husbands, and their families regarded them as conceited. In light of this, the change of attitude that crept over Egyptian society during the 1880s must be reckoned truly remarkable.

In 1892 a survey by the Egyptian Ministry of Education found that parents from the country's new middle class – civil servants and members of the professions – not only favoured sending their daughters out to be educated, but demanded a similar curriculum to that being followed by their sons. An inflexion point was approaching when it went from being socially unacceptable to educate one's daughter to unacceptable not to do so.

One might have expected the country's British administrators to have pushed for girls' education as a dividend from colonial rule; in fact the country's brisk, muscularly Protestant proconsul, Sir Evelyn Baring (later Lord Cromer), and his colleagues regarded mass education of either sex as potentially hazardous and educated only enough Egyptians to fill the government departments. Rather, it was the private (though state-registered) *kuttabs* that most speedily translated Egyptians' softening views on girls' education into a body of literate women, with the number of girls in such establishments, whose curricula also included hygiene, cookery and laundering, rising from 1,640 in 1900 to 17,000 in 1908.[29] On the other hand, total enrolment by both sexes in schools run by the state increased from around 6,000 in 1890 to only 11,000 two decades later, of which just eight hundred were women, though private and mission schools also had several thousand female students.[30]

In 1901, seventy years after Rifaa al-Tahtawi joined the first educational mission of Egyptian boys to the West, the government in Cairo paid for some young Egyptian women to travel to Britain to attend Stockwell Training College, in south London, and Homerton Training College, in Cambridge. Although the young women were chaperoned, controversy dogged them all the same, with critics accusing them of becoming morally debased and their defenders countering that they had not mixed with men, 'as people imagine'.

Pious suspicion of travel as a secularising pursuit was not, of course, without foundation, as the American traveller Edith Butcher discovered shortly before the First World War. At Cairo station she beheld 'a bevy of women ... shrouded up to the eyes', their gaze piously averted from that of any man; once they were safely aboard their Mediterranean steamer the same women made a dramatic entrance to the public saloon, 'unveiled, bare-headed, clad in the latest Parisian travelling fashion'.[31]

It was no coincidence that the middle classes that showed most interest in educating their daughters in schools – the upper classes kept their governesses – also made up the bulk of readers of the women's journals that began to appear in the final decades of the nineteenth century. These publications started in Turkey, spread to Egypt, and were later replicated in Iran. They were a forum for opinion-forming women to discuss their rights and obligations, while the most ardent of these advocates were not afraid to debate the nature of womanhood and femininity in the modern world.

This was the context for the entreaty concerning the innate equality of men and women that a Turkish feminist sent to the weekly *Terakki-i-Muhadderrat* in 1869, and which we came across in the introduction to this book. This and other interventions like it signalled the expanding confidence of the more westernised kind of Turkish women and the possibilities that were opening up for the likes of Fatma Aliye. Letters to *Terraki-i Muhadderat* and other publications might take the form of a diatribe in favour of women's education or against polygamy, or a complaint over the inferior berths assigned to women on Bosporus steamships.[32]

In an indication of the queasiness that was felt by women who were putting their heads above the parapet for the first time, the authors of these letters and articles used pseudonyms like 'A Girl at School' or 'Two Educated Ladies'. The aim of the magazines, as one writer put it, was nothing less than to overturn the standard view of women as inherently deficient in relation to men. 'We are the tribe that men have laughingly derided as long on hair, short on nous,' one editorial declared. 'We are going to try and prove the opposite.'[33]

By the first years of the twentieth century, as the feminists writing in the new magazines had urged, the lifestyle of many urban women in the Middle East had indeed changed. The traveller Elizabeth Cooper compared the Cairo bazaars of the 1870s, which 'rarely saw a woman customer', to the 'clusters of veiled women' out shopping in her own time, on the eve of the First World War. Modern Egyptian women were able to choose their own clothing and ornaments, 'bargaining, chattering, admiring, and purchasing jewellery and finery, which formerly was purchased for them by their husbands'.[34]

As women ventured out, arguments began over the right conditions for them to do so. There were disagreements over whether they needed chaperones and over the veil and body-covers that constituted a kind of mobile harem. Some argued that excessive veiling constricted not only the mobility but also the freedom of women, while others countered with traditional arguments over the preservation of virtue, or that only by covering up might girls and women evade the attentions of lascivious men.

At tram stops situated near the new schools, the girls were indeed prey to unwelcome attention, and according to one Egyptian journal, 'no sooner do women walk in the street than obscenities reach her from all sides, causing her to trip on her skirt. Maybe some of the riff-raff follow her, insult her reputation ... without embarrassment or shame.'[35] It was the beginning of a debate in the Middle East over the merits of veiling as a protection against unwanted attentions, as opposed to the gender discrimination it has come to symbolise.

The veil worn by upper-class Egyptian women was made of translucent white chiffon, like the yashmak in Istanbul, which some believed only accentuated the allure of the wearer. 'It is becoming thinner each year,' wrote Elizabeth Cooper, describing the veil less as dissuasion than 'added attraction, making an ugly face pretty and adding an air of mystery and charm to a beautiful one'.[36]

At a public lecture in 1909, the Cairene poet Malak Nifni Nasif, who is better known by her pseudonym Bahitha al-Badiyya ('Seeker in the Desert'), wondered despairingly where the mania for coquetry would end.

> Our former garment was one piece. When the woman wrapped herself in it her figure was totally hidden. The wrap shrunk little by little but it was still wide enough to conceal the whole body. Then we artfully began to shrink the waist and lower the neck and finally two sleeves were added and the garment clung to the back and was worn only with a corset. We tied back our headgear so that more than half the head, including the ears, were visible ... finally, the face veil became more transparent than an infant's heart. The purpose of our *izar* [a long black cloak] is to cover the body as well as our dress and jewellery underneath, which God has commanded us not to display. Does our present *izar*, which has virtually become a 'dress', showing the bosom, waist and derriere, conform with this precept?[37]

Not only the question of appropriate dress, but also that of appropriate occupations, was energising the new female polemicists. In 1891 a Lebanese newspaper published a criticism of women who expressed dissatisfaction at being confined to domestic duties, and of their presumption that 'equality with men will be achieved only through ... participation in the same kinds of work [as men]'. The article's author, a woman of letters called Hana Kawrani, also criticised the latest (failed) efforts of the British suffragettes to win the vote, and she averred that a 'woman cannot perform work outside the home [and] at the same time ... serve her husband and children'.

The feminist response to Kawrani came in the form of an article in the Egyptian newspaper *al-Nil* ('The Nile') by a woman called Zainab Fawwaz. Her attack on Kawrani's defence of the status quo has been singled out as an early landmark in Arab feminism. It is also a humanist hymn to progress.

Fawwaz began her article by summing up the achievements of the modern human, whose noblest feature is an unshakeable and implacable will. Without that will, 'you would see nothing of the mind-boggling wonders that we witness today; it is through the grace of human intrepidity that conquests have been made and countries have flourished'.

There follows a call to action: woe betide those nations 'through which the illness of laziness has spread and the disease of indolence and apathy has seeped'. One of the secrets of the West's success, Fawwaz argues somewhat optimistically, is the prevailing conviction there that men and women are of equal capacity. There is nothing in Islamic law that prohibits women from 'involvement in the occupations of men'. Nor is natural law an obstacle, and here she name-checks history's female high-rollers – Cleopatra, Queen Elizabeth, Zenobia of Palmyra – before taking the reader to the streets of the modern European city, where there are warehouses full of women 'carrying out commercial occupations – with their requisite book-keeping – and performing the handiwork of craftsmanship – with its requisite perfection'.

For all the increasing currency of feminist views, however, in paternalistic, British-occupied Egypt, women's rights remained men's to confer. The number of women who were sufficiently versed in both Islamic law and Western rights to be able to put forward a vision of how the modern Muslim woman should think and behave remained small, and one of the main obstacles to progress was a conservative interpretation of Islam whose clerics were overwhelmingly men. It was the words of men that were of most significance in these early days of Middle Eastern feminism, and none more so than Qasim Amin (1863–1908), the Darwinian who had responded to Britain's crushing of its Sudanese foes by acknowledging the saliency of natural selection.

Amin was a French-educated bureaucrat in the British administration of Egypt, on the bench of the 'mixed courts', so called because they included foreign and Egyptian judges and used a combination of Napoleonic and Islamic codes to decide commercial cases. In his view the modern competition between nations necessitated the emancipation of Egyptian women so they could take part in a project of national uplift. As much as his interest in the welfare of Egyptian women, it was the enhanced assistance that women could render men – and, by extension, the nation – that turned his attention to women's rights. The question of women was intrinsic to that of national survival; one half of the population had been cut off from productivity and achievement in order to appease the prejudices and fears of the other. As he would write in a famous polemic, *The Liberation of Women* (1899), 'it is impossible to breed successful men if they do not have mothers capable of raising them to be successful'.[38]

The Liberation of Women was in fact a reaction to a diatribe by a foreigner against conditions in Egypt. *L'Egypte et les Egyptiens* was authored by a Frenchman, the Duc d'Harcourt, and it included a harrowing eyewitness account of the entry of a European doctor to the harem of an Egyptian pasha. The pasha's wife was ill but refused to remove her veil and submit to examination. In the end her husband lost patience and 'ended up seizing her, throwing her off the couch and pounding her with his fists and his feet, with the aim of teaching her obedience', which he eventually secured. Notably absent from d'Harcourt's description was any sympathy for the woman in question – or for Egyptian women as a whole, whom he described as 'ignorant, masses of flesh, their faces innocent of the slightest sign of intelligence'.[39]

For all its unappealing tone, the message of *L'Egypte et les Egyptiens* could not be dismissed out of hand by self-respecting progressives like Amin. Their disquiet at the low accomplishments of Egyptian women was aggravated by the cultural superiority that emanated from the British administration, in which some of these progressives, Amin included, held positions.

In *The Liberation of Women* and a follow-up, *The New Woman* (1901), Amin approached the question of female emancipation as someone who had ingested the major arguments over marriage and work that were put forward in the West. He decried the evils of seclusion and loveless marriages and the use of divorce as an instrument of men's desertion of their wives (in Cairo there were half as many divorces in a typical year as there were marriages). Although the custom was not common in Egypt, he also proposed that the tradition of polygamy, legitimised by the sharia, be discarded. 'I do not believe this would be regretted by future generations.'[40] Steps should be taken towards the ending of seclusion, and the face-cover and veil should be set aside.

Unsurprisingly, at a time when very few women enjoyed voting rights in Western countries, Amin contended that at present Egyptian women were not ready for suffrage, but this was the fault of men who had barred women from worldly advance. He neatly identified the logic on which the system rests: 'deeply rooted in men's minds is the idea that an educated woman and a chaste woman cannot be one and the same'.[41] It sufficed to travel in Europe or America, he wrote in *The New Woman*, to appreciate the falseness of these assumptions, and he spoke favourably of those American women who worked as lawyers, ministers of religion and university lecturers. In connection with seclusion of the kind that Huda Shaarawi had experienced, he wrote, 'I do not understand how we can boast about the purity of our women when we believe that they must be protected through the use of guards, fortified locks, and high walls.'[42]

Amin reminds us again of the defensive nature of reform. Almost a century had passed since Napoleon's obliteration of the Mamluks forced Egyptian military planners to overhaul the army completely. The logic in 1899 remained the same – reform or die – but the tone had become stridently pro-Western. Amin accepted the West's claims to its own superiority almost without reserve, and this was a departure from the nuanced approach to civilisation and progress that had been taken by leading figures in the *nahda* such as Rifaa al-Tahtawi and Ahmad Faris al-Shidyaq; it was closer, in fact, to the uncritical admiration of Muhammad Ali. The veneration of all things Western that was evinced by Amin would in time provoke a patriotic and Islamist backlash, with a deleterious effect on his posthumous reputation; even in his lifetime some thirty books and articles were written in response to *The Liberation of Women*, the majority of them critical. But Amin's cooperation with the British should not blind us to the fact that in feminist terms he was a fearless pioneer and it is this aspect of his books, rather than his relations with the colonial power, that accounted for their popularity not only in Cairo but also Istanbul and Tehran.

If one of the spurs to improving the lot of women in the Middle East was shame in the face of Western superiority, this was true to an even greater extent of another area of life that desperately needed over-hauling if the lands of Islam were not to be permanently tarred as sensual despotisms and hostile to universal notions of freedom. At issue was a hoary old Islamic institution, equivalent of an increasingly reviled anachronism in the West.

Slavery among Muslims was in some ways much more humane than the network of commerce and servitude that British abolitionists like William Wilberforce had begun to campaign against in the 1780s and which went on to cause the American Civil War. Indeed, Muslim tradition taught (and most modern historians agree) that the Prophet Muhammad had brought improvements to the lives of slaves in sixth-century Arabia, just as he had raised the status of women. The Muslim take on slavery was that Islam had mitigated an existing evil and turned it into what was for many a tolerable existence.

In the 1840s some 10,000 slaves were being imported openly and legally into the Ottoman Empire each year, and slave markets existed in the major cities;[43] a lesser but still considerable number entered Persia, too, by sea and land routes. (This was still much fewer than the 20,000 per annum that British ships alone had transported to the Americas a century before.) Apart from the fact that it was sanctioned by their religion, the Ottomans believed that slavery was based on principles of humanity and fellowship that exempted it from misleading comparisons with the egregious institution that existed in the West. It was true that Islam assigned obligations to the slave owner and rights to the slave that obtained in neither ancient Rome nor the antebellum Deep South. The Quran proclaimed that to free a slave was one of the most praiseworthy of acts; slaves and freemen were held to be equal in the eyes of God; and the child of a slave was automatically born free. It was common for a slave to be freed after seven years' servitude, by which time the owner had made back what he would have spent paying a domestic servant over the same period.[44]

Western visitors to the Islamic world conceded that there was surprisingly little stigma attached to being an ex-slave. The ancestors of the Mamluk chieftains who ruled Egypt until the French invasion of 1798 had been slaves. The Janissary corps, for centuries the Ottoman Empire's premier fighting force (until Mahmud II disbanded it in 1826), was made up of former Christian slaves who had converted to Islam. The annals of empire were full of slaves who had risen to ministerial office or become top commanders; purchased or captured Circassian beauties virtually monopolised the office of concubine in the imperial harem. There was no tradition of plantation agriculture being pursued on a vast scale under the whip as there had been in the British Caribbean and continued in the southern United States. Egypt was the only province in the Ottoman Empire where slaves were used on the cash-crop estates, although in limited numbers; here the labour force was composed overwhelmingly of free fellahin. The Egyptian army, by contrast, contained large numbers of Sudanese slaves.

In some cases enslavement by a well-to-do family was regarded as a leg-up in life compared to freedom and poverty, as in this Istanbul slave's recollection: 'My mother came to us with joy in her face and said to me: "My children, your father must be having in his favour the ear of the Prophet. Here comes to us a miraculous help. A rich *hanoum* [lady] wishes to buy six or seven little girl slaves. I am going to sell you three little girls, and with the money go back to the mountains to bring up your brothers ... " We were very happy ... '[45]

In the 1850s, Mary Sheil, wife of the British minister in Tehran, reported that domestic slaves in Iran were 'frequently restored to freedom, and when this happens, they take their station in society without any reference to their colour or descent'. Ill-treatment, she conceded, 'must of course sometimes take place when there is unlimited power on one hand, and entire submission on the other ... still it is believed that in general, cruelty, or even harshness, is rarely practised towards slaves in Persia. Their customary treatment is similar to that of the other servants of a family, or even something better ... they are not treated with contempt as in America; there are no special laws to hold them in a state of degradation.'[46]

For all the relative advantages a domestic in Persia had over a cotton-picker in Mississippi, however, slavery was, after all, slavery – a system under which free men and women were seized, transported and put up for sale. It was a flaw in Islam's doctrine of human equality under God, and an affront to the *hurriya*, or liberty, on which a new civilisation was being built.

In the British and Foreign Anti-Slavery Society, the Islamic nations faced their first concerted campaign from a finger-wagging 'human rights' group – the term started coming into currency in the 1830s. Pacifist, vocal and Quaker-dominated, the society received constant reports of slave traffic from its informants around the world, many of them missionaries, and was able to call on armies of letter-writing activists as well as sympathisers in the government.

Pressed by the society, in 1840 – seven years after the Slavery Abolition Act covering most of the British Empire – Britain's foreign secretary, Palmerston, instructed his ambassador at the Porte, Lord Ponsonby, to inform the Ottomans that British support would hence-forth be dependent on progress towards eradicating the trade. Ponsonby's response well describes the prevailing Muslim attitude towards an institution that had been around forever and for whose abolition no convincing reason could be adduced. 'I have mentioned the subject,' the ambassador told Palmerston, 'and I have been heard with extreme astonishment and a smile at the proposition of destroying an institution closely interwoven with the frame of society ... I think that all efforts to give effect to your Lordship's purpose will fail, and I fear they might give offence if urged forward with importunity. The Turks may believe us to be their superiors in the Sciences, in Arts, and in Arms, but they are far from thinking our wisdom or our morality greater than their own.'[47]

For all the Turks' complacent assumptions about the permanence of slavery, however, the trade itself was far from the benign Muslim tradition that it was portrayed as, and not a good advertisement for the reforming monarchy that the statesmen of the Tanzimat were trying to project. For many of the Africans who were seized by raiders or taken prisoner in war, the first experience of servitude was to be driven north from Lake Chad across the Sahara Desert to the Mediterranean slave marts, a death march for many as they succumbed to dehydration, hunger or exhaustion – or else they were immobilised by swollen feet and abandoned to their fate. In perhaps the worst tragedy involving the Saharan caravans, in 1849 some 1,600 slaves and their dealers perished after they reached an oasis whose wells had dried.[48] Georgian and Circassian slaves, comprising the so-called 'white' slave trade, were often transported by boat via the Black Sea. Conditions on board were so bad that there was a clause in the Ottoman tariff regulations whereby dealers were refunded any duty on slaves who died within fifteen days of disembarkation.[49]

For those who survived these ordeals, the ultimate destination was often the slave market of Istanbul itself – situated on European soil, under the puckering nostrils of European ambassadors, missionaries and visitors. Lady Sheil's claim of colour blindness in Persia evidently did not hold in Ottoman Turkey, for there was a definite hierarchy among the slaves at the Istanbul market. The tall, pale-skinned Circassians were at the top, followed by black Africans; the Egyptians, derided as the 'race of Pharaoh', fetched the lowest prices.

In 1843 the British traveller Charles White described the Istanbul market as consisting of a half-ruined quadrangle containing a coffee house and the remains of a mosque, and wrote that the dismal aspect of the place harmonised with the 'degraded condition of its temporary inmates'. Some of the chambers, situated in recesses under the colonnades where the transactions took place, were set aside for 'second-hand negresses (*Arab*), or white women (*beiaz*) – that is, for slaves who have been previously purchased and instructed, and are sent to be resold, perhaps a second or third time'. There were also 'ranges of cells, or rather vaults, infectiously filthy and dark. Those on the right are reserved for second-hand males; the furthest and worst of these dens being destined for those who, from bad conduct, are condemned ... to wear chains.'[50] White witnessed the savage beating of a woman slave by one of the brokers, but dared not intervene for fear that he would be reviled and expelled.

The man who did more than anyone to raise Western hopes regarding the eventual abolition of slavery in the Middle East was Ahmad Bey, the Ottoman governor general of Tunis. Ahmad was a moderniser in the mould of Egypt's Muhammad Ali and he realised the value of acting against slavery as a means of winning Western support for Tunisian independence from Ottoman rule. In 1841 he prohibited the export of slaves from his dominion and closed the market in Tunis, a bombshell that earned him British gratitude and opened the way for him to abolish slavery itself, in 1846 – seventeen years before Lincoln's Emancipation Proclamation of 1863. Indeed, during the American Civil War the mayor of Tunis instructed the American consul general on the economic advantages of abolition, arguing that the productivity of a free person was greater than that of a slave.[51]

The importance of the abolition edict that Ahmad Bey put before the country's parliament lay in the fact that it was full of Islamic legal arguments, rather than Western humanitarian ones. First, it stated, the cruel treatment of the slaves was inherently un-Islamic. Second, to prohibit slavery was to uphold the pious ideal of justice. Finally, the enslavement of Muslims by other Muslims was illegal under Islamic law, and the majority of slaves coming from the bilad al-Sudan – literally, 'lands of the blacks' – were at least nominally Muslim.

Although slavery was perpetuated in Tunis for years after abolition – not least by Ahmad's cousin and successor Muhammad (1855–9), whose harem was reputed to contain more than a thousand female slave attendants – the practice went into decline and aggrieved slaves increasingly threw themselves on the European consuls for support. Ahmad's edict had laid down a progressive Islamic rationale for a ban, a precedent that other Muslim rulers could follow without bringing their own piety into question. And thanks to Ahmad, slavery had become an indelible item on the diplomatic agenda between Islam and the West: it was a question not only of morality and the law but also of influence and pride.

In the middle of the nineteenth century, Egypt, Turkey and Persia could not boast of an abolitionist advocate monarch in the mould of Ahmad Bey; on the contrary, their respective rulers hardly concealed their reluctance to act in a cause that had been foisted on them by outsiders, and which gave the same outsiders more excuses to deepen their interventions. In the event, however, the three main Muslim powers were constrained to limit slavery. With what now seems like extraordinary speed, yet another venerable and apparently unalterable Islamic institution began its collapse. First to act was Muhammad Shah, in 1848, when he banned the entry of slaves from the Persian Gulf (and, later on, overland), followed by the Turks the following decade, who placed restrictions on human imports from Georgia and eventually banned the trade in African slaves outright. Finally, in 1869, Egypt's Khedive Ismail turned his feigned abhorrence of slavery to account by annexing the upper reaches of the Nile, proclaiming to the world that his wish in doing so was to staunch the commodity's source. 'With 3,000 [slaves] in his harem,' wrote the incredulous Lady Duff Gordon, 'several slave regiments, and lots of gangs on his sugar plantations, his impudence is wonderful. He is himself the greatest living slave trader as well as owner.'[52]

In a system where the children of slaves were born free, the survival of slavery clearly depended on continuity of supply; and over the last quarter of the nineteenth century slaves grew rarer and more expensive. Manumission marched on: in Egypt alone, between 1877 and 1889, around 18,000 slaves were enfranchised, part of a trend that led to almost all Egyptian slaves being freed by 1905.[53] (Manumission was not always welcomed by the female slaves, some of whom ended up making a 'free' living as prostitutes.)

Alongside the foreign pressure – and in part drawing from it – a second factor was militating against slavery, and this was the changing moral universe of the more educated and Westernised Muslims. These men and women increasingly considered freedom – not faith – as a prerequisite of human dignity, and bondage, no matter how comfortable, as a defect on the face of the nation. Here, as with the change of attitudes towards seclusion and the rights of women, which was happening at the same time, awareness of anti-slavery in the West engendered both shame and a determination to take away the moral brickbats which the foreigners were using to beat the cultures of Islam.

It would be wrong, however, to depict the decline of slavery solely as the product of self-interest on the part of the Muslims. Some accepted the Western humanitarian argument without demur. In 1860 the early Iranian nationalist Mirza Fath-Ali Akhundzadeh – or Akhundov as he was known in his Russian-occupied home town of Tiblisi – composed a fictional correspondence between a Persian and an Indian prince that contained a highly unusual polemic against the emasculation of young male slaves so they could then enter service in the harems as eunuchs. (This, of course, was one abomination that did not exist on the American plantations.)

There are many humans in Africa who capture young boys, castrate them with great cruelty and then sell them like animals ... in one of the villages near Mecca the slave owners have a hospital for such innocent children, complete with surgeons and barbers. First the barber cuts off 100 percent of the boy's organ, then the surgeon struggles to save the boy. A third of the boys do not survive. The rest are sold at three to four times the price to make up the loss. Who is the cause of such misery of the boys? Muslim pilgrims who purchase them during Hajj and other events.[54]

In spite of the thickening tangle of limits and prohibitions, as well as the slow growth of anti-slavery sentiment among intellectuals like Akhundzadeh, still the traders did not give up, whether they were cramming slaves below decks or doling out bogus manumission certificates to African slaves bound for Anatolia (the documents were taken back on arrival). Furthermore many ordinary Muslims remained convinced that having slaves must be legal because the Prophet had had them.

As late as 1893 the imperial Ottoman seraglio was violating its own laws against trading in free-born Circassians by quietly putting out feelers for girls who had washed up in the Anatolian interior following their expulsion by the Russians, soft pretty ones, of course, preferably with blonde hair and blue eyes. Unfortunately for the sultan, most of the girls of suitable age had become somewhat leathery from the hardships of migration; their parents, in many cases, were reluctant to sell. Taking care not to implicate his master, the sultan's representative hinted that the girls were intended for one of the capital's grander establishments, dangled a large sum their parents' way, and agreed that the girls might be visited. But in all probability no more than twenty such girls were purchased in such swoops, a piffling number for an institution that in its heyday had contained thousands: the days of servitude, and the harem, were coming to an end.[55]

By that time, at any rate among the educated classes, there were fewer delusions over the supposedly enviable conditions of the Muslim domestic slave. Far from focusing in a self-congratulatory manner on the relative physical comfort and security that some slaves enjoyed, Muslim intellectuals had come to appreciate the abomination of enslavement. This seems inevitable in a society that was learning to ascribe value to the individual as distinct from society, finding in her rags of humanity an intrinsic worth that had not been known before.

★

Today there is a fond Western idea, seemingly corroborated by illiberal fundamentalist regimes, that Islamic society views sex with puritanical horror and disapproval. In fact over the centuries this wasn't the case in huge areas of Muslim culture. Sex entered poetry, humour and courtly and urban life, making cheerful havoc in the nooks of classical morality. Medieval Baghdad rejoiced in the story of a man who was tricked by his mother first into sex with her, and, years later, with the daughter he sired by her, and in his groundbreaking novel *Leg over Leg* Ahmad Faris al-Shidyaq amused himself over several pages by listing the various euphemisms for intimate parts of the body that he had found in a medieval Arabic dictionary. The vagina was 'the sprayer', 'the gripper' and the 'large floppy one'; the penis was 'the falcon's stand', 'the big spider' and 'the little man'; and the anus was 'the toothless one', 'the catapult' and 'the whistler'.[56] As for the *Thousand and One Nights*, that great early East–West import (it was the second most popular book in America after the Bible) would be positively skeletal without the sex content – all that 'kissing and clipping, coupling and carousing till day began to wane; when the Mamelukes rose from the damsel's bosoms and the ... slave dismounted from the queen's breast'.

Whatever harm the contained atmosphere of the harem did to the nerves of inmates, it certainly bred fearless talk of sex – and not just talk, with illicitly introduced lovers 'escaping through the roof of the harem, and royal concubines surprised in the basement with adolescent page boys, or half-castrated but still sexually-active eunuchs'.[57]

Such debauch may have tickled Flaubert and some of the libertine French poets, but it offended the Anglo-Saxon morals that entered the region in the baggage of others. George Nathaniel Curzon, who would later become viceroy of India and British foreign secretary, felt a thrill of outrage at the Shia institution of temporary marriage – under which men and women are permitted to marry for a set duration – as it was practised in the supposedly saintly city of Mashhad, in eastern Iran; he described it as 'a gigantic system of prostitution, under the sanction of the [religious authorities]'.[58] This was in 1890, five years before the high tide of Victorian intolerance carried Oscar Wilde away to Reading Jail. The appalled tone of Curzon, the imprisonment of Wilde – these were clear markers of what was acceptable and what was not in the abstemious world of modern virtue.

There was no word for 'homosexual' in the Islamic world, in the sense that was popularised in the 1880s in Europe by the psychologist Richard von Krafft-Ebing – unconventional patterns of behaviour had wound around accepted sexuality and decorum, and no portmanteau was capacious enough to fit them all. There was a canon of male courtship poetry in Arabic, Persian and Turkish, and for many mystic poets the celestial God with which they desired union was made flesh in the rose-lipped pageboy whose face shone like the moon, and not any female object of longing. But these expressions of love were not proof of consummation, or foreplay, or indeed any kind of play at all – as the medieval philosopher al-Ghazali had written, 'the beautiful form is pleasurable in itself even if carnal lust is absent'.⁵⁹ For some Islamic teachers, echoing Plato, the attractiveness of young boys was a divine incentive to aid in the propagation and spread of knowledge, while brute desire for women (by definition inadequate conduits for knowledge) was useful only for perpetuating the species. What some Arabs called an 'inclination to boys', others called a 'sensibility to beauty'; the 'masculinity' of the active partner was contrasted with the 'femininity' of the passive one. These nuances were reflected by the jurists, who devised a rising scale of sin, beginning with the relatively minor transgression of falling in love with a boy, going on to kissing and fondling him, and ending with sodomy itself – which everyone agreed was a major crime, easily as bad as fornication with a woman, and sometimes punishable by death.

For all the examples of chaste desire, sex between Muslim men evidently happened – and pretty often, to judge by the disapproving commentaries of European visitors.

The English mariner Joseph Pitts, who was captured and enslaved in Algiers in 1678, noted after his escape that 'the horrible sin of Sodomy is so far from being punish'd amongst [the north Africans], that it is part of their ordinary Discourse to boast of their detestable Actions of that kind. 'Tis common for men there to fall in Love with Boys, as 'tis here in England to be in Love with Women.'⁶⁰ Two centuries later, in the words of Nasser al-Din Shah's Austrian doctor, the practice of keeping a male concubine was 'so overt that no one makes an attempt to conceal it. In almost every house of standing there is such a boy, even many, who are there to serve this purpose. No one is reserved about introducing them publicly. Indeed, one takes pride in possessing a splendid specimen.'[61] Soldiers from Napoleon's *Armée d'Orient* who fell into the hands of hostile tribesmen during the march from Alexandria to Cairo, if they survived rarely made it back to safety with their honour intact, while female camp followers were killed without being sexually molested. This surprised the French as much as it shocked them.

The harems and baths of Turkey unsurprisingly encouraged female intimacy, the sixteenth-century geographer Nicolas de Nicolay noted, and he wrote that 'there is very great amity proceeding only through the frequentation and resort to the bathes: yea & sometimes become so fervently in love the one of the other as if it were with men'.[62] In Persia women took ardent vows of 'sisterhood', though it is impossible to ascertain whether these relations were typically sexual or not; there does not seem to have been the same tradition of romantic verse that existed among men.

We are obliged to take these lurid foreign accounts of Islamic mores on trust, but from Muslim accounts of Western life we know that there was (and remains) room for egregious misunderstandings. From the naked shoulders of the women he saw in the ballrooms of Europe, for instance, the Iranian traveller Mirza Fattah Khan Garmrudi, who visited Britain in the late 1830s, inferred that they were prostitutes. He also equated the small dogs that ladies of quality carried around with them to sex toys – a necessary supplement given the inability of even the most virile Western male to adequately cover his insatiable brood mare of a woman.[63] Different grooming practices were also a cause of confusion, with some Middle Easterners equating clean-shaven Western visitors with the beardless youths of homoerotic verse, and the Westerners growing manly whiskers in response to correct such misconceptions.

Clearly, however, despite all the room for misinterpretation, there was a tolerance of homosexual behaviour and sentiment in the Muslim world that was at variance with modern Western morality. This tolerance was related to the segregation and slavery that had been inherent in the Middle Eastern social set-up, which rather than one society made up of two sexes, fostered two societies that met for purposes of procreation, and also to the absence of squeamishness concerning boys and sex. There was much more tolerance of rape than now. In the words of a historian of the subject, 'great poets such as Sa'adi and Rumi wrote about the sexual molestation of boys or the castration of former beloveds ... the modern reader cannot escape the fact that classical Persian poetry is brimming with accounts of non-consensual sex with junior male partners'.[64]

But Middle Eastern tolerance – let alone the 'pride' of which Nasser al-Din's doctor spoke – would not survive once contact with Europe was sufficiently intense (and imbalanced) for foreign opinion to matter. To some European observers the homosexual culture in the Middle East was not only a 'sin against nature'; it also conspired to keep women at the margins of society, useful only for reproduction. In the same way that political pressure brought slavery to a close in the Middle East, so the cultural aspersions being cast by Westerners made opinion formers and modernisers in the Islamic world feel ashamed of their sexual culture, and seek to change it.

An example of this kind of shame and embarrassment can be found, again, in the writings of the Iranian traveller Mirza Fatah Khan Garmrudi. He evidently spent much of his visit to Europe in 1838 fending off accusations of pederasty, and he deplored the 'unfair' European stereotype of Iranians as inclined towards beautiful young men. On the contrary, he wrote somewhat defensively, 'the people of Europe are known ... especially for this evil act', and he depicted Europe as awash with rent boys.

A few years earlier Rifaa al-Tahtawi had written approvingly of the French as not inclined 'toward loving male youths and eulogizing them in poetry'. A curious consequence of the French love of women was self-censorship in the translation of homoerotic Arabic verses. 'In the French language,' Rifaa went on, 'a man cannot say: I loved a youth, for that would be an unacceptable and awkward wording. Therefore if one of them translates one of our books he avoids this by saying in the translation: I loved a young female.'[65]

The gradual anathemisation of homosexuality began in the Middle East in the late nineteenth century. It was attributable not only to the importation of Western prejudice, but also to the end of segregation and to the gradual assumption by women of the position of a natural partner, helpmeet and equal of men. Religious traditionalists expressed opposition to increased socialisation between sexes; for them, putting an end to segregated social arrangements was of a piece with ending the veil, and they opposed it vigorously.

For social reformers, the moral and religious imperative of men loving women, and preferably one woman, was now being backed up by a growing appreciation of the link between promiscuity and syphilis. There was an expanding body of literature providing advice for women on how to keep their man happy, and the modern, progressive magazines mercilessly satirised the old institutions of child marriage, same-sex commitment ceremonies, and polygamy. In the 1880s, in an influential book called the *Disciplining of Women*, a male member of the Iranian ruling house depicted the ideal wife as docile and submissive to the extent of imagining a 'garden of flowers' even if her husband pushed her into a fire. She must come to bed 'fully perfumed and clean' and never refuse her husband's demands for sex, or else he would turn to a 'lower-class temporary wife' who would solace him 'in the toilet cubicle or under the stairway'.[66] The feminist riposte came a few years later, in the form of a popular screed enjoining men to be kind and considerate to their wives, and advising women to leave their husbands if they were not.[67]

As a result of Western mores colliding with Islamic ones in the late nineteenth century, Muslim attitudes to sex began to align much more closely with the prevailing Western idea about what was right and what was sinful. Polygamy went out of fashion; it was unfair (on the women) and greedy (of the men) and speedily fell into desuetude among the Middle East's new bureaucratic and intellectual elites. Homosocial 'mentoring' of young boys and men by older father figures came to be considered gross and old-fashioned. At the same time, with the decline of the harem and concubinage men and women began to settle down – on the surface, at least – to monogamous heterosexual relationships as quietly as middle-class people in Europe and America.

There was also a plea from many young people for an end to the old arranged marriages, and in 1889 a young male character in a popular Turkish novel, *Serguzesht*, by the Istanbul writer Samipasazade Sezai, argued that 'the most important right of young people in the world is to marry whom they want'. Eventually that appeal was heard, as more people married partners they themselves had chosen, even if arranged marriages remained the norm among the upper classes for reasons of asset and gene management.

In the final years of the nineteenth century, romantic verse by men and for men was produced in ever diminishing quantities, and in the new century love poetry would be almost exclusively heterosexual in character. By 1925 attitudes had changed so much that an influential history of Arab civilisation authored by the Egyptian writer Ahmad Amin condemned the love of boys as 'the greatest calamity to befall society'. Around the same time, the Iranian social and political reformer Hassan Taqizadeh was pressing for the eradication of 'the shameful practice of unnatural love which has historically been one of the worst practices of our people and which is a major obstacle to civilization'.[68] A strait-laced and puritanical air began to blow through the Middle East, and here as in high-Victorian Britain and the United States the *Thousand and One Nights* was censored in order to excise sexuality of any kind. No more would homosexuality be referred to by the old euphemism 'sensibility to beauty': an Arabic neologism, connoting 'sexual inversion', 'sexual perversion', had arrived in its place.

It was not until the 1990s, and the fraught entry of gay liberation movements to the Islamic world, that the idea of equal sexual rights would surface in the Middle East, and some liberals began to ask whether the old sexual tolerance hadn't been preferable after all.

5

Nation

When we look back from our twenty-first century, it seems surprising to find a time that pre-dates this era of apparently permanent conflict and confusion involving the West and the heartlands of Islam. There was such a time. It was not, as we have seen, one of perfect serenity; on the contrary, from the first major encroachments of Western interests into Muslim lands the nature of the encounter was grating and asymmetric. However, from Muhammad Ali and clerics such as Hassan al-Attar and Rifaa al-Tahtawi in Egypt, to the Crown Prince Abbas Mirza in Iran and even Turkey's Tanzimatists, a tale of gain and useful emulation was slowly embedded in Middle Eastern attitudes towards the West, while some Muslim Westernisers persisted in regarding the objectives of the powers with more optimism than was warranted.

From around the middle of the nineteenth century, when European colonial interests ran up against Muslim resistance from North Africa to India, it is possible to say that a rolling agenda of conflicts between an expanding Western imperium and the Muslims in its path became inevitable. India's subjugation by the British had produced a situation of almost chronic religious revolt, of which the rebellion of 1857, or Indian Mutiny, was a virulent spasm. In the middle decades of the century there were also rebellions against the French in Algeria (and later on in Tunisia, which became a French colony in 1881). The Russian-occupied northern Caucasus was the scene of disturbances aimed at dislodging the newcomers, while Britain's strategy of using Afghanistan as a barrier to keep Russia out of India was bloodily resisted by the Afghans themselves. In the 1880s involvement by the British in Egyptian Sudan embroiled them in a full-scale religious cataclysm, led by a self-proclaimed successor of the Prophet, the 'Mahdi', or right-guided one, which climaxed in the famous massacre of General Gordon's army at Khartoum in 1885.

These disruptions to the smooth establishment of Western colonial supervision were interpreted by many Europeans as the writhing of a retrograde civilisation that had condemned itself to extinction. Yet others considered the agitations and uprisings in a more sophisticated manner. What united these disparate events that were happening in the face of colonial encroachment? Transport had greatly enhanced the mobility of political movements in the Muslim world, with an increasing number making the pilgrimage to Mecca, while the technologies of printing and the telegraph carried ideas in all directions. The borders between the Muslim and non-Muslim worlds were not impermeable, as evidenced by the satisfaction that was expressed by many in Istanbul, Cairo and Tehran when, in 1905, the Russian navy was annihilated by a small Japanese fleet in the Tsushima Strait. From Government House in Calcutta, which, by happy coincidence, was modelled on his family home in Derbyshire, the viceroy Lord Curzon noted that the reverberations of this victory by a small oriental power over a vast imperial one had gone 'like a thunderclap through the whispering galleries of the East'.[1]

By the turn of the century the word 'pan-Islamism' had become a portmanteau to explain the political solidarity that seemed to extend across the Muslim lands in opposition to imperialism. From Cambridge the late-Victorian scholar and Islamophile E. G. Browne deprecated the term as unfairly connoting fanaticism. In his view it was 'certainly no more fanatical than Pan-Germanism, or Pan-Slavism, or British Imperialism, and, indeed, much less so, being, in the first place defensive, and, in the second, based on the more rational ground of a common faith, not on the less rational ground of a common race'. For all that, Browne conceded that 'recent events have done much to create among the Muslim nations a sense of brotherhood and community of interests'.[2]

Pan-Islamism was not the only ideology available to the assertive Muslim living in the eye of change. This 'community of interests' had arisen at the same moment that an impulse to divide the world into smaller, secular units – nations bound by language, history and culture – had spread from Europe and America to the Muslim lands. Clearly there would have to be some kind of truce or accommodation between the two, or they would turn on each other. Room in any system of beliefs that made appeal to a progressive Islamic community would also have to enshrine the controversial trend in Muslim doctrine away from *taqlid*, or the slavish emulation of texts written by men in religious authority, often a long time ago, to *ijtihad*, the exercise of rational faculties in pursuit of dynamic codes of law – in other words, from a reliance on one's 'elders' to a reliance on oneself.

It would take a mind of great flexibility and perhaps deliberate inexactness to come up with an ideology that championed all these notions and at the same time brought together the elements necessary for a revival of Islam on Muslim terms.

This mind belonged to one of the most disputed characters in modern Islamic history – Jamal al-Din Afghani (1838–1897). Expediency and ambiguity were his lodestars, guiding not only the alliances he made, with figures who ranged from the tsar and the Ottoman sultan to the Mahdi of Sudan, but also the beliefs he espoused. Over the course of a long career in the second half of the nineteenth century, this sayyid, or descendant of the Prophet, spent years in the West, became a Freemason, accepted Christian and Jewish disciples, and lamented that Islam had tried to stifle science. He was accused of heresy for allowing his wide reading in secular wisdom to morph into a discourse on the merits of the philosopher over the Prophet. And yet this same man also excoriated the infidel and all his parts, publicly abominated moral licence and anyone who weakened the religious beliefs of the people, and ultimately dispatched an impious sovereign to his death.

It would be surprising if such a personality had not attracted, along with the kind of love one associates with a mystic's submission to the 'pole', or sage, in whom glows the light of esoteric truth, much harsher verdicts. Charlatanism is the least of the accusations that have been levelled at this apparently panoptic man, who seems to have elevated the principle of dissimulation of one's beliefs – a Shia tactic designed to avoid persecution – into an article of faith. He exaggerated his influence and scope, speaking for monarchs who had not asked him to speak for them, discharging commissions where none existed. But the world in the late nineteenth century made room for such independent minds, and afforded them a kind of self-seeding authority; perhaps more so than for any other character in this book it is necessary to view Jamal al-Din in the context of his time. The lands of Islam seemed to hold simultaneously the possibility of their own destruction and renewal, and the promise inherent in Western knowledge was offset by the terrifying advance of the European powers.

Jamal al-Din's modern biographer has written that to accuse him of dishonesty is to judge him by a 'political morality worked out to suit nineteenth century Western liberalism', and there is justification for moral relativising of this kind.[3] Jamal al-Din did not have the leisure to tease a pleasing doctrine from the bramble of ideas. He was negotiating an emergency passage to survival for a civilisation that might disappear at any moment. And so, in this squarely built, black-eyed, chain-smoking ascetic one finds the full mixture of Muslim optimism, doom and fury.

Jamal al-Din was born in western Iran and trained in the seminaries at Najaf, but the young sayyid seems to have adopted the moniker 'Afghani' in order to discourage Sunni Muslims from associating him with the Shia country of his birth, although on occasion he also called himself 'Rumi' ('the Byzantine').

The Indian Mutiny of 1857 found him in India, probably in Calcutta, where he had his first exposure to Western knowledge and watched as the rebels were crushed, engendering both a respect for Western ideas and a hatred of the British. Ten years later, after further travels – including a brief visit to his home town, where his family pleaded in vain with him to settle down – he was in Afghanistan, sporting a goatee beard and shaved head and advising the amir of Kabul on which anti-British stratagems to pursue. 'I am like a royal falcon,' he had told his father, 'for whom the wide arena of the world, for all its breadth, is too narrow for flight.'[4] It was in Kabul in the late 1860s that Jamal al-Din first attracted British notice, which would not flag for the rest of his life. Reports produced for the government of India described him as a 'mysterious personage' who was suspected of being an 'agent of some government', and noted that his lifestyle was 'more that of an European than of a Mussulman'.[5]

He ruminated on his own inscrutability:

> The English people believe me a Russian
>
> The Muslims think me a Zoroastrian
>
> The Sunnis think me a Shia,
>
> And the Shias think me an enemy of Ali [the second Shia imam] . . .
>
> The theists have imagined me a materialist
>
> And the pious a sinner bereft of piety . . .
>
> Banished from the mosque and rejected by the temple
>
> I am perplexed as to whom I should depend on and whom I should fight.[6]

Travelling to Istanbul for the first time in 1869 he found the foremost capital in the Islamic world receiving envoys from Central Asia who demanded aid against Russian expansionism. A man of his experience, erudition and experience of the philosophical traditions (which had been kept alive in the Shia seminaries, while being neglected in the Sunni schools) was swiftly adopted by Turkey's educational reformists, among them men who would be at the forefront of the movement for a constitution a few years later. Indeed, the racy speech he delivered to mark the opening of Istanbul University in 1870 offended orthodox opinion by observing that the statements of philosophers had universal and timeless validity, unlike those of prophets, whose words were affected by the circumstances of the epoch in which they lived. The undoubtedly heretical implication of these comments, which caused considerable disturbance among his audience, was that prophets were not infallible and prophecy was mere craft. His assertion that man's survival was possible by means of technology and the arts and sciences of civilisation also appeared to minimise the need for prophecy.[7]

Jamal al-Din's comments were of a piece with his views, which he seems to have held consistently throughout his life, that prophets are useful because they can communicate the specialness of a religion to the masses – something that philosophers, appealing to the intellect of a small number of people, cannot achieve. Deep in his heart he was an elitist, and he mocked the conventional piety of the ordinary God-fearer, telling the well-known story of the believer who exhorts the unbeliever, 'try to pray regularly for forty days, and see whether you can give up prayer afterwards', but adding the irreverent rejoinder, 'give up praying for forty days, and see whether you can ever resume the practice afterwards!'[8]

It was one thing to believe in a division between religion for the masses and religion for the elites; but publicly suggesting its existence caused a furore among Turkish conservatives who were in any case opposed to educational reform, and who rounded on the reformists' Afghan darling with accusations of atheism. In the spring of 1871 this 'man of unknown parts', as the Ottoman minister of education called him, was expelled from Istanbul. He decided to settle in Egypt, where the next instalment of his peripatetic life would play out amid even greater controversy.

The Egypt which Afghani discovered was in the final stages of the rule of the Khedive Ismail, that proto-European whose locomotive of supercharged development would soon come off the rails, ejecting him safely into exile on the northern side of the Mediterranean and handing the country's debt to Western bureaucrats acting on behalf of the creditors. This early version of today's IMF or World Bank bailout, with all the religious and patriotic reaction it provoked, was some years away when Jamal al-Din took up residence in Cairo in the spring of 1871. With the country still sullenly quiescent under Ismail, in the words of the future grand mufti Muhammad Abduh, 'who would have dared to show his opinion? Nobody, since one could, on the least word, be exiled from one's country or despoiled of his goods or even put to death ... amid this darkness arrived Jamal al-Din.'

To begin with, no doubt chastened by his expulsion from Istanbul, the new arrival concentrated on his natural vocation as a teacher. His erudition, lucidity and optimism in Islam's ability to renew itself drew to his house a range of admirers, including the young Abduh, and Saad Zaghlul, who would become Egypt's pre-eminent nationalist leader of the early twentieth century. To them Jamal al-Din unveiled his longing for the day when Islam, Judaism and Christianity would unite. He differed from the more blinkered clerics in that his conception of human achievement went back further than Mecca at the time of the Prophet. He spoke in reverent terms of the distinctions of the pharaohs, just as in India he would sing the virtues of Ashoka and the Buddha, and in Iran those of the Achaemenids. He did all this not in al-Azhar – an uncongenial home for a man of his unorthodox views – but in his own house, or, holding forth within clouds of cigar smoke, in a Cairo cafe.

This Sunni preacher who had in fact been educated in the Shia seminary went further against the Azharite grain by introducing his pupils to medieval philosophers from the Iranian tradition, as well as their neo-Platonic forebears. Disdaining rote learning – he left behind a slender oeuvre, itself an indication of the faith he put in the spoken word – he pointed out that in the past rationalism, science and fresh interpretations had prospered under Islam, and that while Western learning enjoyed the edge in the present age, the advantage was temporary and the true religion held within it many of the materials necessary for its own rebirth. He believed that Islam was almost unique among the world's religions in 'censuring belief without proof ... its lessons articulate that happiness results from reason and insight'. He read the Frenchman François de Guizot, that apostle of human self-improvement, from whom he adopted the idea of Protestantism as a catalyst for reform. Jamal al-Din often said that Islam needed its Luther, for which role his acolytes did not hesitate to declare him qualified.

'There are two kinds of philosophy in the world,' he was reported as saying; 'one of them is to the effect that there is nothing in the world which is ours, so we must remain content with a rag and a mouthful of food. The other is to the effect that everything in the world is beautiful and desirable, that it does and ought to belong to us. It is the second which should be our ideal ... as for the first, it is worthless, and we must pay no attention to it.'[9]

Notwithstanding Jamal al-Din's isolation from the clerics of al-Azhar, as well as his sobriety of manner and abstemious lifestyle (there are few indications of a sex life of any kind, and he vowed to castrate himself when the Ottoman sultan threatened to impose a wife on him), his unorthodox views nonetheless ensured that he was spoken about – and often in connection with impiety. Zaghlul hid his association with the controversial preacher, while the young cleric Abduh's reputation suffered for what his critics at al-Azhar considered his 'interest in philosophy, his advocacy of certain Mutazilite principles, his prohibition of traditional interpretation, his call for the study of modern sciences, his preference for the science of the Franks'.[10] Abduh and the others had learned these unorthodox modes of thinking from their teacher, whose windows were broken, and whose name was traduced.

Jamal al-Din answered with satire. 'If a philosopher puts on rough clothing, lengthens his rosary and spends his time in the mosque, then he is a mystic; but if he sits in Matatia's coffee-house and smokes the hubble-bubble, then he remains only a philosopher.'[11]

In 1876 Turkey's revolutionaries gained their new constitution from a reluctant Abdulhamid, but then came the disgrace of its author Midhat Pasha, and the democratic forces were scattered. The following year war broke out between Turkey and Russia, and the Egyptians, in Abduh's telling, 'strongly interested in the fate of their suzerain power, followed attentively the march of events'. The war was a disaster for the Ottomans, who had to pay stringent territorial and financial reparations. It was a fillip to the Egyptian press, however, which expanded quickly to answer the demand for news and pro-Ottoman polemic. 'With time,' wrote Abduh, 'the newspapers touched on political and social questions concerning foreign countries and then set boldly to dealing with the question of Egyptian finances, which embarrassed the government.'[12]

The spread of education and the press had created the conditions necessary for the emergence of a modern political culture in Egypt. Now there was a cause in the form of opposition to the spendthrift Europhile Ismail, and Jamal al-Din was heavily involved in encouraging ordinary people to think politically. No longer did he conceal his opposition to Ismail, exclaiming in a speech he delivered to the fellahin in Alexandria, 'Oh! You poor fellah! You break the heart of the earth in order to draw sustenance from it and support your family. Why do you not break the heart of your oppressor? Why do you not break the heart of those who eat the fruit of your labour?'[13]

Aside from his talents as a rabble-rouser, Jamal al-Din had a nose for alliances. He sought partners in the ranks of Egypt's would-be constitutionalist politicians and the foreign diplomatic corps, and he reportedly arranged for the Crown Prince Towfiq – regarded by reformists as a far better prospect than his father – to be inducted into the Eastern Star Masonic Lodge of which he was a member; as in Europe, Middle Eastern rulers regarded the lodges as hotbeds of sedition and anticlericalism. A correspondent for *The Times* (and fellow Mason) depicted Jamal al-Din as the *éminence grise* behind the patriotic opponents of the khedive and the French and British controllers of the debt. He was, *The Times* went on (borrowing from Byron), 'the mildest man that ever scuttled ship or cut a throat'.[14]

To the mysterious sayyid, whose experiences in India, Afghanistan and now Egypt had demonstrated to him the depths of English perfidy, it was necessary for Egypt to end its debilitating reliance on European finance and expertise. In August 1878, at the height of Egypt's insolvency, an Englishman was handed the finance portfolio and a Frenchman was made minister of public works; this 'European' government attracted much patriotic opposition, not least in the assembly, which the khedive dissolved the following year. Jamal al-Din seems to have been banking on Ismail's overthrow or assassination and a big role for himself in an independent Egyptian regime after Towfiq took over, but he was disappointed when Ismail was eventually deposed in June 1879: the new khedive turned out to be scarcely less complaisant in the face of European demands than his father had been.

One evening in the Hassan Mosque in Cairo, before an audience of four thousand, Jamal al-Din gave a powerful speech in which he denounced with a deep prophetic sense the ultimate purpose of British policy on the banks of the Nile. He also showed that the Khedive Towfiq had been compelled to serve British ambitions, and ended his speech with a war cry against the foreigner and a call for a revolution to save the independence of Egypt and 'establish its liberty'. This was too much for Egypt's new ruler and his British backers. In August 1879 Jamal al-Din was expelled from Egypt and his followers, Abduh among them, sent into internal exile.

The expulsion of Jamal al-Din did not kill off the spirit of opposition he had done so much to inspire, and it did not prevent his supporters, dribbling back to Cairo from their places of exile, from continuing to agitate in favour of change. To begin with, some of them, including Abduh, distanced themselves from their master's radicalism; they regarded a strong and stable government that had the confidence of the khedive and the powers as most likely to bring about a satisfactory conclusion to the debt crisis.

In the autumn of 1879 such a government was established, led by a Circassian strongman called Mustafa Riyad Pasha, and the new administration enjoyed a fleeting popularity because it managed to alleviate the tax burden shouldered by the fellahin, in part through cuts to the army budget. But hitting the army created a new force of opposition, and this browbeaten, underfed and demoralised organ found the courage to articulate first its own desires, then those of the country as a whole. The identity of the leader of this new political force was indication of a radical change that would come over the country's elite. He was not a Turk or a Circassian, but a fellah, an Arabic-speaking son of the soil, who, having abandoned his studies at al-Azhar, had risen aged just twenty to the rank of colonel in the khedive's army before his humble background stopped him going further. His name was Ahmad Urabi.

From the career of Sayyid Jamal al-Din Afghani it is now necessary to make a detour into the Urabi rebellion of 1881–2. The sayyid himself was not around to influence events, but Urabi had seen him in the flesh, and, after initial circumspection, went on to form a close association with some of his disciples. Although the Urabi rebellion had an ethnic character that did not sit easily with Jamal al-Din's pan-Islamism, the purposes that animated it, of national revival and liberation from khedival caprice, were his own.

Ahmad Urabi was born in 1841 in the Nile Delta, the son of a provincial cleric. He supplemented the rudimentary education that he received at the local mosque school by learning from his elder brother how to do sums.[15] He was a big, rather ponderous man whose features only came to life when they were infused by emotion or powerful thought, and whose lack of affectation was shown by his habit of touching his hand to his forehead in appreciation even when he was reading a letter. He had been the beneficiary of a conscious effort to lift the fellahin up the military ranks, which went back to Muhammad Ali's decision to bring them into his modern army in the 1820s.

The young Urabi caught the attention of Muhammad Ali's son Said Pasha, who was viceroy from 1854 to 1863, and under whose patronage Urabi experienced his rapid rise up the ranks. It was while he was employed as Said's adjutant in 1861 that he borrowed an Arabic biography of Napoleon from the viceroy, who tossed it dismissively on the ground with the words, 'see how your countrymen let themselves be beaten!' After reading the book Urabi told the pasha that the French had won because 'they were better drilled and organised, and that we could do as well in Egypt if we tried'.[16]

The speed of Urabi's early rise contrasted with the apparent finality with which he clattered into an invisible partition protecting the top ranks. The reason for this was ethnic prejudice. Under Said's heir Ismail, as Urabi would recall, 'everything was put back in the hands of the Turks and Circassians, and the Egyptians in the army got no protection'.[17] The continued dominance of Turks and Circassians over Egyptian life in the middle of the century was an anomaly. They numbered some 100,000 people out of a national population of around 7 million, and they had further damned themselves in the eyes of the fellahin by choosing to rule in hock to religious minorities and foreigners.

Over the 1860s and 70s Urabi watched as his Turkish-speaking comrades were rewarded with promotion after promotion – 'not', as he put it, 'because they knew more than I did', but because they were not Arabs; and for this reason alone the khedive 'bestowed on them ranks, decorations, beautiful slaves, extensive and fertile lands, and spacious houses, he gave them gifts of money and precious jewels sucked from the blood of the poor Egyptians and the sweat of their brows'.[18] The belittlement of Egyptian officers intensified in the early months of Towfiq's rule, when in the name of economy more than a thousand of them were retired temporarily and the rest were barred from promotion; there was not a single non-Egyptian among the retirees.

This was the context for a burgeoning campaign of protest by fellah officers and organised by Urabi. It began in early 1881 with a petition to the council of ministers. When the government tried to have Urabi and his fellow colonels arrested, it turned into a full-blown mutiny that was only defused by the war minister's dismissal and official assurances that there would be no more preferential treatment for Turco-Circassians.

But tensions did not die down, as rumours of revenge by the khedive circulated, and the native Egyptian colonels made further demands for improvements to their conditions. Arabic-speaking landowners had also been inspired by the struggle of their military brethren, and now demanded a share of power from the dominant Turco-Circassian magnates. This led to demands for the assembly that Ismail had dissolved to be recalled – here the indigenous landowners would be able to defend their interests – and its invigoration through a constitution that would permit it, in Urabi's words, to 'guarantee the lives, possessions and honour of the nation'. Demands for a constitution and for a parliament that would function as a proper legislative body (as opposed to the consultative role the assembly had had for most of Ismail's reign) were also being voiced by Muhammad Abduh and other former members of Jamal al-Din Afghani's circle – an alliance on patriotic reforms was in the making.

Another subject that united the malcontents was the need to liberate the country from the Europeans. In Alexandria and Cairo, newspaper editors held up Tunisia's recent incorporation into France's empire as a warning of the fate that might befall their own country. 'Egypt for the Egyptians!' ran the nationalist slogan, and the popular preacher Sayyid Hamza Fathullah ascended his pulpit to reject Europe's monstrous arrogance in claiming to be bringing civilisation to the East. The Europeans should first put their own house in order, he went on; what with anarchists and socialists, civil wars, crime and corruption, they had enough to be getting on with.[19]

In this way, with the addition of new and varied interest groups, an ethnic agitation organised by a few army officers in the summer of 1881 grew into a much wider movement, at once constitutional, pan-Islamist, ethnic and militarist. The khedive tried to scatter the Urabists by arranging the transfer of key army units, but again there was mutiny, which came to a head on 9 September. This time it involved not a handful of officers but some 2,500 men who turned eighteen cannons menacingly towards the neoclassical khedival palace at Abdin – which had been built by Ismail and was a symbol of royal profligacy. Urabi's demands were the dismissal of the government, the restitution of the parliament, and the expansion of the army to 18,000 men – considered the bare minimum for the maintenance of national security. As important as these demands was the manner of presenting them, which was remarkable for its lack of deference to the sovereign. Urabi describes events in his memoir:

> When the Khedive arrived at Abdin he found us occupying the square, the artillery and cavalry being before the west entrance and I with my troops before the main entrance ... and the Khedive called on me to dismount and I dismounted. And he called on me to put up my sword, and I put up my sword; but the officers, my friends, approached with me to prevent treachery, about fifty in number, and some of them placed themselves between him and the palace. And, when I had delivered my message and made my three demands to the Khedive, he said 'I am Khedive of the country I shall do as I please' ... I replied, 'We are not slaves and shall never from this day forth be inherited'.[20]

The khedive had few resources to call on in the face of this overwhelming show of force. He was bereft of military backing and relied on advice offered by the European financial controllers, some American mercenaries who had been looking for work after the end of the Civil War (the head of Egypt's general staff, General Charles Pomeroy Stone, had lost a battle for the Unionists), and the old guard of Turco-Circassian grandees.

After further negotiations Towfiq capitulated. In the glow of success the renegade colonel and his comrades begged leave to kiss the hands of the sovereign they had crushed and humiliated. As the English poet Wilfred Blunt, perhaps the most vocal Western advocate for Egyptian political progress, would recount, 'a cry of jubilation arose such as for hundreds of years had not been heard upon the Nile, and it is literally true that in the streets of Cairo men stopped each other, though strangers, to embrace and rejoice together at the astonishing reign of liberty which had suddenly begun for them'.[21] Indeed it seemed as though the country was on a new path, led by the heroic citizen-soldier Urabi – this 'Egyptian Bismarck' who was now touring the country accepting accolades. In October 1881 elections were held for a new assembly that immediately began work on a constitution. Under the terms of this document, it was true, the assembly's powers would be purely consultative, with the power to make laws residing with an appointed council of ministers, but Urabi advised his supporters to compromise now in the hope of future gains. 'We have waited so many hundreds of years for our freedom,' Muhammad Abduh agreed, 'that we can well afford to wait some months.'[22]

In the chamber itself, meeting for the first time under an elected president (in earlier sessions Ismail had reserved for himself the right to nominate the president), the tone was suffused with optimism, with everyone – the khedive, the council of ministers, even the powers – assumed to be united behind a great common cause: the well-being of Egypt.

That the consensus did not last now seems tragically foreseeable. In any political system that is making the transition to representative government, restraint is unlikely to be much evident among the winners, while panic and defiance are the dominant modes among the losers. This was the case in Egypt in early 1882, with a new military establishment around Urabi settling scores with the Turco-Circassians, a no-holds-barred press campaign in train against the European officials, and an enfeebled khedive showing lamentable tolerance of foreign interference – so long as it diminished his internal rivals.

In the pride and pleasure of modern constitutional arrangements it is easily forgotten that parliament's job is to harry the executive and discharge legislative powers. But the assembly's demands for investigations into inefficiencies and peculation in the European-run departments, and for influence over the budget, caused jitters among the foreign creditors which soon grew into a generalised fear of Muslim hostility. The French occupation of Tunisia had unleashed a fearsome rebellion and colonists were being put to the sword. A trepidation that they would be treated similarly grew among the Europeans in Egypt, while the khedive, dithering and resentful, chafed at the assembly's attempts to box him in.

The answer to the growing wave of hostility to the West, which inevitably had a strong anti-Christian character, was an anti-Islamic crusade in the name of civilisation. This was the view of France's new prime minister, the eloquent barrister and imperialist Léon Gambetta; and he was not alone in believing, with recourse to a convenient backward logic, that Europe was justified in its colonial conquests by the virulent responses they provoked. The measures he envisaged to strengthen Anglo-French control in Cairo were to be an opening salvo in that Western crusade.

In the 'Gambetta note' of 8 January 1882, issued by France and Britain with the aim of settling Towfiq and putting the Urabists on the back foot, the powers assured the khedive of their 'united efforts' to oppose any danger to which he and his government might be exposed.[23] This meant Urabi, who had been painted abroad as a fanatic and a tyrant. But rather than shore up the khedive, the note actually had the effect of weakening him by showing how dependent he was on foreign support. In Egypt, as London's *Fortnightly Review* described it with a perspicacity that was rare among the London press, the Gambetta note was taken to mean that 'the Sultan was to be thrust still further in the background; that the Khedive was to become more plainly the puppet of England and France; and that Egypt would sooner or later in some shape or other be made to share the fate of Tunis'.[24]

The Gambetta note was an ultimatum welcomed by none of the parties in Egypt. It forced divisions into the open; no longer could the Urabists and Towfiq pretend to be on the same side. Soon afterwards the Europeans demanded that Urabi, who had been named minister of war, leave the country. He refused and the government collapsed, while an Anglo-French squadron stood off Alexandria and the khedive fled to Ras al-Tin to wait on events.

Egypt's future was in the balance, and in a public proclamation Urabi accused the khedive of betraying his people by going into league with the enemy. But the Urabists were not strong enough to defend the flimsy structure they had erected. On 11 July 1882, after rioting in Alexandria that left hundreds dead, the British launched a ferocious bombardment that was followed by the landing of an occupation force and the annihilation of much of the city in an inferno that seems to have been caused in part by local arsonists. (By now, the British were on their own; Gambetta had fallen in January and the new French government declined further involvement, claiming prior commitments in Tunisia and Algeria.)[25] In the Place Muhammad Ali, the famous equestrian statue of the country's modern founder remained standing, though all around was a 'quadrangle of lurid flame'.[26]

After the British invasion the outcome of the conflict was no longer in doubt, though it took a full two months for the British to subdue the forces that Urabi had mobilised in Egypt's defence. On 13

September, the patriots were finally routed in the Eastern Desert. The following day Cairo fell without a shot and Urabi surrendered to a British officer, who remarked – with perhaps a hint of surprise – that his captive was neither 'cringing nor arrogant, but acted like a well-bred gentleman'.[27] Gentleman or not, the British could not allow the leader of the Egyptian resistance to stay on, and in December Urabi was exiled to Ceylon. For the British it was the beginning of a colonial involvement in Egypt that would only come to a definitive close seventy years later, through the actions of another patriotic colonel: Gamal Abdel Nasser.

That Whitehall had not desired an occupation is well attested. The British did not relish the addition of another burdensome province to their already unwieldy dominions. But empires bring interests, which in turn need protecting from threats, very often by the accumulation of further interests, and in this way colonisation is pushed on by the logic of acquisition. In the case of Egypt, the British had seen it as their duty to protect their ally the khedive, as well as their control of the Suez Canal, and of course their loans – a subject of personal interest to the prime minister, William Gladstone, who had invested heavily in Egyptian treasury bills. And it was Gladstone who foresaw the multiplier effect that this little war, one among so many in Britain's imperial annals, would have on his country's African possessions. 'Our first site in Egypt,' he speculated, 'will be the almost certain egg of a North African Empire that will grow and grow.'[28]

Undeterred by his unceremonious expulsion from Egypt in 1879, Jamal al-Din Afghani spent the next decade in a blur of international agit-prop. He intrigued in India, Russia, Britain, France and Iran, and whether he was conversing with French Socialists in stiff collar and tailcoat, acting the Shia divine in an Iranian shrine, or entering a mosque in the Deccan to pray in the Sunni manner, he conducted his campaign with his usual flexibility.

By the 1880s the Europeans' thrust for world domination was dictating all major developments in the world; the scramble for Africa proceeded apace while further east the Anglo-Russian contest desta-bilised much of Asia. The military and diplomatic successes of the

Europeans highlighted the gap that existed between the Western and non-Western worlds, and which, despite much progress in the latter, continued to grow exponentially. Those countries that were on the receiving end of imperialism were obliged to make policy on the basis of faits accomplis, which is conducive neither to political planning nor cultural self-confidence. From a defensive starting point the modern Islamic world became a poor producer of original ideas. That's not to say there were no such ideas, and Jamal al-Din was responsible for at least one of them. The Great Game's participants did not consist solely of predators – although it is mostly resourceful Britons and Russians that have been written about in the (mostly British and Russian) literature. The hunted were not inactive, as evidenced by the sage of the East.

The significance of Jamal al-Din's years on the road – as he was being received by crowned heads, statesmen and intellectuals, before, in many cases, being encouraged to move on – is as expository as it is historical. Jamal al-Din did not so much decide events as manipulate and interpret them, and he was one of the first to express the principles that we regard as constituting the main strands of modern Islamic political thought. He espoused, sometimes simultaneously, ethnic and linguistic nationalism, anti-imperialism and violent jihadism, besides, for more select audiences, his usual religious scepticism. Perhaps most significant of all, Jamal al-Din realised the political potential that inhered in the Islamic *umma*, the worldwide Muslim nation that came together to pray, fast, give alms and – for those who could afford it – travel to Mecca. If that immense religious community was mobilised by a modern Muslim activism, a political movement might be created that was capable of standing up to the Europeans. The name of this movement was pan-Islamism.

Today, many of the ideas proposed by Jamal al-Din seem to contradict each other, but this is not necessarily evidence for the sayyid's opportunism or incoherence. It testifies to the hardening of divisions that has taken place over the intervening century and a half. In Jamal al-Din's time the various political colourations of Islam hadn't been adopted in exclusivity by one side or the other; they were part of a general solution in which Islam was suspended. And for all the ambiguous nature of his beliefs, Jamal al-Din never compromised on his main objective: expelling the Europeans, and particularly the British, from the lands of Islam.

Wherever he travelled during the 1880s, British agents reported on his movements and he was accompanied by controversy. In India it was feared that he was on a commission from Ahmad Urabi – whose confrontation with the khedive was unfolding at the time – to foment rebellion. This was untrue, but he heavily criticised Sir Sayyid Ahmad Khan, a prominent collaborationist Muslim leader. The British held, threatened and interrogated him.

In 1882 he went to Paris, where his Anglophobia made him the indirect beneficiary of Anglo-French tensions arising from the British invasion of Egypt (the French perceived Gladstone's egg too). He took a garret room in the Rue de Seize, where the Islamophile William Blunt found him playing host to 'a Russian lady, an American philanthropist and, and two young Bengalis who announced themselves as Theosophists', the conversation consisting of an 'extraordinary jargon about humanity'.[29] His opposition to the British did not keep him away from London, where with typical opportunism he offered the government an Anglo-Muslim alliance provided the British withdrew from the Nile. While in London he accepted the hospitality of Blunt, but Blunt expelled him from his home after two visiting friends of the sage concluded a discussion by beating each other over the heads with umbrellas. 'Jamal al-Din was a man of genius,' the Englishman wrote regretfully, 'whose teaching exercised an influence hardly to be overrated,' but he was a 'wild man ... one must draw the line somewhere'.[30]

Undoubtedly the most significant product of Jamal al-Din's European sojourn was the radical journal, called the *Firmest Bond* in reference to the unifying power of the Ottoman caliphate, that he and his former pupil Muhammad Abduh, who had joined him from Egypt, produced in Paris in 1884. In its short life of just seven months before the money ran out, the *Firmest Bond* gained much influence in the corridors of power around the Muslim world.

The *Firmest Bond* reflected Jamal al-Din's growing conviction that only Muslim unity under the caliph could save the worldwide community of Muslims from being submerged, and the articles it contained tended to downplay the constitutional reforms the sage had advocated earlier in his career. The journal also contained stirring denunciations of the classic Muslim vice of fatalism, and issued appeals for action; and it cheered the military successes being scored against the British by the Sudanese Mahdi, over whom Jamal al-Din, ever the self-aggrandiser, claimed to exercise Merlin-like authority.

Much of the *Firmest Bond*'s output seems to have been produced not by Jamal al-Din but Abduh, who was now downplaying the national character of events like the Urabi rebellion in favour of the pan-Islamism of his master. This no doubt was a factor in the journal's popularity, alongside its espousal of a new and politically charged interpretation of Islam that stressed solidarity against European imperialism. The journal was sent out, free of charge, to key opinion formers everywhere in the Middle East – the equivalent of a coveted invitation-only digest dropping into the inbox of the world's most influential thinkers today. Almost no one of consequence was excluded; even members of the khedival regime in Egypt were on the list. For all the criticism Jamal al-Din levelled at Middle Eastern governments (and particularly their ruling houses), he recognised in them a force that might be harnessed to a movement of his making. That the sultan in his Yildiz Palace on the banks of the Bosporus, the learned men at al-Azhar, the Shia divines of Beirut and Baghdad and the Ottoman functionaries of Mecca (and even Jamal al-Din's relatives in western Iran) had the opportunity to absorb the same ideas at roughly the same time illustrates the revolutionary effect of this journal. The *Firmest Bond* was the perfect expression of a modern, radical, Islamic politics for all the world – perhaps the first media organ that can be called 'Islamist', and offering a surprising contrast to the mass sectarian violence that has marred Islamic unity in the twenty-first century.

The sayyid's earlier denunciations of the tsarist annexation of parts of Central Asia did not dissuade him from spending the years 1887–9 in Russia, where he plotted against the British in India and corresponded with Iranian statesmen on the conditions in his home country. Tsar Alexander II refused to see him except for a private audience, which had no political significance, so the sage made his presence felt in other places. One evening Jamal al-Din attended the Moscow opera in full clerical regalia, making sure he was sitting in a box near the tsar. After the curtain had risen on a sumptuous *mise en scène*, the sayyid dropped to his knees and loudly accomplished the evening prayer. Once he had finished a Russian general was dispatched to find out the meaning of this exhibition, to which Jamal al-Din replied (misquoting the Prophet), 'I have a time with God which has no room for King or prophet.'[31]

The tsar could afford to keep his guest at arm's length, a luxury that was not available to his brother monarch in Iran. On his way to Russia, Jamal al-Din had spent several months in his homeland, where he had alarmed Nasser al-Din Shah by speaking of the need for reform and the rule of law, and, in their first meeting, calling himself a 'sharp sword' that should be employed against foreign governments. This was not what the shah, who would shortly afterwards controversially grant banking, shipping and mining concessions to the British, and who would spend the 1890s saddling his country with foreign debt, wanted to hear. He shunted the unwanted sayyid on to Russia. But even from Muscovy Jamal al-Din continued to insert himself into Iranian affairs, and maintained a correspondence with the country's most powerful statesman, Amin al-Sultan.

The shah had good reason to distrust the sayyid, who in a letter to Amin al-Sultan wrote that Iran was being run by men who were Muslims in outward garb only, and predicted the nation's downfall. When the shah was shown this letter, he wrote that 'such sons of burned fathers, when they have fled the country, remain like vipers, and never become moderate or human'.[32] But then, surprisingly, in November he allowed the viper to return – hoping perhaps that in bringing Jamal al-Din near him he could moderate his behaviour.

By the late 1880s Nasser al-Din appeared to be the great survivor of the Middle Eastern monarchies. Having murdered his reforming prime minister Amir Kabir and seen off the threat posed by the Babi heresy early in his reign, the fourth monarch of the Qajar dynasty had tolerated no further challenge to his prerogatives. The kindest thing that could be said about his stultifying rule was that it was stable. Nasser al-Din had done his patriotic duty by not allowing more Iranian territory to be prised away by the Russians or the Afghans, but he did his best to keep constitutional ideas at bay, even while retaining a lively personal interest in foreign innovations. (He himself might have made a decent living as a portrait photographer.) His naive attitude towards the constitutional arrangements he observed on his foreign trips required subtle parsing by his frightened courtiers. After one such trip he returned to Tehran demanding a system based on a miraculous principle called 'the law'; the ministers to whom he expressed this were struck dumb for fear of disclosing, as one put it, that 'the primary clause of law is the removal of privilege and autonomy from the royal personage'.[33] And so the Qajar state continued to function as it had, as close to medieval as could be imagined in the era of pasteurisation, constitutions and the combustion engine. If the slightest criticism of the Pivot of the Universe was heard in one of Tehran's many coffee houses, all of them were closed down.

Well into the 1880s the national economy had scarcely advanced in comparison to those of Turkey and Egypt. Industry remained almost non-existent, thanks to commercial treaties allowing the entry of European machine-made goods, with cash crops – cotton, rice, silk – being exported to Russia and only tiny quantities of capital goods coming in to build up the productive base. Another Iranian export was working men, across the northern borders into the Russian Caucasus and Central Asia, where they learned about the constitutional movements of Egypt and Turkey and some of them began to revere religious and nationalist heroes such as the Mahdi and Imam Shamil, who had intrepidly led the Caucasian resistance against tsarist Russia in the second quarter of the nineteenth century. Jamal al-Din wrote that considerable numbers of Iranians had emigrated for economic reasons to Turkey and Russia, 'where you may see them wandering through the streets and markets as porters, sweepers, scavengers and water-carriers'.[34]

The shah's own daughter Taj al-Saltaneh later wrote of these tumultuous times that 'the kingdom was in the throes of death, the subjects wretched and destitute, the governors busily wreaking oppression ... the nation was edging closer to the time when the thunderous clamour of the multitudes would tear down and demolish the pillars of the monarchy and release the people from the yoke of continuous oppression'.[35]

In common with the rulers of Turkey and Egypt, Nasser al-Din's main worry was a lack of cash. As we have already seen, his attempt in 1872 to grant an extensive transfer of natural resources and future revenues to Baron Julius de Reuter was cancelled as a result of unrest at home and protest from the Russians. In the late 1880s, egged on by the British minister in Tehran, Sir Henry Drummond

Wolff, a sometime Conservative politician who had also been involved in British machinations in Egypt, the shah had another go at tapping the Europeans. He opened the River Karun, in southern Iran, to British shipping interests, and farmed out a slew of senior posts to plausible foreigners, just as the khedive had done in Egypt. Banking and the exclusive right to issue banknotes were extended to a British bank, angering merchants and money-changers who had been issuing notes. The Russians countered by successfully demanding a banking concession of their own. Another money-spinning scheme was for a lottery concession, which the shah approved at the behest of his wily envoy to London, Mirza Malkum Khan, but was forced to withdraw when the *ulema* protested that it was contrary to Islam. Malkum Khan was dismissed after it was revealed that he had pocketed £40,000 from the would-be concessionaires; this former close adviser of the shah now became one of the monarch's most virulent critics.[36]

Of all the shah's controversial dealings with foreigners, the tobacco concession he awarded in March 1890 would have the most detrimental results. The beneficiary was a Major G. F. Talbot, another British subject, who was given a fifty-year concession over the monopoly, sale and export of tobacco in Iran, at an annual rent of £15,000 plus a quarter of annual profits – and lubricated, it later turned out, by bribes to the sovereign. As the shah's French doctor, Jean-Baptiste Feuvrier, explained in his memoir, this concession was different from the other ones because it affected almost the whole adult population. 'Every Persian smokes, man and woman,' he wrote. 'Along with tea and coffee, the water pipe is presented to all visitors. The Persian does not set off on a journey without his pipe-holder, whom one sees on horseback, water pipes and cake tobacco in high cylindrical holsters, with two stoves hanging on either side of his horse, containing glowing coals.'[37] Apart from its ubiquity, the other thing that made tobacco a potentially explosive subject was that it was picked, dried, packed and sold by Muslims, an intimate and unbroken sequence of transfers that infidel hands now proposed to break, raising the possibility of defilement.

It was some time before the significance of the tobacco concession was fully appreciated. This was a deliberate ploy on the part of Talbot and the shah; anticipating opposition, both parties kept it secret for as long as they could. In the meantime, Jamal al-Din Afghani had returned to Iran in November 1889 and was holding secret meetings with reformist statesmen. He had by now revealed (to his Iranian associates, at any rate) that he was of Iranian origin, which enhanced his appeal among his compatriots and raised the stakes should anyone in authority try to silence him. At the same time, he gave out that he enjoyed Russian confidence, which, even if untrue, seemed to afford him a further layer of protection. News of Jamal al-Din's negotiations may have reached the ears of Amin al-Sultan, who was now convinced that the sage represented a threat to the state. But before the government could act, Jamal al-Din removed himself to the village of Shah Abdulazim, a few miles south of the capital, where in full view of a riveted public a tense stand-off began between the divine and his sovereign.

The shrine at Shah Abdulazim was (and remains) only of secondary importance in Shia Islam, but being so close to Tehran it had acquired much sanctity in the eyes of the capital's inhabitants; the village's other significance lay in the single-gauge line that connected it to the city, representing the sum total of the country's railway capacity. In Shia Islam – as in English Christianity at the time of Henry II and his rebellious archbishop, Thomas à Becket – sanctuary in a holy site was supposed to be inviolable by the civil authorities. (Amir Kabir had tried to dilute this principle during his tenure in the middle of the century). Over the next few months Jamal al-Din used this safe haven to attack the government with unprecedented directness. At the same time dissident publications from abroad, in particular Qanun, or the 'Law', which was edited from London by the same Malkum Khan who had been behind the aborted lottery scheme, broadened its criticisms of the country's ministers to include their boss. 'We have no right to find fault with the Amin al-Sultan,' ran one submission to Qanun; 'if he were to disappear the Shah himself would certainly produce someone of even more obscure origin and detestable attributes.' Over the summer and autumn of 1890 Tehranis trooped out to Shah Abdulazim to hear Jamal al-Din speak against despotism and the foreign powers, and in favour of Islamic unity. Pamphlets were scattered round the capital inciting revolution and an anonymous letter written in the sayyid's trademark overbearing style hectored the monarch for surrendering the country to the

British. Portent became fact in febrile, superstition-filled Tehran, and there was a rumour, allegedly fuelled by the sayyid, that Sir Henry Drummond Wolff had presented the monarch with a copy of the Bible translated into Persian. Sir Henry had to withdraw from the capital until the fuss died down.

When the shah eventually took action against his toxic divine, he did not, like King Henry II, issue vaguely worded orders that led to the priest's murder and brought odium on his name forever. All the same, the disrespectful treatment that the Persian government administered to Jamal al-Din in January 1891 amounted to a scandalous rejection of commonly accepted principles. Horsemen violated the shrine, where they found Jamal al-Din lying ill, and dragged him from his bed. The sayyid's servant Mirza Reza Kermani called out that they were manhandling a descendant of the Prophet, but what resistance his supporters were able to offer was to no avail.

According to Jamal al-Din's account of events, 'the wretch (Amin al-Sultan) commanded me to be dragged ... through the snow to the capital with such circumstances of disrespect, humiliation and disgrace as cannot be imagined ... thereafter his miserable satellites mounted me, notwithstanding my illness, on a pack-saddle loading me with chains, and this in the winter season, amidst the snow-drifts and bitter, icy blasts ... ' Jamal al-Din's travails ended at the border with Ottoman Iraq, across which he was unceremoniously propelled.[38]

But the shah's hope that by distancing Jamal al-Din from the country his pernicious influence might be neutralised was not realised. The abuse suffered by the sayyid had transformed his political opposition to the shah into an abiding personal hatred that had no respect for borders. The mechanics of modern opposition politics also worked in Jamal al-Din's favour. Two of the main threats to Nasser al-Din, the newspapers *Qanun* and *Akhtar*, evaded the shah's wrath because they were published outside the country, and it was a simple matter to smuggle them in despite the best efforts of the secret police.

From their temporary home in Iraq, Jamal al-Din and his assistants were able to incite opposition to the shah effectively unimpeded; Sultan Abdulhamid had no interest in propping up his imperial rival to the east. Furthermore, they now had a perfect base upon which to build Iran's first mass political movement – a cause exerting sufficient pull to unite the varied elements of this notoriously fissiparous country, from highly conservative mullahs to political radicals and the merchants of the bazaar.

The details of the tobacco concession that the shah's government had signed with Major Talbot had become known around the time of the sayyid's expulsion, and they swiftly attracted adverse attention. The farmers grumbled about the price they would be offered for their crop, the merchants fretted for their new status as agents of the concessionary company, and everyone was in agreement with the mullahs that the rights of Muslims were being trampled upon. There was also much criticism of the paltry annual rent of £15,000 against which the shah had signed away some 10 million kilograms of tobacco. Unflattering comparisons were made with the tobacco concession in Turkey that garnered the Porte fully £630,000 a year.

The arrival of Major Talbot himself to take up the concession in February 1891 inflamed an already tense situation. Agents of his Imperial Tobacco Corporation of Persia swarmed across the country to take possession of the entire tobacco crop and to end all trade except within the corporation's aegis. Shiraz and other tobacco-producing centres erupted in fury, which led to the killing of several protesters by soldiers, while the supporters of Jamal al-Din and other exiled opposition figures, including Malkum Khan in London, kept up their barrage of poison pen letters to senior officials. As had been the case with the Urabi protests, the aggrieved tended to express themselves in religious terms, but into the Islamic understanding of justice had seeped the secular concept of rights, which everyone seemed able to grasp.

On 30 August Jean-Baptiste Feuvrier recorded in his diary: 'At Tabriz, proclamations put up by the tobacco company have been torn down from the walls and replaced by revolutionary notices ... the inhabitants of Tabriz ... demand [of the shah] that he not sell to Christians the privileges of Muslims, which runs counter to the Quran, and declare that they are determined to defend their rights to the point of taking up arms.' On 4 September the Frenchman reported that 'a threatening crowd has been stationed for several days before the palace of the Crown Prince, energetically demanding respect for their rights and the Quran'.[39] The protesters were making use of the telegraph network that, almost alone among foreign innovations, the shah had introduced without restraint. The result was a speed of communication among the dissenters that was unprecedented; hardly an advertisement, from the shah's point of view, for further modernising measures.

All the while Talbot's agents, corporate zealots who were not remotely prepared for the task of negotiating with hostile Muslims, conducted spot searches for hidden tobacco stashes. Such violations of the sanctity of the home and private property seemed to recall the Russian sweep for enslaved Christians that had provoked the massacre of the poet Griboyedov and his entire legation half a century before. Now, as then, much of the country was poised between sanity and unreason, and in 1891 there was an insurrection in one of the northern provinces after the authorities tried to arrest a holy seer who had prophesied the shah's death. As a result of his experience with the Bahais – who had not been extirpated, but continued to practise in secret – the shah was in a state of heightened anxiety over any challenge to his authority.

But the tobacco protests lacked a lay leader – the country had no Urabi. Instead it was directed by men of religion who gathered the strands of public anger. The decisive events of the campaign, those that befuddled the shah and forced him into humiliating submission, were of their devising.

Jamal al-Din was responsible for the first such event. In the summer of 1891, while he was under surveillance in Basra, he appealed to the leader of the Shias in Iraq, Hajji Mirza Hassan Shirazi, who had many followers in Iran, to abandon the political quiescence that was his well-established custom and spring into action. Jamal al-Din's letter was extraordinary for its violence, and its declaration of war against a ruler who embodied the divine right of kings must have been terrifying to those Iranians who read it after it was distributed inside the country. The sayyid painted a picture of a ruler who was the epitome of impiety, who had handed the reins of government to a 'wicked freethinker, a tyrant and a usurper' – this was Amin al-Sultan – and who himself 'drinks wine openly, associates with unbelievers and displays enmity towards the virtuous'. It went on to list the assets which the shah was distributing among the 'foes of the faith', not only the tobacco trade, but also – through other concessions, actual or meditated – the banking system, mines, rivers, roadways, and manufactures of soap, candles and sugar. 'This criminal has offered the provinces of the Persian land by auction amongst the Powers,' he went on, 'but by reason of the vileness of his nature and the meanness of his understanding he sells them for a paltry sum and at a wretched price.' He ended his letter with the following clarion call: 'if thou wilt not arise to help this people, and wilt not unite them in purpose, and pluck them forth, by the power of the Holy Law, from the hands of this sinner ... the realms of Islam will soon be under the control of foreigners, who will rule therein as they please and do what they will'.[40]

Jamal al-Din's letter had the desired effect. In December 1891 Shirazi weighed in, sensationally declaring that the use of tobacco was equal to waging war against the twelfth imam, and forbidding it until such time as the concession was withdrawn. The popular obedience that was shown to the pontiff was total, and spoke of the respect that senior clerics continued to enjoy in the Shia world. 'With perfect accord,' Feuvrier wrote in astonishment, 'all the tobacco merchants closed their shops, all the water pipes have been put aside, and no one smokes any more, neither in town, nor in the entourage of the Shah, even in his [harem] ... What discipline,' the Frenchman marvelled. 'What obedience ... !'[41]

With the whole country seething politically (and no doubt suffering from withdrawal symptoms), it was only a matter of time before Major Talbot, the shah and the British government had to give in, and on 5 January 1892, the concession was annulled. Later that month Tehran's town crier announced that Shirazi had lifted the ban on tobacco, and from the urban harem to the rural glade Iranians took up their pipes once more.

The tobacco crisis was over but the country paid heavily for the shah's absence of foresight in awarding a concession he would go on to rescind. In order to compensate Major Talbot and his shareholders, the country was forced to contract its first foreign debt – of half a million pounds – from the British-owned Imperial Bank of Persia; Iran now joined Egypt and Turkey in the dubious club of debtor nations in hock to the West. The newspaper-reading public in Britain had been kept largely in the dark about the seriousness of the tobacco agitation by the over-sanguine reporting of the Reuters news agency, whose owners also happened to own the

Imperial Bank. As for the new loan, the London *Tablet* reported fatuously that this 'satisfactory' arrangement may be 'pretty confidently relied upon to extend the area over which British commerce is supreme'.[42] For Nasser al-Din Shah, who had survived the Babis, Amir Kabir and the machinations of his own harem, the defeat of the concession and the imposition of the loan were about much more than trade. The Pivot of the Universe had been mortally wounded by a simple abstention by his people.

The sayyid who had contributed so fulsomely to his sovereign's humiliation was in England at the moment of victory, staying with his new ally, the disaffected diplomat Malkum Khan. The following summer he went back to Istanbul on the sultan's insistence. It was the last journey he would make before his death five years later – at the age of just fifty-nine – and for all the hopes he had invested in Abdulhamid as the figurehead of a worldwide jihad against the imperialists, the sultan kept him at arm's length for much of his stay, which resembled a period of semi-captivity and was marred by yet more accusations of irreligion. He received visits from old students like the Egyptian nationalist Saad Zaghlul, but he was barred from publishing against the shah, and the houses in which he stayed were watched by police and in one case burned to the ground. In his desire to escape the constricting embrace of the sultan he even tried to secure a British passport. As a figure in world affairs his career appeared to be over.

In fact this accomplished political insurgent had yet to accomplish the last detonation of his life. While he was in Istanbul Jamal al-Din received a visit from his former attendant and acolyte, Mirza Reza Kermani, who had been arrested following the sayyid's expulsion from Iran, and had spent four years in jail. Mirza Reza had suffered greatly during his prison term, which he had spent shackled in chains that had almost paralysed him, and his shaky hands were barely able to hold a cup. According to Mirza Reza's later account, when he described his misfortunes to Jamal al-Din, the sage remonstrated, 'How poor-spirited you were, and how great was your love of life! You should have killed the tyrant. Why did you not kill him?' These words prompted a revolutionary resolution on the part of Mirza Reza, who told himself, 'the Tree of Tyranny must be cut down at the roots, and then its branches and leaves will wither in the natural course of things'.[43]

Jamal al-Din paid Mirza Reza's hospital bills while the latter conva-
lesced in Istanbul before returning to Iran. In January 1896, having
purchased a Russian revolver from a fruit trader, Mirza Reza went to
the shrine at Shah Abdulazim and located the exact place where Jamal
al-Din had been dragged out of the holy place and publicly humiliated
five years before. Mirza Reza had heard that Nasser al-Din Shah would
pray at the shrine on 1 May to give thanks for the fiftieth anniversary
of his accession to the throne. Standing among the petitioners at the
door to an adjacent mausoleum, Mirza Reza intercepted the shah after
he had completed his prayers, and fired his pistol from close quarters.
The shah started. Then, as the assassin testified later, 'I don't know
what happened next.'[44]

What happened is that the dead shah was whisked away and Mirza
was almost lynched by a group of women who seized him and
ripped off his ear; his life was saved by none other than Amin
al-Sultan, who was in the shah's suite. Amin al-Sultan prevented an
immediate breakdown in authority by propping up the shah's body
in the carriage he rode back to Tehran, pretending to hold a conversation with him. Amin al-Sultan's quick thinking prevented the
popular unrest that might have been expected to follow such a
dramatic event; in the capital the Cossacks were deployed to keep
order and the throne passed without incident to Crown Prince
Muzaffar al-Din. During his interrogation Mirza Reza Kermani
claimed that the shah's death had been a necessary blow against
tyranny, but he did not implicate Sayyid Jamal al-Din directly. In
August 1896 the shah's assassin was hanged.

After the death of Nasser al-Din, as the Iranian government
redoubled its efforts to have Jamal al-Din extradited, the sage told
a German reporter, 'surely it was a good deed to kill this bloodthirsty tyrant, this Nero on the Persian throne who destroyed more
than 5,000 people during his reign'. Using language that he knew
would be pleasing to Western readers, he described himself as 'but
a messenger of thought and truth ... I have striven and still strive
for a reform movement in the rotten Orient, where I would like to
substitute law for arbitrariness, justice for tyranny, and toleration
for fanaticism.' And he placed a curse on the lands of Islam that
had not paid sufficient heed to his wisdom, saying, 'the entire
Oriental world is so entirely rotten and incapable of hearing the

truth and following it that I should wish for a flood or an earthquake to devour and bury it.'[45]

Where the Iranian government failed, the sayyid's growing physical feebleness succeeded, and in December 1896, having been thwarted in his diplomatic mission of bringing home the fugitive, Iran's ambassador to Istanbul telegraphed the following news to Tehran: 'Jamal has been attacked by cancer in a very grave manner so that there is no more hope for him. Surgeons have cut off one side of his chin along with its teeth, and he will soon die. The soul of the martyred Shah (may his tomb be sanctified) is finally avenged and Jamal al-Din has been punished for his acts.'[46]

Jamal al-Din succumbed to cancer on 9 March 1897, with just his Christian servant by his side, and was buried in an unmarked grave. Inevitably, given his notoriety, his followers gave out that he had been poisoned on the sultan's orders. In 1944, at the request of the government of Afghanistan his body was moved to Kabul, where finally, in validation of the imposture with which he began his political odyssey, Jamal al-Din became immortally 'Afghani'. His reputation has not suffered as a result of displacement to the periphery of the Muslim world, but has steadily risen, even if his universal message runs counter to the sectarian bigotry of today's militancy. Jamal al-Din embodied the use of Islam as a worldwide ideology of resistance against Western imperialism, knitting the Islamic heartlands together in a way that today seems impossible. He was the godfather of universal, modern Islamism.

As if in vindication of the universal attraction of political freedom, spreading without prejudice between Cairo, Istanbul and Tehran, the turn of the new century was marked by a welter of revolutions, constitutional crises and popular gesticulations. The three major nodes of Middle Eastern life, politics and culture had been brought closer together by a shared experience of modernity, which in turn linked them to a wider world of change and innovation. Integration was the main factor of modern life, whether coerced, voluntary or accidental, and even as the nation states of the modern world began to find their form, the borders between them grew more porous.

Of the various external events that bore on politically aware Muslims, the gradual modernisation of Japan and the inauguration of Russia's first parliament in 1906 were the most significant, sending incipient patriots and future revolutionaries into a tailspin of excitement and emulative zeal. Unlike the French Revolution, which had been heavily muffled for most Muslims, the modernising reforms set in train by the Meiji Restoration of 1868, which climaxed in the humiliation of the Russian fleet in 1905, and the concurrent challenges to the tsar by his disgruntled people, leading to the first Duma the following year, were heard by significant numbers of educated Muslims with unprecedented clarity and immediacy.

The effect of the Japanese victory was especially pronounced on a Muslim civilisation whose experience of modernisation, while productive in many respects, had also fanned a smouldering inferiority complex. After a century of partial Westernisation it was hard to think of any modern endeavour which Muslims were better at than Europeans and Americans, from making rifles to dealing with a bow tie. But 1905 changed perceptions in an amazing and dramatic way, putting up precedents that could be understood by all. (In far away India, even, peasants named their children after the victorious Japanese admirals.) An oriental navy had shown that ideas and technology were indeed communicable and that best practice did not necessarily belong in the West. In Moscow a blow was struck against despotism – even if Nicholas II rallied and dissolved the first Duma after just eleven weeks.

Yet there still remained a dragging sense that what the Japanese and Russians were achieving was somehow beyond the reach of Muslims: that some invisible force – of reaction, or fear, or conspiracy – prevented them from attaining what was clearly the common destiny of all peoples. In Egypt the editors of the progressive journal *al-Muqtataf* regretted that while the Japanese devoted their energies to advancing science, 'most of our [clerics] are still saying a thousand times over what they have been saying for the last thousand years, like cattle chewing their cud; it makes the heart sick'. A Turk posing as a Western observer criticised the Ottomans' failure to wage an uprising against tyranny: 'these Orientals who could not take lessons from the [Western] nations' historical experience, will they once again fail to benefit from the current events in

Russia?'[47] In Iran, from where thousands of migrants had left to find work in the burgeoning Transcaucasian oil centres of Baku and Grozny, the spectacle of proletarian unrest forcing the tsar to retreat served to underline the continued absence of an organised opposition at home.

For all the trepidation and bitter self-doubt that was being expressed, however, social and political pressure was mounting in Iran and Turkey that would prove impossible for their complacent monarchies to resist. New ideas about the dignity of the nation and its inhabitants, along with the necessity of modernisation, were coming together with a militant phobia of foreign powers and a desire to defend Islam. The Qajars and the Ottomans were deemed inimical to this contradictory yet explosive combination of progress and reaction. The mixture would eventually blow up and the result would be revolution.

In Persia the assassination of Nasser al-Din Shah in 1896 had been a warning for the monarchy, and while the dead king's heir, Muzaffar al-Din, behaved a little less arbitrarily than his father, he was sickly and undecided and given to outbreaks of buffoonery; he was all too easily persuaded by his English doctors that frequent immersions in the curative waters of Europe were essential to his well-being and that of the nation. Muzaffar al-Din had inherited a state whose organs, no less than his own, were in the hands of foreigners. In 1898 the country's customs administration was handed over to officials from Belgium, who delivered higher revenues at a cost of dissatisfaction on the part of local merchants who claimed they were being discriminated against. The top Belgian official, the abrasive Monsieur Naus, would go on to become de facto finance minister. In 1900 the country floated its first big Russian debt, which permitted the shah to embark on a lavish European tour; a second loan was contracted in 1902, followed by another fantastically wasteful and inconsequential royal peregrination. The shah reportedly paid £240 a night for his hotel suite in Paris – £26,000 in today's money. While in England he was severely deflated by King Edward VII's refusal to invest him with the Order of the Garter (it was only for Christians, the king maintained, though his mother had awarded it to Nasser al-Din), which gives some indication of the shah's priorities.

There was a further price to pay for the Russian largesse that funded these royal junkets over and above the 5 per cent interest. The Russians arrogated to themselves a right of veto over all future Iranian loans – in effect a bar on borrowing from Britain. In addition, a customs agreement was signed under which Russian goods entered the country almost duty-free.

The country's pivot to Russia had been masterminded by the scheming Amin al-Sultan, the scourge of Jamal Din Afghani, and it involuntarily pulled together the kind of coalition that the sayyid had gathered to defeat the tobacco concession. To the merchants' grumbles and the anti-Christian rabble-rousing of the mullahs was added discontent among more secular-minded men in the civil service and the nascent professions, some of whom were closeted Bahais, and others influenced by socialist propaganda coming in from Caucasia. Maladministration, corruption and oppressive governors were rampant across the country; the magnates hoarded bread, leading to affray; and of the various species of coin and paper money there was usually either a dearth or a glut, depending on the actions of the speculators. Secret societies formed and women hurled themselves at the carriage of the shah, who was periodically rumoured to be dead; his nickname among the foreigners, '*Mauvaise Affaire* al-Din', suggested that politically, he already was.

Into these turbulent waters waded the undaunted, reliably mercantile British, worried for the ramifications of Russia's predominance in Iran on their Indian and Gulf interests and slipping money and encouragement to sympathetic clerics in Iran and Iraq. A pattern was emerging, of an Anglo-Russian rivalry directed not at helping Persia to greatness but bossing her infirmity, with the powers alternating in the role of sadistic nursemaid.

An Iranian constitutionalist, Nazem al-Islam Kermani, described one riot that particularly exemplified the feverish political temper of turn-of-the-century Tehran, a city whose lattice of adobe lanes and wind towers suggested that it was much more immobile than it actually was. At issue was an attempt by a Russian bank to build a branch on consecrated ground belonging to a religious foundation, which contained a cemetery and seminary. The establishment in question was dilapidated and had been abandoned, and after failing to persuade a leading religious authority to validate the proposed acquisition the

Russians bribed a lesser divine to issue the necessary permit. The bank now bought out the inhabitants of shacks that encircled the land, and two hundred workers began to erect a splendid new building, sparkling with multifaceted mirrors of magnificent workmanship, contrasting with the inferior dross all around.

The government had stationed police to protect the building site but the ecclesiastics persevered. On the last day of Ramadan a prominent preacher ascended his pulpit and railed against the egregious breach of Islamic law that had taken place, the unearthing of recently buried Muslim bodies (including that of a woman) during construction, and their unseemly disposal in a well, and the likelihood that usury would soon be practised over hallowed Muslim ground. No sooner had his sermon ended than the congregation surged furiously to the partially completed bank, which, in Nazem al-Islam's words, 'in a matter of an hour was so comprehensively obliterated as to lead one to believe it had never existed'. Nazem arrived a little later to find children picking over the remains, and he 'knew then that the spiritual power of the people is a superior force of God'.[48]

For all the apparent conservatism of Tehran at the turn of the century, in fact the spring of constitutionalism was being wound for the first time, and, as would become apparent, very fast. Cairo's workings had got stuck in 1882; for the Egyptians every dream of future emancipation was predicated on a hypothetical British departure. In Turkey, a quarter of a century had uncoiled disappointingly since the Ottomans' first experience of semi-democratic government ended almost as soon as it started. After dispensing with Midhat Pasha, Namik Kemal and the other constitutionalists, the autocratic Sultan Abdulhamid had applied himself to a programme of retrenchment mixed with elements of modernisation that included the expansion of the education system (the future Istanbul University was founded in 1900). Malcontents were exiled or jailed and all hopes of representative government suspended as the sultan exercised absolute power.

Having gathered authority as much as possible into his own hands, Abdulhamid presented his subjects with an uncompromising vision, of an Ottoman patriotism that kept him, the sultan-caliph, at its centre. This held obvious appeal for the empire's Muslim subjects, but it was not at all enticing to the Bulgarians, Armenians, Greeks and other minorities whose periodic lunges for independence were mediated by the powers. The second half of the nineteenth century was the high noon of European clientelism, with the Russians adopting the Armenian and Bulgarian causes and the French that of the Maronites of Mount Lebanon, while the British stood up for the Druze in Lebanon and the Greek-speaking Cretans. Abdulhamid was obliged to devote much energy to neutralising alliances that were being struck between the empire's non-Muslim minorities and their mighty foreign sponsors, which would chip pieces off the empire and fatally damage relations between him and millions of his people. He also resorted to violence and terror, particularly in the 1890s when forcefully smacking down Armenian agitations in southern Anatolia; these police actions and pogroms earned him the sobriquet 'Red Sultan'.

A striking feature of the sultan was the distrust he felt for his own subjects – particularly those he had taken such pains to educate, and who, in some cases, used their new skills to plot against him. The sultan needed no spur to feel threatened in the Yildiz, his vast and rambling complex of palaces and kiosks on the slopes of European Istanbul, punctuated by cedars and oriental planes and populated by a vast, caterwauling menagerie, from which fear of assassination persuaded him seldom to venture. Such was his terror that assassins might acquire the plans to his residence that he was constantly walling up doors, opening new ones and introducing bulky furniture and other impediments into the corridors.[49] The legs of his chair were insulated to ward against electrocution by lightning bolt. He deliberately misinformed his attendants over what room he would sleep in on a given night.[50] Military recruits were not allowed to use live ammunition. In the hands of this monomaniac reposed one of the biggest empires in the world.

Not that Abdulhamid's terror of violent death was entirely without reason. Between 1881 and 1908 no fewer than seven heads of state were assassinated around the world (including King Umberto of Italy, President William McKinley and, of course, Nasser al-Din Shah) and the sultan himself was unsuccessfully targeted on several occasions: there was an attempted stabbing in 1904 and his carriage was dynamited the following year. The rare public appearances he did make were sometimes spoiled when students, despite having been carefully chosen and instructed to shout 'Long Live Our King!', gave vent to 'Down with Our King!' instead. A pervasive sense of decline made for a jumpy middle class, especially those staff college graduates who were the victims of swingeing expenditure cuts insisted upon by the country's European creditors. Turkey was famously a police state, with spies everywhere and a plethora of reports, some of them concocted, feeding the sultan's insatiable appetite for intrigue. Censorship was so stringent that when, in 1903, the King and Queen of Serbia were assassinated, the newspapers in Istanbul put the double regicide down to indigestion for fear that the people would get ideas.

For Abdulhamid, as for so many Muslims who wished to modernise without copying Europe, Japan was the model to follow, and he declared that 'none of our ills is incurable and we have in us qualities and forces which make us capable of a complete recovery'.[51] But in practical terms the success of his sultanate was dependent not on the distant Japanese but the much more proximate Europeans. For all the sultan's brave affirmations of Ottoman and Islamic pride, the benefits of his reign were mostly produced by the very Europeans whose influence he wanted to escape. The British expanded the postal service; the French extended the telegraph network; and by the end of his reign in 1909, thanks to German engineers and financiers in Europe, it was possible for a pious Ottoman to travel to Medina by train and an operatic one to Vienna. Like many subsequent Muslim rulers, Abdulhamid tried to limit Europe's cultural penetration, and like them he tried to distinguish between useful technology and destructive mores, a distinction as impossible to sustain then as it is now. Circulars emanating from the palace urged ever greater emphasis on religious education, but in practice geography, economics and geometry could not be displaced from the new schools that were appearing in provincial towns across the empire, while European languages and sciences slipped into the curriculum of the War Academy – supposedly the last bastion of the sultan's orthodoxy.[52]

It could be argued that this was a propitious time for revolutions, just as 1848 had been. In Mexico a decade of unrest started with the agrarian insurrection of 1910 and the following year the Chinese threw out the Qing dynasty and declared a republic. It was certainly a good time for nationalism, with patriotic movements spreading a mass base in Russia and Austria–Hungary, Sinn Fein emerging as a popular political party in Ireland, and a growing sense of nationhood among Dutch settlers in the Transvaal who collided with British expansionism in the Boer Wars.

The Muslim Middle East was not immune from these trends. Here, as elsewhere, nationalism and constitutionalism were the dominant political currents. What was new and startling in the Middle Eastern context was that Iran, whose position so far in this story of Muslim modernisation has been that of an idler staring out of the window and turning in his homework late, suddenly sat up, took notice, and shot to the top of the class.

Iran's Constitutional Revolution of 1905 wasn't simply the first sustained mass engagement with pluralism and the modern politics of rights to take place in the country; it was the first such engagement in the whole of the Middle East, and it incorporated nationalism, anti-monarchism and a political morality that was heavily informed by the Shia values of justice and sacrifice. That a modern Iranian political consciousness came into being so quickly, and achieved such success, was in part down to the secure base of national identity underpinning it and which had yet to develop fully in Turkey and Egypt. It was also attributable to the leading part that was played in events by Shia clerics, some of whom were influenced by the strikingly modern political doctrines of Bahaism.

On the whole, the Iranian mullah did not share the Sunni sheikh's high regard for monarchy as the form of government best suited to the *umma*; in Shiism it was the clerics who were closest to the real political leader of the community, the temporarily absent twelfth imam, and they were quite prepared to pass judgement on a sovereign who could only aspire to be a stopgap before his reappearance. The clerics had already asserted themselves during the tobacco protests, and the turbaned Sayyid Jamal al-Din Afghani was remembered as the inspiration behind Nasser al-Din's assassination. In 1905 their prestige rose further still.

The Iranian Constitutional Revolution started in December of that year, when some sugar merchants in Tehran were bastinadoed after a dispute with the governor over prices. In order to express solidarity with them, and to protest against gubernatorial abuse elsewhere in the country, a number of other merchants then took *bast*, or sanctuary, in the royal mosque in Tehran, where they were joined by two prominent clerics, Abdullah Behbehani and Muhammad Tabatabai. The sanctuary-takers, or *bastis*, listened to the impassioned words of a preacher, who had just completed his denunciation of the governor's tyranny and was warning the shah to pay heed when a pro-government stooge in the congregation started raining curses on him, calling him godless and an apostate and yelling, 'Kill! Imprison! Strike this Babi!'[53] This was a signal for other planted thugs to emerge from the shadows holding sticks, daggers and even revolvers, and there was pandemonium as Behbehani, Tabatabai and the other clerics were whisked from the mosque in fear for their lives. The following day, rather than risk another confrontation with the government's goons, the clerics and their followers slipped away to the scene of so many recent Iranian convulsions, the shrine at Shah Abdulazim, where they dug in for a protracted battle.

Over the next six months, this small group, whose initial demand was the government's dismissal, and whose leaders were at pains to demonstrate their loyalty to the shah, became a mass movement that won the country a constitution and a parliament and spoke out with unprecedented bluntness. In January 1906 the shah, embarrassed by the forthrightness of the opposition that had established itself at Shah Abdulazim, and disquieted by strikes in the bazaars, agreed to convene a 'House of Justice', a body made up of influential men that would adjudicate on the complaints of the people, dimly inspired by the (banned) Babi councils of the same name. The shah also signed supplemental laws putting himself below parliament and designating the people as trustees of the powers he held – remarkable concessions given the enduring influence of the divine right of kings. Believing they had won the day, the *bastis* duly made their way home. But when the government did not give effect to the reforms that had been promised, there were more protests, this time leading to the shooting of a young seminarian who had been trying to free a preacher imprisoned for speaking out against autocracy; the young student's body was carried through the streets, which generated more unrest and led to many more deaths. There were also bread riots in the holy city of Mashhad where several protesters were killed by police.

Barely a century after modern ideas arrived in Istanbul for the first time, this was the scene on the bridge spanning Istanbul's Golden Horn: a bustling, snorting, chugging maelstrom of modern ideas and technologies that gave rise to social novels, political parties, feminism, nationalism, and total war.

Royal Caprice: much taken with the tutus he had seen at the Paris ballet, Iran's Nasser al-din Shah ordered the women of his harem to abandon their traditional attire in favour of a supposedly balletic ensemble of flared jacket, knickerbockers and white socks. But the heyday of the harem was coming to an end.

The vogue for portraiture saw Muslim women strike risqué poses for male photographers who were often non-Muslims. Traditionalists bemoaned the increasing flimsiness of the face veil worn by Turkish and Egyptian women, which had become, as one Cairene put it, 'more transparent than an infant's heart'.

Islam's 'wild man of genius': in the course of a career of international agitation that took him to Turkey, Egypt and Iran, the shadowy man of religion Jamal al-Din Afghani embodied the revolutionary potency of Islam and turned it into a modern political tool.

Russia and Britain operated a reciprocal veto on any infrastructure project that would give the other a strategic advantage in Iranian affairs. This single narrow-gauge railway, bringing the people of Tehran to their favourite shrine just outside the city, was the sum total of track in the entire country.

As demands for political liberty grew, so social mores also began to change, and the hoary old practice of male concubinage became vilified by proponents of monogamous heterosexual marriage on the western model. This cartoon satirises the practice of 'brotherhood vows' between comely boys and their older mentors.

Almost a century after Abbas Mirza started modernising the Iranian army, the country's forces remained primitive and poorly equipped. But militias such as this one, seen here training in Tabriz, heroically resisted the Russian invasion of 1908.

Progressive priests: leading the reformist movements of Egypt and Iran respectively, Muhammad Abduh, on the left, and Hassan Taqizadeh, faced bitter opposition by conservatives as they strove to capitalise on a moment of liberal opportunity.

Among the practices that were deplored by western visitors to Iran was the bastinado, or beating of the soles of the feet, an excruciatingly painful form of punishment. It was the bastinado of sugar merchants at the Tehran bazaar that sparked Iran's Constitutional Revolution of 1905-6.

In 1908 the Ottoman Sultan Abdulhamid II garnered fleeting popularity by restoring the constitution he had abrogated more than three decades earlier, but even his opportunism did not staunch the popular yearning for political freedom. In April the following year he was deposed in a military-led uprising.

Educationalist, patriot and aviator, Halide Edib (the sole woman in this group) seized opportunities that were becoming available at the beginning of the Turkish Republic. Her garb in this photograph seems conservative now; but this and her posing amongst men would have earned her pious opprobrium only a few years earlier.

After the Second World War, Iran was fertile ground for a reaction against the decline of traditional culture. The influential thinker Jalal al-e Ahmad (seen here with his wife, the author Simin Daneshvar) roamed between third-world nativism, nostalgia for a lost Iran, and distaste for the vacuity of western culture. His sentiments influenced the generation that launched the Islamic Revolution of 1979.

'I have killed the Pharaoh!' With these words, the jihadi assassin of Egypt's President Anwar Sadat, Khalid al-Islambouli, struck against tyranny and impiousness in 1981 and brought the Islamic world into a new age.

From his new place of refuge in a mosque in Tehran, Ayatollah Tabatabai addressed the shah: 'Majesty! The Kingdom is in ruins, the subjects are distressed and begging, the trespassing hand of the governors and officials is outstretched ... they obey the power of their wrath and lust, whatever it desires and demands, in beating, killing and destroying.'[54] But Muzaffar al-Din's health had taken a turn for the worse and the government had no intention of carrying out his promise to set up a House of Justice. Luckily for the protesters it was now, as stalemate threatened, that geopolitics intervened.

For some time the British had been ruing the decline of their influence over Persian affairs and the rising fortunes of Russia and its Belgian ally, so when the protesters approached the British chargé d'affaires in July 1906 and sounded him out about taking *bast* inside the legation, the better to pursue their demands, the envoy replied encouragingly. What happened next is testimony to the extraordinarily quick growth of Iran's movement for emancipation: within a few days no fewer than 12,000 people had taken up residence in the grounds of the legation, and this expansive property in the middle of Tehran, dotted with English-style cottages and overshadowed by oriental plane trees, was transformed into a subversive camp that served as a nursery of modern politics.

'Imagine', the young British diplomat Walter Smart would recall the scene, 'the Legation Garden with tents in every available place, and crammed with thousands of all classes, merchants, ulema, members of all the guilds ... sitting there day after day with stubborn patience, determined not to leave the shelter of the British flag until their demands were satisfied. They policed themselves in a most remarkable manner, and, considering their numbers, gave little trouble ... they extemporised a rough kitchen behind the guardroom, and every day a circle of enormous cauldrons was to be seen cooking the meals of this vast multitude.' Smart pointed out the unfamiliarity to a Westerner of a revolution – 'for it is surely worthy to be called a revolution' – being directed by clerics: 'The priesthood have found themselves on the side of progress and freedom. This, I should think, is almost unexampled in the world's history ... are we witnessing the Dawn of Liberty in Persia?'

Yet only a few years before, whiling away the final years of his life on the banks of the Bosporus, the revolutionary Sayyid Jamal al-Din Afghani had identified religion not as an impediment to civilisation but the only way to achieve it. 'If we consider the reasons for the transformation in the condition of Europe from barbarism to civilisation,' he had told his disciples in the 1890s, 'we see it was only the religious movement raised and spread by Luther ... he reminded [Europeans] that they were born free, and so why were they submitting to tyrants?'[55] Here was the very question that occupied clerical and lay *bastis* alike inside the legation, who were able to consult diplomats like Smart on the precepts of constitutional government. As the constitutionalist Nazem al-Islam wrote, 'the Legation had taken on the role of a school, for under each tent and in every corner groups sat together and were instructed by someone versed in politics ... words reached their ears that hitherto no one had dared utter'.[56]

The government's ill faith as a negotiating partner was so badly disguised that the protesters would no longer be satisfied merely with a house of justice; the call now was for a legislature drawn from the different sections of society. With the British playing a mediating role, draft constitutions were batted between the royal court and the *bastis*, and the radicals among the latter were sophisticated enough to foresee that to call the new assembly 'Islamic', as the government insisted should happen, would amount to excluding progressives from the new body. In the event, 'Islamic' was replaced by 'National', which also opened the way for representatives of the country's Armenian, Jewish and Zoroastrian minorities to sit in the new chamber.

On 9 August 1906, agreement was finally reached on the formation of a national consultative assembly. The previous month the shah had summoned the courage to sack his tyrannical prime minister. The *bastis* now poured out of the British legation and the bazaars reopened and were strung with bunting and lights as if for a religious holiday. The following month elections were held. A collegial electoral system operated in the provinces, while in Tehran the elections were direct. They were far from ideal reflections of the popular will, however, being held under a limited franchise that excluded women, the poor and other undesirables. In Tehran, Tabriz and other places where political awareness was high, voter turnout exceeded 90 per cent.

Iranians were by most measures politically inexperienced, but they sensed nonetheless that by changing the terms of their relationship with the monarch they were changing other relationships too. An Iranian correspondent told E. G. Browne the story of a builder who had come to the house of a minister to repair an iron fireplace. 'On entering, he saluted the Minister. The Minister's servant bade him do obeisance. He replied, "Knave, do you not know that we now have a Constitution, and that under a Constitution obeisances no longer exist?"'[57]

The birth of modern Iran over the course of 1906 did not strike much of the rest of the world as very significant in comparison to other events. The launch of HMS *Dreadnought* in February had sparked an intensified race for naval supremacy between Britain and Germany, in April the Russian state Duma had, as we have seen, convened for the first time, and in October the United States had invaded Cuba. As Walter Smart of the British Legation rued, 'the English papers practically ignore the "Land of the Lion and the Sun", and Persian news is generally relegated to small, out-of-the-way paragraphs'.[58]

'On New Year's Day, 1907,' Browne wrote in *The Persian Revolution*, 'the Constitution, signed at last by the dying Shah, under the strong suasion of the clergy (who bade him remember that he was about to meet his God, and should strive to take into that awful Presence some deed of great merit ...) was taken to the National Assembly by the Prime Minister.' All the approaches to the assembly building and the gardens around it 'were thronged with an enthusiastic concourse of spectators, many of whom wept with joy as they exchanged embraces. Commemorative poems ... were recited, the city was illuminated for two successive nights, and joy and gratitude reigned supreme'.[59]

Browne's words recall the similarly rapturous reaction of that other Islamophile Englishman, Wilfred Blunt, to Urabi's success in facing down the Khedive Towfiq outside the Abdin Palace in 1881. Yet there were big differences between the two cases. The political base of the Iranian revolution was wider than that of Egypt, and, again in contrast with Egypt, for a few lucky months the powers were undecided as to how to react to it, leaving Iran's decisions to be taken by Iranians. As a result, the twenty-month life of Iran's first parliament passed in a firestorm of radicalism, decision and opportunity, for the dying Muzaffar al-Din had signed away the magic of Iranian kingship and there was a new powder, that of democracy, to sprinkle over the land.

Iran was now a constitutional state whose document of foundation, or 'fundamental law', borrowed liberally from those other new constitutional states – Belgium, Bulgaria, even Russia – and whose ministers were no longer responsible to the sovereign, but to the nation's representatives in parliament. Among the significant early actions of the deputies was to award themselves the right to veto all major financial transactions, including loans from foreign powers, and devolve powers to new provincial assemblies around the country. Shortly after this, parliament showed its independence from the shah by turning down a proposed £400,000 loan from Britain and Russia; it went on to act contrary to the government's wishes in other ways, securing the dismissal of M. Naus, the much disliked Belgian head of customs (who had aggravated feelings against him by attending a fancy-dress party dressed as a mullah), incorporating a raft of civil rights into supplementary constitutional laws, and cutting the pensions that were given to members of the royal family.

All this went on in an environment of almost unbridled freedom of speech, with scores of new publications subjecting the sovereign and parliament to an unflinching and in many cases satirical scrutiny. At the same time the roots of modern Iranian feminism were being planted by women activists who took the opportunity presented by the continued erosion of the harem to come out of seclusion and set up schools, health clinics and orphanages. There were reports of women creating human shields to protect the constitutionalists at crucial moments in the political struggle that had brought about the constitution, and widows now flocked to hand in earrings and bracelets to fund the national bank that was opened in January 1907 in the patriotic spirit of self-sufficiency.[60]

In the spring of the same year the British minister in Tehran reported to his government that 'in every town there is an independent Assembly which acts without consulting the Governor or the [parliament] at Tehran. One after another, unpopular Governors have been expelled, and the Central Government and the Tehran Assembly have found themselves powerless to resist. A spirit of resistance to oppression and even to all authority is spreading through the country.'[61]

If these currents of irreverence had unsettled Muzaffar al-Din, who died a week after promulgating the constitution – his 'deed of great merit' safely accomplished – they excited a visceral aversion in his son and heir, the corpulent, generously moustachioed, forbidding Muhammad Ali. While growing up in Tabriz in the 1870s and 80s, Muhammad Ali had come under the sway of the Russians, who maintained a strong diplomatic and commercial presence in the city. His sinister Russian tutor had been a Crimean Jew called Shapshal Khan, who is generally credited with poisoning the Crown prince's mind towards constitutionalism. An American critic would later call Muhammad Ali 'perhaps the most perverted, cowardly, and vice-sodden monster that had disgraced the throne of Persia in many generations. He hated and despised his subjects from the beginning of his career, and ... easily became the avowed tool and satrap of the Russian government.'[62] For the moment, however, assuming the throne of a nation that was aquiver with constitutionalism, the new shah could only hope not to be submerged by forces that were opposed to everything he represented.

The transformation that came over Iran after the granting of the constitution was an unlikely and dramatic one, touching life far from the capital and the traditional elites. Appropriately enough for the town that had seen the first serious programme of Westernisation in Iranian history, it was Abbas Mirza's former bailiwick of Tabriz that flew the standard of revolutionary radicalism. A multitude of popular associations were set up there, some propagating socialist and republican ideals, and giving birth to military units for the constitution's defence. According to the Tabrizi historian Ahmad Kasravi – the same religious student whose observation of Halley's Comet turned him towards scepticism – the bazaars of his home town 'would close every evening and chintz dealers, rock sugar sellers, coppersmiths, used goods vendors and merchants ... would rush off to their houses, change their clothes, pick up a rifle, head for the local barracks, and drill there with the rest. Every evening the sound of drum and bugle ... rose from every borough.'[63] In their defence of modern constitutionalism and their use of modern arms, these Tabrizis showed how much the city had changed since Abbas Mirza's first, furtive attempts at military drilling a little under a century earlier.

Under the influence of left-wing ideas coming in from the Caucasus, parts of northern Iran staged revolts of their own in 1907, as peasants formed associations that expelled the landowners' over-seers and refused to pay taxes. Parliament and the newspapers received complaints from around the country of the tyrannical behaviour of local magnates and their representatives, and in some towns the telegraph office, that all-important means of communication with the outside world, displaced the mosque as the preferred place of sanctuary. In the far north of the country, along the lush, subtropical strip that divides the Alborz Mountains and the Caspian Sea, the country's olive, jute, fishing and silk industries were shaken by strikes against the foreign interests that controlled them, while in Anzali, the country's main northern port, workers occupied the customs bureau.

Iran's nascent women's movement also took important strides forward. The well-heeled Durrat al-Muali, a member of the patriotic Association of the Ladies of the Homeland, organised campaigns to boycott Western commodities, along the lines of the swadeshi movement in India. But desire for emancipation was not confined to the lettered. Mahrukh Gowharshenas, a Tehrani woman of little education, was not untypical in joining a revolutionary women's association that set up a girls' school, and in hiding her activities from her husband. When he found out, he accused her of stepping outside 'religion and virtue', and of bringing disgrace to her family. But she persisted nonetheless, and later the gates of her school were opened to boys as well.[64] All the while, in the pages of the country's most radical new publication, the satirist Ali Akbar Dehkhuda wrote scathingly against seclusion, polygamy and arranged marriages. It was the golden age of Iranian journalism, and soon every town in the country had at least one newspaper.

Few people embodied the new spirit of resistance and enquiry more completely than the youthful parliamentary deputy Hassan Taqizadeh. Born in 1878 (twelve years before his fellow Tabrizi Ahmad

Kasravi), his father was a noted ascetic whose life, Taqizadeh wrote, was passed 'entirely in devotion'. His intellectual journey had begun with the traditional sciences of the seminary at which he had shown preternatural promise, finishing the Quran at the age of five.[65] In adolescence a 'hankering for the rational sciences' turned his attention first to medieval thinkers like Nasser al-Din Tusi, then to modern medicine, for which he learned French in secret – just as the Turkish writer Fatma Aliye had done. Shortly before his death, the old man discovered his son's guilty secret, and, in Taqizadeh's telling, 'gave me much grief'.[66]

The young Taqizadeh's reading – in Persian, Arabic, French, Ottoman Turkish and English (he had also found time to attend an American missionary school) – which he described as concerned with 'political affairs, modern civilisation, political freedom, women's liberation, and especially freedom of thought', amounted to a manifesto of *fin-de-siècle* sedition. He absorbed the essays of Malkum Khan, the talented if unscrupulous Europhile who in the course of a long exile in London had published the dissident newspaper *Qanun*, and who was one of the first Iranians to issue a call for a constitutional regime. He also examined the journals of Turkish dissidents living in Paris and translated a book of astronomy by the French popular scientist Camille Flammarion. He and his friends opened a school, a chemist's shop selling German medicines and a bookshop – but the first was considered too modern by the more traditional denizens of Tabriz and was closed, while the last was placed under surveillance by the then Crown prince, Muhammad Ali.

As if all the learning he could take in while sitting in Tabriz was not enough, in 1904 Taqizadeh completed his education by travelling. In the Caucasus, that fertile cultural amalgam of Iran, Russia and Turkey, he visited newspaper offices and was perhaps over-inclined to compare anyone interesting he met to Molière and Tolstoy (he closely followed the Russian's experiments with farming and community formation). In Istanbul he took a room in the Iranian quarter and spent the autumn buried in the works of Namik Kemal. One wonders what he made of that roar of national awakening, *Homeland or Silistria*. The books he was reading had been banned, of course. 'It was the time of Sultan Abdulhamid,' Taqizadeh recalled in his memoir, 'and one couldn't breathe.'[67] He returned to Tabriz the following year and immediately became one of the town's leading revolutionaries.

Taqizadeh was immaculately dressed in a clerical bluish-grey *aba* (gown) and turban when the British diplomat Walter Smart met him in Tehran's parliament building in 1907. 'There is something so sympathetic in his face,' Smart wrote, 'so attractive, that it escapes all definition ... if I am not mistaken, he is of those whose genius is capable of inspiring great enthusiasms, great sacrifices, and whose influence leaves a lasting impression on the history of nations.'[68] Smart was not alone in admiring the deputy for Tabriz. The more he spoke in the new parliament, the higher his stock rose, and 'many was the time', as the Iranian recalled, that fellow passengers on the horse-drawn cart home 'said that Taqizadeh excelled himself in parliament today – without knowing that I was sitting right next to them!'[69] He combined the attributes of religious and secular leader in a way that, for some Iranians, reconciled those uncompanionable bedfellows of Islam and liberty, and regularly led the evening prayer at the edge of the bazaar. His integrity was legion. On one occasion a well-wisher tried to make him the offering of an expensive rug, but Taqizadeh insisted on buying it from him. The following evening Taqizadeh returned the rug, saying that he had had it priced and that it was worth three times what he had paid for it.[70] In the personable, impassioned, honest Taqizadeh it seemed as though the new Iran might have found its spokesman.

The Constitutional Revolution had taken place in a blaze of popular fervour and goodwill, allowing radicals like Taqizadeh to assume national prominence. Still, reaction had a deep well of dogmas and assumptions from which to draw. Clearly, for Iran, with its long and intersecting traditions of governance, society and faith, the new constitution represented a brutal severance with the past. For all the many who welcomed the changes, others felt profound unease at this unruly force that was sweeping them towards the unknown.

The reaction was organised by Muhammad Ali Shah and helped gratefully along by conservative clerics who saw in the tenets of constitutionalism a set of shears for their own emasculation. The most prominent of these reactionaries was Fazlullah Nuri, a learned ecclesiastic from Mazandaran, in the north of the country, who had been part of the constitutional movement in its early days only to grow disenchanted with its secularising aims and jealous of its heroes. For Nuri the constitution was a trail that if followed would lead into sin and the mire. As he wrote to his son, 'one word was uttered in the [constitution] on freedom of the press and all the mischief of the newspapers resulted. What would have happened if ... there was to be freedom of beliefs?'[71]

Nuri was influential and he used his clerical authority to neutralise the effect of the civil rights that Taqizadeh attempted to enshrine in the supplementary laws. Nuri ensured that these rights only entered the statute as part of a much wider importation of Islam into the mechanics of government. In this way the principles of free education, free association and free speech were made conditional on these freedoms being consistent with the sharia. The job of adjudicating whether a given law was consistent with the sharia or not fell to the *ulema* – to Nuri himself.

The radical democrats were opposed to mixing religious precepts with secular ideas which they believed needed to be kept pure. 'They are bringing forth autocracy, reaction and deception,' one protested, 'in order to challenge the freedom and justice that we have managed to achieve with so much sacrifice.'[72] These lines can be read today as a prediction of more than a century of failed attempts to reconcile Islam and civil rights. In 1920, in a famous statement that the Egyptian secularist and women's rights campaigner Qasim Amin would no doubt have seconded, Taqizadeh would take the principle of non-dilution to its logical conclusion when he declared that 'Iran must both in appearance and reality, both physically and spiritually, become Europeanised and nothing else'.

Over the course of 1907 Nuri turned decisively against the liberals, provoking riots in Tehran when he attempted to take over the congregational mosque and withdrawing to the shrine at Shah Abdulazim, from where he denounced the revolutionary associations as seedbeds of blasphemy and moral licence. He also used his goons to incite disorder around the country, which did not require much effort – the provinces were already suffering from the smaller revolutionary agitations, an emptying exchequer (revenues came in irregularly, if at all), and an opportunistic incursion by the Turkish army into the northwest of the country.

The violence that flared up in Tehran during this period strengthened the impression of a country that was having difficulty looking after itself. In August 1907 the reinstated prime minister, Amin al-Sultan, who had until now shown impressive longevity, was assassinated by some combination of his plentiful foes. On another occasion a bomb was thrown at Muhammad Ali's car (the vehicle was wrecked but the monarch was not inside); and four months later there was an inconclusive stand-off between armed democrats and royalist Cossacks who had designs on the parliament building.

All this went on in an atmosphere of venomous invective and soaring emotions. Nuri was denounced in a radical newspaper for spouting 'any nonsense that the devil advocated, calling the fifteen million people of this nation atheist and deceitful while only he and his followers were seen as true Muslims'.[73] And surveying the retreat of the royalist forces following the stand-off around parliament, Taqizadeh exulted, 'glory to God, we have seen that the union of the people made the whole world tremble'.[74]

Internal disorder and chaos are the inevitable and perhaps even necessary concomitants of revolution, but they are also standing invitations to outside forces to intervene under the guise of restoring order. The British claimed they had received such an invitation in Egypt in 1882, with the result that the Egyptian revolution died in infancy. In Iran a quarter of a century later, it was the Russians who, despite their own internal problems and their humbling loss to Japan two years earlier, in alliance with their client Muhammad Ali Shah exploited and aggravated the chaos which prevailed internally for much of 1907.

One thing could perhaps have stopped the savage attack that Russia and the shah launched against the constitutionalists: a continuation of the same frigid imperial rivalry that had somehow preserved Persia's independence for many decades. But on 31 August 1907 – coincidentally, the same day as Amir al-Sultan's assassination – that rivalry officially ended with the signing in St Petersburg of the Anglo-Russian Convention. In global terms the convention was recognition that the world's top powers needed to gang up more closely if they were to offset the threat posed by a surging Germany. As far as Eurasia was concerned, the two nations came together to arbitrate their respective rights and privileges from the Pamirs to the Caucasus.

The Persians, and other nations that came under the purview of the agreement, notably Afghanistan, naturally saw it less as a pacific endeavour than an annexation. The accord divided Iran into two zones of influence, a Russian one covering the north of the country and extending as far south as Isfahan, and a British one in the south-east incorporating the approach to India. (The centre and south-west of the country were in theory to be kept neutral.) Both imperial signatories rendered up the usual platitudes about respect for Iran's independence, but the fact was, as patriots in Tehran and liberals (such as E. G. Browne) in London noted with dismay, that the country had been chopped up without being consulted. The Persian newspaper *Habl al-Matin* predicted that 'the signing of this agreement will be shortly followed by the end of Persia's independence and autonomy'.

Events internationally seemed to concur, setting precedents for further blows against the Iranian patriots. In 1905 Lord Curzon had partitioned Bengal in the latest manifestation of divide and rule, while in Russia the democratic opening of the following year had been brought to a close through Nicholas II's closure of the Duma and the suppression of regional rebellions. British foreign policy had become the hostage of Russophiles led by the foreign secretary, Sir Edward Grey, who would, as Browne put it, 'gracefully ignore the courts-martial, the hangings, and farm-burnings of their new ally, and simulate, at least, some enthusiasm for "Holy Russia"'.[75]

In Tehran it was the deciding moment in the struggle between Iranian autocracy and constitutionalism, when relations between the shah and the assembly were at breaking point and the democrats were in sore need of pressure in their favour from the outside world. Instead, on 2 June 1908, as the country threatened to tip into chaos, the Russian minister in Tehran and his British counterpart made an unprecedented joint representation to the Iranian foreign minister, in the course of which they asserted that the life of the shah was in jeopardy and that the constitutionalists had 'transgressed all bounds'. These sinister forces, they contended, 'now wish to depose the Shah. This we cannot tolerate, and, should it happen, Russia will be forced to interfere, and will do so with the approval and sanction of England.'[76]

Here, then, was the Iranian equivalent of the Gambetta note that had paved the way for the invasion of Egypt, and the shah took immediate and full advantage of Britain's abandonment of the constitutionalist cause. The following day he let loose two regiments on the capital, 'shooting, shouting and slashing, and creating a general panic', while he himself profited from the chaos to emerge from his palace in a cloud of dust and speed off to one of his gardens outside the town.[77] The meaning of the shah's flight, as all partisans of the assembly knew, could only be ominous.

In the early hours of 23 June, General Liakhoff, commander of the Russian-officered Cossack Brigade – a force some 1,500-strong, and one of Nasser al-Din's few significant innovations – deployed infantry, cavalry and artillery around the assembly building in conformity with orders he had received from the shah the previous evening. A tense stand-off ensued between the Cossacks and constitutionalists, some of whom were armed with rifles, inside the assembly building and in the adjacent mosque. The Cossacks ordered the constitutionalists to disperse. The constitutionalists made no move. Then an ancient mullah wearing the black turban of a sayyid, and seated on an ass, heaved into view, followed by hundreds of people who were evidently intent on joining the constitutionalists. The Cossacks warned him to stop, but he went on, stolidly, until shots rang out and the beast dropped to its knees, throwing its rider to the ground. At that moment a Russian officer unholstered his pistol and fired a shot into the air, and this, Ahmad Kasravi wrote in his history of events, 'was the signal for battle, and the Cossacks began firing as one. From the other side the [constitutionalists] gave reply and in this way the bloodshed began.'[78]

Thus began a pitched battle that the deputies – among them mullahs who did not conceal their terror at the bullets and bombardment – could not hope to win. For all their inferiority in numbers and equipment, however, some of the armed constitutionalist associations put up a gallant fight, firing down on the Cossacks from the minarets of the mosque and disabling three enemy artillery pieces. That left the Cossacks a further three, however, with which they continued to pour shrapnel on the defenders, destroying the parliament roof and punching holes in its rear. The battle lasted no more than four hours and cost perhaps a few hundred lives – by any reckoning a modest toll for a tragedy that would resound through modern Iranian history.

The immediate upshot of the destruction of Iran's first parliamentary regime was the arrest and execution of several leading constitutionalists, the flight into exile of several more (including

Taqizadeh, who went to Cambridge, where he was the guest of E. G. Browne), and the installation of a military dictatorship by Liakhoff in the name of the shah. But the democrats and other anti-shah forces had not admitted defeat, and rebellions began immediately, most spectacularly in Tabriz, where for ten months after the destruction of the Tehran parliament the associations that Kasravi had observed drilling were able to put their skills and patriotism to good use, first against royalist forces, whom they all but expelled from the city, and then against the famine that set in after the roads closed. The defence of Tabriz is justly remembered as one of the great blood-soaked epics of modern Persian history, and the chief commanders of the local patriotic forces gained legendary status on account of their bravery. In April 1909, however, Russian troops forced an entry into the city and the guns fell silent – even though conflict intensified at other points around the country, where the mood of insurrection and anarchy continued to rise.

One of the features of the constitutional movements of the Middle East was the indifference, shading into scorn and contempt, with which they were held by the foreign powers. As late as the 1960s, the main British historians of the Urabi uprising did not take it seriously as an expression of national awakening, while British support for the Iranian constitutionalists did not survive the jealousy of Russian prestige on which it was predicated. *The Times*, despite the considerable international repute that it enjoyed, did not deviate from its belief that the Iranians –in common with the Egyptians, the Indians and other benighted oriental peoples currently basking in the rays of colonial rule – were unfit for self-government. For *The Times* and a large body of Conservative opinion, Iranian self-government was a distraction from the august imperative of maintaining Europe's balance of power, and the paper scolded the Persians for their reluctance to incur further indebtedness to their 'two powerful neighbours'.[79]

For all their scepticism, however, and bearing in mind the hold that the constitution had taken on the Iranian imagination, and the counterproductive nature of Muhammad Ali's policies of unadulterated repression, the powers urged the shah to restore the assembly and proclaim an amnesty for all political offences – a pill they proposed to sweeten with a joint loan of £200,000.

Muhammad Ali agreed but it was too late. On 13 July, two separate revolutionary armies converged on the capital, neutralising Liakhoff and his Cossacks, while the shah was forced to flee to the Russian legation, where three days later he abdicated in favour of his twelve-year-old son Ahmad. After this extraordinary twist it only remained for elections to be held to the country's second parliament, completing the democrats' triumph. And yet, the inauguration of another parliament under another shah would not bring Iran's political epic to an end. The revolution had unlocked the impulses that would compete for control over Iranian society, even though none was strong enough to achieve victory.

The first of these impulses was in the direction of a constitutional regime under which the monarch's role would be tightly circumscribed, though a split soon appeared between liberals like Taqizadeh – who, having returned to Tehran after the triumph of the nationalist forces over Muhammad Ali, was now insisting on complete equality between religions – and moderates from among the orthodox clergy. The second insisted on giving the mullahs veto power over policy and legislation. And there was a third major force, gliding opportunistically between the two: the shah's desire to resist encroachments on his prerogatives, and particularly his purse. Some reactionaries and conservatives continued to promote royalism even after Muhammad Ali sailed away to Baku in September 1909, from where a Russian train took him to Odessa, on the Black Sea, his place of exile. The divine writ of kings remained fresh in everyone's mind, fresh enough for attempts to be made to restore it.

In the atmosphere of recrimination that was generated by Muhammad Ali's treachery, anticlericalism of the kind that was privately expressed by Ahmad Kasravi was able to burst into the public sphere. In July 1909 this tendency climaxed in an event that was unprecedented in the history of modern Iran: the execution of the most learned of all Tehran's ecclesiastics, the arch-reactionary Fazlullah Nuri. For much of parliament's first term Nuri had opposed constitutionalism as a blasphemous innovation. During the worst period of Muhammad Ali's despotism he had written in justification of the bombardment of the assembly and he had been involved in organising the defence of Tehran against the constitutionalist forces that eventually took the capital. Now Nuri was tried for involvement in the murder of four constitutionalists who had taken sanctuary at Shah Abdulazim, and the satirists duly lampooned his alleged willingness to sell Persian honour to the highest bidder. As one verse ran:

> My countrymen I loathe and execrate,
> My country is the object of my hate!
> I represent the Monarch wise and great,
> Who to my hands commits the nation's fate!
> 'Tis time for breakfast. Put this business through!
> Who bids? Who bids? Come Sir, a bid from you![80]

In fact, in accepting Russian support Nuri had not overcome his aversion to throwing himself on the mercy of an infidel government, and he had signally avoided following his monarch into the safety of the tsarist legation when he had the chance. He approached death with calmness and dignity, predicting that those who had judged him would themselves answer for their deeds on the Day of Judgement, before turning to his executioners and saying, 'Do your work.' He was hanged in his turban and cloak, an eloquent tableau of clerical authority subordinated to profane law. It is a telling commentary on the spread of constitutional ideas that the sentence was endorsed by many of the senior *ulema* of Iraq, as well as Nuri's own son, Mahdi, who 'stood at the foot of the gallows, reviling his father, and urging the [executioners] to bring this sad business to a speedy end'.[81]

As the execution of Fazlullah Nuri gave notice, Iran's second parliament, which was elected shortly after his death, gave voice to nonconformist views, but the mood soon turned confrontational between the radical and the moderate constitutionalists, while the reactionary current that had been represented by Nuri not only survived its leader's death, but drew moral fervour from it.

Fluidity is the default aftermath of revolution, with counterrevolution and new upheavals always a possibility, often under the influence of meddling outsiders. It was not until the collapse of the Second Empire in 1870 that the French Revolution can be said to have come into port. That Iran's Constitutional Revolution left behind conditions of uncertainty and the promise of further instability is no cause for surprise, particularly given that Britain, the influential outside power that had initially shown a benevolent interest in Iranian political development, had turned hostile.

For all the sincere feelings of goodwill harboured by individual diplomats like Walter Smart, Britain's early support for constitutionalism had in any case been opportunistic. And the constitutionalists, for their part, in spite of their stated admiration for Western ways of doing things, represented the multitude in desiring to end the country's dependency on Britain and Russia. The methods of these revolutionaries were not conducive to peace, quiet and the accumulation of foreign debt, as *The Times* so earnestly desired. They could not be pushed around by Britain and Russia. The opposite was true of the shahs as the Qajar dynasty negotiated the demands of the new century. Isolated, impecunious and ridiculously fond of foreign travel, they were a diplomatic pushover, and it's no wonder that the powers favoured dealing with them over the more problematic constitutional politicians.

Thus, in the years after the Constitutional Revolution, all the while professing their sternest esteem for Persian independence, Russia and Britain deepened their incursions into the nation's life in conjunction with the shahs. It was with unease that the powers viewed the appointment of a courageous and incorruptible American customs official, Morgan Shuster, to reorganise the country's finances, in 1911. Shuster was the disinterested representative of a rising world power that had no history of colonial involvement in the Middle East; many in the region regarded the US as their natural ally against the established European powers. Clean-cut, able and naive, Shuster arrived in Iran in May 1911 to take up the position of Persian Treasurer-General, only to run up against Russian and British efforts to sabotage his mission. In particular they stymied his efforts to set up a tax-collecting gendarmerie that would increase revenues and threaten their own military supremacy over Iran. Two months after Shuster's arrival the Russians allowed Muhammad Ali – wearing false beard, accompanied by a suite of uniformed officers and a consignment of rapid-fire cannon labelled 'mineral water' – to 'escape' Odessa and re-enter Iran with the aim of seizing back the throne. The nationalist government in Tehran was plunged into panic, but in the event the deposed shah's forces were defeated and he slipped away again, this time never to return.

Still, the powers refused to allow the constitutionalists to achieve their aim of independence, and they correctly identified Shuster as a major obstacle to their designs. In November 1911 the Russians issued an ultimatum demanding the American's dismissal. The sombre deputies rejected the ultimatum even though they knew they were condemning the country to invasion. In Shuster's recollection, the deputies came forward after a moving debate, their hands trembling, and 'when the roll call was ended every man, priest or layman, youth or octogenarian, had cast his own die of fate, had staked the safety of himself and family, and hurled back into the teeth of the great Bear from the North the unanimous answer of a desperate and down-trodden people who preferred a future of unknown terror to the voluntary sacrifice of their national dignity'.[82] A thousand miles away in the Ottoman parliament, the Turkish minister of foreign affairs remarked delicately that Persia's independence could not be under threat as it had been guaranteed by the Anglo-Russian Agreement. And this, Shuster wrote, at a time when 'some 12,000 Russian troops were occupying the entire northern part of the empire'.

In the days that followed, the parliamentary vote of a boycott of English and Russian goods was observed everywhere, while telegrams and messages of support from Muslim associations and communities arrived in Tehran from around the world – a manifestation of pan-Islamic unity of which Jamal al-Din Afghani would have heartily approved. But where was the strong, well-equipped army to defend this gallant sentiment? Where were the munitions, fodder and money? The sad fact was that some eighty years after Abbas Mirza's first attempts to build a deterrent force capable of defending Iran, the country remained pathetically dependent on foreign military clout. Even if one included those men who now constituted Shuster's treasury gendarmes (under American officers), the nationalist forces could not repel the Russians.

Again the constitutionalists consulted Shuster, this alien whom they'd come to trust; after three hours of parley the American felt compelled to 'express the reluctant opinion that if a single hostile move were made against the Russian troops north of Tehran, the 50,000 Cossacks who would be poured into Persia when the snows melted the following spring would crush out the last spark of Persian liberty and leave, perhaps, not even widows and orphans to mourn at soldiers' graves'.[83]

Shuster was right, and with this grim realisation the ruin of Iran's second parliament was assured. On 21 December, Persia accepted the Russian ultimatum. Parliament was suspended, Shuster and his American colleagues left Iran, and the radical constitutionalists went into hiding or, as in the case of Taqizadeh, into exile once more. Russian forces spread death and terror in Tabriz, hanging constitutionalists and abrogating laws, and the tsar's officials began extending their authority throughout the north of Persia, even demanding control over the area's mineral resources.

In the south, the British made similar strides towards establishing a de facto colony, setting up a police force called the South Persia Rifles that was soldiered by Indians, and, in 1914, bringing the Anglo-Persian Oil Company, a private enterprise that a British prospector had set up to exploit Iran's oil resources, under government guarantee. In 1915, the 'neutral' zone envisaged under the Anglo-Russian agreement was formally incorporated into the British zone occupying the south of the country.

The condition of Iran in the second decade of the twentieth century indeed gave cause for gloom to anyone who had observed the Constitutional Revolution and longed for the consolidation of the gains it had brought. Parliament remained closed, the press was censored, and power was now in the hands of cabinets operating under vigilant Russian and British supervision. The new shah, Muhammad Ali's teenage son Ahmad, was not a tyrant as his father had been, but nor was he purposeful or committed, and, like his grandfather Muzaffar al-Din and great-grandfather Nasser al-Din before him, he had a fatal yen for foreign travel on credit. The constitutionalists' dream of a financially independent Iran run according to the rule of law had been realised all too briefly. It is hardly to be wondered that from the wreckage of the chamber of Iran's second parliament emerged, vengeful and bloodied, yet more virulent manifestations of national expression.

Nationalism can be said to be the joint gift of Britain and Russia to the Iranian nation, and yet it was the people themselves who gropingly worked out what it meant to be modern and Iranian. Even before the Constitutional Revolution, and influenced by the romantic nationalisms of Europe, with their myth-making and redis-covery of long (and in many cases deservedly) forgotten heroes, a small number of influential Iranians had begun sifting symbols of the glorious past for beacons to light the national future. This too was in reaction to foreigners. Over the course of the nineteenth century, the activities of European archaeologists and explorers – energetic men in pith helmets picking their way through the Achaemenid ruins at Persepolis, or being lowered in baskets in order to decipher Old Persian cuneiform carved into the sheer limestone of the Zagros Mountains – had aroused first the puzzlement, then the interest, and finally the pride of these Iranians. The medium of photography enabled the country's ancient wonders to be seen by more people than had previously known of their existence, and in this way Iranians became aware of what their ancestors had been and what they had built.[84]

The new discovery of old greatness had complex effects on the nascent national sense. Much had been achieved, yes, but how far one had since fallen! In their mesmeric uniformity, the Achaemenid soldiers parading up the steps of the Apadana at Persepolis in perfectly drilled battalions were nothing if not a shattering reminder of the ill-disciplined rabble that all too often passed for a modern soldiery. The question was how to bring historic achievement into the service of the present.

On a personal level the Qajar shahs had actually started this process quite early. From the 1840s onwards, they had commissioned inscriptions and reliefs, inspired by the Achaemenids and Sasanians, which were cut into the rocks around Tehran and showed their prowess at war or in the saddle. To some of the mullahs such representations of the human form were an abomination and against Islam; but their disquiet was heeded only in the matter of an eques-trian statue whose heritage is traceable to the Bronze Horseman depicting Peter the Great in St Petersburg via the famous represen-tation of Muhammad Ali in Alexandria. Having commissioned this piece, Nasser al-Din ended up keeping it discreetly in his garden. It was later melted down, not for religious reasons, but competitive dynastic ones.

The historical point that needs to be made here is that Shia Islam and Arab culture were no longer being seen as contributory to the national sense, but inimical to it. On the contrary, it was the Persians' separate, pre-Islamic heritage that would supply the materials of national apartness.

Iran did not have many scholars who were capable of fashioning the older heritage into a new identity capable of withstanding the Europeans as well as the country's traditional cultural rivals. One of the few was the Babi dissident Agha Khan Kermani, who established himself in Istanbul in the late 1880s, from where he wrote pamphlets and articles in praise of Darwinism and modern science, and lambasted the Arabs. Although the cultures of Islam tend to emphasise the unifying force of religion over the divisive effects of race, there had for a long time been anti-Arab sentiments. One doesn't need to go very far into medieval Iranian poetry to come across spicy references to emaciated Arabs skulking around the desert as white-skinned Persians recline on divans sipping iced water. Kermani drew scornful contrast between the noble Aryans of the Iranian plateau and the savage 'lizard-eating' Arabs, in this way preparing for a lasting cultural divorce that would set up the Persians on a pedestal of their own.

Pride in ancient Iran and a growing sense of distinctness from the Arabs beyond the River Karun were two layers of Iranian identity that began to solidify in the early decades of the twentieth century. A third factor was literary. The constitutionalist lionheart Hassan Taqizadeh was among the first to understand the potency of the country's written heritage, and in particular that of the national epic, the *Shahnameh*, which details in relatively 'pure' (that is, un-Arabised) Persian the exploits of Iranian kings, both mythical and historical. During his second, much longer, period of exile lasting from 1910 to 1924, Taqizadeh and a group of like-minded émigrés produced what is now recognised as one of the most significant publications in the history of modern Iran. The name of this journal, *Kaveh*, itself had meaning. Kaveh the blacksmith was one of the few non-royal heroes in the *Shahnameh*, who raised a rebellion against the foreign demon Zahak in order to restore the legitimate Iranian monarch Fereydun – an event that was commemorated in a lithograph on the magazine's cover which showed the doughty blacksmith raising his apron in triumph.

A mixture of history, geography and politics, *Kaveh* contained some of the earliest writing by modern Iranians about their cultural heritage, in particular the Achaemenids and the Sasanians, as well as the pre-Islamic new year, Norooz, which falls on the spring equinox and is celebrated using elements that come from Zoroastrianism and other pre-Islamic beliefs. Inevitable reference was made to works of Western orientalist scholarship, not with the intention of denouncing their authors as part of a sinister plot of subjugation, but out of regret for the lack of Iranian researchers with similar competences and interests. Here a home-grown scholarly tradition, exploring and explaining the past to the present, was being held up as an essential feature of modern nationhood.

One of the most symbolic features of *Kaveh* was that each edition was dated according to the 'Yazdegerdi' year. Yazdegerd III was the last king of the Sasanians, defeated by the Arabs in the Battle of Ctesiphon, in what is now Iraq, in 637. This battle laid the Persian plateau open to the Arab armies, and within a few years the Sasanian Empire was completely destroyed and its leading figures scattered. The Yazdegerdi calendar was therefore a timepiece of humiliation, counting the years since the fall of the last legitimate Iranian king. Yet in this way Taqizadeh and his colleagues also showed their disdain for every Iranian dynasty that had ruled the country since the Islamic conquest – including the Qajars who now, in this period of accelerated change, were hurtling towards extinction.[85]

Of the three major dynasties of the Middle East, it was the oldest and most powerful – the house of Othman – that appeared to have best survived the ravages of the belle époque. Abdulhamid had stayed alive while Nasser al-Din had not; and the sultan had carefully caged the *éminence grise* behind his brother monarch's assassination in one of those waterfront villas that served so well as gilded prisons, where Sayyid Jamal al-Din Afghani eventually died in 1897. The sultan had likewise avoided the fates of his vassals in Egypt, with the Khedive Ismail spending his declining years in Constantinople, ever the high-roller (his parties were legendary), and the present ruler, Towfiq, squirming under the eye of Lord Cromer.

In truth, Abdulhamid was not as inept as his critics maintained, and thanks to improvements in infrastructure (railways, telegraphs and all-weather roads), and booming exports (not just foodstuffs and textiles but sought-after metals such as chrome, borax and manganese), economically the empire wasn't in bad shape at the turn of the century. For all the shame of suffering foreign mandarins to control the finances, the French-run Public Debt Commission established in 1881 had introduced efficiency and regularity to the lucky dip of Ottoman revenue collection, while British-run Egypt proved a more reliable tributary than Ismail's had been.

Even the Red Sultan's absolutism was less absolute than his opponents liked to claim. With the exception of Midhat Pasha's strangling, presumably on the sultan's orders, in 1884, Abdulhamid tended to exile his political opponents rather than kill them, creating what one historian has called an 'international cadre of elite enemies'.[86] All the while he skilfully played the international power game with the aim of blocking Balkan and Armenian nationalism – which, as we have seen, he was also prepared to use murderous force to suppress.

His major innovation in geopolitics was to outflank Britain and Russia by making friends with Germany, whose impulsive kaiser, Wilhelm II, did not tire of reiterating his esteem for the sultan-caliph and his worldwide following of Muslims, many of whom, in a show of Afghani-style pan-Islamism, helped fund that quintessential Turco-Germanic project, the Hejaz railway to Mecca. Also with German help, the sultan was able to begin constructing the first Middle Eastern army of real substance, as demonstrated in the brief Greek war of 1897, when Turkey's efficient, German-reformed infantry units, armed with the latest repeating Mausers, overwhelmed their inferior opponents before Russia intervened to impose an armistice.

But these puffs of achievement were of little consequence before a screaming gale of ill tidings. On a typical day the dispatches received at the Yildiz Palace from Abdulhamid's network of spies might tell of riots in Crete, plotting in Beirut, and a mutiny over back pay by army units in Mesopotamia. Even the empire's victories were occasion for more prying by the powers. In 1903 the sultan's vigorous suppression of a partisan uprising in Macedonia proved just the excuse Tsar Nicholas II and Emperor Franz Joseph of Austria–Hungary needed to impose an international gendarmerie to police the territory – another blot on the fairy tale of Ottoman sovereignty.

Unsurprisingly, given his obsessive micromanagement and advanced delusions over his own indispensability, the suspicious, inscrutable sultan himself was held responsible for the parlous state of affairs. In Paris groups of exiles known as the Young Turks schemed against him. They were divided between those, including Armenians, who welcomed European intervention as a necessary guarantee of reform, and others who vigorously opposed it as a loss of independence.

Ahmet Riza, a former Ministry of Agriculture official who had gone into exile in frustration at his inability to make headway in the imperial bureaucracy, was one of these dissidents, and his opposition newspaper *Mesveret* (meaning 'consultation', a word with clear parliamentary overtones) was smuggled into the empire much as Malkum Khan's *Qanun* had been brought into Iran before the Constitutional Revolution. On its pages the sultan was described variously as a hangman, scourge of God, bloody Majesty and wolf guarding the fold. The Young Turks drew particular inspiration from the revolution across the border, many of whose leading lights – Hassan Taqizadeh, for instance – were Azeri Turks with whom they shared much cultural and linguistic heritage.

The more radical of the Young Turks were certainly capable of equalling their Iranian counterparts when it came to shocking impiety. Ahmet Riza, for instance, had written to his sister, 'were I a woman, I would embrace atheism and never become a Muslim ... keep this religion away from me'. Another influential dissident, Abdullah Cevdet, anticipated Taqizadeh's famous pro-Western sentiments when he declared, 'the West is our teacher; to love it is to love science, progress, material and moral advancement ... to be an industrious and thankful disciple of the West – that is our lot!'[87]

Riza and Cevdet were among a group of Young Turks who came together in 1907 to set up a revolutionary society called the Committee for Union and Progress, or CUP, which adopted a secretive cellular model and required its adepts to pledge their lives over a sword and the Quran.[88] The committee's demand that the sultan revive the constitution exercised a strong appeal on Turkish army officers staring morosely into their raki in Macedonia (where the humiliation of foreign supervision was most keenly felt) and the cafe-hopping Parisian exiles alike. All were in agreement that to fail to arrest the decline of the empire would lead ineluctably to its death, and that the spirit of entente created by the Anglo-Russian accord, which had already led to the bombardment of the Iranian parliament, would strangle the Ottomans too. In the summer of 1908, the sense of imminent catastrophe was compounded by reports that the tsar's fleet was manoeuvring along Turkey's Black Sea coast.

The Turkish revolution began at the end of June with the flight of some two hundred officers and men into the hills of Macedonia. As the mutinies spread a CUP telegram to Yildiz attached a demand to the agitation: the constitution must be restored. Few of the rebels can have anticipated the sultan's surprising response to their demands; rather than reject this challenge to the autocracy he had spent the past three decades carefully constructing, Abdulhamid made out that the constitution's revival had been his ardent wish all along. On 24 July he announced parliament's recall, the abolition of censorship, and an amnesty for political prisoners. The embodiment of Ottoman despotism could now take the credit for its dismantlement.

Following the emperor's announcement there was a brief pause in Istanbul while people took the measure of events – followed by the delirium of a city that thought it had found a panacea for all evils. A few days into the revolution the feminist writer Halide Edib entered the city, where 'the scene on the [Galata] bridge caught me at once ... the tradition of centuries seemed to have lost its effect'. In 1798 Napoleon had tried and failed to persuade the people of Cairo to don the symbol of the French Revolution, the tricolour cockade; now, by contrast, swilling over the Golden Horn, was a 'sea of men and women all cockaded in red and white' (the colours of the Ottoman flag). Distinctions of sex seemed to have been abandoned, as 'men and women in a common wave of enthusiasm moved on, radiating something extraordinary, laughing, weeping in such intense emotion that human deficiency and ugliness were for the time completely obliterated ... it looked like the millennium'.[89]

The contrast that the revolution offered from the old arrangements was certainly dramatic. There was the unaccustomed sight of men standing on chairs on street corners and addressing anyone in earshot, and Edib noted a delegation of butchers issuing solemnly from the Sublime Porte, whither they had gone to assure themselves of the permanence of the new regime, to which they had in a matter of just a few hours become passionately attached. An old man swore to sacrifice all he held dear for the 'sacred cause'.[90] But what did he know of this cause? Not very much, in all probability, and Edib wrote tellingly of an exchange between the influential committee member and future educator Riza Tevfik, who rode about the place keeping order (Abdulhamid's police had slunk back into the shadows), and some illiterate porters. 'Tell us what the constitution means,' the porters yelled. Tevfik replied, 'Constitution is such a great thing that those who do not know it are donkeys.' 'We are donkeys!' the porters roared back good-naturedly.[91]

It was hardly surprising that there was confusion over how to define the new words that were being bandied about; ambiguities invariably abound in the wake of popular regime change. Debtors thought 'constitution' meant the remission of debts. Labourers thought it meant the doubling of wages. Customers of the Bosporus steamship company confused it with free passage across the straits. One woman refused to pay the toll when crossing the Galata Bridge. 'Have we not liberty now?' she demanded. A Muslim who was condemned to death for killing a Christian considered this, too, an affront to his new freedom. Porters on the waterfront struck for workers' rights. Everywhere people refused to pay their taxes.[92]

The importance of the Turkish revolution was not lost on Ottoman neighbours who were fighting their own constitutional battles. On 4 August 1908, news of the overthrow of Turkish despotism reached the constitutionalists of Tabriz, then suffering the effects of a siege by royalists and their Russian allies, and placards appeared declaring that for the freedom-loving Tabrizis 'the Sultan would be as good a sovereign as the Shah'.[93]

The continued success of Sultan Abdulhamid's legerdemain depended on maintaining the impression that the new parliament was his gift, and when he inaugurated its first session, on 17 December 1908, he duly congratulated his people on having attained the political maturity that had allowed him to restore it. 'I have directed my efforts to promoting progress in all parts of the country,' ran the sultan's rhetorical pat on his own back; 'thanks to God, this end has been attained and, owing to the propagation of public instruction, the degree of culture in all classes of our population is increased.'[94]

Like its short-lived forebear, the chamber was a reflection of the empire's cosmopolitanism: it contained 140 Turks, 60 Arabs, 25 Albanians, 23 Greeks, 12 Armenians, 5 Jews, 4 Bulgarians, 3 Serbs and 1 Vlach. But the vision of unity in diversity that had brought the inhabitants of Istanbul onto the streets at the beginning of the revolution – with the sultan, the Committee of Union and Progress and Ottoman subjects of all stripes ganging purposefully together – was immediately exposed as an illusion. In the aftermath of 8 June the newly liberated got down to politics.

As had been the case with Iran, the forces in Turkey were arrayed at different points along a line between secularism and the sharia, with the monarch shifting position carefully according to short-term advantage, but in the long run siding with the reactionaries. The difference with Iran at the equivalent moment in its revolution was that Turkey already had a constitution, the notoriously conservative document of 1876, whose fifth clause declared the sultan to be sacred and unaccountable.

The CUP put a novel gloss on this clause, which, according to them, meant that Abdulhamid was above politics and could not be burdened with responsibility. And the new parliament, over which the CUP had much influence, soon gave notice of an unwonted radicalism of spirit.

In Ahmet Riza, the president of the chamber, many Ottoman Muslims saw a future unfixed from the frame of Islam, embodied in this positivist half-breed (his mother was Bavarian) who alluded to his opponents as 'wretches'.[95] The sultan courted the radicals by wining and dining them at the Yildiz (personally helping Riza to his favourite mineral water), but they threw back his hospitality and offered public criticisms of the royal personage that were without precedent. When money was found to have disappeared from a fund raised through a bazaar at the Yildiz, one deputy thundered: 'This money has been stolen and squandered, and the responsibility lies with the highest personages in the empire.' Another recommended that the sultan hand over his palaces to compensate the people for the millions he had squeezed out of them. (This suggestion did not get far, but the civil list was cut, as it had been in Iran.) All the while, the rampant CUP conducted a massive purge of royalist elements. 'Bureaucrats and clerks are being fired everywhere,' the CUP organ, *Tanin*, trumpeted, and the newly liberated press casually branded hundreds of employees of the imperial administration as spies.[96]

For all the CUP's vigour, however, Turks' first experience of modern politics did not lead to unanimity over what kind of place they wanted to live in, and the task of forging a consensus was further retarded by repeated humiliations on the diplomatic front. If Iran's constitutionalists could claim that the Anglo-Russian Accord was the enemy of domestic reform, creating instability and ultimately leading to General Liakhoff's bombardment of the parliament, things were almost as bad for the Ottomans, whose polity was shrinking before their eyes as the empire's peripheries continued to prise themselves away from Istanbul.

Over a few ghastly days in October 1908, Bulgaria's Prince Ferdinand declared that he was henceforth tsar of an independent nation, Austria annexed Bosnia–Herzegovina (still officially an Ottoman province), and Crete announced union with Greece. Taste the fruits of constitutionalism! the Young Turks' opponents crowed – and the backlash began.

It was some months in coming – during which an organisation of pious Muslims, the Society of Muhammad, denounced the CUP for deviating from the sharia, and its mouthpiece, the newspaper *Volkan*, raged that along with the incessant cries of 'Long Live Liberty!' none of their opponents was to be heard shouting 'Long Live Islam!' At the same time, the army rank and file were seething at new Prussian-style discipline that made no allowance for the call for prayer; they also reviled CUP measures to cut their number in the name of economy. Objections were raised to the proliferation of theatres attended by women and to the establishment of a girls' school on the Bosporus – this too was religiously impermissible, the hardliners maintained.[97]

As Sheikh Fazlullah Nuri had done in Tehran, the Society of Muhammad demanded that legislation be compatible with the sharia, with many others – ordinary soldiers, fearful for their future; widows and orphans, regretting the sultan's diminished largesse; religious students – adding their voices to a growing murmur of dissatisfaction. Even the feminist Halide Edib was critical of the CUP's disdain for views other than its own – though she continued to contribute articles on women's emancipation to *Tanin*, in defiance of death threats. In the meantime the Society of Muhammad continued to grow, setting up branches in provincial towns as the CUP had done. In this way the Ottomans got their first experience, however unruly, of party politics.

Upon assuming power – but not office; they were never more than a government within a government – the Young Turks had taken the telegraph office at the Yildiz out of commission, in this way cutting the sultan out of the intelligence loop that had been his virtual monopoly. All the while, units of the CUP were set up around the country; and thus the CUP became arguably the first modern political party in the Middle East. But a reaction was gathering force. A preacher called Blind Ali led a crowd to the rambling palace complex of the Yildiz, where the sultan appeared at his window. 'We want a shepherd!' the crowd cried; 'a flock cannot exist without a shepherd!' A pious journal declared that photography was nothing but heresy.[98]

The counter-revolution began on 13 April 1909, when officers in Istanbul were overwhelmed by a revolt in the ranks. Within a few hours, thousands of soldiers and NCOs had convened on the parliament building, where they were joined by a flotsam of religious students and junior imams. To the ominous accompaniment of trumpet blasts from the square outside, parliament received a delegation of *ulema*, accompanied by armed soldiers, which harangued the deputies. The rebels' demands included the restoration of the sharia, the removal of CUP ministers and the cashiering of many officers – and as if to ram home their point the mob outside lynched a deputy who had been trying to enter the chamber.

Over the next few days there was more terror. Ministers were assassinated. Progressive newspapers were sacked (including *Tanin*). Officers were killed by their soldiers in their homes and in front of their families. The pro-CUP captain of an imperial cruiser was brought in an open carriage to the Yildiz, where he was murdered in the sultan's presence.

Abdulhamid is not thought to have been behind the counter-revolution, but he was not slow to take advantage. After the nightmare of CUP rule, pro-monarchy loyalists took over the government and the key army and navy ministries. Regional governors were informed by telegraph that the sharia had duly been restored. One might as well forget all about the constitution – it was as if the Tanzimat reforms had never taken place.

But in true revolutionary fashion, fortune swung back again. The mutineers had overplayed their hand. The retribution had been too hard, and the CUP sought revenge of their own. From Macedonia, a force of Young Turks set out to subdue the sultan. The leaderless rabble that had taken over the city were no match for General Mahmud Shevket Pasha and his new Action Army, which stormed the capital on 24 April, and was stopped only by the royal guard at the Yildiz, which had been fortified for just such a contingency.

'At sunset,' wrote one eyewitness, 'when the flag was hauled down, the shout of *padshahim tchok yasha* ("Long Live the King!") showed that Abdul-Hamid still reigned, but when darkness descended on the scene there began along all the roads that converged on the Yildiz a sinister rattle and rumble that lasted without intermission all night long. It was the rattle and rumble of the advancing Macedonian cannon.'

Caged in his palace, abandoned by his servants and his sons (the eunuchs and the ladies subsided into hysterics), Abdulhamid had no alternative the following morning but to receive the parliamentary delegation that was sent to inform him of his impending fate. Two days later the parliament that had been terrorised reconvened to deprive Abdulhamid of his throne.[99] He was exiled to Salonica, a city he hated because it was the birthplace of the subversion that had been his undoing, and where he occupied himself with cabinetmaking (he was a skilled carpenter) and fondling his angora cat. In 1912 he was brought back to Istanbul, where he died six years later, bitter and unlamented – an autocrat who, although he had been much more exposed to Western ideas of modernity than his contemporary Nasser al-Din Shah, was in the end no better equipped to fend them off. Modernity was relative, in any case, as the Irish journalist Francis McCullagh indicated in his posthumous assessment of the sultan: 'as is the case with Nicholas the Second, he was probably in advance of his predecessors, but his people had progressed so much owing to the infiltration of western ideas that he seemed retrograde'.[100]

The strange events of 1908–9 in Istanbul provide another proof of the folly of expecting a chaotically modernising society to attain political 'maturity' overnight. At the beginning of this period the

Ottomans found themselves thrust into the soft sands of democratic politics, and at the end of it they were still searching for their footing. In the summer of 1908 security was provided by the constitution. In April 1909 it was the sharia – not only for the mutineers, but also for many other Ottoman Muslims, who worried that everything they held dear was in the process of disintegrating. This is not as illogical as it might seem. The public understanding of these concepts was limited, but both, because they were spoken of with reverence and ascribed mighty powers, gave the impression of a superhuman agency floating above the people and able to right all that was wrong with their lives. It is no accident that much of the poetry that has been composed in praise of democracy, rights and constitutional politics conveys the same sense of bliss and ecstasy that one finds in religious texts. Both answer to a yearning for a solution to the emptiness that is part of the human condition. So it went with the Turkish revolutionaries. Demonstrating the fickleness of their attachment to phrases that promise more than they can deliver, the people flew from the constitution to Islamic law and back again without being aware of the inconsistency that this suggests to a modern sensibility. A similar oscillation happened in Egypt during the Arab Spring of 2011, and it will no doubt happen again when a pious society trampolines from entrapment to liberty, and liberty disappoints. After all, a constitution is only a document. The sharia is only law. In order to be worked into a means for ordering society, both require wisdom and ingenuity of an order that, in 1910, no Turkish leader possessed.

During the nineteenth century, as we have seen, the Ottoman Empire's Christian subjects used the examples set by modern European nationalisms to press for rights and autonomy. Over the same period the empire's Muslim leaders continued to insist on the viability of an exotic big yurt arrangement called Ottomanism. This was a direct descendant of the view that the early Arabian Muslims had espoused when they, a tiny minority, had set out to conquer millions of subjects of the Persian and Roman empires in the middle of the seventh century. It allowed for the coexistence under Islamic law of Muslims and non-Muslims, with the Muslims in control – a power structure that was in the Ottoman case surmounted by the person of the sultan-caliph. As early as the reign of Mahmud II, however, and then deepening in complexity with the Tanzimat reforms, the Ottoman government had undermined their own supremacy over this arrangement by granting rights to non-Muslims.

If the minorities were becoming more privileged, and even gaining access to the corridors of power (in the early years of the twentieth century the Ottoman cabinet contained Armenian members), then why did benign Ottomanism fail? The answer is that it wasn't a secular idea; and in the modern world secular labels, not religious ones, were being adopted as a means of identification and separation. The powers defined themselves as national not religious states, and this secularisation of identity was transmitted to the sultan's Christian subjects, with the Greeks, Bulgarians and Armenians agitating for political independence over and above the religious independence they already enjoyed. Eventually the nationalist contagion reached the sultan's other non-Turkish-speaking Muslim subjects, and Constantinople became home to revolutionary cells not only from the Balkans and Armenia, but also from Syria, Kurdistan and Albania.

The empire's core group, the Turks, were left to figure out where they fitted in. That the 'Turks' were a nebulous sort of group anyway, sometimes unkindly defined as the dregs of the Muslim peasantry, and genetically compromised after centuries of miscegenation with Iranians, Arabs, Kurds, Armenians and Greeks; that their culture went from the earthy and often idolatrous utterances of the mountain herdsman to the pedantry and piety of the Pasha in his braids; that the Turkish 'look' ranged from blue-eyed Salonican blonds to moon-faced steppe-folk and swarthy Middle Eastern types – these considerations were secondary in the view of those Ottoman Muslims who, at the turn of the twentieth century, realised that a world of nations was engulfing them and that they hadn't one of their own. The Armenians had political parties that were agitating for autonomy and independence. The Greeks had a new country founded on memories of the old. So (as of 1908) did the Bulgarians. All had national languages, songs, myths. Why not the Turks?

The man who answered this question, and in doing so set the parameters of the future Turkish nation, was Ziya Gokalp, a quiet, modest, intermittently inflamed south-easterner. He was 'fat, short,

and very dark', in the account of his friend Halide Edib, with a forehead that bore 'a mark like the sign of the cross ... which caught
one's attention at once'. This, she went on laconically, was the residue
of a 'bullet which he had tried to lodge in his brain at twenty, but
whose effect he had somehow survived'.[101] Ziya's youthful suicide
attempt has been blamed on the early death of his father Tevfik and
the subsequent efforts of his uncle, a man of religion called Hasip
Efendi, to force him to marry his daughter Cevriye rather than go to
Constantinople to complete his studies. It can also be seen more
broadly as the climax of a disorderly childhood that left him existen-
tially adrift.

He was born in 1875, the eve of the empire's tumultuous year of
three sultans, and the son and grandson of civil servants in Diyarbakir,
the administrative centre of south-eastern Anatolia. For much of its
history this ancient city famed for its basalt walls had been ruled by
Arabs and Persians; now, three centuries after it had been brought
under Ottoman control, its biggest communities were Kurds and
Armenians. Ziya was brought up knowing the Kurdish language, and
he was probably at least partly Kurdish – an awkward position from
which to launch a project of Turkish nationhood, but far from irre-
trievable, as a passionate nationalism often grows strongest in the
breasts of the ethnically 'impure'. Before he died, his father instilled
in the young Ziya a love of reading, an attachment to Namik Kemal
and a sense of the cultural dilemma that bedevilled all educated
Muslims in the age of rampant nationalism. This was exemplified by
an exchange between Tevfik and his friends when a decision needed
to be made over whether to send Ziya abroad to study. 'I am afraid,'
Tevfik confided, 'that in Europe he might become a *gavur* (unbeliever).'
One of the friends asked, 'What will happen if he stays here?' Tevfik
replied: 'He will become an ass.'[102]

For the young orphan, voracious and sensitive, growing up in
Diyarbakir was both inspiring and confusing. In this remote outpost,
rubbing against the empire's Iranian and Russian neighbours, he was
able to learn Arabic, Persian and French, besides conversing in his
native Turkish and Kurdish, and, presumably, knowing some words
of Armenian. Hasip Efendi taught him Islamic philosophy and the
religious sciences, while from the notorious CUP atheist and physician
Abdullah Cevdet, who was sent to Diyarbakir in 1892 to help deal

with a cholera epidemic, he received a no doubt unflinching lesson in the imperative of progress and the perils of backwardness.

Cevdet must have been something of a freak in turn-of-the-century Diyarbakir, where religion of one kind or another permeated almost everything. The CUP activist believed that opponents of Darwinian theory – turbaned and otherwise – should have their heads smashed, and a few years later he did not hide his euphoria when the first Turkish aviator was killed, because it was proof that the Turks were approaching European levels of fearless enquiry. 'When the European explorers went to the Arctic,' Cevdet wrote, 'and their aviators flew in the skies, we used to laugh at them and say, "Look how these stupid Europeans get themselves eaten by polar bears and blown to pieces in plane crashes." We did not realise that by these "stupid" acts they realised their domination over the world. Now our men too have begun to crash. This is not something to grieve over. We must rejoice! For me, it is the sign that we are regenerating and that we shall not die!'[103]

Not surprisingly, Hasip Efendi forbad Ziya to see this dangerous freethinker, but the meetings went on – and with happy results, for it was Cevdet who saved Ziya's life after the latter's suicide attempt. Another medical man, the Greek Orthodox Dr Yorgis, opened Ziya's mind to Western philosophy, while his mystical inclinations – he was a devotee of the medieval Sufi poets Ibn Arabi and Rumi – lit still another possible path between the poles of religion and reason that his father had identified.

The crises that followed on from this impossibly conflicted upbringing wound about Ziya's adolescence and led to 'insomnia which continued for several years and left me almost a skeleton. I did not have any organic disease, nor had I any social discomfort. The source of my trouble was my thoughts. I used to believe that if I were able to reach what I called the Great Truth, I would be relieved from all pain. But where could I find it?'[104]

In 1896 he went to Constantinople, again in the teeth of his uncle's opposition, where he enrolled at the veterinary college (the only institution of higher learning that offered free board and tuition), and was soon donating what little money he had to the underground CUP. He read Léon Cahun's *Introduction à l'Histoire de l'Asie*, a work of orientalist scholarship that describes in epic terms the westward spread of the Turks and Mongols; and he met up again with Dr Yorgis, who had settled in Constantinople and who encouraged him to carry out a thorough sociological examination of the Turkish people, the better to align the coming revolution with their needs. In this way a Frenchman and a Greek began teaching a presumed Kurd the significance of being a Turk.

In 1897 Ziya was arrested by Abdulhamid's secret police; his year-long incarceration, he wrote, 'delivered me for ever from my psychological depressions'.[105] After his release he was exiled back to Diyarbakir, where he finally married Cevriye and settled down; he continued to read French philosophers, psychologists and sociologists. Ziya's public career appeared to be over before it had begun – until Abdulhamid's downfall presented him with unexpected opportunities to expose his ideas. In 1909 he received a fateful invitation to attend the congress of the CUP in Salonica, half a continent away on the Aegean Sea.

For centuries this much coveted port city had been considered the epitome of Ottoman diversity. Within its walls Iberian Jews (descendants of families that had been expelled during the Inquisition), Christians and Muslims (some of them actually secret Sabbateans, followers of a Jewish messianic figure who had been persecuted in the seventeenth century) had coexisted, if not with love, then for the most part without hate.

By the time Ziya got there, however, Salonica's religious patchwork was being unpicked by national identity. It was becoming of supreme importance whether one spoke Bulgarian, Greek, Vlach or Armenian, and whether one supported the Slavic claim to Macedonia (the Ottoman provinces of Salonica, Monastir and Uskub), or that made by the Greeks. All the while, partisans of Zionism were in town spreading the revolutionary idea of the Jews as a modern nation. 'The Turkish people have proven their spirit of tolerance for religions,' argued one such proselytiser among the city's Jews, Vladimir Jabotinsky, on a visit to the city in 1908. 'When they will learn that nationality has also to be tolerated, they will also respect this.'[106]

From this seedbed of nationalisms – where Ottomanism had no more of a future than it did back in south-eastern Anatolia – Ziya sent up shoots of his own. Overcoming his natural shyness and a conspicuous Diyarbakir accent, he quickly impressed the CUP high command with his obvious intelligence and wide reading, and he was elected to the party's powerful central council, becoming a good friend of the future grand vizier Mehmed Talat Pasha. Settling in the city, he gave private classes on the French sociologists Gabriel Tarde and Gustave Le Bon, who were endeavouring to understand the instincts of the masses, and he was appointed teacher of sociology at the city's main secondary school – which made him probably the first teacher of the new science in the Ottoman Empire.

Salonica was a living experiment in the formation of new collective identities and it prompted Ziya to abandon Ottomanism. In this crucible of nations he started to develop the ideas that would grow into a powerful ideology to rival those of the Greeks, Slavs and Zionists – and which could, like theirs, be used to advance claims to exclusive identities and territory. The name of this ideology was Turkism, and it would be indissolubly linked to the somewhat withdrawn pamphleteer and journalist who in 1911 began to use the symbolic pen name 'Gokalp' by which he is known today. This word is composed of the Turkish words for 'sky' and 'hero', and it expresses a longing for the steppe from which all Turks – Ottoman and otherwise – had originally sprung.

According to Ziya, one of the factors acting against the emergence of a coherent Turkish nation was localism. Watching the empire's successful minorities, he noted an enviably broad-based solidarity that had helped them acquire economic and social power (Greek bankers, for instance, numbered among the richest men in the empire). For the Turks, he wrote, 'notions of solidarity, patriotism and heroism did not transcend the confines of the family, the village, and the town'.[107] As a result, in crafts, trade and finance, the Turks were not as powerful as the minorities.

Ziya's fascination for Turkish myths and folklore would have been easily understood by the European Romantics. He considered the everyday language and customs of ordinary Turkish people to be distinct from the artificial overlay of Ottoman civilisation and expressive of a noble culture spanning the whole of the Turkic world. He named this world Turan, as it is called in the Iranian epic the *Shahnameh* (though for Iranian nationalists such as Hassan Taqizadeh the word had negative connotations, evoking a kind of eternal enemy in the steppe to the north). He even toyed with the idea of a cultural union extending throughout Central Asia.

Ziya's first concrete proposals towards forming a nation concerned the Turkish language itself. Even after the changes initiated in the 1850s and 60s by Ibrahim Sinasi, this schizophrenic tongue continued to divide Turks into two mutually unintelligible populations. The first was made up of metropolitan Turks speaking Ottoman – a blend of Turkish, Arabic and Persian, increasingly seasoned with French. The second was the everyday, earthy Turkish of the common people. In Ziya's view the aim should be a hostile takeover of the first by the second that would produce a simple language reflective of the Turkish experience but enabled through acquisition to deal with science and religion. It was essential to get rid of Arabic and Persian words if there existed a Turkish equivalent; outbreaks of foreign grammar (the Arabic plural, for instance) must be stamped out. If words for modern concepts could not be found among the existing stock, new ones should be invented.[108]

Although the mature Ziya was not a particularly religious man, he regarded Islam as an important part of national identity and the translation he made of the Quran into Turkish was probably more a patriotic than a religious gesture, designed to entrench Turkish in sacred as well as secular life. Like Jamal al-Din Afghani, Ziya the moderniser also believed that Islam needed to go through a reformation of the kind that had allowed Europe's Protestant nations to advance and which would inevitably separate the religious and public spheres.

Such ideas were clearly anathema to the Islamists who emerged as Ziya's adversaries when the extent of his nationalist project became apparent. For them the very notion of a human identity that venerated artefacts from the pre-Islamic past was grotesque; the last thing they wanted was for a community of so-called 'Turks' to set itself up as a rival to the *umma*. Nationalism, thundered the Islamist scholar Ahmed Naim, was a 'foreign innovation as deadly to the body of Islam as cancer is to man ... at a time when the enemy has set foot on our breasts it is madness to divide Islam into nationalities'. And he scoffed at those bogus nationalists 'in whose veins not a single drop of Turkish blood remains ... to learn the Turk's past is not needed'.[109]

The final pillar of Ziya's tripartite conception of nationhood was 'civilisation', by which he meant Western civilisation, and which he – in common with other Middle Eastern modernisers – believed should be adopted in its entirety. 'For us today,' he wrote, 'modernisation means to make use of the battleships that the Europeans are making and using.' Only when the Turks no longer needed to import knowledge and goods from Europe could they consider themselves truly modern.

Nowadays it seems obvious that Ziya's three components of Turkishness – language, religion, civilisation – would end up fighting and cannibalising each other. But he himself saw no contradiction, and in an article published in 1913 he concluded a virtuoso summation of the national condition with the bald statement, 'the Turkish nation belongs to the Ural-Altai [language] group of peoples, to the Islamic *umma*, and to Western internationality'.[110]

By the eve of the First World War, Ziya stood at the height of Turkish intellectual and national life. Political adversity and human suffering had helped turn the jottings of a provincial intellectual into the most potent political philosophy of the time. The calamity that pushed nationalism to the forefront of Turkish life began with another Balkan conflagration – this one so consuming that it all but ended the Ottoman presence in Europe.

The fighting started in March 1912, when Bulgaria, Serbia, Greece and Montenegro ganged up against their former Ottoman master. Provinces which had been Ottoman for five centuries fell in weeks; Bulgaria and Greece raced each other to Salonica (the Greeks got there first); Albania declared independence. Thousands of Balkan Muslims were slaughtered and hundreds of thousands were driven towards Constantinople with the Bulgarians on their heels. A British diplomat who observed the Ottoman flight wrote, 'the track of the invading Bulgarian army is marked by 80 miles of ruined villages'.[111] In general, however, there was little sympathy in Western capitals for Muslim suffering.

The Ottoman capital, seething with refugees, was saved by a heroic counter-offensive and the stressed Bulgarian supply lines. But the fighting led to 34,000 Ottoman casualties. 'The Bulgar, the Serb, the Greek,' wrote one of Ziya's fellow Turkists in the stunned aftermath, 'our subjects of five centuries, whom we have despised, have defeated us.'[112]

The Balkan debacle was the beginning of Turkey's 'long Great War', which would see it strike an opportunistic alliance with the

Kaiser's Germany and end up forfeiting its Arab lands and, briefly, Istanbul itself. The Great War was the moment when the Turks came of age as a modern nation, congregating, huddled but defiant, on the soil of Anatolia.

The man who crystallised these intentions was an Ottoman war hero from Salonica called Mustafa Kemal – who would later call himself Atatürk. In May 1919, following the invasion of Anatolia by the victorious allies, he slipped away from Istanbul to raise a nationalist army from the remnants of Ottoman forces. When his ship sailing eastwards along the Black Sea was checked for smuggled goods by the occupying British, he reportedly muttered that they were 'fools ... we are not taking contraband or arms, but faith and determination. But they cannot appreciate a nation's love of independence.'[113] Four years later, having proved his point by driving out the British and the other occupying powers, the government that Atatürk had set up signed the Treaty of Lausanne with the Allies, delineating the extent of a new Turkish Republic in place of the defunct Ottoman Empire. The irony was that Atatürk had achieved in a few months what the powers had been trying to do for centuries, in the process definitively answering the 'Eastern question'. But Atatürk was the quintessential modern nation-builder and he did not regret the empire.

An important chronicler of the rise of the Turkish nation over the long Great War was Halide Edib. Following the revolution of 1908 she had grown disenchanted with the CUP, but her national feeling, in common with that of many other Turks, had not abated. Far from it; in the wake of the Balkan humiliation of October 1912 –when Istanbul was a refugee camp, Haghia Sophia a cholera infirmary, and men lay dying in the ice-bound mosque yards – she directed achingly intense feelings towards what we would recognise as a national identity built on an attachment to land and fellowship. The futuristic novel she wrote during this grim period, which was called *The New Turan* and described an awakening of Turkish sentiment from Istanbul to Mongolia, made her famous. She was called 'mother of the Turks' by her fellow nationalists and several cafes were given the name The New Turan to cash in on the book's popularity.[114]

A passage from Edib's memoir showed how the privations of that terrible winter galvanised national feeling: the identity formulated by Ziya Gokalp was becoming flesh.[115] In the aftermath of the Balkan defeat Edib would go each day to a small hospital to care for the wounded soldiers. She would bring newspapers to the invalids despite the fact that they reported only disaster, and put on a brave face for the benefit of the soldiers – for she knew 'how those Anatolian eyes would look at me, proud in spite of the tragic curiosity and anxiety in their childish depths'.

A man from Ankara stayed in her mind, she wrote, a 'symbol of the Anatolia of those days. He must once have been a fine specimen of manly beauty. He had those dark greenish eyes and long lashes and the tall physique of his region, but now he had turned into a huge skeleton. He had gone from Albania to Yemen, and after seven years of it he had been sent home some three months ago, broken with malaria and hardship, his intelligence almost extinguished. Hardly had he arrived in Constantinople when he was sent to the Balkan front.'

Now this smashed and splintered man needed repair. His heart was in no state to bear chloroform, and the operation was to happen without anaesthetic. The doctor, Edib reported, 'made him understand that he was not to move his leg during the operation'. As the doctor cut and incised, the brave soldier 'remained rigid, as if he were a piece of unyielding iron. He closed his eyes, clenched his teeth, and lay as still as a dead man crushing my hand, which he always humbly asked to hold in his.'

It was then, in that moment of intimacy as close as any bond of blood, that Edib 'saw how an ordinary Turkish soldier who has lost all except his sense of manhood bears pain'. And the moment of recovery, when she felt that he would be all right, was linked to the land itself. 'During the last days of his convalescence,' she wrote, 'he recovered his memory and interest in life to a certain degree, and got me to write his letters to his village. He was going back and wanted his fields got ready for barley sowing.' In her recollection of the event, Edib elevated the convergence of her humanity with that of an uneducated man – and their shared concern for the future of the land – into the symbolic birth of a nation.

That winter she realised 'the extent of my affection and love for my people and my land. I cannot make out which I loved best, but I felt my love was … incurable and had nothing to do with ideas, thoughts, or politics, that in fact it was physical and elemental.' Crossing Sultan Ahmed Square she contemplated 'with infinite sadness of an alien army marching toward it. I had a foolish desire to stoop and kiss the very stones of the place, so passionately did I love it. No force could have dragged me away from Constantinople. I belonged to the place, and whatever its fate, I meant to share it.'[116]

This unaffected and spontaneous spinning of threads between Halide Edib and her fellow man, as she places one person in relation to another, standing on the same land, is almost unbearably moving. The feeling is noble; the narrator is interested in elevating the individual rather than bringing him down. And yet raising someone to a position of pride and ownership almost always involves lowering someone else, a rule for which it is possible, in events that took place just three years later on the Anatolian littoral, to find one of history's most hideous examples.

In 1915 Ziya Gokalp's old friend from Salonican days, Mehmed Talat Pasha, who was serving as interior minister, ordered the mass deportation of the Armenians of Asia Minor. Here was a community that had inhabited Anatolia long before the Turks, and which had intermittently prospered under Ottomanism. But the Armenians had become conscious of being a modern nation before the Turks. Long before tsarist Russia – Turkey's foe in the First World War – promised them an independent Armenia if they helped it defeat the Ottoman army, the yearning for an independent home in Anatolia had grown in Armenian hearts.

The deportations began in May and it did not take long for Talat's claim that the Armenians would be safely escorted to new homes far from the Russian front to be exposed as fraudulent. At least a million people died in death marches and massacres over that spring and summer, and the age-old Armenian presence in Asia Minor was all but eradicated. Young Armenian women were forcibly converted; the Armenians' farms and homes were taken over by their Kurdish and Turkish neighbours. Generations later, the consensus among many historians and jurists – disputed by the Turks, of course – is that what happened in 1915 was genocide.

It is easy to see how the sufferings of Ottoman Muslims in 1912 clarified the patriotic feelings of people like Halide Edib. But shared culpability can be as effective a nation-builder as shared suffering, and for decades after 1915 the modern Turkish state never admitted the character or scale of the Armenian outrages. Ziya Gokalp, founder of modern Turkishness, supported the treatment that was meted out against the Armenians. So did Halide Edib. So did Atatürk. Everyone did, for the nascent Turkish nation had convinced itself that killing off the Armenians was a condition of its own survival.

In this way, amid war and revolution, nationhood came to the Middle East. For the Iranians, in conceptual terms, the process was relatively simple. It involved plucking attractive fruit from the branches of pre-Islam while at the same time carrying on with the same Shia beliefs and practices that set the majority of the inhabitants of the Persian plateau apart from their Sunni neighbours. And it involved continuing to speak Persian. For those modernists who took the opportunity to turn their backs on religion – like Taqizadeh and Kasravi – this too could be presented as an expression of national self-regard. For them, the religion they were rejecting was a reminder of Arab achievement and Iran's subjugation in the Islamic conquests of the seventh century. The point of nationhood was to feel more Persian – to luxuriate in the culture of one's forefathers, not that of one's forefathers' conquerors. Finally, in letting go of Arab culture and getting closer to that of the West, these Persians were advancing their other objectives which were to be modern and free.

For modern Turks like Atatürk much of the above held true, even if the blocks of identity needed much work before they would fit together to form a nation. An important stay on nationhood had been the historic responsibility of the Ottoman sultan to provide leadership to the worldwide community of Muslims, which was naturally incompatible with the wholesale rejection of Arab culture and language. But with defeat and dismemberment in the First World War, and in default of the old sprawling Ottoman expanse, a neat, compact, logical and ethnically cleansed Turkish nation came into being – feeling Turkish (Atatürk's school books disseminated an extreme Gokalpianism) and separated from its neighbours by the Turkish language. (Again, Atatürk's cultural policies were responsible; his teachers taught only in Turkish, even in polyglot Diyarbakir.) In the 1920s Atatürk abolished the Ottoman dynasty and the caliphate. This severed the Turks from their former Arab subjects. In 1928 the Arabic script was replaced with the Roman one, and other,

Gokalp-inspired measures of linguistic rationalisation were implemented with the aim of distancing the people from their multilingual
past. Atatürk, that freethinking, card-playing Salonican soak (as his
adversaries considered him), even decreed that the call to prayer
should be sung out in Turkish.

For the third and largest of the region's groups, the Arabs, a lot
of this cultural spring-cleaning was neither possible nor desirable.
Nationalism could hardly involve the negation of Islam, for that
would amount to self-negation. Islam was the supreme contribution
of the Arabs to humanity, and the Quran was its moral and literary
seed. As a result, few modernisers in Egypt or elsewhere in the
Arab world turned their backs on Islam. While reformers in Turkey
and Iran thought about it less and less, in Egypt they thought about
it more and more. If the horse and cart of modernity and nationhood could not be driven around Islam, it would have to be driven
through.

Sheikh Muhammad Abduh (1849–1905), whom we met earlier in his
role as an acolyte of Sayyid Jamal al-Din Afghani and a participant in
the Urabi uprising, was the man who worked tirelessly to effect this
tricky manoeuvre. Abduh and Afghani had gone their separate ways
after their shared exile in Paris, for reasons that have been lost, and
in 1888, after a spell as a schoolteacher in Beirut, the younger man
was accepted by the Khedive Towfiq back into Egypt, where he
re-entered government service as a provincial judge.

The circumstances of Abduh's return to Egypt may shed light on
his split with Afghani. Just as the master was approaching the great
anti-colonial gesture of the Iranian tobacco agitation, the pupil was
making his peace with the aliens that Afghani so completely loathed.
In the event it was none other than Lord Cromer, Egypt's de facto
ruler between 1882 and 1907 – and a man whose past career in the
Indian colonial administration alone would have qualified him for the
sayyid's odium – who secured for Abduh the khedival pardon that
allowed him to come home. This act of benevolence was the beginning of a relationship between Cromer and Abduh that epitomised
the latter's pragmatic line towards his country's occupiers. While he
remained vocally opposed to the British occupation, like many nationalists in India he maintained a cordial working relationship with the
colonial power. Abduh's tightrope act brought benefits and risks. It

helped him rise as a public figure but in the long run condemned the Islamic reformation on which he had set his heart.

Like Hassan al-Attar and Rifaa al-Tahtawi before him, Abduh was a trained cleric versed in classical Islamic scholarship who believed that Islam was ripe for regeneration. Despite the efforts of these earlier reformers, the citadel of Sunni Islam in the heart of Fatimid Cairo had received little air since Attar's innovations were stifled back in the 1830s. The curriculum at al-Azhar continued to lean heavily away from history, philosophy and science, and Sheikh Muhammad Ilish, who became rector in 1881, disputed the idea that human reason was capable of distinguishing between good and evil. Ilish also took a notably narrow view of mind-broadening improvement, ruling that travel to the Christian nations was 'improper' and that the only appropriate knowledge centred on Islamic law.[117]

Abduh was a rebel against much of what Ilish stood for. While teaching at the modern Sultaniya school in Beirut he had delivered a series of lectures, later collected in a book called *The Theology of Unity*, and published in Cairo in 1897, which amounted to a manifesto for modernist Islam. In his prolegomena, Abduh ran briskly through the history of Islam, showing favour to the 'middle course' of the Asharites, the followers of the tenth-century Ab'ul Hassan al-Ashari, who had based their doctrine 'rationally on the laws of the universe'.[118] His regret was that the obscurantists had since gained the upper hand, destroying 'the remaining traces of the rational temper which had its source in the Islamic faith', while the seminary education had been reduced to 'mere wrangles about words ... complete intellectual confusion beset the Muslims'.[119]

For all Abduh's dissatisfaction, *The Theology of Unity* was a broad-shouldered, optimistic book. It contained little of the Quranic nitpicking that old-school sheikhs employed in order to bamboozle anyone who challenged their authority, and it campaigned against *taqlid*, or adherence to precedent. Offering up a grand, self-confident statement of principles, Abduh proposed a reimagining of Islam back to the time of the *salafs*, or 'ancestors'– the men and women who practised the new religion at its dawn.

Such desires put Abduh in awkward company, for now those who proclaim themselves to be followers of the Salafs, called Salafists, are associated with a dry-as-dust Islam that rejects human reasoning and is associated with fanaticism. Abduh agreed that early Islam had a purity that needed to be recaptured, and that much of subsequent scholarship was guff and accretion. He was also, like the modern Salafists, firmly opposed to the worship of saints, which had proliferated at a popular level. But he differed from them in that he believed Islam had been characterised at the outset by the most complete respect for human reasoning evinced by any faith, and that, far from promoting backward thinking, it encouraged people to cease clinging to precedent. Using the same asinine imagery as the father of Ziya Gokalp, Abduh asserted that 'man was not created to be led by a bridle'.[120]

Next to the borderline-atheistic utterances of the Turkish and Persian modernist iconoclasts, *The Theology of Unity* is a vehement assertion of faith, a defence of Islam as giving meaning to the modern world. After his return home to Cromer's Egypt and his entry into the judiciary – first upcountry, then in Cairo where in 1890 he was appointed to the court of appeal – Abduh strove to give flesh to this assertion, and in the process became perhaps the most significant clerical voice in Islam. As a member of al-Azhar's governing council, a teacher and a journalist whose columns reached into new middle-class homes, he moved easily between the legal and political worlds.

In 1899 Towfiq's successor as khedive, Abbas Hilmi, who ruled from 1892 to 1914, named him Grand Mufti. Besides bringing automatic membership of several prominent bodies enjoying advisory or executive powers, this appointment put Abduh at the top of the sharia courts. Inextricable from his official duties was the mufti's prestige; he was a 'magnate', Cromer wrote, 'of whose spiritual authority the temporal rulers must take account'. At the peak of his powers he was being received by the khedive twice a week and passing on all the political gossip to the political networker and poet Wilfred Blunt. On the eve of the new century Blunt exulted that his friend, 'having been imprisoned for his Liberal opinions, and exiled by the Anglo-Khedival restoration of 1882, has gradually been recognised for what he is, by far the most able and most honest man in Egypt'.[121]

Not that his fame was confined to his native land. His progressive and enlightened views were read in Turkey by Gokalp and in Iran by Taqizadeh. He was an inspiration to reformers at the venerable school of Zeytoun, Tunisia's version of al-Azhar, while the Malayan *ulema* debated his blending of jurisprudence from all four schools of law – a rejection of the supposedly sacrosanct divisions between them.

Whenever Abduh wanted to hold up the example of an institution that would ruin Islamic civilisation, he would point a derisive finger at his old school, describing long years of 'sweeping the dirt of the Azhar from my brain'. For all the efforts of Hassan al-Attar to reform al-Azhar, the institution that Abduh knew was as fractious and filthy as it had ever been, besides being vastly more overpopulated: there were now more than 10,000 students, up from an estimated 3,700 at the time of the Napoleonic invasion.[122] The dormitories were overpoweringly smelly; anyone going under the loggias had to pick his way between snoring men and pools of standing water; rodents snaffled decaying food that lay about the place.

In the citywide cholera epidemic of 1896, an infected student was unsurprisingly discovered inside the school, but his fellows responded to efforts to remove him to hospital with protestations that 'all who go to the hospital die', and by throwing planks, rocks and other missiles at the authorities till the police were called in. The policemen were ordered to tear down the locked gate by their (British) commander, and they entered the adjoining mosque shod and with bayonets at the ready – an infidel violation that prompted comparisons with the *Armée d'Orient*'s irruption into the same sacred space a century before.

The cholera riot, because it laid bare the school's complete unfamiliarity with modern educational ideas, lent impetus to efforts at reform, which Abduh and his allies put into effect the same year. School terms were introduced, as well as teaching hours; salaries were formalised for the sheikhs, and attendance insisted upon for the students – they were now required to complete eight years' tuition before they could become a primary-school teacher or imam. Discipline was tightened, time-wasting forbidden (Azharite students were famously long-winded), and running water introduced. The ancient school was acquiring some of the characteristics of a modern educational institution.

These reforms could not have happened without the support of Abbas; the khedive also funded the teaching of new subjects, including maths, algebra, geography and composition, which in time permitted graduates to get employment as teachers in civil schools. No longer were only brilliant autodidacts such as Rifaa al-Tahtawi able to cross the divide between the ecclesiastical and lay worlds. The introduction of secular subject matter into al-Azhar marked the narrowing of the divide itself.

Abduh's reformist views were aired in 'debates' that were published between 1900 and 1902 by a protégé, Rashid Rida, and which were aimed at winning converts to the mufti's position. In these debates an anonymous reformer argued against a traditionalist that 'emulation' of learned sheikhs should give way to *ijtihad*, or the use of independent reasoning, in order to determine God's will. This was the same *ijtihad* whose gates the Ottoman jurists had slammed shut back in the sixteenth century; Muhammad Abduh and his allies were flinging them open again. In one of these 'debates', the reformer declared that he was able to perform *ijtihad* thanks to the reading he had done of the Quran and his knowledge of the *salafs*. Clearly it wasn't necessary to be a stickler for exegesis, gloss and marginalia to understand what God wanted. Any educated Muslim with a Quran in his hand could perform his own *ijtihad*.

The significance of Abduh's proposals was colossal. For the majority of Muslims the licensed holy man, whether a village sheikh in the Nile Delta or a Shia ayatollah in Najaf, or the unlicensed one, such as a Sufi 'pole', was an indispensable conduit for sacred wisdom and the law. But Abduh was dispensing with the indispensable, and in doing so he had called into question the very need for a clerical intermediary between God and worshipper. The parallels with Calvinism, with which Abduh no doubt came into contact when he took courses at Geneva University, probably in 1894, are inescapable.

Abduh's daring approach to dogma in his six-year period as mufti did not stop at rejecting *taqlid* and embracing *ijtihad*. He also revived the old Mutazilite idea that the Quran was created, not eternal, from which it followed that it was open to interpretation according to time and circumstance, and might contain errors introduced by humans. He spoke out against the already ailing institution of polygamy, not on religious grounds (polygamy is sanctioned in the Quran) but in the name of domestic harmony. And he railed against the prevalent belief in predestination, arguing that it was the reason behind Egypt's decay. He also had no problem with evolution, which he incorporated into his conception of natural law.

It is hard to overstate the radicalism of Abduh's thoughts, but what made him doubly controversial was his style, which ran unashamedly counter to the closed and cautious traditions of his caste. Whether citing European scientists on the organisation of ants, crossing the Mediterranean to take the waters at Evian, or rifling through manuscripts in the Bodleian Library (he was particularly taken by the medieval correspondence that Frederick II of Sicily carried on with the Andalusian philosopher Ibn Sabin), Abduh was a blast of modernity into the cloth ears of Sheikh Ilish.

It had not crossed the mind of Sheikh al-Jabarti to learn the language of the invaders back in 1798. Abduh perfected the same infidel tongue by reading *The Count of Monte Cristo* – in fact, the Egyptian's French grew so good, that it was later described as 'faultless in its grammar, and almost Parisian in its intonation'.[123] He read Schiller, Goethe and Schopenhauer in French translation, as well as Herbert Spencer (at the time the most celebrated philosopher in the world), whose influential book *On Education* he translated into Arabic, and whose opposition to rote learning Abduh made his own. (The two men met in 1903, in Brighton, and the Englishman was pleased with Abduh's description of God as a 'being', not a 'person'.)[124] His famous ecumenism extended as far as befriending a Protestant clergyman, the Reverend Isaac Taylor, whose ambition was to unify Islam and Christianity; Abduh told his fellow divine that the day would come when the two religions would 'take each other's hand'.[125]

According to one of his most distinguished students, the historian Taha Hussein, Abduh's approach to teaching marked a 'complete break' with the literal-minded tradition of al-Azhar. Abduh, Hussein wrote, was 'exaggeratedly negligent as regards everything connected with words, and extremely meticulous as regards everything connected with ideas'.[126] Those ideas acted like a pneumatic drill on the fossilised nostrums of the school. For the traditional *ulema*, a Quranic verse in which some Jews respond to the Prophet's invitation to convert by saying they prefer the religion of their forefathers was an opportunity to point out the folly of the Jews in rejecting the true path. For Abduh it was an opportunity to criticise the idea behind their words, which was of course *taqlid*, or emulation; and he went on to say that nowadays it was the Muslims who were excessively attached to their forefathers.

A round, brown, cuddly man with a beard like an Elizabethan ruff, he would ease into a chair facing the prayer niche (illuminated by the modern marvel of gas lighting) before beginning his lesson for the day. 'Nothing,' Taha Hussein recalled, 'can efface from my mind the memory of that voice, the gentleness with which he recited passages from the Holy Book, the sincerity of his interpretation, or the strength of his conviction that nothing he said was in contradiction with the discoveries of modern science, or at variance with the demands of Western civilisation. He was listened to with a passionate interest and admiration which verged on religious ecstasy.'[127]

Abduh's best-known interventions in the lives of Muslims were his fatwas – opinions that carry sufficient authority to overturn or refine existing interpretations of Islamic law. In 1901 he authorised property insurance, hitherto considered forbidden on the grounds that it was a form of gambling. He also permitted the depositing of religious endowment funds in interest-paying accounts in the new national bank – a move that many considered a contravention of the Islamic ban on usury. In his famous 'Transvaal' fatwa of 1903 – so called because it responded to questions from Muslims living in the South African territory of that name – he ruled that it was permissible for a Muslim to wear a brimmed European hat unsuitable for prayer so long as 'this did not indicate an intention of copying the Europeans in their religion'. In the same fatwa he also allowed Muslims to eat meat slaughtered by Christians – in practice, by Boers who killed animals with an axe rather than slitting the animal's throat as stipulated in Islam. This last fatwa was a striking recognition that the contexts in which Islam was practised had proliferated and grown fantastically varied since the time of the Prophet, and that for Muslims living or travelling in a non-Muslim country it might be impossible to get hold of halal meat.

Whether he was glossing over a specific restriction against eating animals killed by a violent blow (as in the Transvaal fatwa) or combining elements of the four legal schools to come up with a more humane application of the divorce law, Abduh evidently felt that relaxing long-held technicalities was legitimate because of the practical benefits accruing to the Muslim community. His instinct was invariably towards the most liberal interpretation of the law, which would harmonise with the lives of increasing complexity that were being led by Muslims around the world. It was also towards friendship with peoples of other faiths. He was Islam's great liberal.

The problem was that liberalism was deeply suspect to those who saw the religion's interests as served by accentuating the barriers between the faiths, not breaking them down. Abduh's opposition to saint-worship also upset many ordinary Egyptians, while his friendship with foreigners displeased young firebrands like Mustafa Kamil, whose National Party declared the British the enemies of the Egyptian people and demanded an immediate end to the protectorate. For all Abduh's continuing advocacy of constitutional government, the mufti was heavily implicated in a colonial regime in which the Egyptian component was only advisory. The fact was that in terms of democracy Egypt had gone back to Ismail and the country was no more independent than it had been under Napoleon.

By 1901 the Khedive Abbas had become frustrated by his plainly subordinate position to Cromer, who believed that the Egyptians were nowhere near being capable of running their own country. Relations between Abbas and Abduh also deteriorated; the khedive suspected the powerful mufti of trying to emasculate him. Anti-British feeling was on the rise more generally, expressed through nationalism and Islamic conservatism. What better target existed for these various resentments than the famous and distinguished friend of the British, a man whose mission was to make forbidden things permissible?

The ferocious campaign that was waged against Abduh between 1901 and his death in 1905 was in many ways a rerun of the vilification of Hassan al-Attar three-quarters of a century before, which had driven the earlier divine to his death – except that on this occasion the campaigners wielded a modern weapon in the form of the press.

In early 1901 the satirical journal *Humarat monyati*, which means 'she-donkey of my desire', and which was owned and edited by a muckraker called Muhammad Towfiq, heaped shame on the sheikh for ruling in favour of interest-paying bank accounts. That summer Abduh went to Europe and returned to an even more devastating broadside. In the pages of *Humarat monyati* Towfiq remonstrated to a fictional friend, 'You saw yourself that the Mufti of Islam went one year to look at the Paris Exhibition, and one year he went to bathe in who-knows-what baths. If you were to ask him about the *Kaaba* he would say he'd never seen it.' Towfiq continued, 'What's wrong with the pilgrimage ... is it part of "civilisation" that the people must go to Europe yearly and not ... perform the duties to Our Lord?'[128]

The demonisation of Abduh by *Humarat monyati* reached a climax in March 1902, when the periodical published a photograph purporting to show him leaning familiarly towards a European woman with whom he was conversing – part of a scandalously mixed group of revellers in the open air. The photograph is grainy and the ensemble somewhat disjointed, which led to conjecture that it had been faked. But the damage was done: a leading divine of Islam had been exposed as a hedonist and possibly a pervert. As one contemporary chronicler described it, Muhammad Towfiq filled the same issue with 'the most awful and most hateful speech ... he attacked him [Abduh] with two poems, the likes of which no one has uttered before or since. The enemies of the Sheikh proceeded to read those poems to every passerby from the masses and low class inhabitants of the Azhar district ... they even placed copies of the paper near Abduh's sitting area at the Azhar mosque and on his dining table.'[129] Just when it seemed that things couldn't get any worse for the sheikh, an illustrated scandal sheet appeared showing him embracing a European woman while a dog pawed his robe, rendering him ritually impure.

Abduh was the object of xenophobic and conservative emotions that were easy enough to whip up in a subjugated Egypt whose vital infrastructure, notably the Suez Canal, was in foreign hands. But much of the fault for what happened lay with Abduh himself. He had clearly not appreciated that his privileged position in society, acquired so easily, could be taken away from him just as easily, and he had done little to placate the conservatives without whose support his Islamic reformation was impossible. There followed a messy trial of Muhammad Towfiq in which the unrepentant editor gleefully depicted the Grand Mufti of the Egyptian Realm as a pawn of British interests.[130] (Towfiq received a three-month sentence for damaging the mufti's reputation – not, however, for slander.) Meanwhile, other wolves gathered around the wounded sheikh. A new pro-nationalist newspaper funded by the khedive painted the Transvaal fatwa as inadmissible intellectual freelancing. His old sparring partners at al-Azhar called him a 'heretic'. Only Cromer stood between the sheikh and dismissal.

Reliance on the occupying power must have been a horrendous predicament for a man whose patriotism seems to have been genuine, but it was typical of his uninterrupted receptivity to foreign ideas that in 1904, in the midst of his demonisation, he wrote an admiring letter to Tolstoy in which he noted that 'in our skies the suns of your ideas have risen, making a bond of friendship between the minds of the intelligent here and your mind'.[131]

In January 1905 he fell ill, with cancer of the kidney, and died quickly, at the age of fifty-six. There was a state funeral, as befitting a man who had died in high office, but the khedive berated one of his courtiers who had the temerity to mourn. 'Don't you realise that this man was the enemy of God,' he exclaimed, 'the enemy of the Prophet, the enemy of religion, the enemy of the doctors of the faith, the enemy of the Muslims, and the enemy of himself?'[132]

In Muhammad Abduh, the Sunni Islamic tradition had shown unprecedented flexibility to Western ideas and their exponents, while at the same time attempting to retain its cultural authenticity. In his willingness to throw over aspects of Islamic orthodoxy in the name of ecumenism and progress, he was the consummate exponent of an ideological and cultural blending that for many alongside him smacked of surrender and betrayal. The general impetus continued to lie with modernity, Westernisation and ideas of liberal origin. But Abduh's destruction at the hands of chauvinists was the harbinger of a huge reaction that would be released by the fast-approaching conflagration of the First World War: Islam's Counter-Enlightenment.

6

Counter-Enlightenment

By the First World War, a liberal modernising tradition had emerged strongly in the three intellectual and political centres of the Middle East, generating and attracting ideas that in turn spun off into the adjacent regions. This tradition was not without competitors. Militarism, royalism and traditional and revivalist forms of Islam all joined the struggle, but the institutions they vied to control were no longer those of the medieval Islamic principality or empire – they were the liberal institutions of the post-Enlightenment nation state as it had evolved in Europe and the United States. In Egypt, Iran and Turkey, some trappings of medieval royalism had been permitted to remain (and in the former power-sharing arrangements were an inevitable bone of contention with the colonial government), but politics were increasingly democratic. Alongside the ideas themselves – the freeing of knowledge, individual fulfilment and secular rights – the methods and institutions that would be used to plant these ideas had also advanced. In less than a century the region had leaped politically from the medieval to the modern, and the Egypt of 1910 was a place Jabarti would have had trouble recognising.

The idea of a popular franchise had developed considerably since 1876, when membership of the first Ottoman assembly had been determined for the most part by electoral colleges that were themselves elected by electoral colleges; when Iranians voted in the first parliament of the constitutional era, in 1906, elections in the capital were direct, even if suffrage was confined to property-owning males (a common enough restriction at the time). Egypt had been denied constitutional oxygen by Lord Cromer and his successors, and elections to a lower house with serious legislative powers were put off until 1924, when all male adults were able to cast a vote. The Muslim countries were not remarkable in denying women the vote. Many European states only introduced female suffrage after the First World War, and some of these, including Britain, continued to place limits on women's involvement in the democratic process well into the 1920s.

In Turkey, Iran and Egypt people and beliefs consolidated into parties, officers were appointed, and signs went up over rented doorways. Well before the First World War, the Committee of Union and Progress had boasted an executive body and branches in provincial towns across the western Ottoman Empire. In Egypt after the close of hostilities the National Party of Mustafa Kamil (who died in 1908) was soon eclipsed by the Wafd, or 'Delegation', led by Jamal al-Din Afghani's former disciple, the nationalist lawyer Saad Zaghlul. Along with the Iranian Democrats and Moderates that were elected to the Tehran parliament in 1909, these groups reflected a region-wide trend towards establishing modern parties.

Women's participation in public life more broadly continued to grow. Following the war an influential group of Egyptian women were heavily involved in the nationalist struggle led by Zaghlul's Wafd, whose achievement was the country's independence in 1922 – a stunted foal, however, for Britain kept control over Egypt's foreign and military affairs. Huda Shaarawi and other upper-class women played supporting roles in this movement, running the gauntlet of army units when coming out into the streets to agitate against the arrest of Zaghlul and the other Wafdist leaders in 1919, taking part in a series of strikes and riots that paralysed the country, and organising a boycott of British goods and banks. Increasingly Huda's political activities were dominated by her struggle for women's equality, particularly after the death of her husband, Ali Shaarawi (himself a prominent Wafdist) to whom she had been married so uncongenially twenty-one years before.

In 1923 this 35-year-old widow, child of the harem, caused a major shock when she returned from a feminist meeting abroad and pulled back the veil from her face before a substantial crowd.[1] Such nakedness had rarely – if ever – been seen from a respectable woman in the capital of the Arab world, and there was no millennial belief to help explain it away as there had been in the case of Qurrat al-Ayn.

Across the Mediterranean that other Muslim feminist, Halide Edib, took stock of the challenges and opportunities thrown up by the end of the war. During the fighting in Anatolia, Edib had organised hospitals and schools, itself an expansion of the role she had assumed in peacetime. Her response to the Allied invasion of Anatolia at the close of the war was to step even further out of the boundaries imposed by her sex, and like Huda Shaarawi she made her mark in a public manner and at the nadir of her country's fortunes. In May 1919, the nation was dazed and the patriotic forces had scattered; warplanes of Britain's Royal Air Force flew between the minarets of Istanbul while news came in of a Greek invasion of the Aegean coast, attempting to recreate the Hellenic hegemony of yore. This period of uncertainty and panic, Edib wrote, was 'one of almost continuous public speaking for me'. This banal-sounding phrase only achieves genuine force if it is placed in the context of the time; when Edib was born in 1884 it had been inconceivable for a woman to address a mixed assembly of strangers.

Her most famous performance came on 6 June 1919, at a patriotic rally attended by 200,000 people in the Byzantine hippodrome. In her speech Edib coupled Islam – 'not the Islam entangled by super-stition and narrowness, but the Islam which came as a great spiritual message' – with her beloved Turkey: a wronged and martyred nation, whose spiritual and moral force 'no material agency can destroy'. She also coined a phrase that encapsulated the tortuous feelings of many Turks towards the world's powerful countries, and which would become an unofficial national slogan. 'The peoples are our friends,' she declared, 'the governments our enemies.' Her audience thrice swore that they would 'not bow down to brute force on any condition'.[2]

Even Egypt, denied Turkey's and Iran's experiences of electoral politics, was developing institutions that might, if permitted to mature, hold up a liberal political regime. These included the some-what anarchic press that had ruined Muhammad Abduh, and the Egyptian University (later renamed Cairo University), which Abduh had pressed to be formed, and which finally opened in 1908. For all the opposition that the more traditional-minded Egyptians had shown their progressive sheikh, Egypt after the First World War continued to hear voices of reform. In 1925, a year after Atatürk caused shock among Muslims by abolishing the caliphate, a disciple of Abduh called Ali Abdel Razeq provoked a further storm of protest by arguing that the very idea of Islamic government was a fiction and that the caliphate had been a 'plague for Islam and the Muslims'.[3] The central theological contention of Abdel Razeq's book, *The Caliphate and the Sovereignty of the Nation*, was that Muhammad's sole function had been a prophetic one, and that he had not made a system of law that would be the basis for human government. This ran counter to an understanding of Muhammad's mission that had been largely uncontested in orthodox Sunni and Shia thought for hundreds of years; if it was followed to its conclusion it would remove religious dogma from public life and secularise Islam entirely. It did not, and in the controversy that followed publication a council of leading Azharites pronounced Abdel Razeq unfit to hold any public function.

The following year, Taha Hussein, Abduh's brilliant blind follower who had become one of the first Islamic scholars to examine the Quran as a work of literature, suggested that some Arabic poetry hitherto held to be pre-Islamic had in fact been falsified. The critical method he used, if applied to religious texts, could similarly cast doubt on their authenticity. Again, this line of thinking could have had a defining effect on Islam, opening the way for Quranic studies to become a branch of literature and history – as had happened to biblical studies in the West. Again, it did not. Hussein's thinking was still that of an outlying minority. He was denounced as a heretic and lost his job as a professor of Arabic literature.

Although Hussein and Abdel Razeq were punished and abused, it is notable that neither of these unorthodox thinkers was killed or hounded abroad, as many subsequent doubters would be. Indeed, in later years, both men would be sufficiently rehabilitated to occupy public office.

From an Egyptian nationalist perspective the First World War brought medium-term advantages at a price of immediate pain. Egypt had gone through the first decade of the century as an Ottoman province whose effective incorporation into the British Empire it was in no one's interest to acknowledge – not the

Ottomans', whose prestige would suffer; nor the khedive's, whose powerlessness would be exposed; nor that of the British, who thrived on such ambiguities in order to exercise power without accountability. But the war threw Egypt's overlapping suzerains against each other. Turkey's entry on the side of Germany prompted the British to declare Egypt a protectorate and to depose the pro-Axis Khedive Abbas II, replacing him with his uncle, Hussein Kamil, given the fancy new title of Sultan. When Hussein Kamil died in 1917 he was replaced by his brother Fuad.

This constitutional sorcery allowed Britain to impose martial law and commandeer the economy to serve the military, but many Egyptians were deeply opposed to their unsolicited involvement in a war against the caliph, whose religious authority they continued to recognise (at least until Atatürk abolished the office in 1924). The British suppressed nationalist activity during the war and tranquillised opinion by promising to hold discussions over self-government after the cessation of hostilities. These discussions duly began in 1919, were bedevilled by arguments over who represented the Egyptian people (eventually – to British displeasure – the task fell to Zaghlul's Wafd), and ended in the paper independence of 1922. For all the limitations of this arrangement, however, the new Egyptian King Fuad, the Wafd government and the revived parliament were given the freedom to discuss and control domestic affairs. The hated capitulations, under which foreigners had been subject to their own laws on Egyptian soil, were finally abolished, and in 1936 an Anglo-Egyptian treaty allowed the Egyptians theoretical control over their own foreign and military matters, even if, in practice Britain continued to wield much unofficial influence.

The Great War, then, brought about an amelioration in Egypt's internal situation, which might have been expected to strengthen liberal institutions under the aegis of a state that would in time witness a further nibbling at the king's prerogatives and Britain's continuing control of the Suez Canal. In fact, the relatively benign outlook in Egypt was not replicated elsewhere in the Middle East, where the First World War was an unmitigated catastrophe – and even Egypt's own development was knocked back as a result.

In contrast to the deadly torpor of the Western Front, the Middle East between 1914 and 1918 was an almost limitless stage for the rapid deployment of technologies old and new; it was fought at frenetic speed with armoured cars, biplanes, dreadnoughts, river steamers, steam trains, camels and horses. On their circuitous career to collapse, Ottoman armies hurried from the Caucasus (where just 18,000 out of 100,000 Turkish troops returned from a brutal winter campaign against the Russians) westwards to repulse an Allied invasion at Gallipoli, down to Iraq where they fought an Indian army force and again westwards to try and extinguish the Arab Revolt that the British had ignited in the Hejaz and Syria. Alongside the human tragedies of the Armenian genocide and the Gallipoli campaign, the disruption of governance was felt agonisingly in all areas of life. The Turkish word for mobilisation, *seferberlik*, became synonymous with 'crop failure, inflation, disease, famine, and death among non-combatants on an unprecedented level'.[4] Mortality rates across the empire ran to an astonishing 20 per cent, as compared to the worst per capita figure on the Western Front, France's 3.5 per cent.[5]

Persia, officially neutral, was violated with impunity, its strategic value heightened by the British-controlled oil industry since Churchill, in an inspired fit of out-of-the-boxism, modified the British fleet to run on oil and not coal. (This made British ships several knots faster and allowed them to refuel at sea.) Turkish, Russian and British armies, besides Armenian irregulars and German agents, ran amok on Iranian soil. Parliament scattered, no fewer than eight different prime ministers formed sixteen different cabinets, and hecatombs of non-combatants dropped from starvation even as the country's more fertile provinces overflowed with wheat and rice. By the close of hostilities, belying all the advances of the Constitutional Revolution, Persia can be said barely to have existed.

The most important material consequence of the First World War in the Middle East was the destruction of the Ottoman Empire. This raised the possibility that the region would be reconstituted on the increasingly universal principle of the nation state. The signs were quite hopeful. The Turks under Atatürk were resigned to making their future in Anatolia, the Egyptians were edging towards independence, and the newly liberated Arabs of Arabia, Syria, Palestine and Mesopotamia were eager to determine their own futures. Iran was already a nation though it needed to rebuild the state.

The question now was whether Europe's empires would facilitate the process of Middle Eastern state-building, and hopes rested to an unrealistic degree on President Woodrow Wilson, the first American to impinge significantly on the destiny of the region. Like his compatriot Morgan Shuster, he was a well-meaning failure.

Wilson was a fervent Presbyterian whose early picture of the Middle East had been as a backdrop for missionary activity. The collapse of the Ottomans, the formation of a Bolshevik state to the north, and the growing importance of oil necessitated a closer understanding on the part of the United States. Having contributed militarily to Germany's defeat, besides financing much of the Allied war effort, American prestige was at an all-time high, and as hostilities drew to a close Wilson adumbrated aims, summarised in his 'Fourteen Points', which he hoped to impose on his fellow victors. As far as the Middle East was concerned, the most important was point twelve, which contained the stricture that Turkey's former subject peoples should enjoy an 'absolutely unmolested opportunity of autonomous development'. In February 1918 Wilson announced that Middle Easterners were no longer to be 'bartered about ... as if they were chattels', and that post-war territorial settlements must be 'in the interest and for the benefit of the populations concerned'.[6]

The president's statements concerning an equable settlement for everyone electrified the political classes. Everyone from the Iranians to the Kurds and the Armenians wanted his ear when he travelled to Paris at the end of 1918 to preside over the peace conference and a chance to impress the justice of their claims on the man who promised autonomy for all.

Halide Edib's famous speech in May 1919 was in fact directed at Wilson: the mass meeting she was addressing had been organised to draw attention to the opening clauses of the president's twelfth point, namely that 'Turkish portions of the present Ottoman Empire should be assured of a secure sovereignty' (this as the British warplanes circled overhead).[7] In Cairo the patriotic anger of Huda Shaarawi and her fellow women protesters had been aroused by the refusal of the British to let the Wafd go to Europe to put its case; instead the British imprisoned its leaders, including Zaghlul, in Malta. Iran, too, felt that the country's suffering in the conflict qualified it for a place at the table, and from his temporary home in Germany Hassan Taqizadeh issued a detailed memorandum on Iran's wishes, which included membership of the League of Nations (another of Wilson's pet ideas), the evacuation of foreign troops, the abolition of capitulations, and a large loan with which to reconstruct the state.[8]

Wilson's idealism did not lessen his fellow victors' desire for territory. A feeding frenzy got going over the carcass of Asia Minor, as British, French, Greek and Italian forces attacked from different angles, settled only by the Treaty of Lausanne of 1923. A US commission that went to Syria in June 1919 and discovered much resistance to the prospect of European rule was similarly powerless to prevent annexation by France the following year. Lebanon was hived off as a separate, Christian-majority unit.

In Egypt, meanwhile, the continuing efforts of the nationalists to air their grievances only contributed to the formalisation of the status quo. In the spring of 1919 the Wafd were finally admitted to the peace conference, but were disappointed when the United States endorsed the British protectorate. As for the Iranian delegation that travelled from Tehran to Paris, they didn't even get a hearing.

The day was ending for European colonialism but at sundown there was a binge in the Middle East. At the Paris conference, Britain took Palestine, Iraq and Transjordan (soon to become Jordan), while France got Syria and Lebanon. In theory the imperialists had been reborn as mandatory powers fulfilling the covenant of Wilson's League of Nations. The mandates were to be a form of trusteeship under which the powers oversaw 'peoples not yet able to stand by themselves under the strenuous conditions of the modern world', and whose well-being would be 'a sacred trust of civilisation'. But by the time the mandates had been agreed, in 1920, Wilson himself was incapacitated by illness, the Senate had rejected America's own membership of the League, and the country was retreating into isolation. Without America and Russia among its members, Wilson's bequest to the world became a league of empires, and its Permanent Mandates Commission, which was supposed to look after the interests of the mandated territories, a means of expanding Pax Britannica into Pax Mundi.[9]

The conduct of the powers in the mandate era anticipated much of their behaviour in later, post-colonial times. Into these confected countries they implanted friendly Arab leaders in the hope that their own interests would be advanced. Faisal, third son of the emir of Mecca, Hussein, whom the British had enlisted into the Arab revolt against the Ottomans, was made King of Syria before the French kicked him out. Nothing daunted, he assumed the throne of neighbouring Iraq, which he went on to rule with laudable even-handedness. In 1932 his efforts to wriggle out of Britain's embrace were crowned with Iraq's accession to the League of Nations, though, as in the Egyptian case, this form of independence meant accepting a long-term military partnership with Britain. Faisal's brother Abdullah got Jordan (which today is still run by a Hashemite, Abdullah's great-grandson). But their father, the patriarch Hussein, lost British support and his throne after he rejected the post-war settlement. In 1926 his kingdom was seized by another British client, Ibn Saud, founder of the modern state of Saudi Arabia.

Iran was independent and had not been occupied; but it, too, found itself under the imperial parasol. In 1919, Britain and a triumvirate of Iranian statesmen concluded a secret deal that effectively imposed a protectorate on the country. The architect of the Anglo-Persian Agreement, as it was called, was Britain's foreign secretary Lord Curzon, who boasted that 'no more disinterested and single-minded attempt was ever made by a Western power to re-establish the existence and secure the prosperity of an Eastern country'.[10] But there was disquiet among Persian patriots – particularly after it became known that Curzon had paid £130,000 to the triumvirs – which, when added to the famine, brigandage and Bolshevik insurgencies that were rampant at the time, made the country even more ungovernable. In 1921, Reza Khan, an Iranian officer with the Cossack Brigade, which had come under British control, seized the reins of government. Four years later, having chased Ahmad Shah, the last of the Qajar monarchs, into exile, Reza became shah.

In later years, the cupidity and arbitrariness of British and French conduct would gradually be reduced to a single tagline, Sykes–Picot, after the secret pact, agreed in 1916 by the calamitous amateur Sir Mark Sykes, and the French colonial officer François Georges-Picot. (When they declared their caliphate in Iraq and Syria in 2014, ISIS gloated that they were 'smashing Sykes–Picot'.) In fact, Sykes–Picot was far from being the most consequential of a plethora of treaties, declarations, gentlemen's agreements and coronations that were imposed on the region, and which, being ill-considered, self-interested and indifferent to the desires of its inhabitants – in short, as distant from Wilsonian ideals as it was possible to be – created a belt of instability from Sinai to Anatolia.

An idea of Britain's insouciance towards the peoples that had fallen into its hands may be gleaned from the personal styles of the men drawing the borders. Looking over a map, Sykes famously proposed dividing the region into British and French zones along a line running from the 'e' in Acre to the final 'k' in Kirkuk. Churchill boasted that he had created Transjordan 'with the stroke of a pen, one Sunday afternoon in Cairo'. The zigzag that even today adds variety to Jordan's border with Saudi Arabia is said to have been the consequence of post-prandial trapped wind forcing its exit as the colonial secretary's pudgy hand moved across the map – 'Winston's hiccup', as it is called, though it is always possible that another orifice was involved. Churchill also created Iraq, with its oil fields in mind; he was indifferent to the difficulty of unifying a country composed of Shia and Sunni Arabs and Kurds.

Perhaps most fateful of all, the First World War also bore witness to the Balfour Declaration of 1917 promising the Jews a national home in Palestine, an act of imperial overstretch that led to the creation of Israel under conditions that virtually all Arabs regard as colonial in character.

The administrators of the new mandates did not shrink from stamping their authority on their new lands. Meeting opposition to their rule in Syria in 1925, the French repaid the 'sacred trust of civilisation' by levelling Damascus. Also in the 1920s Churchill approved a policy of bombarding ('air policing') rebellious Kurds in northern Iraq. Even these events did not induce a sense of rueful self-criticism in the colonial officials involved, but a search for someone to blame. They alighted, inevitably, on Wilson; the uprisings, sniffed Maurice Hankey, Lloyd George's cabinet secretary, stemmed from his 'impossible doctrine of self-determination'.[11]

Later judgements have been harsher on the British and their French accomplices in the carve-up of the Middle East. For all the losses that the region experienced as a result of the fighting, what had an even more devastating impact were the structures and political trends that were engendered by incompetent imperialism.

The post-war settlements created nations that were too rebellious to be good clients and too divided to be good states. Although the powers were not strong enough to prevent independence, their evident desire to delay and limit it created ill will and hostility in local populations. Native rulers favoured by the colonisers unsurprisingly lacked popular legitimacy, and neither the British-backed monarchies in Iraq and Egypt nor the republican regime that the French established in Syria survived decolonisation.

Another product of the fighting, while not directly attributable to Britain and France, also had a damaging impact. The First World War ushered in oil as a determinant of joy and misery in the Middle East; its weight as a strategic commodity skewed development towards rentier economies and ensured the continued meddling of the West. Finally, the carve-up of the Middle East brought into existence a new Arabian state that injected a bigoted and unimaginative discourse into world Islam: Wahhabism.

In the light of the subjugation of so much of the Middle East following the First World War, it is not surprising that many of its inhabitants began to seek political means to express their distrust of the West. No longer would it be possible for a Muhammad Abduh to defend an optimistic view of relations between the two worlds. The West seemed more determined than ever to trample on the lands of Islam and humiliate their inhabitants. This revulsion found expression in ideologies of resistance that would mark the Middle East in the twentieth century, and the first to be tried out on a significant scale was militarist nationalism.

Between the wars, Turkey and Iran became the standard-bearers of this new approach, for reasons that are readily comprehensible. The two neighbours had evaded colonisation or mandate status by tight margins. Atatürk continued to regard with suspicion the powers he had at such great cost expelled from the country, while Reza Shah, having been brought to power with British connivance, spent his reign in a glowering terror that London might try and undo him. Both leaders repressed internal opposition in order to tranquillise states that they aimed to found anew.

In doing so they drew on existing traditions – the martial tramp of Muhammad Ali and Abbas Mirza, the materialism of Besir Fuat, and

Gokalp's patriotic fervour – taking them to their farthest, least flexible conclusions. The origin of these ideas was of course Western; and the underlying belief was that the East needed to become indistinguishable from the West in order to avoid being overrun by it. No longer would room be given to the illusory idea that Islam could be reformed in order to give the East internal coherence and strength. Nor would naive nostrums such as tolerance of opposing views and rule by consensus enjoy official airtime. The militarist nationalists of the Middle East were convinced that reform must be quick, compulsory and backed up by force of arms. In this they had much in common with European fascism.

Another thing that united these men was their contempt for the credulous rabble that it was their unhappy lot to command. A good illustration of this was provided by Reza Shah's court minister Abdolhossein Teimurtash, who believed that his compatriots 'should be struck, should be ridden, should be held by the stirrup-leather'.[12] Teimurtash was a leading member of a class of mandarins that formed around both Atatürk and Reza Shah: fast-track progressives just out of army uniform, many of them Western-educated, who were actuated by a sense of shame at their countries' backwardness.

Turkey advanced the faster. Atatürk's policies of ethnic and cultural homogenisation (the annihilation of the Armenians had given him a head start) got going in 1923 with the forcible exchange of more than a million Anatolian Greeks for 380,000 Muslims, mainly from Macedonia and Crete. Then he turned his attention to the rebellious Kurds, and between 1924 and 1938 the Turkish armed forces took part in no fewer than seventeen campaigns and engagements in Turkish Kurdistan. Many in the new republic were glad of the relative stability that was eventually obtained, with strategic parts of the economy in state hands and protection for new industries such as steel and textiles. Atatürk died in 1938 but his policy of neutrality was perpetuated by his successor, Ismet Inönü, who kept Turkey out of the Second World War.

Atatürk wasn't simply concerned with externals. He tried to make the Turks think as he believed modern people should think. To be modern meant to be secular, and as part of his campaign to relegate Islam to the status of a private moral compass he closed dervish lodges and the religious brotherhoods, pressed the mosques into a stifling new bureaucracy, and oversaw the promotion of unveiled women into medicine, the civil service and the law. He completed the secularising legal reforms that the Tanzimatists had begun and the CUP had continued, introducing parity between men and women in matters of divorce and inheritance. His discarding of the old Arabic alphabet in favour of a modified Roman one was more than a break with the script of the Quran: it was a cultural blindfold making it impossible for Turks to read the literature of their forefathers, or even their gravestones. Atatürk was an after-dinner intellectual who proposed that the Turks were the originators of all language and that the ancient inhabitants of Anatolia had not been Urartian, Greek or Armenian at all, but true-blood Turks. Luckily these theories were not taken seriously.

The effects of Atatürk's top-down engineering were felt even in the villages and provincial towns, where girls put on pinafores to attend brand-new schools, men exchanged fezzes for Western-style hats, and women exercised their new right to vote, even if only one party – Atatürk's – was allowed to win. 'Civilisation is a fearful fire which consumes those who ignore it,' the president growled at a rural crowd he had ordered to give up their old-fashioned garb, and the clerical freelancers who had made a living by teaching, officiating at marriages, rubber-stamping land sales and administering quack remedies became irrelevant. In time the jack-of-all-trades provincial sheikh was superseded by white-collar specialists: lawyers, teachers, notaries and doctors.

Atatürk's wrenching changes had been made possible by the First World War and the clean break it represented with the Ottoman past. Turkey was now a republic governed by Western-style institutions and disburdened of its old desire to lead the Islamic world. In Ankara there was scarcely a mosque in sight; the new capital was a shop window for the new laws, clothes and language. New technology and skills allowed a truly independent Turkish Republic to build more industrial capacity in a few decades than the Ottoman Empire had managed over the whole of the nineteenth century. But a heavy price was paid for the forward movement. Internal exile, censorship and political murder were the less appealing features of Atatürk's rule, and it was only in 1950 that the republic staged its first free elections.

Atatürk's autocratic style ended up driving liberals like Halide Edib from his side. Having euphorically joined 'our George Washington' as the leader's press secretary in 1920, she later made it clear that her obedience to him was conditional on his continuing to serve the cause she believed in – to which he responded with a threat: 'you shall obey me and do as I wish'. In 1925, after Atatürk shut down the opposition party that she had helped found, Edib went into exile, only returning to Turkey after his death.[13]

A thousand miles to the east, the Iran of Reza Shah was following a similar path. At the beginning of the century the Iranians had preceded Turkey into constitutional government. In the 1920s and 30s political exports generally went the other way, as Reza replicated many of Atatürk's legal, educational and social measures.[14]

During his period as prime minister under Ahmad Shah, Reza had used the country's oil revenues to build a new army that was then deployed to smash the refractory tribes – ending the dazzling seasonal movements of man and beast that had been a feature of Iranian life for millennia. Those who had herded found themselves herded into villages and told to plant beans. He banned the photographing of camels, for fear that foreigners conclude that Iran was backward. His coronation in 1926, gently savaged by Vita Sackville-West (her husband was at the British legation), was a poor imitation of King George V's. The mongrel ceremonials were at once Persian and European, one part Muslim and one profane. Behind Reza Shah's furious reforms lay a furious inferiority complex.

Reza's success at pacifying the country allowed him to introduce a great many of these changes over his sixteen-year reign. He brought in secular codes to replace the sharia, got rid of the old Arabic and Turkish months, and changed the international name of the country, from Persia (a European name from antiquity) to Iran (which is what the people called it). He built schools, factories and a cumbersome civil service. Fixated by the powers' historic collusion in denying Iran a modern transport network, he levied taxes on tea and sugar to finance a north–south railway from the Caspian Sea to the Persian Gulf, laying the last rail himself in 1938. It turned out to be of more use to the Allied armies that invaded the country three years later than to Iranian traders and travellers, who more often needed to get across the country rather than up or down, and used roads to do so.

In matters of dress Reza went even further than Atatürk and outlawed the chador. This had a calamitous effect on social life, and many Iranian women did not set foot out of doors until the law was rescinded following the shah's fall from power in 1941. He was a destructive antiquarian, razing medieval town centres and building instead town halls and marble bank branches in the style of Persepolis. Unlike Atatürk, who cared above all for glory, Reza was venal, seizing the most fertile 10 per cent of agricultural land in the country, as well as any palatial home that took his fancy. He slept little (on the floor – his luxurious bed was too soft) and worked hard. But he was not rewarded with the love of his people, only their fear.

Parallel to Atatürk's Turkism, Reza Shah consciously elevated Iran's national heritage over its Islamic traditions, setting up a department of antiquities to check the flow of pre-Islamic treasures that had been leaving the country, commissioning a Frenchman to build a museum in Tehran to house the archaeological treasures, and putting up a memorial to the author of the *Shahnameh*. The mullahs were still an irritation, glowering at him from the shrine city of Qom, where their seminaries were increasingly concentrated, but they played less of a role in public affairs than at any time since the rise of the Safavids four hundred years earlier. Reza's loathing for Islam was visceral and well known. Nor did he encourage splinter movements such as Bahaism. 'I shall not permit any prophets during my reign,' he vowed.

Reza was not as strategic a reformer as Atatürk, whose clearly expressed preference was for an orderly transition to democracy. Reza, by contrast, got harder the further his rule advanced; he imprisoned thousands and killed hundreds of his opponents. Again in contrast to Atatürk, who died at the zenith of his global reputation, having established a stable new republic where once had been sliding zones of interest, the Iran that Reza bequeathed remained acutely vulnerable to foreign interference.

This was not entirely Reza's fault. The country's most promising new industry was oil. It was firmly under the control of the Anglo-Iranian Oil Company, which paid Iran a nugatory royalty. At the beginning of the Second World War, Reza was foolish enough to flirt with Hitler's Germany, provoking first warnings on the part of the Allies, and then, in 1941, a full-scale invasion. Fearing for the survival of his dynasty, he went into exile. His son, Muhammad Reza – a callow 21-year-old who had grown up in terror of his father, and would be driven by a desire to out-shah him – took his place.

By the erratic standards of Middle Eastern reform, the dictatorships of Atatürk and Reza Shah were stunningly productive. The nation states they bequeathed were in many ways unrecognisable from the semi-ruins they had found. That two new countries seemed to have been born and then leaped forward a century in the space of twenty years earned their leaders much praise from abroad. But there was a jarring dissonance between the identity that Atatürk and Reza wished to impose and the identity to which the people continued to cling. In their fanciful appeals to the ancient past, and their championing of a national, rather than a religious destiny, the dictators went against Islam, that most demanding and encompassing of religions. There was unease among the people as Atatürk waltzed and womanised and Reza horsewhipped the mullahs and impoverished them, turning them into a laughing stock. Atatürk was remembered in a secular mausoleum with marching, fascist column orders. Reza put up pastiches of Persepolis. But the people never loved these temples to human vanity. They remained stubbornly spiritual. At the weekends, they went to the old shrines, mouthed the same prayers, and slowly – imperceptible to those who considered the struggle long won – were born the conditions for reaction.

When they looked at Egypt in the first half of the twentieth century, regarded by many as the 'leader' of the Arab world, it appeared to many observers that the chances of an Islamic reaction checking the country's progress towards an increasingly Westernised identity were virtually nil. Confidence in the continuing secularisation of the Middle East was part of a world view that had formed around Max Weber's idea of humankind moving away from the 'great enchanted garden' of traditional belief and culture. Even in the 1960s, by which time the Middle East had been caught up in a Cold War involving two ideologies, communism and capitalism, that were not of its making, the historian Arnold Toynbee would argue that the religions of the world were 'experiencing the same crisis of faith and allegiance that the Western Christian churches had begun to experience before the close of the seventeenth century', implying that these religions found themselves on the same course as Christianity, if a few furlongs behind.[15] It even seemed possible that the crisis would advance more rapidly in the Middle East, which was being courted by two ideologies in broad agreement on the obsolescence of religion as a factor in public life. One only needed to take a stroll through the modern quarter of any Middle Eastern capital, where women went out to work or study, alcohol was available, and suits and ties were worn, to conclude that the process was irreversible. Referring to the long struggle between traditional Islamic practice and secularism, one scholar wrote in 1963 that 'this particular war is over in the great majority of Middle Eastern states'.[16]

Islamism as we know it is the harvesting of Islam for political use and the manipulation of religious dogma in order to create ideologies suitable for modern politics or revolutionary activity outside the established political order and cutting across national boundaries. Sayyid Jamal al-Din Afghani was perhaps the first to sense Islam's capacity for militancy of this kind, but he was an ego, not an organiser, and his legacy was more heat than light. Perhaps the strongest claims to fathering the Islamist movement as we know it now belongs to the later, more strategic, Hassan al-Banna, a solidly built, frizzy-haired horologist from the village of Mahmudiya in the Nile Delta.

Banna was born in 1906 to a father who, aside from pursuing the watch-mender's trade that he passed on to his son, had also been student at al-Azhar. Young Hassan's religious upbringing in Mahmudiya was a combination of conventional Quranic studies – he began his education at a *kuttab* religious school –and the emotional discipline imposed by Sufism approached through the writings of Abu Hamid al-Ghazali, whose skewering of philosophy and pursuit of spiritual 'extinction' in the eleventh century had proved damaging to the speculative tradition in Islamic thought.

The most significant impetus acting on the young Banna, however, was a politics of resistance lifted from Colonel Urabi and steeled by the terrifying speed and apparently uncontrollable nature of social change in Egypt in the first quarter of the twentieth century. At the age of thirteen (by which time he had memorised the Quran) Banna became the secretary of a local, Sufi-inspired organisation, the Hasafiyya Society for Charity, whose aims included checking the progress of American missionaries in the Delta, of whom he wrote suspiciously, 'they were preaching Christianity in the guise of teaching embroidery work and providing asylum to the orphan children'. Another aim of the society was the promotion of Islamic morals: already at the age of ten Banna is reported to have campaigned successfully for the removal and destruction of an 'obscene' statue of a semi-naked woman displayed on one of the Nile boats.

Banna's political development was also marked by the popular uprising that followed the arrest of Zaghlul and his fellow Wafdists in 1919 – in which Huda Shaarawi played a part in Cairo. 'I still remember the scenes of the demonstrations, strikes and processions,' Banna wrote years later, and nor did he forget the slogans of the protesters as they were chased and beaten by the British: 'Love for the homeland is a duty of our faith … if we fail to gather in Independence, then we shall surely meet in paradise!'[17]

It is a significant pointer to the diminished role of clerics in modern Islamism that Banna did not follow his father to al-Azhar, but instead carried on his studies at Cairo's modern teacher training college.[18] A shock awaited him when he moved to his new home in 1923, for if the delta was being eroded by Western interests and mores, the penetration of the capital was of an entirely different order. One senses in Banna's appalled reaction to his new environment the same crawling of the flesh, mingled with fascination, that millions of other new city-dwellers also experienced in this period of mass, worldwide urbanisation.

Cairo in the 1920s was unequal, consumerist, irreverent and cosmopolitan – everything Mahmudiya was not. Cinemas, theatres, unveiled women and department stores formed a gaudy backdrop to an untameable bazaar of ideas, with the Wafdists squaring up to their political rivals, the Liberal Constitutionalists, and nihilistic winds sweeping in from Atatürk's Turkey. It was exactly the kind of place where progressives like Ali Abdel Razeq would feel emboldened to bring out an argument against the legitimacy of Islamic government –

Banna duly took part in protests that greeted the publication of *The Caliphate and the Sovereignty of the Nation* in 1925.

The cultural and economic assault of the West was seemingly unstoppable, however. In Cairo the wedding of the daughter of the chief rabbi was attended by Muslims and a myriad of variously denominated Christians, all speaking French. The magnates – again, overwhelmingly foreign or members of the religious minorities – sucked on lobster at clubs whose appointments were the equal of Pall Mall. Meanwhile, on the fringes of this carnival of opulence, the majority lived without running water or electricity; half the city's children died of diarrhoea and malnutrition before entering their sixth year.

Here in whetted form was what Banna later described as the 'fierce attack of Western thought and culture ... armed with wealth and the outward temptations of life'.[19] Banna's upbringing had not equipped him to turn modernity's weapons back on itself. Not for him the vengeful avant-gardism through which the Turkish novelist Halid Ziya Uşakligil had delivered his condemnation of the new life in *The Blue and the Black*. Nor were the old arbiters of affairs even close to appreciating the enormity of the threat that faced them. Banna went to al-Azhar to plead for effective action against the rot. But the old school was torn between trying to retain the favour of the sovereign and carrying out its traditional scholastic functions, and the sheikhs were apparently resigned to the 'missionary and atheistic currents' disrupting society.[20]

Banna was transfixed by the unravelling society around him, and shared his feelings with a group of like-minded friends. 'No one but God', he wrote, 'knows how many nights we spent analyzing the state of the nation ... analyzing the sickness, and thinking of the possible remedies. So disturbed were we that we reached the point of tears.'[21]

Banna did in fact reach a solution: one of the most important in the recent history of the Islamic world. It took flight in the Suez canal settlement of Ismailia, where Banna was appointed to teach in a primary school in 1927. From the British army's nearby garrisons and the signage in English, not Arabic, to the juxtaposition of lavish houses for foreigners and hovels inhabited by lowly Egyptian workers, Ismailia embodied cultural and material disequilibrium. Banna took to the coffee houses, as Afghani, whose activism he greatly admired, had done in 1870s Cairo, addressing his audience in general terms about Islam before ushering those who showed particular interest into a side room for more detailed discussions of the nature of God, the correct way to worship, and the duty of all believers to promote virtue and combat vice.

Banna soon had a reputation in the poor quarters of Ismailia, and in March 1928 he was approached by six labourers working for the British garrison who required guidance. According to Banna's later account, they told him that they were 'weary of this life of humiliation', without 'status' or 'dignity', and that they desired to be of service to 'the fatherland, the religion and the nation'. They also committed themselves to the 'road to action as you perceive it'. Banna was moved by their sincerity and he and the men took an oath to become 'troops for the message of Islam'. Banna thought up a name for the group. 'We are brothers in the service of Islam,' he said. 'Hence we are the "Muslim Brothers".'[22]

This was the beginning of what would become the most influential Muslim organisation of the twentieth century, a combination of service provider and consultant on the big questions of life – and all with the aim of restoring confidence to a community that felt battered by the European assumptions of cultural superiority being taken to their conclusion by Atatürk and Reza Shah. On the contrary, Banna argued, Islam could not be bettered as a system for life, and he acknowledged his debt to Salafism, which was not yet the marker of Islamic militancy it would become but rather a restatement of Islam's undiminished applicability as a complete approach, in no need of amendment by Western ways.

Over the next few years Banna spent much time – alongside his work as a teacher – touring the country, preaching and raising funds for mosques, schools and clinics which brought tangible change to people's lives – an approach that was adopted by his followers. (In the foundation story of the Brotherhood it is hard not to hear echoes of those Christian missionary groups, with their blending of proselytisation and practical help for society's losers, which Banna had so hated in Mahmudiya.) Whether it was running night classes that taught correct Islamic practice and mores, promoting self-help through aid to members who had lost their jobs or had otherwise fallen on hard times, or raising money for good works, the Brotherhood was an innovation in the Muslim world. Here was a non-governmental social organisation run for the most part by laymen, and determined, as its ubiquitous, hard-working, unfailingly good-humoured founder put it, to avoid any entanglement with the apparatus of power that had plunged the country into such difficulties in the first place.

Banna described the Brotherhood as a 'political organization, an athletic group, a cultural-educational union, an economic company and a social idea', a gamut of activities whose apparent desire to take over all aspects of life recalled communism, fascism and other totalitarian systems of social organisation. Despite the Salafism, and despite the conservative message, in many ways the Brotherhood was not a throwback to the past but a reflection of its modern rivals, with attributes that would allow it to take on such ideologies and defeat them.

By 1936 the Brotherhood boasted a hundred branches around the country, a newspaper full of good news stories about Egyptians helping themselves, and a youth organisation, the 'rovers' – Boy Scouts with biceps and a prayer mat. (In another direct aping of the Christian adversary, in 1927 Banna and others in Cairo had set up a Young Men's Muslim Association.) The engine of this extraordinary spurt of growth was the movement's founder himself. Always in motion, a man of action rather than theory (he hardly wrote anything), this genial spreader of the faith would greet his admirers with a 'big open smile', according to one, 'and a verse from the Quran, then a line or two from a poem, and finally, a laugh full of life and energy'. When Banna addressed his supporters, another reported, 'the old and the young, the highly cultured, the illiterate, and the ignorant understand him ... in his voice there is a deep resonance and from his tongue comes magic'.[23]

And yet, for all his disavowal of politics, in 1936 Banna chose to address the new king, Fuad's son Farouk, in an open letter full of advice. The deceased monarch had been avaricious, authoritarian and contemptuous of his subjects, and there were hopes that his handsome, pious, sixteen-year-old son, the first member of the dynasty of Muhammad Ali to speak good Arabic, would preside over Egypt's flowering as a truly independent nation. In his letter, which was distributed to the heads of all Arab governments, Banna demanded that the country gain its liberty and compete with the other nations to make 'social progress', but not by following the West, whose political foundations were being 'razed by dictatorships, its economic foundations battered by crises'. In contrast to some earlier reformers who had written in praise of the Protestant work ethic, Banna rounded on the capitalist order, the root, as he saw it, of European materialism, aggression, and greed. 'Humanity,' he wrote, 'is in dire need of the purifying waters of true Islam,' and he counselled the new king to spoon out 'the Quran's medicine to save this sick and tormented world'.[24]

Banna's letter, which was also circulated among many ordinary people, was one of the opening manoeuvres in Islam's counter-Enlightenment. For perhaps the first time since the beginning of the transformation of the Middle East at the turn of the nineteenth century, here was the leader of a modern Islamic movement pouring scorn on the West and its pretensions to superiority – indeed, publicly rejecting the very materialist principles that reformers like Rifaa and the Tanzimatists had expended so much energy trying to reconcile with Islamic ideals. Now Banna, leader of a resurgent Egyptian, Sunni Islam, was announcing that this job of synthesis was over, and that simpler Islamic values like thrift, equality, conservative social values and traditional Islamic economics – which offer a seductively middle-of-the-road blend of incentive and social conscience – were the most effective ways to deal with the modern world.

The Islamism of Hassan al-Banna contained both elements of modern politics and a hankering for the past. Far from being a reflexive reactionary, Banna clearly appreciated that the Muslim world had changed irrevocably, and by laying emphasis on education, the need for investment in science and technology, and the active roles open to women under Islamic government, he drew heavily on the achievements of earlier reformers. Nor did the layman Banna seek to reverse the clerical decline that had seen the sheikhs of al-Azhar lowered from their former positions as arbiters of society. He also remained aloof from those of his compatriots who were involved in an abortive attempt to reconstitute the caliphate in Cairo, with Farouk as caliph. Having adopted these modern ideals – banking them, as it were, as authentic Islamic capital – Banna called for a resurgent civilisation that was ready to challenge the West, not as Atatürk and Reza Shah had done, on Western terms, but in the honeycomb of Islamic culture.

The Brotherhood wasn't just about good works and moral uplift, however. The Islamist message in later years has been lent great poignancy by the suffering of its adherents; but the objective of those who suffer is to gain power in the name of Islam, if necessary by force of arms. This line of thinking was discovered by the Brotherhood in the late 1930s, when it developed a paramilitary apparatus, whose eventual purpose, Banna announced to the Brotherhood's conference in 1939, was to bring the current phase of 'preparation' into a new one – of 'execution'. And he closed his speech with a condemnation of political parties – associated with division, easily exploitable by Islam's enemies – and colonialism. 'Death is better than this life,' he said, 'a life of slavery and oppression!'[25]

The Muslim Brotherhood's entry into politics led to increasingly bitter disputes with the country's political establishment, particularly the by now bloated and corrupt Wafd, as it became clear that the two sides did not enjoy an identity of interests. King Farouk himself was less devout than he had seemed, and grew similarly bloated and corrupt. His reign degenerated into poker, debauch and practical jokes, with the country's top officials locking up their daughters to keep him from pawing them and his fleet of red cars – including a Mercedes presented by Hitler – startling the populace with an array of custom-ised klaxons.[26]

The Second World War placed intolerable strain on Egypt's flimsy semi-democracy. The British once again used the country as a base of operations, imposing martial law and, in 1942, leaning on the king to topple a pro-Axis government. As an inflexible opponent of colo-nialism, his loathing for Britain sharpened by the advance of Zionism in neighbouring Palestine (still a colonial mandate), Banna found himself in British cross hairs, and in 1941 he was briefly arrested. Banna also tried to run for parliament during this period, but the electoral process was rigged against him. The mutual mistrust between Islamism and democracy was crystallising.

Also taking shape in the turbulent years that followed the Second World War were the ideals that would vitalise modern Islamism, notably government according to the sharia, the anti-colonial struggle exemplified by the struggle against Zionism, and opposition to domestic tyranny. The indifference that was shown by a pro-palace government to the fate of the Palestinians in the 1930s – exemplified by the use that Jewish settlers were able to make of an Egyptian port as a disembarkation point – convinced Banna that the monarchy and the magnates shed only crocodile tears for their fellow Arabs. After the war decolonisation movements got under way from India and Indonesia to Kenya and Cyprus, but in Egypt the British refused to pull out of the Canal Zone while next door the Jewish colonists' struggle for a homeland bore fruit with the United Nations partition plan of September 1947.

In conditions of almost unbearable domestic and international tension, Brotherhood militants activated their military plans – the extent to which Banna himself was involved is not quite clear – lobbing grenades and blowing up bombs in British installations and assassinating political figures they considered insufficiently patriotic. In 1948 Muslim Brothers took part in the failed campaign that was waged against the new Jewish state by the Arab nations – most ignominiously, by King Farouk himself, who, having reviewed his troops on a white charger, retired to the gaming table. Although the Brotherhood volunteers distinguished themselves with their bravery, the effort to smother the infant Israel was an unmitigated disaster and the new state emerged with more prestige and land than it had begun with.

In the ruins of defeat, the prime minister, Mahmud Nuqrashi, banned the Brotherhood. No longer could the establishment tolerate a paramilitary opposition movement with revolutionary tendencies whose supporters were estimated to number as many as one million souls.

A few weeks later, and probably without Banna's foreknowledge, a young Brother assassinated Nuqrashi. Banna admitted that the Brotherhood had made mistakes, and even consented to its dissolution. But he was not arrested – an official oversight that he prophetically described as tantamount to a death warrant. On 12 February 1949, he was shot dead on the steps of the headquarters of the Young Men's Muslim Association in Cairo.

It was the beginning of the Muslim Brotherhood's experience of state repression. Banna went to his grave escorted by tanks and armoured cars, and by July 1949 some four thousand Brothers were behind bars. The organisation's assets were also sequestered. But the sense of anger and yearning for justice that had animated Banna and his supporters did not die. On the contrary, they burgeoned in the years that followed, as the Brotherhood established branches in Syria, Jerusalem, Transjordan, Iraq and North Africa, and seeded yet more movements of national uplift and Islamic revival.

That Islamism should take flight in the turbulent interwar period is not altogether surprising. The emergence of a dynamic political movement championing the counter-Enlightenment was borne of reaction – it was a response to the arbitrary settlements that had been imposed by the victors in the First World War and which reached a nadir in the creation of Israel, and to the continuing frustration of projects of national self-realisation that had been kept hanging since Colonel Urabi.

The paradoxical situation of imperialists advocating democracy had always been a flaw in the modernisation of the Islamic Middle East. A century and a half into efforts to smooth it out, either by forgiving the Westerners their cupidity because of the strengths of their ideology, or by presenting the ideology as reheated Islam, the impossibility of dividing message from messenger had become painfully obvious. In his dismissive attitude towards political parties, Banna showed his scepticism towards a system of government that was constantly being sold by the West, and which, when it operated as imperfectly as it did in Cairo, seemed only to produce divisions that the West could come in and use. Western-style democracy, for which Islamic reformers had struggled for decades, was indelibly associated with international exploitation.

A sign of the cynicism that now sprang up in the Middle East with respect to the intentions of the West can be found in reactions to the formation of the United Nations after the Second World War. Not for Hassan al-Banna the unrealistic hopes that earlier Muslim nationalists had lodged in the League of Nations and Woodrow Wilson's excessively sanguine vision of a future of mutual respect. As a founder member of the Security Council, Britain was able to prevent meaningful discussion of Egyptian independence, and in November 1947 the General Assembly passed its controversial resolution partitioning Palestine. No more would the Muslim states repose trust in international bodies created by Western countries. If Islamic civilisation were to revive and grow strong once more, it would have to do so under its own energies, in the glow of its own purity.

This was the Islam promised by Hassan al-Banna. 'When asked what it is for which you call,' he told his followers, 'reply that it is Islam, the message of Muhammad, the religion that contains within it a government, and has as one of its obligations freedom. If you are told that you are political, answer that Islam admits no such distinction. If you are accused of being revolutionaries, say, " . . . we are permitted by God to defend ourselves against your injustice."' Islam, from its origins, built institutions that were predicated on an assumption that the religion would drive all before it and assume power. It was, as a modern Islamic scholar has written, 'programmed for victory'.[27] Since then, with the arrival of Western ideas, this assumption had been pummelled and trampled on. Now it was back on its feet.

An unlikely figure – an avant-garde poet and bureaucrat who heard about Banna's murder while brushing up his English in Washington DC – would harden the ideology of the Muslim Brotherhood into a revolutionary creed capable of stunning acts of militancy.

His name was Sayyid Qutb and the long journey he took to Muslim martyrdom, via erratic verse and some of the most influential Islamist tracts of the twentieth century, began in the village of Musha on the flood plain of the upper Nile. In this brick-and-adobe settlement two hundred long miles from Cairo, his perspective bounded by limestone and desert on either side of the cultivable strip, Qutb was born in 1906 and raised by a family of struggling landowners and minor Azharites.

Qutb later wrote about his childhood in a memoir that shows how important nostalgia can be as a catalyst for anger. The Musha that is depicted in *A Child from the Village* is the kind of earthy, un-monetised sort of place where each house has its own oven and selling bread is a crass breach of mores, and which the annual flood turns 'into a group of islands interconnected only by small boats and light skiffs'.[28] In this sociable, meddlesome, enchanted society the principal terrors for a young boy were an encounter with the dervish Naqib, who would 'tear his clothes to shreds and then roll in the mud or pour dust over his head and naked body'; an assault by malicious sprites (the death of Qutb's own baby brother is blamed on such a 'twin'); or simply the hours of night, when the village streets become black and 'one approached every corner expecting some unknown danger'. The balancing forces of good and evil in the universe, the resignation of people to tragedies ordained by fate – here is the cosmic architecture of Musha.

And yet this same Musha, seemingly impervious to the rational values that have impregnated life and belief in the cities, is itself being transformed by a brusque modernity. The young Qutb attends a clean, well-equipped school paid for by the state (blotting paper supplied), and he is glad to do so because his experience of the rival *kuttab* is of a primitive establishment whose teachers are slovenly rumour-mongers. Qutb memorises the Quran before he is ten, on top of his other schoolwork, all the while building a library eclectic enough to feature a medieval devotional poem, the risqué verses of the *Thousand and One Nights* and Arabic translations of Conan Doyle. Thus the hound of the Baskervilles howls in Musha – happy result of Muhammad Ali Pasha's efforts to introduce printing to Egypt a century before.

Musha has been hauled out of comfortable obscurity and into the official account books, but this isn't necessarily a good thing as far as Qutb is concerned. There is consternation among the children when they receive a visit from a government doctor. He pricks them with a needle and demands urine and faeces specimens – to what purpose they cannot guess. And there is terror when government soldiers raid the village as part of an operation to confiscate illegal weapons. Faced with an ultimatum to give up guns they don't possess the poorer villagers sell cattle, food and jewellery in order to acquire them.

'The countryman', Qutb laments, 'is always oppressed by the rulers, oppressed by the taxes on his small bit of earth, oppressed by the endless demands of the [headman] to meet the orders of the government, which include donations for charitable associations ... tickets for the Red Crescent ... then there is the corvée labour on the dykes and in the fields of the rich to clear the caterpillars, and guard duty outside the village, and the struggle against locusts, and countless other "tasks" besides these, which make the villager feel like a beast of burden forever.' Finally, he writes, 'there is the burden of tradition – especially on the woman, who is never more than a commodity in the eyes of the man'.²⁹

It was with a strong sense of injustice – but giving little warning of his later Islamic militancy and social puritanism – that the young Qutb went to Cairo in 1921, where, after attending secondary school, he entered teacher training college a couple of years after the same institution bade farewell to Hassan al-Banna. Graduating in 1933, Qutb began his career as a primary school teacher in the salubrious spa suburb of Hulwan, a slight, primly moustachioed figure in suit and tie who was adept enough at bureaucratic slithering to gain promotion to the Education Ministry's prestigious office of General Culture. The Egyptian novelist Naguib Mahfouz, a friend of Qutb at the time, later depicted him in a semi-autobiographical book, *Mirrors*. It is not a flattering portrait. The Qutb character is described as a 'polite conversationalist', who 'never spoke about religion, pretended modernity in his ideas and dress, and adopted European habits'. Something about him troubled Mahfouz's narrator, for 'while he always showed me generous fraternity, I was never comfortable with his face or the look in his bulging, serious eyes ... I was disturbed by his opportunistic side, doubting his integrity. A permanent revulsion, despite our friendship, settled in my heart.'³⁰

Mahfouz was part of a circle of secular *littérateurs* whom Qutb met frequently in the 1930s – poets and critics whose work reflected a society at odds with itself. Qutb felt particular reverence for the neo-Romantic Abbas Mahmud al-Aqqad; he also admired Abduh's disciple, the controversial educationalist Taha Hussein. Trying to deal with the alienation that flickered over the new Egypt, drawn to the Muslim Brotherhood's dynamism, but not its theocratic ideas, Qutb sketched the lines of a civilisation not living up to its promise of achievement. 'Why do our arts not depict an atmosphere of strength and energy?' he asked. 'Have we fought and won a battle against our enemies? Have we opened a new era for the world? Have we gained our independence? Can we breathe freely? Have we made any industrial breakthrough that we can be proud of?'³¹

His verses were either effusive and jejune, or else starkly political –
commentary on a 'dark age' of colonial subjugation.[32] 'We are exiles,'
he wrote after the death of his mother in 1940; 'we are the small
branches whose roots have withered after their estrangement from
their native soil. And how far are the branches from establishing
themselves on foreign soil!'[33]

It seems likely that Qutb's frustration was aggravated by a lack of
romantic fulfilment. His tendency was to idealise the opposite sex
while at the same time regarding the unveiled women he came across
as unworthy of his attention. His sexual experiences may not have
extended beyond those of the hero in his novel *Thorns*, who sees the
object of his desire in her underclothes, when 'many things made him
want to approach her, but many other things prevented him from
doing so'.[34]

For all his sense of Egypt's unused potency, Qutb believed that the
country possessed a moral as well as a political integrity, and that its
inhabitants, Christian as well as Muslim, were the possessors of an
innate spirituality marking them out from the materialist and indi-
vidualist West. He distanced himself from Taha Hussein in 1938, when
the latter argued (as Hassan Taqizadeh had done for Iran) that Egyptian
modernisation should take its lead from Europe; on the contrary, Qutb
argued back, Egypt was part of an Eastern tradition to whose instinct
for the transcendent Islam had given practical form. He was now
inching towards the argument, which he would go on to articulate in
his most influential book, *Milestones*, that since the lands of Islam
could not compete with Europe in material ingenuity, 'we must have
some other quality, a quality that modern civilization does not
possess'.[35]

What was that quality? What would allow Egypt to demonstrate
its genius? In the 1940s, appalled by Zionism and the bacchanals of
Farouk, he came full circle and landed on the sacred text he had
committed to memory while a child in Musha. Qutb was now
acclaiming the Quran for its peerless literary qualities; his writing
in this period delineated an Islam that was both God-given and
aesthetically delightful. Still, however, Qutb's view of a political
order based on Islam lay within the reformist tradition of Namik
Kemal – adopting the Enlightenment concept of progress with the
Quran at its heart.

Qutb was poised between an Islamic and a universal solution to the questions of human fulfilment when, in the autumn of 1948, the Egyptian government sent him to the United States to study American educational methods. For the influential Middle Eastern thinkers who had preceded him westwards, a prolonged Western sojourn had had an exemplary effect. Think of Mirza Saleh, returning to his Iranian homeland with one of the first printing presses ever used there, Namik Kemal emerging from the British Museum library imbued with the values of that Enlightenment institution, and Taha Hussein, whose descriptions of studying in France were coloured by his evident desire to rise to the rigorous standards of French scholarship. America did the opposite to Sayyid Qutb. How come this traveller conceived such a profound disgust for the West while his predecessors had received such a favourable impression?

That Qutb's mind was already working along Manichaean lines of destructive mutual opposition is apparent from his reaction to the preaching of a Christian missionary on the Atlantic crossing – which prompted him to lead retaliatory prayers for Muslim passengers and members of the ship's company. The advances of a 'beautiful, tall, semi-naked' woman, whom he expelled from his cabin, and who promptly fell down, dead drunk, alerted him to the forked tongue of Western sensuality, while New York, emerging like a chrysalis from its wartime skin, glistening with shows, shopping and sex, was symbolised by the 'roaring cars and thunderous traffic, which surged forward as if it were the Judgment Day', and the 'hurrying crowds rushing feverishly in search of their prey', giving out 'sharp and sparkling looks filled with greed, desire, and lust'.[36]

There is a disagreeable whiff of prurience to these descriptions, sharpened by the unaccomplished desires of the virgin from Musha, and while in Washington DC, where he enrolled on a language course and was treated in the George Washington University Hospital (he suffered from respiratory problems), he was apparently the object of another advance, this time from a nurse who tried to titillate him by describing the ideal qualities of her lovers. Between humid appreciations of the typical American woman's 'thirsty lips ... bulging breasts' and 'smooth legs', Qutb seized the civilisational high ground; he professed himself unimpressed by the 'defective pedagogy' employed at his college and wrote to a friend yearning for 'someone to talk to about topics other than money, movie stars, and car models'.[37]

For most of these impressions and incidents Qutb's writings are our only source, and his version appears partisan and incomplete. His claim that employees at the George Washington University Hospital rejoiced at Hassan al-Banna's assassination is especially dubious as it credits them with a greater awareness of Middle Eastern politics than seems possible in 1940s America.

Of all the wholesome, quintessentially American places that might have let the air out of Qutb's swelling prejudice, the ranching town of Greeley, Colorado, where he went in the spring of 1949 in order to audit teaching techniques, was promisingly placed. Pious, morally vigorous and alcohol-free, the kind of place, as the State College of Education put it, where 'the handshake is firm' and the greeting 'sincerely cordial', this spacious, tree-lined settlement of barely 10,000 souls boasted a score of churches while, at the same time, attracting enough foreigners to justify an international club whose annual dinner featured something called 'Arabian cuisine'.

In Greeley, Qutb clearly did not betray the militant feelings for which he would later be known. A fellow member of the international club recalled that his Egyptian friend enjoyed Western classical music; and he never saw Qutb pray. Qutb even joined a church club in order to experience community life. One can only assume that he was also the recipient of many acts of consideration and kindness.

But Greeley must have seemed infinitely distant from the convivial bustle of Egypt, and for Qutb it came to exemplify the atomised, superficial nature of American life – he was particularly saddened by the inordinate amount of time its inhabitants spent caring for their lawns. The church club dance he attended again brought out the salivating prude in him, as the hall 'convulsed to the tunes of the gramophone and ... arms circled waists, lips met lips, chests met chests ... the atmosphere was full of passion'.[38]

Qutb's depictions of America tell a remarkable story of the disappointment of an Islamic intellectual with the Western Shangri-La, and they are of course as much a window into Qutb as the failings of the West. From his lip-smacking denunciations it is clear that he felt plagued by all the sexuality on display; in contrast to earlier Muslim travellers, who, while feeling little affinity to Western mores, did not regard them as a threat to their personal salvation, one detects in Qutb a horror of moral contagion. It's notable that Mirza Saleh was able to praise the virtue of the Devon girls he mixed with in the early nineteenth century. No such virtue seems possible to Qutb in the diabolical America of 1949, and to today's reader his words are a warning that morality was preparing to slip its religious moorings and become truly secular. The sexual permissiveness that began to trans-form Western society in the late 1960s would repel many mainstream Muslims because it ran counter to the family values that were the bedrock of Islamic society.

Qutb drew the opposite conclusion of earlier Muslim reformers who accepted that the inventions of the West stemmed from human ingenuity unleashed by the Enlightenment; instead he asserted that there was 'no correlation' between America's advanced material civi-lisation and the people who created it. 'I fear', rang his final indictment, 'that when the wheel of life has turned and the file of history has closed, America will have contributed nothing to the world heritage of values.'[39]

He was on firmer ground when damning racial prejudice in the United States, having doubtless learned of the fate of the Ute people of western Colorado (whom Congress had dispossessed of their vast ancestral lands in 1880). During his stay in Greeley, Qutb was barred from a cinema for being black. Upon learning that his customer was not, in fact, African American, but Egyptian, the manager apologised, but Qutb refused to enter on principle. 'In America,' he wrote after his return home in August 1950, 'they talk about the white man as though he were a demi-god ... they talk about coloured people, like the Egyptians and Arabs generally, as though they were half human ... we must nourish in our school age children sentiments that open their eyes to the tyranny of the white man.'[40] He was not, however, free from prejudices of his own, belittling jazz as 'a type of music invented by Blacks to please their primitive tendencies and desire for noise'.[41]

The Egypt to which Qutb returned had entered a period of political ferment that would end in revolution – and that he, enjoying the success of a bristling new polemic, *The Battle of Islam and Capitalism*, observed with growing excitement. In 1951 the government abrogated the Anglo-Egyptian Treaty and armed groups led by the Muslim Brotherhood stepped up their harassment of British forces in the Canal Zone. The following January there were mass riots against foreign interests in Cairo; arson and looting consumed the European city that Ismail had conceived, as cinemas, restaurants, liquor shops and other Western interests were torched and trashed. 'It was as though all earth's atoms were screaming at once,' Naguib Mahfouz wrote; 'repressed anger, stifled despair, pent-up tension, all that had been brewing inside the people burst forth, erupting like a whirlwind of demons.'[42]

In the absence of a political solution to the crisis with Britain, the fury consumed more pillars of the old order. In July 1952 a coup led by Colonel Gamal Abdel Nasser, and with a Brotherhood-approved Islamist, General Muhammad Naguib, as its figurehead, toppled King Farouk. Within a year Egypt was a republic. Qutb had been closely involved in preparations for the coup; and he had formally joined the Muslim Brotherhood, renouncing his earlier, secular writings. Now, as a liaison between the officers and the Brotherhood, he confidently anticipated an Islamic regime. But in February 1954 Naguib was sidelined and in Nasser, who now took over the country, there was more of Muhammad Ali Pasha than there was of the Prophet Muhammad. Another secularising modern-iser had arrived to save Egypt.

'I was born in 1951,' Qutb would later say, referring to the moment when he finally joined the Brotherhood, but it could be argued his real rebirth arrived during the conflict that now crackled into life between the Islamists and the army. Land reform, not Islamic rule, interested Nasser, and his preferred form of international coopera-tion against Israel and Britain was Arab unity under Egypt, not Islamic unity under the Brotherhood. On 26 October 1954, while addressing a throng, Nasser was fired at by a member of the Brotherhood's secret apparatus, an assassination attempt that gave him a useful pretext to demolish the organisation. Six senior brethren were executed and many imprisoned. When Qutb came to court he raised his shirt to show the marks of torture on his body. 'Abdel Nasser has applied to us in jail the principles of the revolution,' he said. He was sentenced to twenty-five years' hard labour.

In fact for the next nine years Qutb languished in the notorious Tura jail, and he was able to establish himself as the most important theorist of militant Islam. This was in part down to the negligence of the government, which continued to permit him to publish new works from behind bars, in part to the solitary, unmoderated hostility he now conceived for the godless republic sprouting outside. But in Nasser he had a strong and successful enemy. The country's new *rayyis*, or chief, was popular – because he fought and won battles against the country's enemies, because he was a man of the people opening a new era for the world. In 1956 he succeeded where the old regime had failed, engineering a sensational defeat for the British by nationalising the Suez Canal and seeing off a ham-fisted military intervention by Britain, France and Israel. Two years later Egypt and Syria formed the United Arab Republic, which was supposed to be a partnership of equals but was in fact dominated by Nasser (Syria ended up seceding); and in 1961 Egypt became a founder member, along with Yugoslavia, India, Indonesia and Ghana, of the Non-Aligned Movement, an anti-imperialist bloc that nonetheless wished to avoid inclusion into the Soviet Empire.

At home, Nasserism was about planning, redistribution and dam-building; in Hulwan, Qutb's fragrant former home, the air grew thick with dust and fumes from new steel mills, car factories and cement factories.[43] Egypt's cacophonous semi-democracy was shut down and voices of dissent were silenced amid the aura of invincibility that surrounded the *rayyis*. Over the next few years the Nasserite model proved sufficiently attractive for it to be adopted in part or in full from Algiers to Baghdad – half a dozen new presidents holding forth on socialist development and Arab unity all the while building radio masts and torture chambers. Most galling of all, to Qutb, the mass of Egyptians, desperate to believe in the success of Nasser's great movement, acquiesced in his 'tyranny'.[44]

There was not much room for Islam in all this, or for Western-style liberalism. Liberalism had been discredited because it was associated with a colonial order newly swept away, and Islam was quiet amid the Nasserite mania for industrial progress, female education and international dress codes (the short-sleeved safari suit was all the rage in the nationalised company boardrooms). But political Islam, or

Islamism, was evolving into an ideology of resistance whose enemy now included tyrants within. The foundations for Islam's resurgence in its most virulent and politicised form were being laid – to a substantial degree in the Tura jail.

Suffering and virtue are vital to Islamism, which its theorists link neatly to the grim early days of Islam, when the Prophet's mission had seemed on the verge of extinction by pagan and Jewish forces. In the early 1950s these admired qualities were embodied by the suppressed Muslim Brotherhood and their outstanding stoic Sayyid Qutb. He passed on ideas in the prison exercise yard, and in the filthy, infested cells he interpreted small evanescent joys – for instance a beam of light, 'no bigger than a penny', in which he and his fellow brethren took turns to stand – as signs from God. In 1957 he was in the infirmary when the authorities slaughtered twenty-one refractory Muslim Brothers in their cells, but Qutb's faith in final victory never wavered. 'I have not surrendered my weapon,' he wrote in the massacre's aftermath, 'if the armies of darkness encircle me ... I will avenge my Lord and my religion.'[45]

God, he believed, had given people the choice of whether or not to strive to establish a sublime order on earth, and there could be no piecemeal implementation of a programme that only made sense in its totality. He turned his fire on the rationalists he had once stood alongside. Muhammad Abduh, he wrote, had 'poured Islam into the foreign mould of philosophy', elevating reason to the same status as revelation.[46]

Here Qutb – as fingers rest on the nuclear trigger and as man pushes off into space – restates Hassan al-Ashari's bromide, *bila kayf*, or 'without asking how', and goes against Sayyid Jamal al-Din's belief in the timeless validity of philosophy and the limitations of prophets. In doing so he attempts to roll back 150 years of the slow advance of reason. 'Who knows better,' he hectors the doubters, 'you or God?'[47]

Of all the books Qutb wrote in this final, productive period of his life, first in jail, then following his release in 1964 (at the behest of Iraq's president, a fan), none has been more effective in steering Muslims towards radical militancy than *Milestones*. This tract begins with a prognosis followed by a prescription. 'Mankind today is on the brink of a precipice, not because of the danger of complete annihilation which is hanging over its head – this being just a symptom and not the real disease – but because humanity is devoid of those vital values which are necessary not only for its healthy development but also for its real progress ... it is essential for mankind to have new leadership!'[48]

This must of course come from Islam, but not the current, degenerate Islam that one finds in the world, one that is shot through with *jahiliyya*, a condition of ignorance and benightedness that has not been so oppressively prevalent since the dawn of Muhammad's mission. *Jahiliyya* is our 'whole environment, people's beliefs and ideas, habits and art, rules and laws', and the discussion that follows tars all of today's so-called 'Muslim' societies as counterfeit. Under the influence of the West, Qutb argues, their way of life has become a hybrid made up of Muslim and alien values, and they have passed over the title of lawmaker, which belongs to God, to men in councils and in parliaments.[49]

A vanguard needs to be formed (here Qutb shows a debt to Lenin's revolutionary ideas), advancing the cause of Islam until it takes over the world and an authentic Islamic government can be brought in to implement the sharia. At the start of the process it is necessary for today's Muslim to read the Quran with the same sense of literal enquiry as his or her forebear in early Islam, not 'for the purpose of acquiring culture and information, nor for the purpose of taste or enjoyment', but to find out 'what the Almighty Creator had prescribed for him ... as a soldier on the battlefield reads "Today's Bulletin" so that he knows what is to be done'.[50]

Of course Qutb anticipates bloodshed. He derides the current, wishy-washy thinkers, products of the 'sorry state of the present Muslim generation', who have 'laid down their spiritual and rational arms in defeat', saying, '"Islam has prescribed only defensive war!"' This is the kind of pacifist interpretation to which Abduh inclined, along with the Indian collaborator Sir Sayyid Ahmed Khan, and which Qutb now refutes. 'It would be naive to assume', he asserts, 'that a call to free the whole of humankind throughout the world may be effected by preaching and exposition of the message alone.' On the contrary, wherever Muslims live under 'the political tyranny of an absolutist state, the socio-economic system based on races and classes, and supported by the military might of tyrannical governments' (i.e. everywhere), Islam logically has no recourse but to remove these governments by force.[51]

Milestones speaks a lot about freedom, the same *hurriya* that Sheikh al-Jabarti used to signify freedom from slavery – itself a misinterpretation of the French *libération*, meaning political autonomy. How does the father of Islamism understand the word? Qutb does not emphasise the freedom of the individual to do as he wishes, but his is a freedom from human political dominance in order to obey unthinkingly the rules of God. Divine bondage in place of human bondage, in other words, though nowhere does the author of *Milestones* lay out how this would look in practice, nor which human structures would be erected to implement God's will and laws. Qutb doesn't approve of parliaments, so even if people were prepared freely, through elections, to entrust their affairs to a parliament of lawmakers, this would be forbidden under Qutbism. In a striking demonstration that his is a post-Reformation Islamism, he rejects the idea of a ruling priesthood, which he equates with the Church, or the idea that 'some spokesmen of God become rulers, as is the case in a theocracy'.[52]

Among Qutb's targets were the senior Azharite sheikhs, whose school Nasser had placed under state control in 1961, and who dutifully bolstered the regime against its detractors. In this way, by hugging the old school too close, Nasser discredited any claims it might have had to independence from the temporal power.

Milestones appeared in November 1964, when Qutb was not only out of jail, but busy mentoring a group of Islamists who were preparing for armed conflict with the state. The egalitarian Utopia promised by Nasser was now being exposed as a sham, with state housing shoddily built, the minorities hustled before unsympathetic Muslim judges, and educational standards plummeting even as the number of graduates soared. (In 1950 the ratio of teachers to students at Cairo University was 1:6; a decade later it was 1:60.)[53] When it came to his troublesome Islamists, Nasser's attitude oscillated between martial vigour, his desire to co-opt opposition to his regime, and his need to accommodate demands for clemency being directed at him by other non-aligned leaders. In the event, when *Milestones* came out, Nasser himself intervened to ensure that this unabashedly revolutionary screed got past the censors. The Egyptian public showed their appreciation by buying the book in droves – which no doubt contributed to the fate of its author. 'If you want to know why Sayyid Qutb was sentenced to death,' wrote one of Qutb's followers, Zeynab al-Ghazali, 'read *Milestones*.'[54]

In August 1964, less than a year after his release, Qutb was rearrested. Thousands more brethren and sympathisers followed him into jail, and many of them were tortured. Qutb admitted that he had wished to change the regime, but by persuasion. 'Nationalism is a flag whose historical time has passed,' he told Egypt's spy chief.[55]

When he received news of his death sentence for trying to overthrow the country's legitimate regime, Qutb said, 'praise be to God, I performed this jihad for fifteen years until I earned this martyrdom'.[56] He refused official offers of a pardon in return for contrition, and was hanged, along with two other Islamist militants, in the early hours of 29 August 1966.

In their bravery, Qutb and his fellow martyrs set a standard for defiance in the face of political tyranny that is engraved on the hearts of Islamists to this day. Victory doesn't go to the last man standing, but to him who dies best. And when, a few months after Qutb's execution, Nasser's army was humiliated by Israel in the Six-Day War, the imprisoned Zeynab al-Ghazali cawed bitterly, 'it is because of your departure from the Quran and the Sunna that you are defeated, miserable and sinking ... for there is nothing in disobeying God except humiliation, misery, defeat, weakness, fire and an everlasting punishment'.[57]

Qutb died, but not Qutbism. It was helped by the initial emollience of Nasser's successor as president, Anwar al-Sadat, who came to power on the death of the *rayyis* in 1970, and it was steeled by Iran's 1979 revolution and the Soviet invasion of Afghanistan. From Qutb's *jahiliyya*, an all-purpose denunciation of the tyrants of the age, was drawn the doctrine of *takfir*, the declaration of a state, or an individual, to be apostate and deserving of death. For the vast majority of Muslims, including today's Muslim Brotherhood, *takfir* is un-Islamic and unacceptable, but without it there would be no Islamist terrorism as we know it – *takfir* is integral to the armoury of the modern Islamic radical. And so it was for Egypt's al-Jihad, a group founded in 1979 and inspired by the thirteenth-century jurist and anti-rationalist Ibn Taymiyya, whose leader Abd al-Salam Faraj wrote that 'it is obligatory for Muslims to raise their swords under the very ideas of the Leaders who hide the truth and spread falsehoods'.[58]

President Sadat himself was an example of Islam's 'near enemy', Faraj argued (the 'far enemy' being the West). Although Sadat's forces had given a good account of themselves against Israel in the Yom Kippur War of 1973, six years later he angered many Muslims by making peace with Israel in return for closer ties with the West – all the while cracking down on domestic opposition. In October 1981 Sadat became a victim of *takfir* in action, wasted by his own soldiers during a military parade. As he hurled his grenades into the tribune where Sadat stood, taking the salute, the al-Jihad militant Khalid al-Islambouli shouted, 'I have killed Pharaoh!'

Sadat's assassination was a fanfare announcing the arrival of militant Islamism as the major new factor in Middle Eastern politics, which would either have to fight it out or come to an accommodation with the impulses to modernise and emulate the west that had been gradually taking over the Egyptian body politic since the time of Muhammad Ali. At the other end of the Middle East, on the Persian plateau, the Iran of Shah Muhammad Reza Pahlavi was heading towards an even more dramatic Islamist cataclysm: a movement by Iranians of all persuasions seeking to stamp out those same impulses. When it came, in the 1979 revolution that bundled the shah out of power and welcomed Ayatollah Khomeini to set up the modern world's only theocracy, an Islamic Republic was formed that claimed to be operating according to universal values. But the Iranian Revolution would not be successfully exported, as its architect had hoped it would be. It never escaped its Iranian origins.

For all that, the Islamism of Qutb and the Islamism of Khomeini would become the world's two most influential modern Muslim movements, injecting rage and a doctrine of martyrdom into the war to liberate Afghanistan after the Soviet invasion of 1980 and leaving their mark on Islamist militancy to the present time. That these two strands of Islamic militancy never coalesced belied their claims to universality, showing how much their proponents subscribed to a national identity sharpened by sectarian differences.

There was another gap between rhetoric and reality. Neither Khomeini's revolutionaries nor the Muslim Brotherhood were able to dispense with electoral democracy, a sure sign that these avowed returnees to pre-modern values were in fact riddled with recent ideas of Western provenance about representative government. Notwithstanding all the pious talk of Islam crossing borders and the merits of archaic forms of 'consultation', nationhood and democracy proved impossible to abandon. To its intense irritation, Islamism itself was shot through with Enlightenment values.

How Iranians came to raise their revolution of 1979 is a story that blends such modern values with mass mobilisation and religious zeal – a tale of dislocation, betrayal and a popular reaction whose consequences few had foreseen. In Iran in the middle of the twentieth century, the young Muhammad Reza Shah strove like Farouk to gain purchase on an unreliable landscape of nationalist, leftist and revivalist sentiment. (In the interests of royal solidarity, the two men in fact became brothers-in-law in 1939, though the marriage between Muhammad Reza and Farouk's sister Fawzia did not last.) Muhammad Reza's accession to the throne in 1941 had led to the relaxation of some of his father's more stringent anti-religious policies, and in 1946, in a sign of burgeoning Islamic chauvinism, the doctrinaire secularist Ahmad Kasravi was slain while answering charges that he had 'slandered Islam'. Kasravi had already been the subject of an assassination attempt by Mojtaba Navvab-Safavi, an Iranian militant who had good relations with the Muslim Brotherhood in Egypt, and a rising cleric called Ruhollah (later Ayatollah) Khomeini demanded decisive action against the 'illiterate Tabrizi'. (Whatever he was, Kasravi was far from illiterate, and he infuriated the *ulema* by delivering his sharpest rebukes to Islam in Arabic.) In the course of the final hearing, goons affiliated to Navvab-Safavi's organisation, the Devotees of Islam, entered the courtroom and, using guns and knives, killed Kasravi and his faithful amanuensis Muhammad-Taqi Haddadpour. The killers were apprehended but the trial that followed was a farce because witnesses refused to testify and the government eventually bowed to clerical pressure and set them free.[59] The euphoria with which the murderers' release was greeted was a sure sign that the godless days of Reza Shah were finished, and over the next decade the Devotees of Islam were able to exploit the support they enjoyed among the radical *ulema* to carry out a series of high-profile assassinations, most notoriously that of a serving prime minister, Hajj Ali Razmara, in 1951 – a career of violence and fanaticism that finally hit the buffers with Navvab-Safavi's execution in 1956.

In the 1940s and 50s the world of Islam was not riven by the murderous Sunni–Shia enmity that we know today, and Iran's new radicals were for the most part welcomed into a worldwide Islamic network that extended from Indonesia to North Africa, held its annual AGM in the sidelines of the hajj, and crystallised around opposition to Israel and colonialism more widely. Cross-sectarian amity was also shown to Iranian secularists such as Muhammad Mossadegh, a European-trained lawyer who had been a young supporter of the Constitutional Revolution of 1905, almost lost his life to Reza Shah's dictatorship, and bitterly regretted how little progress had been made in uprooting colonialism and domestic tyranny. In May 1951, after becoming prime minister, Mossadegh sensationally nationalised the oil industry – a British asset seized by the natives in a whirlwind of self-assertion. That winter Mossadegh was invited to Cairo, itself aflame with anti-British sentiment, where he was feted by large crowds and advised the government, in a clear reference to the (still foreign-controlled) canal, to reclaim their 'property'.[60] His patriotic adventure ended less happily than Nasser's, however; two years later the British teamed up with the Americans, whom they had convinced that Mossadegh was a cat's paw for the Communists (he wasn't), to topple him in a coup that returned the industry to Western control.

For both sides the oil dispute was about much more than economics, and in aborting Mossadegh's premiership, the plotters from MI6 and the CIA also ended Iran's best chance since 1905 of having a constitutional regime independent of the great powers. Chastened by his experience of the abrasive Mossadegh, whom he believed to be a republican (he wasn't), the shah now began gathering power; henceforth no elected prime minister would be able to bid for political primacy at the monarch's expense.

In the 1950s and 60s Muhammad Reza Shah subscribed to the top-down reform and economic planning that had been given the status of a new orthodoxy across the developing world. Dam-building, land distribution, state-led industrialisation – for all the shah's horror at Egypt's republican revolution, and his dislike for Nasser, his programme had much in common with republican Egypt's. But the shah, unlike his bête noire on the Nile, was no believer in non-alignment, and with the British in retreat as a world power he steered the country into Washington's slipstream. America now became Iran's main source of hardware and expertise, keeping the shah supplied with oil platforms, economic plans and the latest methods of torturing dissidents – the latter adopted and even expanded upon by the shah's American-established secret police, Savak.

With oil revenues rising and a spending splurge getting under way in the 1960s, imbalance became one of the outstanding features of the shah's Iran. Industrialisation proceeded apace and per capita income soared, but agriculture suffered from underinvestment and Iran's villages, the traditional unit of the nation's life, started to empty as people sought urban employment and amenities. Migration on such a scale was more than Iran's immature infrastructure could withstand, and the matrix of prosperity, expectation and distribution was skewed and maladjusted. The shah, meanwhile, brooked no opposition to his civilisational long leap. In 1963 he bloodily put down a short-lived agitation inspired by Khomeini and other mullahs, and after that the 'black reaction', as he liked to call the clerics, were for the most part quiescent, either bought off like Nasser's Azharites or else silenced – as happened to Khomeini, who was sent into exile.

There was also a psychological malaise that the economists and planners didn't care to see. Internal migration, rising education levels, and a new consumer culture induced a sense of dislocation, of being an observer of one's own unravelling destiny. For those who were caught up in it, the country's sprint towards modernity was a race without a finishing line – a race against Iran itself.

The Iran of the 1960s was a country undergoing social transformation according to a foreign model. This might have spelled the triumph of the Islamic Enlightenment. That it did not, and that the shah's hubristic new Iran would, in fact, be overturned in a revolution, demonstrate that the shah's rule lacked the political suppleness and ability to accommodate dissent that is intrinsic to any modern system of government. Simply put, Iran was brittle. But the shah's failure also signalled that there is no single pattern of modernisation, but rather a general thrust or tendency that must be balanced with the existing host culture. The shah's pell-mell lunge towards an entirely new way of living was interpreted as a sign of his embarrassment at Iran's Islamic heritage and the way of life of ordinary Iranians; and the monarch didn't understand the revulsion people felt for the foreign interests now crowding in for a piece of the economy. The tobacco protest of 1891 had been propelled to victory by a fear of non-Muslims handling a stimulant that would go near Iranian lips. Now, three-quarters of a century later, things had got much worse. Foreigners touched, directed, orchestrated and passed comment on almost every area of the country's life, generating a sense of powerlessness and self-loathing among the people who watched it happen.

The other trouble was that, as Sayyid Qutb had noted, Western material culture was banal. It gave no quarter to the transcendent and it casually obliterated centuries of tradition. Was this really the culmination of a century and a half of hard-fought social and political struggles – those revolutions of the mind that brought out the first modern soldiers' drill on a square of Tabriz scrub, saw the harem condemned and a Constitutional Revolution fanfared into being? Could one fit all this into a bottle of Pepsi? What upset many educated people was that progress, a grand idea ostensibly directed at allowing people to achieve their potential, seemed to have been perverted, emptying man of culture and feeling and filling him with an idiotic love of glitter. It was this sham progress that the shah seemed intent on bringing into Iran, a shah who showed his abhorrence for his people by doing what custom and practice told them was wrong: keeping dogs as pets, retaining his shoes when entering a peasant's hut, raising Bollinger toasts to foreign dignitaries and their bosomy wives.

It was against this backdrop of material advance and spiritual impoverishment that a new kind of Iranian disquiet came up, which, like that of the early Qutb, harked back to a simpler, more human mode of existence, and yet, in contrast to the intransigence of the late Qutb, interpreted the country's Islamic identity with a very human flexibility.

This kind of disquiet was the *raison d'être* of Jalal Al-e Ahmad, one of Iran's most significant and (for the shah) troublesome thinkers of the twentieth century. He was born in Tehran in 1923 and he spent his childhood under Reza Shah's unbending regime. The son of a mullah (like Ahmad Kasravi), he learned good Arabic and enough French to translate Camus and Sartre. Like the Muslim Brotherhood's Hassan al-Banna he became a schoolteacher, but he was the first to see the flaws in his own arguments, and this made him an unconvincing proselyte – he knew he was a member of the country's intellectual elite and suffered nobly for it. 'I don't know what I am,' he would tell an audience of students in Tabriz late in his life, and since 'nothing can be begun with certainty, it's better we begin with doubt'.

Over the course of the 1940s and 50s he went from being a Communist to a Mossadeghist but he also wrote lovingly of Shia Islam. He was the kind of traditionalist who dared chat up a woman on a long-distance bus journey and later marry her. (This was the novelist Simin Daneshvar, to whom he referred in essays as 'Simin'– an unusual public intimacy.) And he was the kind of proud Muslim who still took up an official invitation to visit Israel. But one shouldn't hold these contradictions against him. One of the reasons for his success as a public intellectual was his frank acceptance of his own fallibility.

It didn't harm either that he had an attractive, accessible persona, and that when he wasn't teaching or travelling around the countryside researching pieces, you might easily find him holding court at the Cafe Firouz, a stone's throw from the British Embassy (where the plot to depose Mossadegh had been hatched), all elbows and knees, his upper lip grown over by a shop-floor moustache, his black hair parted by a belt of grey.

The work that first brought him prominence, an autobiographical novella called *The School Principal*, which was published in 1958, is about a modern structure – in this case the school – that is supposed to do one thing but is found out by reality and embarrassed into doing something else. In Al-e Ahmad's depiction Iran's education system is completely undermined by an event as random as a fall of rain, which turns the world into mud and results in a tenfold increase in absenteeism. 'Before this,' his narrator confesses, 'I had read a lot of rubbish about what the basis of education is: teachers, blackboard cleaners, proper toilets or a thousand other things. But here, quite simply and primarily, the basis of education was shoes.'[61] In another passage he deplores the provision of a modish handicrafts class that will, he knows, have no effect on the country's chronic dependence on mass-produced foreign goods and the commensurate decline in local production. 'We import jigsaws by the donkey load,' he writes, deliberately using an archaic unit of measure, 'along with safety pins, porcelain toilets, water piping, enema pumps', but just one person in a thousand thinks to do something productive like open a framers' or an inlay shop.

Relations between individuals and society are rendered all the more complex and intractable by the insertion of a third party: God. In another short story a weak-minded bazaar broker called Amir-Reza reneges ineptly on the obligations of the Ramazan fast; so thirsty does he become, and so desperate to avoid detection by his pious fellow bazaaris, he takes a bus all the way to the neighbouring town of Karaj, where he can slake his thirst anonymously. But Amir-Reza's wife discovers his deception when he fails to show sufficient enthusiasm for the evening breakfast, and she coruscates his want of virility, piety and good sense. 'Don't you feel any shame to have spent four *tomans* to go all the way to Karaj just to drink a glass of tea and break your fast into the bargain? And in the afternoon at that, when you could have waited only two or three more hours! How can you hope for God's mercy now? You're not even man enough to keep His fast! Who said you had to fast anyway?' The story ends with the stars pulsing in the night sky; 'perhaps', writes Al-e Ahmad, 'they had been overcome by laughter in the face of all this wretchedness and stupidity and were winking at each other in mockery of us'.[62]

In 1962 Al-e Ahmad wrote a book that shook up the disaffected of Shia Iran – just as the Martiniquean intellectual Frantz Fanon had thrilled France's disengaging colonies with his influential work, *The Wretched of the Earth*, in 1961, and as Sayyid Qutb's Sunni constituency would be galvanised by *Milestones* in 1964. The name of Al-e Ahmad's contribution to this troika of anti-Western diatribes was *Gharbzadegi*, which has been variously translated as 'Westoxication', 'Weststruckness', 'Euromania' and 'Occidentosis', a mysterious debilitation he defines in agricultural terms that are easily comprehensible to Iran's still partially rural society. 'It's at least as bad as sawflies in the wheat fields,' he writes. 'Have you ever seen how they infest wheat? From within. There is a healthy skin in places, but it's only a skin.'[63]

What is the cause of this terrifying de-substantiation? The answer is the machine – both in its physical manifestation and the dehumanisation and political subservience it signifies. The shah's programme of industrialisation runs counter to Iran's very humanity and ancestral pattern. 'As the machine entrenches itself in the towns and villages,' Al-e Ahmad goes on, 'be it in the form of a mechanized mill or a textile plant, it puts the worker in local craft industries out of work. It closes the village mill. It renders the spinning wheel useless. Production of pile carpets, flat carpets, felt carpets is at an end.'[64]

Al-e Ahmad divides the world into developed Western countries that have the machinery and capital to turn out finished goods and undeveloped Third World ones that are condemned to supply oil or iron ore and buy back whatever the West manufactures. If this sounds like a familiar, one-sided arm-wrestle between the producers of raw and refined products – 'dependency' as had been experienced by the cotton farmers of Turkey and Egypt and the loom towns of northern England in the nineteenth century – think again. It's more sinister: this new disequilibrium also transforms creativity and metaphysics. The epic stories, the foundations of belief, music and even the loftiest climes of religious thought are not exempt from *gharbzadegi*; the 'aggregate of events in life, culture, civilization, and mode of thought' is robbed of its supporting tradition and whatever it is that makes Iran Iranian folds or implodes. This degeneration has its source in a dismal history of contacts with the outside world – notably the West's attachment to Iranian oil. In Al-e Ahmad's Manichaean conception of history, Iran is placed at the wrong end of a continuum of opposites, between 'wealth and poverty, power and impotence, knowledge and ignorance, development and desolation, civilization and savagery'.[65]

Al-e Ahmad's vision of Iranian decline is linked to the pull of the cities and the slow death of village life. Industry and building sites are pulling in labour from the countryside, and he likens the peasant's migration from the village of his forebears to being 'snapped from the ground', a phrase that recalls the severance of the believer from God – reed from reed bed – that the medieval poet Jalal al-Din Rumi evoked in his masterpiece, the *Mathnavi*, or 'couplets'. Today's emptying villages, Al-e Ahmad regrets, are themselves victims of the raw-goods/manufactured product nexus, receiving tractors that trample indifferently over the ditches between the plots and are the cause of violent disputes; of these 'bloody encounters', writes this occasional chronicler of rural life, 'I have an archive'.

The peasant's uprooting is completed in the city itself, where soft furnishings and alien victuals and entertainments (sandwiches, the cinema and transistor radios) have an effeminising effect. Iran's sons of the soil are reduced to lusting over Raleigh bicycles, Fiat cars and tinned food from the Antipodes. 'In our clothes, our houses, our food, our civilities,' Iranians are a tribe 'estranged from itself'.[66]

The figurine atop this meringue culture – the role model to which the new arrivals look – is the 'West-stricken' man, the shah's unthinking cipher and functionary. Al-e Ahmad comes close to implicating the monarch directly when he introduces the target of his derision as a member of the nation's 'ruling establishment'.[67] (For this lese-majesty he was rewarded with attention from Savak, which obliged him to present himself to its offices at periodic intervals.) The modern Iranian mandarin is the kind of villa-dwelling, car-worshipping, record-playing, *Time*-reading non-entity who whiles away his time in government commissions, pleads a dust allergy in order get out of visiting the countryside, and rhapsodises about the neon lights and internationalist architecture that are turning Tehran into a version of everywhere else. Needless to say, 'mosque and *mehrab*' – the niche indicating the direction of Mecca – have been forgotten. Our shell-Iranian believes in neither God nor man.

One man's (the shah's) progress is another man's (Al-e Ahmad's) horrendous dystopian nightmare. Al-e Ahmad's horrified reaction to the machine age would perhaps have been the reaction of the Turkish author Halid Ziya Uşaklıgil, whose description in his novel *The Blue and the Black* of the lithograph press in 1890, with the chief typesetter 'broken and exhausted by binding and unbinding the ideas at his fingertips', demonstrated the dehumanising possibilities of the machine.

Al-e Ahmad's concerns in *Gharbzadegi* overlap heavily with his fellow anti-Westerners. Shades of Sayyid Qutb and his loathing for the appetite-driven Western life show through his contempt for the leisure pursuits of Tehran's new bourgeoisie, which consist of calls to the barber, tailor, shoeshine and whore.[68] Although Frantz Fanon shows a naive faith in the Nasserite pan-Arabism that will, in fact, burn itself out in just a few years, and his polished faculty French is a contrast with Al-e Ahmad's rhetorical plunges, the instinct of both men is to meld culture and resistance, building a hearth, as Fanon puts it, 'that glows with passionate emotion'. The native intellectual 'not only turns himself into the defender of his people's past; he is willing to be counted as one of them'.[69] The Martiniquean might have been talking of the Iranian.

Yet although it shares ideas and themes with these other polemical and analytical works, *Gharbzadegi* remains a distinctly Iranian cry against the impersonal forces of globalisation that have in a few years obliterated vast deposits of custom, expression and belief – the culture of a nation.

The perennially dissatisfied nature of Al-e Ahmad's mind was again demonstrated by his distinctly catholic travel itinerary for the years 1963–5, taking in Israel, Harvard and Mecca. His and Simin's Israeli trip was perhaps the most surprising of these forays, for while the shah had implicitly recognised the Jewish homeland – Nasserism was their shared enemy – it remained for the majority of Muslims an unacceptable colonial implant. But Al-e Ahmad's admiration for this communitarian state sanctified by martyrdom and implementing socialism overrode other, specifically Islamic concerns. The couple stayed on a kibbutz where they sank beers and discussed Castro and Mao with their fellow toilers. Al-e Ahmad came out of Yad Vashem, the Holocaust memorial in Jerusalem, in tears, and concluded that Israel was an appropriate response to the Jews' tragic history. It was also an example of what could be taken from the West without losing one's identity. 'Israel,' he wrote, 'with all its faults and all the contradictions concealed in it, is a base of power, a first step, the herald of a future not too far off.'

Sayyid Qutb and other proto-jihadis would have been disgusted by Al-e Ahmad's praise for the Israelis, no less than by his largely positive account of Harvard, where he spent the summer of 1965 attending the International Seminar of which Henry Kissinger was the organiser (supported, it later emerged, by the CIA). Between lectures and classes, ploughing through *Huckleberry Finn* and *The Naked and the Dead* (he heard Norman Mailer speak, describing him as a man 'of middling stature, rotund, with his hair blown around like wheat'), Al-e Ahmad obviously relished the cosmopolitan atmosphere conjured by American soft power. Among his fellow seminarians was an opinionated Pakistani intellectual who astonished him with her never-ending collection of saris (this was before Pakistani Muslims rejected the sari as a badge of Hinduism) and a young Japanese man whose father and grandfather had both committed hara-kiri, and who described this as an act of defiance. Whether he was appraising a beautiful German woman, enjoying 'significant' conversations with the habitués of a working-class bar, or slipping from awkward English to better French when the *mot juste* eluded him, he clearly revelled in the opportunity to hear opinions drawn from varied contexts. Al-e Ahmad's Harvard was as stimulating and light as Qutb's Greeley had been clammy and obnoxious.

That the two Middle Easterners retained such different impressions of the United States was in part down to their differing personalities, but Americans themselves had changed since 1949, becoming less conformist, and Al-e Ahmad appreciated the avenues for opposition and resistance that were being cut from American culture itself. At the time of Al-e Ahmad's Harvard residency, more than 15,000 US soldiers were involved in the Vietnam War and he joined heated discussions on the subject – though not, apparently, with Kissinger himself, who manipulated a forum he chaired 'in such a way that there was no attack on American policy'.[70] Race was the other hot topic (the Civil Rights Act went through during Al-e Ahmad's stay), and he won the attention of the black writer and campaigner Ralph Ellison – author of the acclaimed novel *Invisible Man* – by deploring the protective cocoons that American blacks had spun themselves. 'Christianity and jazz,' he declared; 'if these two refuges didn't exist, perhaps the problem would have been solved by now.'[71] Ellison doesn't seem to have minded this deliberate provocation (he was an accomplished jazz trumpeter); 'he's sturdy', Al-e Ahmad wrote approvingly, 'and he smiles'.

Al-e Ahmad's largely favourable account of Harvard did not, however, add up to a reversal of his earlier denunciation of America's influence in *Gharbzadegi*. What was natural in Americans would only produce Potemkin Americans if transplanted elsewhere – like the man without qualities in *Gharbzadegi*. Culture needed the strongest and deepest roots if it was to survive the Western onslaught, and these roots, he gradually realised, must reach into the metaphysical.

For a man who had deprecated Christianity as retarding civil rights in the US, Al-e Ahmad's pivot to Shia Islam towards the end of his life is perplexing. Certainly his Islam had little in common with Sayyid Qutb's militant demands for the literal application of the Quran and the overthrow of rulers on the grounds of their impiety. Al-e Ahmad had not moved beyond the nation state as Qutb had; for him Shia Islam was an essential element of the Iranian identity and the most effective 'vaccine' against *gharbzadegi*. Compared to the aura of resistance that had attached to Shiism ever since Iran became a Shia state in the sixteenth century, and the feverish emotions that were generated by expectations of the reappearance of the occulted twelfth imam, it may be that the fatalistic creed of Christianity that was practised by many black churches in the United States smacked to Al-e Ahmad of Marx's 'opiate of the masses'.

His appreciation of Islam was bolstered by a growing conviction that Iranians had been let down by excessively Westernised intellectuals, the products, in part, of the secularism promoted by Reza Shah. Again surprisingly for someone who as a young man had admired Ahmad Kasravi, he now felt an answering warmth towards the *ulema*. Reflection on Jamal al-Din's mobilisation of the top clerics against the Tobacco Concession in 1891, the mullahs' sufferings under Reza Shah, and, more recently, Khomeini's anti-regime heroics had convinced him of the clerics' utility. In *Gharbzadegi* he had gone so far as to rehabilitate Sheikh Fazlullah Nuri, the former constitutionalist who turned against the impieties of radicals such as Taqizadeh and was executed in 1909; to Al-e Ahmad's mind the real villains were the secularists who had mocked and cheered him to his grave.

In 1965 he went on the hajj, and there is still a great deal of the detached, sidling outsider in his deprecation of the neon lighting and 'multi-coloured mini-skyscrapers' with which the Saudi Arabian government had decked out the holy city in its bowl between the granite peaks of western Arabia. (He would have been shocked to see the canyons of bling that now tower over the birthplace of Islam.) Between these ironic asides, however, between gripes and stomach aches caused by the weather and the food, Al-e Ahmad experienced that dissolution within the multitude that is the experience of so many who travel to Mecca, who abandon national and class differences for the white, unbraided uniform of the hajj, and carry out the same rituals for the same God. 'I began my prostrations,' ran Al-e Ahmad's description of the ritual prayer in the great mosque at Mecca, and 'by the time I raised my head again the entire population ... was lined up, from one end of the porticoes and rooftops to the other. The greatest assembly of human beings under this sky who came together in one place in response to a command. And, after all, there must be some meaning to this gathering.'[72]

And so there was. The Pakistani woman he had befriended in the US had told him that intellectuals in her country were backing away from a secularism that cut themselves off from ordinary people and were re-engaging with their Muslim identity. This is the manoeuvre that Al-e-Ahmad executed towards the end of his life. He remained a far from perfect believer, for all his praise for the clergy (reciprocated by Khomeini), and for all the satisfaction he derived from the Meccan pilgrimage, and when in 1967 he was asked for his views on evolution and creationism he replied as if he had been asked whether he preferred dates or honey. 'Between the two – that is, between the supposition or speculation [of evolution] and the story [of creation] – I like the story. Why? Because it is poetry ... accept whichever version you like.' Expecting a more categorical answer that let in light on Al-e Ahmad's religious convictions – a more Qutbian answer – some of those present interjected, 'Not acceptable.'[73]

In 1969, aged just forty-six, his hair by now quite white, Al-e Ahmad succumbed to a heart attack. He had been grieving for a political ally who had recently died, he was bitter at his and Simin's inability to have children, and he mourned, as the intellectual historian Roy Mottahedeh has put it, 'for a cultural heritage that seemed irremediably doomed to extinction ... his hope was failing'.[74]

THE ISLAMIC ENLIGHTENMENT

In the event, despite the apparent solidity of the shah's rule backed by America, Al-e Ahmad's hopes for an axis of resistance uniting the *ulema* and a class of intellectuals who recognised themselves in the looking glass of Iranian culture would materialise rapidly. Royal hubris, an overheating economy and the unbridled entry of Westerners carrying their values (some 25,000 Americans were living in Iran in the mid-1970s) saw to that. Revenues soared eightfold thanks to the oil price rises of 1972 and 1973, and the world's salesmen converged on Tehran. Like his former brother-in-law, Egypt's King Farouk, like the Khedive Ismail back in the 1860s, Iran's late-twentieth-century monarch misinterpreted his power as a general licence for excess. He indulged fantasies that are only available to dictators: changing the calendar, setting up a one-party state, and hosting an unfeasibly silly party for world leaders in the ruins of Persepolis. And – sure sign of the incorrigible boy racer in him – he ordered not one, but two Concordes.

The shah lost control of the boom. In the middle of the 1970s inflation rose, measures were introduced to curb credit, and growth oscillated wildly. Investment fell off and many of the young people who had been expensively educated found themselves either jobless or working menially. All the while many poorer Iranians – those who had stayed in Al-e Ahmad's beloved villages, those who crowded into the shanties on the edges of the big towns – were living without basic amenities like running water.

Al-e Ahmad had been too full of doubts – too much a product of the Enlightenment – to offer a solution to the problems he identified in *Gharbzadegi*. In the event it fell to another public intellectual, the sociologist and lay preacher Ali Shariati, to marry the anti-colonialism he had learned in Paris in the 1960s – he had been a student of the French orientalist Louis Massignon and translated Fanon into Persian – with the Shia concept of resistance against injustice, in the process coming up with a revolutionary ideology to politicise the middle classes and sweep the country towards revolution.

Born in 1933 – a decade after Al-e Ahmad – Shariati was a clean-shaven, balding tie wearer whose wife and daughters were the object of pious sniping because they kept their hair uncovered. To the big audiences who gathered to hear him speak in prosperous north Tehran in the early 1970s (in a lecture hall financed by the Iran representative of the Dodge Motor Company), Shariati revealed an Islam that drew on the martyrdom of the imams to become an agent of revolt. Islam, he said, was both 'an ideology and a social revolution which intended to construct a classless and free society'.[75] A dictatorship, he went on, could only be shifted by force. Clearly Shariati's Islam was intended to act as a steroid, not an opiate, and his nostalgia for Al-e Ahmad's 'authentic' Iran was strengthened by militancy. In response to the shah's hankering for Iran's ancient empires – exemplified by the revels at Persepolis – Shariati wrote that 'our people remember nothing from this distant past ... for us a return to our roots means not a rediscovery of pre-Islamic Iran, but a return to our Islamic, especially Shia roots'.

Feared and distrusted by the government, which harassed and arrested him without cease, the combative Shariati also picked fights with the Shia clerics who were now divided over whether to oppose the shah or live with him. Although he himself was the son of a mullah, Shariati had arrived at his religious convictions not by parsing religious texts but by treading in the path of 'nonreligious or even antireligious scientists. I travel along this road and I speak with the same language which ... renounces religion or negates its metaphysical roots'.[76]

Downgrading the religious texts also meant downgrading the men who guarded them, and Shariati, in contrast to Al-e Ahmad's generally positive feelings for the clergy, denounced their 'closed monopoly, despotic, stifling and petrified'.[77] This conception of God without the priests drew on a long tradition of scepticism of the sheikhs' claim to authority. Back in the 1870s Jamal al-Din Afghani had considered himself a potential Muslim Luther, but the success of the Tobacco Protest had depended on the rulings of the chief clerics, and Jamal al-Din himself – a freelancer with a position neither at al-Azhar nor the Shia seminaries – had ended up neglected and obscure. From Ahmad Kasravi railing against the deceit that was the cleric's 'hallmark', to the preparedness of Sayyid Qutb to dispense with al-Azhar while reprogramming Islam for action, the modern faith was being shaped by forces outside the sheikhs' control. The latest of these was Shariati (who was inspired by Qutb), but for all his success at twinning Shia Islam with resistance he was unable to establish anticlericalism as a central plank of the gathering movement against the shah.

Iran's space-age Luther died in exile in June 1977 from a heart attack. The following January, by planting a scurrilous attack on Ayatollah Khomeini in a newspaper, the royal court inadvertently sparked protests that gathered power and intensity over the following twelve months, leading to the shah's flight from Iran on 16 January 1979. Shariati's absence from the stage allowed Khomeini and others in the revolutionary vanguard to appropriate his ideas about Shiism's revolutionary potential and ally them to a spellbinding clerical authority. The mass of ordinary Iranians, it turned out on 1 February 1979, when huge crowds greeted Khomeini on his return from sixteen years of peripatetic exile, were not ready for Islam without clerics. The landing of the ayatollah's chartered Air France 747 at Mehrabad Airport was inevitably compared to the return of the occulted twelfth imam.

The fugitive shah was taken in by his friend President Sadat of Egypt, where he died of cancer in July 1980 – fifteen months before his host was himself gunned down. In the meantime Khomeini set up his Islamic Republic. With its disdain for Western materialism and zeal for holy war, which would now be prosecuted against the godless Baathism of Saddam Hussein's Iraq, in a horrendous conflict that lasted from 1980 to 1988, the world's first Islamic theocracy was widely interpreted as a signal that Iran was returning to the medieval age.

This was incorrect. The shah's displacement marked the culmination of Iran's struggle to limit the monarch that had begun with the premiership of the cook's son Amir Kabir in the 1850s and led to the Constitutional Revolution and its turbulent postscript. Regime change itself was a major innovation; it went against a millennium and a half of Islamic orthodoxy, which regards such upheavals as displeasing to God. The Islamic Republic, furthermore, had recognisable modern features. It was heavily informed by nationalism – anti-Arab feeling ran high during the Iran–Iraq War, when Saddam was supported by his fellow Arab states – and socialist ideas about redistribution shone through the planned economy. For all the talk of divinely ordained government, the institutions of the new state, with an elected presidency and parliament, and ministries and departments, were versions of a universal, modern theme – a theme running all the way back to Napoleon's consensual diwan of notables governing Cairo in 1798. And while many of the incidental gains of the Islamic Enlightenment, such as women's rights, were henceforth either stationary or went into reverse (the hijab, for instance, was made compulsory), the pressure for further forward movement would be irresistible. It would be the Islamic Republic that educated unprecedented numbers of young Iranian women – by the mid-2000s more than half of university graduates in the country were female – and brought the country into the nuclear age.

For all that, there is no denying that the Islamic Revolution was a setback for many of the values that are associated with the Enlightenment. Iran exchanged one kind of repressive state for another and for the first time in history Shia mullahs ran a country. Many of Khomeini's supporters were nostalgists like Al-e Ahmad, militants like Ali Shariati, and bigots like Sayyid Qutb. Theirs was a cry against modern forms of cultural and political imperialism, and it was taken up by people who had had enough of being treated like chattels and longed instead for spiritual enchantment and cultural authenticity.

In Turkey, the traditional crossing point between the cultures of East and West, the riddle of Islam and modernity in the second half of the twentieth century engendered a kind of politics that was not revolutionary but entailed the peaceful takeover of the state. Revolutionary Islamism did not enjoy mass appeal in a young country that had been born out of trauma and had grown up obsessively attached to the reassuring structures of the state. On the contrary, a limited amount of Islamic piety was valued even by the ruling 'Kemalist' establishment (so called because of its adherence to the ideas of Mustafa Kemal Atatürk) because it was an ideological wall against communism.

In the 1960s and the 70s Turkish revolutionaries tended to be Marxists or Trotskyites, and the pious majority were, on the whole, deeply conservative. If Turkey at that time did not produce a thinker as influential as Sayyid Qutb, or as original as Jalal Al-e Ahmad, this is because the country's Islamists were less concerned with elaborating theories of Islamic government or nativist resistance than figuring out how to convert their considerable popular support into actual power.

The gradual repudiation of Atatürk's legacy took shape after the Second World War – which Turkey, under Ismet Inönü, had cleverly managed to avoid. The Cold War, however, proved less resistible, and the state bequeathed by Atatürk became unambiguously Western-orientated, committing a sizeable contingent of soldiers to the anti-Communist side in the Korean War of the early 1950s – from which some 2,500 Turkish soldiers never returned – and joining Nato in 1952. All the while, as the elected politicians politely undermined the legacy of Kemalism, the cat's cradle of secularism, democracy and piety was exposed.

The inception of multiparty politics in the late 1940s furnished an opportunity to resolve the strands, and as soon as the electorate was given the chance to vote into power a pious opposition party, the Democrat Party, in 1950, they promptly did so, and the result was a slow, cautious retrenchment of religious values. In 1933 Atatürk had outlawed the call to prayer in Arabic and insisted it be done in Turkish instead; this measure was reversed (almost overnight the Arabic call to prayer was adopted across the country), and religious education and mosque construction both took off.

The opponents of Turkey's new Islamists were the Kemalist establishment, supporters of Atatürk's unitary, secular state, who constituted a ruling elite centred on the army and the bureaucracy. As in Egypt, and much more so than in Iran, the Turkish military retained immense power over civilian politics, and on three occasions between 1960 and 1980 the generals overthrew elected governments that were, in their view, either too Islamist or leading the country to chaos. Permitted to take part in politics provided they paid lip service to Kemalism, liable to be arrested by the military and thrown into jail, Turkey's Islamic-leaning politicians developed a modus operandi that stressed infiltration, not revolution; they suborned the state rather than overthrew it.

The last and most consequential of Turkey's three military coups inadvertently helped the Islamists achieve their goal. In May 1980 the Turkish military overthrew the unstable centre-right government of Suleyman Demirel, following which some 650,000 people were taken into custody and more than 1.5 million people were barred from public sector employment. Torture was widely practised and much of the country lived in terror. Although Islamists were among those affected,

Turkish leftists bore the brunt of the repression, and this, compounded by the end of the Cold War in 1989, killed Turkish Socialism as a major political force. Whereas before 1980 Turkey's Islamists had been engaged in a vicious struggle with the leftists, now they were able to concentrate on infiltrating Kemalist institutions such as the military, the police and the civilian bureaucracy. Within a quarter of a century the ramifications of this gradual movement of men and ideas would be felt not in revolution, as in Iran, nor in gusts of unrest and repression, as in Egypt, but in the legal takeover by Turkish Islamists of the levers of government.

Conclusion

With the failure of democracy in Egypt, the revolution that took place in Iran, and the rise to power in Turkey of a strain of Islamism that later turned authoritarian, the story of the Islamic Enlightenment, including its dissonant coda, the counter-Enlightenment, seemed to have come to an end by around 1980. Nowadays it is hard to discern any general movement in favour of liberal, humanist principles in the Middle East, but rather a slippage towards violence and sectarian hate. Indeed, with the failure of the Anglo-American occupation of Iraq in 2003, the aborted Arab Spring of 2011, and Turkey's evolution under Recep Tayyip Erdogan from a progressive new society to a corrupt authoritarian one, it is tempting to conclude that the Islamic Enlightenment was an interesting idea that ended in failure; that the great movements of thought, modes of living, and political organisation that have been described in this book did not, in the end, amount to more than the weight of tradition and conservatism they were supposed to overturn.

The idea that the struggle between faith and reason has been won by the former is misleading, however – and not simply in the light of the exceptionalism displayed by Iran, which continues to be dominated politically by a vigorous reformist faction. In fact the terms of the confrontation between tradition and modernity have been redefined. As is exemplified by the tortured disputes over what constitutes 'real' Islam, claims and counter-claims permeate the modern Islamic identity. Rarely in Islamic history has Sunni zealotry so insistently proclaimed that the Shia are heretics deserving death; other Muslims state baldly that these same zealots practise not Islam but barbarism; and all the while, technology, literacy and the modern cult of the individual have permitted people to practise Islam according to their own tastes.

Homogenisation has opposed variety for much of Islamic history. The urban centres of the Ottoman Empire were made up of communities living side by side; but propinquity did not necessarily bring sympathy, let alone emulation.[78] Religious and secular authorities alike tried to reduce the practice of the faith to a limited number of schools and comportments. Sheikh Abdulrahman al-Jabarti strongly disapproved of the saint worship practised by many of his compatriots, while the violent reaction of Nasser al-Din Shah to Babism and Bahaism showed a hypersensitivity to the threat posed by modern prophethood. More recently, homogenisation has been challenged by technology and an ethic of personal emancipation that has crossed from the secular to the religious sphere. The emergence of individualistic versions of the faith is in part a consequence of the weakening of the traditional Sunni clergy that occurred throughout the nineteenth and twentieth centuries. In part it stems from the dislocations of modern life.

A British Muslim of Pakistani origin may consult radical online screeds rather than accompany his parents to hear a traditional, apolitical sermon in the local mosque. For alienated French Muslims, Islam may be less a code of belief than a response to racism and Islamophobia, and they may know little of the faith they espouse. What, if anything, links these angry, often ill-informed Muslims to the entrepreneurial Iranian Americans who hold Sufi prayer meetings and engage in philanthropy in suburban Los Angeles, or the followers of Fethullah Gulen, a Turkish preacher, whose network controls hundreds of schools around the world, preaches inter-religious amity, and is accused of trying to overthrow the Turkish state? It is far from certain whether these people belong to the same community or different, opposing ones. What is called 'Islam' is a very broad church indeed.

And then, of course, there is an unquantifiable number of people whose world view has been shaped by Islamic beliefs and practice and who, while respecting the moral precepts they have received from their forebears, are lax in matters of observance. They, too, may identify themselves as Muslim; in their secular world view and relatively liberal values they represent the successful part of the Islamic Enlightenment.

These examples show that the breakdown of geographical boundaries between the Islamic and non-Islamic worlds has had a big effect on the variegated Islam we now see around us. Islam is no settled entity. It has burst its banks and seethes with discontents and desires that are immediately recognisable as the consequence of a painful engagement with modernity. Many of the suicide bombers who have done their work on European soil are pitifully ignorant of Islam; their abominations are more the product of psychological instability and a wider failure to reconcile Islamic values with those of modern society in the libertine and materialistic form it has assumed since the 1960s. The phenomenon of the suicide bomb is indissoluble from the media that report it; recorded by smartphone or body camera, broadcast through the social media, these acts may be considered extreme selfies – they are to some degree an authentic product of our narcissistic age. Some of the worst 'Islamic' attacks that have taken place in the West have been committed by men whose lives had been chaotic, criminal and hedonistic. It is hard to attach the label 'Muslim' to people whose engagement with the faith is so superficial. These miracle-grow Muslims have been incubated in the hothouse of modernity.

And yet, for all the apparent suspension of the Islamic Enlightenment, the historic shifts associated with it grind on. In the summer of 2009, Iran's Green Movement mobilised millions of people in spectacular protests against a fraudulent election result manufactured by the country's hardline leadership; in Tehran I was told by protesters (a large number of whom were women) that the aims of the Constitutional Revolution were finally being achieved. Two years later the Arab Spring promised similar delayed gratification for peoples that had been denied self-determination by European colonialism at the end of the First World War and had since been ruled by tyrants drawn from the military. In Cairo revolutionaries told me they had been emboldened by the toppling of the political despotism of Hosni Mubarak to undermine long-standing hierarchies closer to home; no established structure, whether the family, the workplace or the university, seemed immune from Egyptians' desire to re-examine their deferential attitudes to authority. Then in 2013 Turkey erupted in protests of a similar size and intensity against Erdogan's intolerant form of government.

That none of these demonstrations of popular will has achieved its goal does not of course mean that the motivations animating them have gone away. Iran's Greens were first crushed, then vindicated five years later by the election of the moderate reformist President Hassan Rouhani. Inept, distrustful of democracy, the government that the Muslim Brotherhood set up in Egypt in 2012 was itself overthrown the following year in a military-led counter-revolution; and the protests in Turkey gave Erdogan all the pretext he needed to round on his domestic adversaries. In the meantime, civil war in Syria, Libya and elsewhere, along with poverty and climate change, pushed millions of Muslims into Europe. All but an infinitesimally small minority of these people did not come to the West in order to turn it into an Islamic caliphate. They came in order to avail themselves of the fruits of an Enlightenment that had gone wrong in their own countries.

Much of this book has been about the relationship between the Islamic world and ideas that were first elaborated in Europe. This relationship was gusty and volatile back in 1798, and it remains so today, but I hope I have demonstrated that many of the ideas, such as the value of the individual and the benefits of law, science and representative government, were adopted rapidly – so seamlessly, in fact, that they are now authentic features of Islamic thought and society.

Of course, the West itself has not stood still during this process of integration and assimilation, stretching the limits and possibilities of humankind in ways that none of the characters in this book can possibly have imagined. Some manifestations of post-Enlightenment life, whether sociological, such as the condemnation of the traditional family, or cosmic, such as science's seductive promise of immortality, speak to many Muslims of a repugnant hubris. For post-religious Christian society Islam remains a younger sibling that, while it has internalised many modern ideas, continues to insist on a spiritual dimension that has been largely lost in the West. This is Islam after the Enlightenment, sketched by Jamal al-Din Afghani and Muhammad Abduh, humanised by Jalal al-e Ahmad and pumped up by Sayyid Qutb, never at rest, beset by contradictions. It is certain to continue to needle and perplex us.

Acknowledgements

I spent three years in libraries researching and writing this book, largely in silence. One might expect this way of working to incur lighter debts of gratitude than a journalistic book dependent on the goodwill of living characters – their stories, their tolerance and their beds for the night. Surprisingly, I am seriously in the red as a result of writing *The Islamic Enlightenment*, for although the idea was mine and the words are my own, without the wisdom, encouragement and criticism of a great many others it would never have come about. *The Islamic Enlightenment* is as collaborative a book as it is possible to imagine by a single author, written, for the most part, in a single room in the British Library.

No bibliography, nor a spattering of footnotes, can do justice to the inspiration and information I have derived from a great many writers. Now is the time to acknowledge my debt to the roving intellect of Juan Cole, the innovative social history of Janet Afary and the judicious modern analysis of Max Rodenbeck. If Peter Gran had not done all the hard work, my section on Hassan al-Attar could not have been written; I am similarly indebted to Daniel Newman's introduction to his fine translation of Rifaa al-Tahtawi's travelogue for my account of the father of modern Egypt. Ehud Toledano's books were indispensable to my account of the decline of slavery; and without Nikki Keddie the passages on Jamal al-Din Afghani would have been skeletal. My understanding of Iran in the nineteenth century has benefitted from the scholarship of Abbas Amanat, while Niyazi Berkes was my constant companion in the Turkish sections. Philip Mansel's studies of Istanbul and Alexandria enriched my understanding of these cities while Malise Ruthven, Richard Mitchell and John Calvert introduced me to modern Islamism. If through my text glow older insights, they emanate from such stars as Marshall Hodgson, Albert Hourani, Patricia Crone, Homa Katouzian, Roy Mottahedeh and Bernard Lewis. There is no dearth of brilliant writing about the Middle East.

No less vital was the personal aid I received from scholars, students, friends and fellow writers, sometimes in the form of a suggestion of a book I should have paid attention to, but had not; and sometimes by introducing me to a train of thought or a conversation that was enlightening and stimulating. In no special order, and with apologies to those I have forgotten, they include John Gurney, Negar Azimi, Eugene Rogan, Hussein Omar, Norman Stone, Murat Siviloglu, Christina de Bellaigue, Eric de Bellaigue, Nader Hashemi, Danny Postel, Mohsen Milani, Paul Luft, Ali Dehbashi, Hugh Eakin, Abbas Milani, Roger Cohen, Jeremy Harding, Nicholas Burns, Tessa Boteler, Sheila de Bellaigue, Behrouz Afagh and Muhammad-Hossein Zeynali. My journalistic work with the BBC in Egypt and Tunisia during the Arab Spring, and with the *Guardian* and the *New York Review of Books* in Turkey and Iran in subsequent years, have permitted me not to lose sight of the contemporary while writing about the past. So, thanks to my editors in these enterprises, Robert Silvers, Innes Bowen, and Jonathan Shainin – who bravely allowed me to trial my ideas in 2015 in a Guardian Long Read, 'Stop Calling for an Islamic Enlightenment'.

I should also like to thank Arlene Callender-Blake and Marie Lewis of the Asia and African Studies Reading Room in the British Library. As librarians they were model professionals, but it was their mischief and humour that kept me buoyed on the long winter afternoons.

The Islamic Enlightenment is a big book that covers a lot of ground. When I delivered my first draft, it was slobby and unkempt. Liveright's Bob Weil, an editor in the grand tradition, cajoled and slapped and caressed it into shape. The scrawls and curlicues he trailed over my unsuspecting manuscript are works of art. Next up were Jörg Hensgen and Anna-Sophia Watts of the Bodley Head, who under the benign tutelage of Stuart Williams went through the text with forensic dedication, questioning and improving in a quest to render it as transparent and coherent as possible before handing over to copy-editor Katherine Fry. In New York Steve Attardo designed a sumptuous jacket and the book was prepared for publication by Phil Marino, Peter Miller and Marie Pantojan, while in the UK I owe thanks to

Julia Connolly, for her arresting jacket design, and to Aidan O'Neill for taking on the publicity brief.

The primary job of an agent is to find the best publisher, and in this regard I cannot fault Peter Straus and Melanie Jackson. But they are much more than good matchmakers. The more I am exposed to their love of writing, the more honoured I feel to be represented by them.

Dearest of all, my wife Bita has lived the Islamic Enlightenment as it unfolded. My debt to her cannot be repaid.

List of illustrations

Mehemet Ali (1769–1849), by Louis Charles Auguste Couder, 1840 (oil on canvas). Château de Versailles, France/Bridgeman Images.

The Battle of the Pyramids 21 July 1798, by Louis Lejeune 1806 (oil on canvas). Château de Versailles, France/Bridgeman Images.

Personnages egyptiens, Duterre, from *Description de l'Egypte,* E.M., vol. II, pl. B. The New York Public Library. 'Costumes et portraits. 1. Le poëte; 2. L'astronome.' The New York Public Library Digital Collections, 1809 - 1828. http://digitalcollections. nypl.org/items/510d47e0-21d1-a3d9-e040-e00a18064a99

The Inauguration Procession of the Suez Canal at El-Guisr in 1865, from *Voyage Pittoresque à travers l'Isthme de Suez* by Marius Fontane, engraved by Jules Didier, by Edouard Riou 1869-70 (colour litho). Bibliotheque des Arts Decoratifs, Paris, FranceArchives Charmet/Bridgeman Images.

Crown Prince Abbas Mirza, attributed to Mehr Ali, early 19th century. Golestan Palace, Tehran. Photographer: Abbas Kowsari.

Iranian military band, late 19th century, artist unknown (on tiles). Golestan Palace, Tehran. Photographer: Abbas Kowsari.

Amir Kabir, by Abul-Qassem Taki Nuri, c. 1851. Golestan Palace, Tehran. Photographer: Abbas Kowsari.

Execution of Mirza Reza Kermani, with shadow of camera and photographer, Antoin Sevrugin, 1896. Collection of Azita Bina and Elmar W Seibel.

Materialistic Science on Display at the Imperial Military Academy, Abdullah Frères, Library of Congress, Prints and Photographs Division, Abdulhamid II Collection, LC-USZ62-77267 http://www.loc.gov/pictures/collection/ahii/item/2002716937/

Constantinople (Istanbul) c. 1900: sailboats on the Bosphorus / Photo © PVDE / Bridgeman Images

★

View from the Galata Bridge, Constantinople, Turkey (coloured photo), French School, (20th century) / Private Collection / © Look and Learn / Elgar Collection / Bridgeman Images.

Persian lady in Indoor Costume © The British Library Board. Ella C. Sykes, *Through Persia on a Side-saddle*, London, MacQueen, 1901, 10077.e.37., p.17.

Dame turque voilée, 1880. Pierre de Gigord collection of photographs of the Ottoman Empire and the Republic of Turkey. Series I. Large format albums, 1852-1920. Digital image courtesy of the Getty's Open Content Program. Getty Research Institute 96.R.14(A25). http://hdl.handle.net/10020/96r14d1058

Portrait of Seyyed Jamal al-Din Afghani from *The Persian Revolution of 1905–1909* by E. G. Browne, (Frank Cass, 1966).

Railway to Shah 'Abol al-'Azim Shrine, 12 km south of Tehran, Antoin Sevrugin, late 19th century. Collection of Azita Bina and Elmar W. Seibel.

'Now they perform Brotherhood Vows', *Molla Nasreddin* (Iranian journal), 2 May 1910.

Portrait of Muhammad Abduh. Alchetron http://alchetron.com/Muhammad-Abduh-1183849-W

Gymnasium at Drilling Ground, Tabriz, Antoin Sevrugin, late 19th century. Collection of Azita Bina and Elmar W. Seibel.

Portrait of Hassan Taqizadeh from *The Persian Revolution of 1905–1909* by E. G. Browne, (Frank Cass, 1966).

Abdulhamid II cheered by crowd after restoring the constitution. *The Graphic: An Illustrated Weekly Magazine*, London, 8 August 1908.

Bastinado, unknown photographer, late 19th century. Collection of Azita Bina and Elmar W. Seibel.

Halide Edib before an aeroplane flight at the front © The British Library Board. *The Turkish Ordeal*, London, John Murray, 1928, 10607.ccc.17., p.16.

Jamal Al-e-Ahmad and his wife Simin Daneshvar, c. 1956, from the collection of Ali Dehbashi. © Abdullah Amin.

Egyptian soldiers fire on Egyptian President Anwar Al-Sadat while reviewing a military parade in honour of The October 1973 War, on 6 October 1981 in Cairo. The assassination is attributed to Muslim extremist group Muslim Brotherhood. MAKARAM GAD ALKAREEM / AFP / Getty Images.

Grateful acknowledgement is made to the Azita Bina and Elmar W. Seibel Collection.

Notes

Introduction

1   Cole, Juan, *Modernity and the Millennium*, 9.
2   Lyons, *The House of Wisdom*, 124.
3   Rodenbeck, *Cairo*, 151.

1 *Cairo*

1   Herold, *Bonaparte in Egypt*, 97.
2   Al-Jabarti, cit. Rodenbeck, 152.
3   Al-Jabarti, *Chronicle of the French Occupation*, 31.
4   Al-Jabarti, *Merveilles biographiques et historiques ou chroniques*, vol. 6, 74–5.
5   Ibid., 111.
6   Al-Jabarti, *Merveilles biographiques et historiques ou chroniques*, vol. 1, 13.
7   Al-Jabarti, *Chronicle of the French Occupation*, 43.
8   Raymond, *Artisans et commerçants au Caire au XVIIIe siècle*, 346.
9   Al-Jabarti, *Chronicle of the French Occupation*, 29.
10   Ibid., 33.
11   Loc. cit.
12   Cole, *Napoleon's Egypt*, 159.
13   Fourier, *Description de l'Egypte*, vol. 1, 516.
14   Ibid., xvi.
15   Ibid., iii.
16   Al-Jabarti, *Merveilles biographiques et historiques ou chroniques*, vol. 6, 223.
17   Al-Jabarti, *Chronicle of the French Occupation*, 76.
18   Gran, *Islamic Roots of Capitalism*, 79.
19   Ibid., 189–90.
20   Marsot, *Egypt in the Reign of Muhammad Ali*, 273.
21   Lane, *An Account of the Manners and Customs of the Modern Egyptians*, vol. 1, 129.
22   Marsot, *Egypt in the Reign of Muhammad Ali*, 127.
23   Paton, *A History of the Egyptian Revolution*, vol. 2, 97.
24   Hamont, *L'Egypte sous Méhémet-Ali*, 437.
25   Tucker, *Women in Nineteenth-Century Egypt*, 27.
26   Ibid., 88.
27   Paton, *A History of the Egyptian Revolution*, vol. 2, 243.
28   Mansel, *Levant*, 61–3.
29   Ibid., 68.

30   Hamont, L'Egypte sous Méhémet-Ali, ii, 336.

31   Paton, vol. 2, 286.

32   Lane was moved to write his classic Account of the Manners and Customs of the Modern Egyptians not by a desire to capture the new Egypt – which he conceded regretfully would come unavoidably into being – but to record the Egypt that was being swept away. His book would have been better titled 'An Account of the Manners and Customs of the Medieval Egyptians'. The Scottish artist David Roberts also contributed to the Flaubertian image of Egypt with the panoramic views of the medieval city that he painted in the 1840s. For many foreigners the most alluring Egypt was the unchanging one of the imagination.

33   Gran, Islamic Roots of Capitalism, 103.

34   Delanoue, Moralistes et politiques musulmans, vol. 2, 353.

35   Gran, Islamic Roots of Capitalism, 106.

36   Ibid., 105.

37   Galland, Tableau de l'Egypte, volume ii, 2.

38   Delanoue, Moralistes et politiques musulmans, vol. 2, 347.

39   Livingston, 'Shaykhs Jabarti and Attar', 97.

40   Clot, Aperçu général sur l'Egypte, vol. 2, 410.

41   Hamont, L'Egypte sous Méhémet-Ali, ii, 91.

42   Paton, vol. 2, 287.

43   Gran, Islamic Roots of Capitalism, 128.

44   Ibid., 130.

45   Delanoue, Moralistes et politiques musulmans, vol. 2, 355.

46   Silvera, 'The First Egyptian Student Mission', 14.

47   Ibid., 9.

48   Tahtawi, An Imam in Paris, 261.

49   Ibid., 150–2.

50   Ibid., 246.

51   Ibid., 233.

52   Ibid., 249.

53   Lane-Poole, Life of Edward William Lane, 70.

54   Tahtawi, An Iman in Paris, 252.

55   Burlamaqui, Principles of Natural Law, 3.

56   Tahtawi, An Imam in Paris, 323.

57   Ibid., 324.

58   Ibid., 49.

59   Delanoue, Moralistes et politiques musulmans, vol. 2, 450.

60   Tahtawi, An Imam in Paris, 182.

61   Delanoue, Moralistes et politiques musulmans, vol. 2, 362.

62   Jabarti had used hurriya to mean freedom in the sense of the opposite of slavery. For Rifaa it meant 'justice and equity'. Only later would it echo the French word liberté, with its sense of political and social freedom. With the rise of European imperialism, hurriya came to denote freedom from the colonial power, before returning to its earlier, more limited sense in time for the Arab Spring.

63   Tahtawi, An Imam in Paris, 92.

64   He was less successful when he turned to a peculiarly European concept, the weather. This was signified in French by the word for 'time', temps. Rifaa duly employed the Arabic word for time, al-zaman, to mean the same thing. It never caught on.

65   Tahtawi, An Imam in Paris, 46.

66   Hourani, Arabic Thought in the Liberal Age, 71.

67   Tahtawi, An Iman in Paris, 359.

68   Delanoue, Moralistes et politiques musulmans, vol. 2, 482.

69   Ibid., 449.

70   Ibid., 429.

71 Ibid., 426.
72 Ibid., 433.
73 Kyle, Keith, *Suez*, 14.
74 De Leon, *Egypt under its Khedives*, 160.
75 Douin, *Histoire du règne du Khédive Ismail*, vol. 2, 41.
76 Ibid., 461.
77 Mansel, *Levant*, 114.
78 No doubt because of the criticisms that Jabarti had levelled at the founder of the khedival dynasty, it wasn't until 1879 that the authorities permitted the *Marvels of Deeds in Annals and Lives* to be published in the homeland of its author.

2 *Istanbul*

1   Lewis, *The Emergence of Modern Turkey*, 66.
2   Temperley, *England and the Near East*, 272.
3   Langles, *Diatribe de l'ingénieur Séid Moustapha*, 52.
4   Ibid., 36.
5   Finkel, *Osman's Dream*, 435.
6   Jouannin/Gaver, *Turquie*.
7   Temperley, *England and the Near East*, 19.
8   Jouannin/Gaver, 428.
9   Ibid., 429.
10 Heyd, *Foundations of Turkish Nationalism*, 75.
11 Adnan, *La Science chez les turcs ottomans*, 160.
12 Bianchi, 12.
13 White, *Three Years in Constantinople*, vol. 1, 127.
14 Ibid.
15 DeKay, 153–4.
16 Ibid., 117.
17 Panzac, *La Peste dans l'Empire ottoman*, 292.
18 On the whole, evasive action seems to have been more widespread among *dhimmis* such as the Greek Orthodox, for whom the catastrophe was a divine malediction that could be stayed by flight, prayer or, *in extremis*, a pogrom against the Jews.
19 Panzac, *La Peste dans l'Empire ottoman*,
20 Al-Jabarti, *Merveilles biographiques et historiques ou chroniques* vol. 9, 19.
21 Panzac, *La Peste dans l'Empire ottoman*, 468–74.
22 Ibid., 475.
23 Temperley, *England and the Near East*, 27.
24 cit. Berkes, 105.
25 Gibb, *A History of Ottoman Poetry*, vol. 6, 19.
26 Mansel, *Constantinople*, 252.
27 Ibid., 260.
28 Davison, *Reform in the Ottoman Empire*, 97.
29 MacFarlane, *Constantinople in 1828*, vol. 2, ii, 267.
30 Mason, 234.
31 Repression of a different kind was the lot of many of the empire's heterodox Muslims, including proto-Shia groups like the Alevis; without *millet* status or a foreign power to protect them, they were at the mercy of any official who took a dislike to them.
32 Berkes, 149.
33 MacFarlane, *Turkey and its Destiny*, volume II, 268.
34 Ibid., 295.
35 Gibb, *A History of Ottoman Poetry*, vol. 5, 3.

36   Mardin, *The Genesis of Young Ottoman Thought*, 266.

37   White, *Three Years in Constantinople*, vol. 2, 157–9.

38   Walsh, *A Residence at Constantinople*, vol. 2, 283.

39   Gibb, *A History of Ottoman Poetry*, vol. 5, 22.

40   Tanpinar, *Asir Türk*, 169.

41   Mardin, *The Genesis of Young Ottoman Thought*, 265.

42   Lewis, *The Emergence of Modern Turkey*, 144.

43   Sinasi, *Makaleler*, 6–10.

44   Ibid., 23.

45   Ibid., 103.

46   Macaulay writes in the same vein of the earliest street lighting in London, patented by an ingenious 'projector' called Edward Heming, and says that in spite of the obvious improvements it brought to the lives of the inhabitants, 'the cause of darkness was not left undefended. There were fools in that age who opposed the introduction of what was called the new light as strenuously as fools in our age have opposed the introduction of vaccination and railroads ... many years after the date of Heming's patent there were extensive districts in which no lamp was seen.' (*History of England*, vol. 1, Longman, Brown, Green and Longmans, 1861, p. 565.)

47   Ebuzziya, *Sinasi*, 150.

48   Ibid., 253.

49   Ibid., 233.

50   It has since been lost; there are rumours that it was burned though it is possible that it lurks unidentified in a French library.

51   Tanpinar, *Asir Türk*, 165.

52   Siviloglu, 'The Emergence of Public Opinion in the Ottoman Empire', 171–3.

53   Budak, *Munif Pasa*, 547.

54   Lewis, *The Emergence of Modern Turkey*, 147.

55   Davison, *Reform in the Ottoman Empire*, 34.

56   Ibid., 85.

57   Ibid., 75.

58   Findley, 117.

59   Unlike the early advocates of the Protestant faith, who had immediately seen in Gutenberg's moving type an excellent means of propagating their ideas, the devout among Muslims denounced print as an aggressor from which the most sacred of word combinations should be protected. It wasn't until 1874 that the first Arabic Quran was printed, some two hundred years after the same book, in English and French translations, emerged from the presses in Oxford and Paris.

60   Siviloglu, 'The Emergence of Public Opinion in the Ottoman Empire', 160.

61   Davison, *Reform in the Ottoman Empire*, 69.

62   Kuntay, *Namik Kemal*, vol. 2, 164.

63   Kaplan, 113.

64   Substitute Turkey for Italy, and the values that Verdi's departing warrior Rolando prescribes for his son would have been applauded by Kemal himself. 'Tell him he is of Italian blood,' Rolando instructs the boy's mother, 'and after God teach him to respect the homeland.'

65   Tanpinar, *Asir Türk*, 324.

66   Berkes, 209.

67   Davison, *Reform in the Ottoman Empire*, 204.

68   The generally unsatisfactory coupling of two ideas, Islam and democracy, can be observed in the waxing religiosity of the Pakistani constitutions of 1956, 1962 and 1973, in the foundation document of the Islamic Republic of Iran, which came into force after the 1979 revolution, and in Muhammad Morsi's constitution of 2012, which lasted just seven months before Egypt's first Muslim Brotherhood head of state was felled in a military coup.

69   Kuntay, *Namik Kemal*, vol. 2, 535.
70   Lewis, *The Emergence of Modern Turkey*, 142.
71   Kaplan, 106.
72   Ibid., 129.
73   Berkes, 212–13.
74   Davison, *Reform in the Ottoman Empire*, 224.
75   Kaplan, 80.
76   Kaplan, 90.
77   Kuntay, *Namik Kemal*, vol. 2, 527.
78   Davison, *Reform in the Ottoman Empire*, 152.
79   Siviloglu, 'The Emergence of Public Opinion in the Ottoman Empire', 218.
80   Hawgood, *Modern Constitutions since 1787*, 140.
81   Finkel, *Osman's Dream*, 488.
82   Midhat, *The Life of Midhat Pasha*, 213.
83   Davison, *Reform in the Ottoman Empire*, 403.
84   Lewis, *The Emergence of Modern Turkey*, 170.

3 Tehran

1   Greaves, 'Relations with European Companies', 353.
2   Algar, *Religion and State in Iran*, 38.
3   Tabatabai, *Dibachei dar Nazariyeh-ye Enhetat-e Iran*, 221.
4   Morier, *A Second Journey*, 199.
5   Drouville, *Voyage en Perse*, 251.
6   Morier, *A Second Journey*, 217; Kotzebue, *Narrative of Journey into Persia*, 153.
7   Green, *The Love of Strangers*, 8.
8   Atkin, *Russia and Iran, 1780–1828*, 110.
9   Ibid., 135; Wright, *The English Among the Persians*, 50.
10   Wright, *English Among*, 51.
11   Morier, *A Second Journey*, 213.
12   Drouville, *Voyage en Perse*, 255.
13   Morier, *A Second Journey*, 209, 210.
14   Ouseley, *Travels in Various Countries of the East*, vol. 3, 16.
15   Atkin, *Russia and Iran, 1780–1828*, 137.
16   Wright, *The Persians Among the English*, 73.
17   Ouseley, *Travels in Various Countries of the East*, vol. 3, 16.
18   Green, *The Love of Strangers*, 3.
19   Mirza Saleh, *Majmueyi Safarnamehha*, 92–3.
20   One such earlier chronicler was the trader and cleric Abdul-Latif Shushtari, who at the turn of the century had put down much information gleaned from Britons he met while living in Calcutta and Bombay, though his physics was unreliable – he predicted that the digging of the Suez Canal would flood the world and cause it to sink.
21   Saleh, *Majmueyi Safarnamehha*, 113.
22   Green, *The Love of Strangers*, 9.
23   Saleh, *Majmueyi Safarnamehha*, 245.
24   Green, *The Love of Strangers*, 72.
25   Saleh, *Majmueyi Safarnamehha*, 277.
26   Ibid., 283.
27   Ibid., 285.
28   Ibid., 293.
29   His sources are likely to have included David Hume's standard *History of England*.
30   Tabatabai, *Dibachei dar Nazariyeh-ye Enhetat-e Iran*, 271.
31   Saleh, *Majmueyi Safarnamehha*, 435.

32   One might compare this to the ease with which the Khedive Ismail had been able to drive the Boulevard Muhammad Ali through the centre of Cairo in time for the opening of the Suez Canal.

33   Saleh, *Majmueyi Safarnamehha*, 295.

34   Green, *The Love of Strangers*, 302.

35   Farman Farmayan, 'The Forces of Modernisation in Nineteenth-century Iran', 123.

36   Ibid., 122.

37   Green, *The Love of Strangers*, 310.

38   Amanat, *Pivot of the Universe: Nasir al-Din Shah and the Iranian Monarchy*, 75.

39   Wright, *Persians*, 82.

40   Kelly, *Diplomacy and Murder in Tehran*, 193.

41   Adamiyat, *Amir Kabir va Iran*, 54.

42   Amanat, *Pivot*, 77.

43   Ibid., 112.

44   Ibid., 123.

45   Encyclopaedia Iranica, Algar, Hamid, *Amir Kabir, Mirza Taqi Khan*

46   Algar, *Religion and State in Iran*, 134.

47   Adamiyat, *Amir Kabir va Iran*, 188.

48   Sheil, *Glimpses of Life and Manners in Persia*, 249.

49   Ibid., 251.

50   Ibid.

51   Ibid.; Amanat, *Pivot*, 162.

52   Adamiyat, *Amir Kabir va Iran*, 495–6.

53   Some seven years after the amir's death, when an Austrian doctor in the shah's service visited the palace of Fin, he found the wall of the bathhouse still spattered with the dead man's blood.

54   Modern Bahaism's international and ecumenical qualities are well expressed by its biggest place of worship. The Lotus Temple in New Delhi, so called because it is composed of massive petals, was designed by an Iranian, funded by an Indian, and constructed by a British firm out of Greek marble. In 2001 more than 70 million people visited it, the majority of them Hindus, making it one of the most popular attractions in the world.

55   Amanat, *Resurrection and Renewal*, 133.

56   Ibid., 148.

57   Amanat, *Pivot*, 217.

58   Browne, *Materials for the Study of the Babi Religion*, 270.

59   Ibid., 139.

60   Bahaism's starting point was not out of place in the pottage of heterodox beliefs, including occultism, mysticism and reincarnation, that had been stirred by the Victorian age. There was communication between the different groups. In 1911 Bahaullah's son and successor Abdulbaha would address the Theosophy Society in London, reiterating his father's belief in the unity of faith and of humanity, which the Theosophists shared.

61   Cole, *Modernity and the Millenium*, 73.

62   Ibid., 36.

63   Ibid., 60.

64   Ibid., 41.

65   Amanat, *Resurrection and Renewal*, 297.

66   Ibid., 299.

67   Nabil, *The Dawn-Breakers*, 270.

68   Mottahedeh, 'Ruptured Spaces and Effective Histories', 64–5.

69   Ibid., 66.

70   Shock tactics of this kind are not confined to the Islamic tradition. When his wife Kali went on an unstoppable rampage of murder and beheading, the

Hindu god Shiva found that the only solution was to lie down in her path – and indeed she came to her senses after improperly touching him with the soles of her feet.

71   Hatcher and Hemmat, *The Poetry of Tahirih*, 13–14.
72   Decades later Sarah Bernhardt commissioned the French playwrights Catulle Mendès and Henri Antoine Jules-Bois to write a play about Qurrat al-Ayn – though it was never performed.
73   Hatcher and Hemmat, *The Poetry of Tahirih*, 15.

4 *Vortex*

1   Pamuk, *The Ottoman Empire and European Capitalism*, 17.
2   Issawi, *An Economic History of the Middle East and North Africa*, 152.
3   Ibid., 95–6.
4   Cole, *Colonialism and Revolution in the Middle East*, 198–200.
5   Mansel, *Constantinople*, 328.
6   Findley, 181–2.
7   Cole, *Colonialism and Revolution in the Middle East*, 198.
8   Berkes, 292.
9   Elshakry, *Reading Darwin in Arabic*, 110.
10 Ibid., 76.
11 Ibid., 87.
12 Berkes, 292.
13 Okay, *Besir Fuad*, 80–3.
14 Ibid., 77.
15 Ibid., 100.
16 My material on Ahmad Faris-al Shidyaq is drawn from Robyn Creswell's excellent essay, 'The First Great Arabic Novel', *New York Review of Books*, 8 October 2015.
17 Cresswell, 'The First Great Arabic Novel'.
18 Finn, *The Early Turkish Novel*, 13.
19 Ibid., 19.
20 Lewis, *What Went Wrong?*, 132.
21 Baron, 'Unveiling in Early Twentieth Century Egypt', 373.
22 Amin, *New Woman*, 153.
23 Cooper, *The Women of Egypt*, 183–4.
24 Ettehadieh, *Zanani ke zir-e maghnaeh kolahdari nemudeand*, 20.
25 Amanat, *Taj al-Saltana, Crowning Anguish*, 197–8.
26 Shaarawi, 57.
27 Fahmy, 'Women, Medicine, and Power in Nineteenth-Century Egypt', 40.
28 Baron, 'Unveiling in Early Twentieth Century Egypt', 81.
29 Tucker, *Women in Nineteenth-Century Egypt*, 127.
30 Cole, 'Feminism, Class and Islam in Turn-of-the-Century Egypt', 401.
31 Edith Louise Butcher, *Things Seen in Egypt*, London, 1910, cit. Baron, *Unveiling in Early Twentieth Century Egypt*, 381.
32 Cakir, *Osmanli Kadin Hareketi*, 60.
33 Ibid., 65.
34 Cooper, *The Women of Egypt*, 29.
35 Baron, 'Unveiling in Early Twentieth Century Egypt', 377.
36 Cooper, *The Women of Egypt*, 129.
37 Badran and Cooke, *Opening the Gates*, 232.
38 Amin, *The Liberation of Women*, 22.
39 Harcourt, *L'Egypte et les Egyptiens*, 100.
40 Amin, *The Liberation of Women*, 86.

41 Ibid., 31.
42 Ibid., 53.
43 Toledano, *The Ottoman Slave Trade and its Suppresion*, 279.
44 Ibid., 79–80.
45 Ibid., 18.
46 Sheil, *Glimpses of Life and Manners in Persia*, 243–4.
47 Toledano, *Slavery and Abolition in the Ottoman Middle East*, 116–17.
48 Toledano, *The Ottoman Slave Trade and its Suppression*, 112.
49 Ibid., 42.
50 White, *Three Years in Constantinople*, vol. 3, 280–3.
51 Toledano, *The Ottoman Slave Trade and its Suppression*, 277.
52 Tucker, *Women in Nineteenth-Century Egypt*, 174.
53 Ibid., 166.
54 Afary, *Sexual Politics in Modern Iran*, 115; Akhundzadeh, *Maktubat-e Kamal-ul Dowleh*, 73.
55 Toledano, *The Ottoman Slave Trade and its Suppression*, 186–91.
56 Cresswell, 'The First Great Arabic Novel'.
57 Amanat, *Taj al-Saltana, Crowning Anguish*, 41.
58 cit. Afary, *Sexual Politics in Modern Iran*, 65.
59 El-Rouayheb, *Before Homosexuality in the Arab-Islamic World, 1500–1800*, 94.
60 cit. El-Rouayheb, 1–2.
61 cit. Afary, *Sexual Politics in Modern Iran*, 104.
62 cit. Andrews and Kalpakli, *The Age of Beloveds*, 173.
63 Afary, *Sexual Politics in Modern Iran*, 112.
64 Ibid., 95.
65 El-Rouayheb, 2.
66 cit. Afary, *Sexual Politics in Modern Iran*, 120.
67 Afary, *Sexual Politics in Modern Iran*, 123.
68 Ansari, *The Politics of Nationalism in Modern Iran*, 63.

5 Nation

1   Mishra, *From the Ruins of Empire*, 1.
2   Browne, *The Persian Constitutional Revolution*, 1.
3   Keddie, *Sayyid Jamal ad-Din 'Al-Afghani'*, 80.
4   Ibid., 34.
5   Ibid., 41, 45.
6   Ibid., 54.
7   Berkes, 187.
8   Kedourie, *Afghani and Abduh*, 15.
9   Ibid., 14.
10 Ibid., 12.
11 Ibid., 14–15.
12 Keddie, *Sayyid Jamal ad-Din 'Al-Afghani'*, 95.
13 Kedourie, *Afghani and Abduh*, 25.
14 Keddie, *Sayyid Jamal ad-Din 'Al-Afghani'*, 116.
15 Wright, *A Tidy Little War*, 16.
16 Ibid., 27.
17 Blunt, *Secret History of the English Occupation of Egypt*, 368.
18 cit. Wright, 19.
19 Scholch, *Egypt for the Egyptians!*, 159.
20 Blunt, *Secret History of the English Occupation of Egypt*, 114.
21 Ibid., 117.

22   Scholch, *Egypt for the Egyptians!*, 202.
23   Rogan, *The Arabs*, 129.
24   cit. Wright, 42.
25   France's abstention would later harden into outright opposition to British rule over Egypt.
26   cit. Wright, 109.
27   Ibid., 262.
28   cit. Wright, 103.
29   Blunt, *Gordon at Khartoum*, 209.
30   Ibid., 500–1.
31   Keddie, *Sayyid Jamal ad-Din 'Al-Afghani'*, 304.
32   Ibid., 298.
33   Adamiyat, *Ideoloji-ye Mashrutiyat-e Iran*, 12.
34   Browne, *The Persian Revolution*, 27.
35   Amanat, *Taj al-Saltaneh, Crowning Anguish*, 188.
36   Algar, *Mirza Malkum Khan*, 177.
37   Feuvrier, *Trois ans à la cour de Perse*, 310.
38   Keddie, *Sayyid Jamal ad-Din 'Al-Afghani'*, 331.
39   Feuvrier, *Trois ans à la cour de Perse*, 311–12.
40   Keddie, *Sayyid Jamal ad-Din 'Al-Afghani'*, 343–4.
41   Keddie, *Religion and Rebellion in Iran*, 96–7.
42   Browne, *The Persian Revolution*, 58.
43   Keddie, *Sayyid Jamal ad-Din 'Al-Afghani'*, 408.
44   Nazem al-Islam Kermani, *Tarikh-e Bidari-ye Iranian*, 85.
45   Keddie, *Sayyid Jamal ad-Din 'Al-Afghani'*, 411–12.
46   Ibid., 420.
47   Sohrabi, *Revolution and Constitutionalism in the Ottoman Empire and Iran*, 80.
48   Nazem al-Islam Kermani, *Tarikh-e Bidari-ye Iranian*, 295.
49   Despite his excellence as a marksman he was apparently not confident of outshooting two assassins standing abreast.
50   McCullagh, *The Fall of Abd-Ul-Hamid*, 255–60.
51   Mansel, *Constantinople*, 317.
52   Deringil, *The Well-Protected Domains*, 98.
53   Nazem al-Islam Kermani, *Tarikh-e Bidari-ye Iranian*, 276.
54   Kasravi, *History of the Iranian Constitutional Revolution*, 104.
55   Keddie, *Sayyid Jamal ad-Din 'Al-Afghani'*, 392.
56   Nazem al-Islam Kermani, *Tarikh-e Bidari-ye Iranian*, 435.
57   Browne, *The Persian Revolution*, 127.
58   Ibid., 119.
59   Ibid., 133.
60   Afary, *Sexual Politics in Modern Iran*, 179.
61   cit. Afary, *The Iranian Constitutional Revolution*, 63.
62   Shuster, *The Strangling of Persia*, 21–2.
63   Kasravi, *History of the Iranian Constitutional Revolution*, vol. 1, 269–70.
64   Afary, *The Iranian Constitutional Revolution*, 189.
65   Taqizadeh, *Zendegi Tufani*, 24.
66   Ibid., 26.
67   Ibid., 43.
68   Browne, *The Persian Revolution*, 144.
69   Taqizadeh, *Zendegi Tufani*, 63.
70   Katouzian, 'Sayyed Hassan Taqizadeh', 2.
71   Afary, *The Iranian Constitutional Revolution*, 100.
72   Ibid., 110.
73   Ibid., 135.

74   Browne, *The Persian Revolution*, 167.
75   Ibid., 194.
76   Ibid., 201.
77   Ibid.
78   Kasravi, *Tarikh-e Mashrouteh-e Iran*, 636.
79   Browne, *The Persian Revolution*, 247.
80   Browne, *The Press and Poetry of Modern Persia*, 215.
81   Afary, *The Iranian Constitutional Revolution*, 259.
82   Shuster, *The Strangling of Persia*, 182.
83   Ibid., 191.
84   It would be unjust to include the shah himself in this number. Nasser al-Din's interest in the digs that were being conducted by the Europeans was primarily commercial.
85   Ansari, *The Politics of Nationalism in Modern Iran*, 57–8.
86   McMeekin, *The Ottoman Endgame*, 35.
87   Berkes, *The Development of Secularism in Turkey*, 357.
88   McMeekin, *The Ottoman Endgame*, 45.
89   Edib, *Memoirs*, 258–9.
90   Ibid., 259.
91   Ibid., 260.
92   Sohrabi, *Revolution and Constitutionalism in the Ottoman Empire and Iran*, 175, 186.
93   Browne, *The Persian Revolution*, 250.
94   McCullagh, *The Fall of Abd-ul-Hamid*, 13.
95   Ibid., 65.
96   Sohrabi, *Revolution and Constitutionalism in the Ottoman Empire and Iran*, 190, 197.
97   Ibid., 233.
98   Berkes, *Development*, 341.
99   McMeekin, *The Ottoman Endgame*, 54.
100   McCullagh, *The Fall of Abd-ul-Hamid*, 271.
101   Edib, *Memoirs*, 317.
102   Heyd, *Foundations of Turkish Nationalism*, 22.
103   Berkes, *Development*, 395.
104   Gokalp, *Turkish Nationalism*, 38.
105   Ibid., 40.
106   cit. Mazower, *Salonica, City of Ghosts*, 283.
107   Gokalp, *Turkish Nationalism*, 73.
108   Ibid., 83–5.
109   Berkes, *Development*, 375.
110   Gokalp, *Turkish Nationalism*, 76.
111   McMeekin, *The Ottoman Endgame*, 72.
112   Berkes, *Development*, 358.
113   Mango, *Atatürk*, 218–19.
114   Thompson, *Justice Interrupted*, 101.
115   In an article he had written the previous year, Ziya had drawn on Emile Durkheim when describing the process by which institutions are invested with emotional or spiritual meaning. 'We regard an object as "sacred",' Ziya had written, 'whenever we feel a religious attachment to that object; we call something "good" for which we experience a moral feeling; we call something "beautiful" which stimulates an aesthetic emotion.'
116   Edib, *Memoirs*, 335–7.
117   Gesink, *Islamic Reform and Conservatism*, 97.
118   Abduh, *The Theology of Unity*, 35–7.
119   Ibid., 38.
120   Ibid., 126–7.

121 Blunt, *My Diaries*, vol. 1, 418.
122 Gesink, *Islamic Reform and Conservatism*, 16.
123 Sedgwick, *Muhammad Abduh*, 74.
124 Blunt, *My Diaries*, vol. 2, 69.
125 Sedgwick, *Muhammad Abduh*, 62.
126 Mahmoudi, *Taha Husain's Education*, 29.
127 Ibid., 28–9.
128 Gesink, *Islamic Reform and Conservatism*, 182.
129 Fahmy, *Ordinary Egyptians*, 85.
130 Gesink, *Islamic Reform and Conservatism*, 186.
131 Blunt, *My Diaries*, vol. 2, 455.
132 Sedgwick, *Muhammad Abduh*, 113.

6 *Counter-Enlightenment*

1 Shaarawi, *Harem Years*, 7.
2 Edib, *The Turkish Ordeal*, 31–2.
3 Hourani, *Arabic Thought in the Liberal Age*, 185.
4 Rogan, *The Fall of the Ottomans*, 291.
5 McMeekin, *The Ottoman Endgame*, 481.
6 Fromkin, *A Peace to End All Peace*, 258–9.
7 Edib, *The Turkish Ordeal*, 30.
8 Ansari, *The Politics of Nationalism in Modern Iran*, 69.
9 Pedersen, *The Guardians*, 17.
10 de Bellaigue, *Patriot of Persia*, 51.
11 Fromkin, *A Peace to End All Peace*, 399.
12 de Bellaigue, *Patriot of Persia*, 82.
13 Thompson, *Justice Interrupted*, 109–11.
14 Even further east, Afghanistan's King Amanullah was doing much the same; a standard template was emerging for modernising a Muslim country.
15 Mitchell, *The Society of Muslim Brothers*, viii.
16 Halpern, *The Politics of Social Change in the Middle East and North Africa*, 130.
17 Thompson, *Justice Interrupted*, 154.
18 A contemporary of Banna who also had a great influence on the rise of Islamism, the Pakistani Sayyid Abul-Ala Maududi, was, by contrast, educated in a religious school, but he excelled at science and mathematics as well as religious studies. The acceptability of applied science in modern Islamist circles is a distant consequence of the success enjoyed by nineteenth-century thinkers like Hassan al-Attar and Sanizadeh Ataullah in convincing their co-religionists that there is no opposition between Islam and scientific knowledge.
19 Thompson, *Justice Interrupted*, 156.
20 Mitchell, *The Society of Muslim Brothers*, 71.
21 Ibid., 5.
22 Ibid., 8.
23 Thompson, *Justice Interrupted*, 161.
24 Ibid., 163.
25 Ibid., 168.
26 Rodenbeck, *Cairo*, 194.
27 Ruthven, *Islam in the World*, 92.
28 Qutb, *A Child from the Village*, 113.
29 Ibid.
30 John Calvert, *Sayyid Qutb and the Origins of Radical Islamism*, 115.
31 Ibid., 78.

32   Ibid., 68.
33   Ibid., 66.
34   Ibid., 110.
35   Ibid., 96.
36   Ibid., 143.
37   Ibid., 145.
38   Ibid., 150.
39   Ibid., 153.
40   Ibid., 149.
41   Ruthven, *Islam in the World*, 81.
42   Rodenbeck, *Cairo*, 199.
43   Ibid., 219.
44   Calvert, 195.
45   Ibid., 203.
46   Ibid., 208.
47   Ibid.
48   Bergesen, *The Sayyid Qutb Reader*, 35.
49   Ibid., 40.
50   Ruthven, *Islam in the World*, 89.
51   Ibid., 92.
52   Bergesen, *The Sayyid Qutb Reader*, 37.
53   Rodenbeck, *Cairo*, 221.
54   Ruthven, *Islam in the World*, 96.
55   Calvert, 258.
56   Ibid., 261.
57   Ibid., 268.
58   Ibid., 283.
59   Manafzadeh, *Ahmad Kasravi*, 194.
60   de Bellaigue, *Patriot of Persia*, 185.
61   Mottahedeh, *Mantle of the Prophet*, 297.
62   Al-e Ahmad, *Iranian Society*, 57.
63   Mottahedeh, 296.
64   Boroujerdi, *Iranian Intellectuals and the West*, 70.
65   Al-e Ahmad, *Gharbzadegi*, 7.
66   Ibid., 36.
67   Ibid., 71.
68   Ibid., 47.
69   Fanon, *The Wretched of the Earth*, 175.
70   Al-e Ahmad, *Karnameh*, 111.
71   Ibid., 102.
72   Al-e Ahmad, *Iranian Society*, 305.
73   Mottahedeh, *Mantle of the Prophet*, 301.
74   Ibid., 323.
75   Rahnama, *An Islamic Utopian*, 236.
76   Boroujerdi, *Iranian Intellectuals and the West*, 107.
77   Buchan, *Days of God*, 133.
78   Where unregulated mingling did take place, such as in the rural Balkans, Islam, Christianity and Judaism produced syncretic traditions that later purists frowned upon and stamped out.

Bibliography

Abduh, Muhammad, *Rissalat al-Towhid: Exposé de la religion musulmane*, translated and with an introduction by B. Michel and Moustafa Abdel Razik, Librairie Orientaliste Paul Geuthner, 1925

Abduh, Muhammad, *The Theology of Unity*, translated by Ishaq Musaad and Kenneth Cragg, with an introduction by Kenneth Cragg, George Allen and Unwin, 1966

Abu-Taleb, Mirza, *Westward Bound: Travels of Mirza Abu Taleb*, Oxford University Press (Delhi), 2005

Abul Hassan Khan, *A Persian at the Court of King George, 1809–10*, translated by Margaret Morris Cloake, Barrie and Jenkins, 1988

Adamiyat, Fereydun, *Amir Kabir va Iran*, Amir Kabir, 1955–6

Adamiyat, Fereydun, *Ideoloji-ye Mashrutiyat-e Iran*, Payam, undated

Adnan, Abdulhak, *La Science chez les turcs ottomans*, Librairie orientale et americaine, 1939

Afary, Janet, *The Iranian Constitutional Revolution, 1906–1911: Grassroots Democracy, Social Democracy, and the Origins of Feminism*, Columbia University Press, 1996

Afary, Janet, *Sexual Politics in Modern Iran*, Cambridge University Press, 2009

Ahmed, Leila, *A Quiet Revolution: The Veil's Resurgence, from the Middle East to America*, Yale University Press, 2011

Akhundzadah, Mirza Fath-Ali, *Maktubat-e Kamal-al Dowleh*, Elm, 1985

Aksit, Elif Ekin, 'Fatma Aliye's Stories: Ottoman Marriages beyond the Harem', *Journal of Family History*, 35/3 (July 2010)

Al-e Ahmad, Jalal, *Gharbzadegi*, Naghl va Tarjomeh-e Azad, 1962

Al-e Ahmad, Jalal, *Iranian Society: An Anthology of Writings*, ed. Michael C. Hillman, Mazda, 1982

Al-e Ahmad, *Karnameh-e Seh Saleh*, Zaman, n.d. [*c*. 1968]

Algar, Hamid, *Religion and State in Iran, 1785–1906*, University of California Press, 1969

Algar, Hamid, *Mirza Malkum Khan: A Study in the History of Iranian Modernism*, University of California Press, 1973

Al-Jabarti, Abd-al Rahman, *Chronicle of the French Occupation*, trans. Shmuel Moreh, Markus Wiener, 2004

Al-Jabarti, Abd-al Rahman, *Merveilles biographiques et historiques ou chroniques*, translated by Chefik Mansour Bey, Abdulaziz Kalil Bey, Gabriel Nicolas Kalil Bey, Iskender Ammoun Effendi, Imprimerie Nationale, 1890

al-Tahtawi, Rifaa Rafi, *An Imam in Paris, Account of a Stay in France by an Egyptian Cleric (1826–1831)*, translated and introduced by Daniel L. Newman, Saqi, 2011

Aliye, Fatma, *Yasami-Sanati-Yapitlari ve Nisvan-i Islam*, Mutlu, 1993

Amanat, Abbas, *Pivot of the Universe: Nasir al-Din Shah Qajar and the Iranian Monarchy*, IB Tauris, 2008

Amanat, Abbas, *Resurrection and Renewal: The Making of the Babi Movement in Iran, 1844–1850*, Cornell University Press, 1989

Amanat, Abbas (trans. and ed.), *Taj al-Saltana, Crowning Anguish: Memoirs of a Persian Princess, from the Harem to Modernity*, Mage, 1993

Amin, Qasim, *The Liberation of Women and The New Woman: Two Documents in the History of Egyptian Feminism*, translated by Samiha Sidhom Peterson, The American University in Cairo Press, 2000.

Andrews, Walter G., and Kalpakli, Mehmet, *The Age of Beloveds: Love and the Beloved in Early-Modern Ottoman and European Culture and Society*, Duke University Press, 2005

Ansari, Ali M., *The Politics of Nationalism in Modern Iran*, Cambridge University Press, 2012

Atkin, Muriel, *Russia and Iran, 1780–1828*, University of Minnesota Press, 1980

Avery, Peter, Hambly, Gavin, Melville, Charles, *Cambridge History of Iran. Vol. 7: From Nadir Shah to the Islamic Republic*, Cambridge University Press, 1991

Ayalon, David, 'The Historian Al-Jabarti and His Background', *School of Oriental Studies Bulletin*, 23 (1960), pp. 217–49

Baron, Beth, 'Unveiling in Early Twentieth Century Egypt: Practical and Symbolic Considerations', *Middle Eastern Studies*, 25/3 (July 1989)

Badran, Margot, and Cooke, Miriam, *Opening the Gates: An Anthology of Arab Feminist Writing*, Indiana University Press, 2004

Barr, James, *A Line in the Sand: Britain, France and the Struggle for Mastery of the Middle East*, Simon and Schuster, 2011

Barrett, Alan H., 'A Memoir of Lieutenant-Colonel Joseph D'Arcy, R.A. 1780–1848', *Iran*, 43 (2005), pp. 241–74

Bell, Charles, *Khedives and Pashas: Sketches of Contemporary Egyptian Rulers and Statesmen*, Sampson Low, Marston, Searle and Rivington, 1884

Bell, Gertrude, *Safar Nameh*, Richard Bentley and Son, 1894

Bergesen, Albert J. (ed.), *The Sayyid Qutb Reader: Selected Writings on Politics, Religion and Society*, Routledge, 2008

Berkes, Niyazi, *The Development of Secularism in Turkey*, McGill University Press, 1964

Bianchi, Thomas-Xavier, *Notice sur le premier ouvrage d'anatomie et de medicine, imprimé en Turc, à Constantinople*, L. T. Cellot, 1821.

Blunt, Wilfred Scawen, *Gordon at Khartoum*, Stephen Swift and Co., 1911

Blunt, Wilfred Scawen, *My Diaries; being a personal narrative of events, 1888–1914*, Martin Secker, 1919

Blunt, Wilfred Scawen, *Secret History of the English Occupation of Egypt*, Alfred A. Knopf, 1922

Booth, Marilyn (ed.), *Harem Histories: Envisioning Places and Living Spaces*, Duke University Press, 2010

Boroujerdi, Mehrzad, *Iranian Intellectuals and the West: The Tormented Triumph of Nativism*, Syracuse University Press, 1996

Broadley, A. M., *How We Defended Arabi and His Friends*, Chapman and Hall, 1884

Browne, E. G., *The Persian of Revolution 1905 –1909*, Frank Cass, 1966

Browne, E. G. (ed.), *A Traveller's Narrative Written to Illustrate the Episode of the Bab*, Cambridge University Press, 1891

Browne, E. G., *A Year amongst the Persians*, Adam and Charles Black, 1970

Browne, E. G., *Materials for the Study of the Babi Religion*, Cambridge University Press, 1918

Browne, E. G., *The Press and Poetry of Modern Persia*, Cambridge University Press, 1914

Buchan, James, *Days of God: The Revolution in Iran and its Consequences*, John Murray, 2012

Budak, Ali, *Munif Pasa: Batililasma Surecinde Cok Yonlu Bir Osmanli Aydini*, Kitabevi, 2004

Burlamaqui, J. J., *Principles of Natural Law*, translated by Mr Nugent, J. Sheppard and G. Nugent, 1776

Bury, J. B., *The Idea of Progress*, Macmillan, 1920

Butcher, Edith Louise, *Things Seen in Egypt*, London, 1910

Cakir, Serpil, *Osmanli Kadin Hareketi*, Metis, 2013

Calvert, John, *Sayyid Qutb and the Origins of Radical Islamism*, Columbia University Press, 2010

Chambers, Richard L., 'The Education of a Nineteenth-Century Ottoman Alim, Ahmed Cevdet Pasa', *International Journal of Middle East Studies*, 4 (1973)

Chardin, Sir J., *Voyages en Perse, et autres lieux de l'Orient*, ed. Langles, Lenormant, Imprimeur-Librairie, 1811

Clot Bey, A-B., *Aperçu général sur l'Egypte*, Fortin, Masson et Cie, 1840

Cole, Juan, *Colonialism and Revolution in the Middle East: Social and Cultural Origins of Egypt's 'Urabi Movement'*, Princeton University Press, 1993

Cole, Juan, 'Feminism, Class and Islam in Turn-of-the-Century Egypt', *International Journal of Middle East Studies*, 13 (1981)

Cole, Juan, *Modernity and the Millennium: The Genesis of the Baha'i Faith in the Nineteenth-century Middle East*, Columbia University Press, 1998

Cole, Juan, *Napoleon's Egypt: Invading the Middle East*, Palgrave Macmillan, 2007

Cook, Michael, *A Brief History of the Human Race*, Granta, 2003

Cooper, Elizabeth, *The Women of Egypt*, Hurst and Blackett, 1914

Corbin, Henri, *Histoire de la philosophie islamique*, Gallimard, 1964

Cragg, Kenneth, *The Call of the Minaret*, Oxford University Press, 1964

Cresswell, 'The First Great Arabic Novel', *New York Review of Books*, 8 October 2015

Cromer, Earl of, *Modern Egypt*, Macmillan, 1908

Davison, Roderic H., *Reform in the Ottoman Empire, 1856–1876*, Princeton University Press, 1963

de Bellaigue, Christopher, *Patriot of Persia : Muhammad Mossadegh and a Very British Coup*, Bodley Head, 2012

De Kay, James E., *Sketches of Turkey in 1831 and 1832*, J. & J. Harper, 1833

Delanoue, Gilbert, *Moralistes et politiques musulmans dans l'Egypte du XIXième Siecle (1798–1882)*, Institut francais d'archéologie orientale du Caire, 1982

De Leon, Edwin, *Egypt under its Khedives*, Sampson Row, Marston, Searle and Rivington, 1882

Deringil, Selim, *The Well-Protected Domains: Ideology and Legitimation of Power in the Ottoman Empire, 1876–1909*, IB Tauris, 1998

d'Harcourt, Duc, *L'Egypte et les Egyptiens*, Librairie Plon, 1893

Di Amicis, Edmondo, *Constantinople*, trans. Stephen Parkin, Oneworld, 2010

Dodwell, Henry, *The Founder of Modern Egypt: A Study of Muhammad Ali*, Cambridge University Press, 1931

Douin, G., *Histoire du règne du Khédive Ismail*, Société Royale de Géographie d'Egypte, Cairo, 1933.

Duff-Gordon, Lucie (Lady), *Letters from Egypt, 1863–65*, Macmillan, 1865

Durant, Will, *Outlines of Philosophy: Plato to Russell*, Ernest Benn, 1962

Drouville, Gaspard, *Voyage en Perse*, Librairie nationale et étrangère, 1825

Ebuzziya, Ziyad, *Sinasi*, ed. Huseyin Celik, Iletisim, 1997

Edib, Halide, *Memoirs*, Century Co., 1926

Edib, Halide, *The Turkish Ordeal*, Century Co., 1928

El-Rouayheb, Khaled, *Before Homosexuality in the Arab-Islamic World, 1500–1800*, University of Chicago Press, 2005

Elshakry, Marwa, *Reading Darwin in Arabic*, University of Chicago Press, 2013

Ettehadieh, Mansoureh, *Zanani ke zir-e maghnaeh kolahdari nemudeand*, Tarikh-e Iran, 2009–10

Fahmy, Khaled, 'Women, Medicine, and Power in Nineteenth-Century Egypt', in Lila Abu-Lughod (ed.), *Remaking Women: Feminism and Modernity in the Middle East*, Princeton University Press, 1998

Fahmy, Ziad, *Ordinary Egyptians: Creating the Modern Nation through Popular Culture*, Stanford University Press, 2011

Fakhry, Majid, *Islamic Philosophy*, Oneworld, 2009

Fanon, Frantz, *The Wretched of the Earth*, Penguin, London, 1969

Farman Farmayan, Hafez, 'The Forces of Modernisation in Nineteenth-century Iran', in William R. Polk and Richard L. Chambers, *Beginnings of Modernisation in the Middle East*, University of Chicago Press, 1968

Faurrier, et al., *Description de L'Egypte, ou Recueil des Observations et des Recherches qui ont été faites en Egypte pendant l'Expédition de l'Armée française*, Imprimerie Imperiale, 1809–28

Feuvrier, Jean-Baptiste, *Trois ans à la cour de Perse*, F. Juven, 1900

Findley, Carter Vaughn, *Turkey, Islam, Nationalism, and Modernity : A History, 1789–2007*, Yale University Press, 2010

Findley, Carter Vaughn, 'Fatma Aliye: First Ottoman Woman Novelist', in *Histoire économique et sociale de l'empire ottoman et de la Turquie (1326–1960)*, Collection Turcica, vol. VIII, Peeters, 1995

Finkel, Caroline, *Osman's Dream: The Story of the Ottoman Empire, 1300–1923*, John Murray, 2005

Finn, Robert P., *The Early Turkish Novel, 1872–1900*, Isis, 1984

Fromkin, David, *A Peace to End All Peace: Creating the Modern Middle East, 1914–1922*, André Deutsch, 1989

Galland, Antoine, *Tableau de Egypte pendant le séjour de l'armée française*, Cerioux, Galland, an XI

Gesink, Indira Falk, *Islamic Reform and Conservatism: Al-Azhar and the Evolution of Modern Sunni Islam*, IB Tauris, 2010

Gibb, E. J. W., *A History of Ottoman Poetry*, Luzac, 1907

Gokalp, Ziya, *Turkish Nationalism and Western Civilisation*, translated and edited by Niyazi Berkes, George Allen and Unwin, 1959

Gran, Peter, *Islamic Roots of Capitalism: Egypt, 1760–1840*, University of Texas Press, 1979

Greaves, R., 'Relations with European Companies', in Avery, Hambly and Melville (eds), *Cambridge History of Iran. Vol. 7: From Nader Shah to the Islamic Republic*, Cambridge University Press, 1991

Green, Nile, *The Love of Strangers: What Six Muslim Students Learned in Jane Austen's London*, Princeton University Press, 2016

Guizot, F., *Lectures on European Civilisation*, translated by Priscilla Maria Beckwith, John Macrone, 1837

Gutas, Dimitri, *Greek Thought, Arabic Culture*, Routledge, 1998

Hatcher, John S., and Hemmat, Amrollah (eds), *The Poetry of Tahirih*, George Ronald, 2002

Halpern, Manfred, *The Politics of Social Change in the Middle East and North Africa*, Princeton University Press, 1963

Hamont, P. N., *L'Egypte sous Méhémet-Ali*, Leautey et Lecointe, 1845

Hanioglu, M. Sukru, *Blueprints for a Future Society: Late Ottoman Materialists on Science, Religion and Art*, from Ozdalga, Elisabeth (ed.), *Late Ottoman Society*, Routledge Curzon, 2005

Hanioglu, M. Sukru, *Bir Siyasal Dusunur olarak Doktor Abdullah Cevdet*, Ucdal Nesriyet, 1966

Hanioglu, M. Sukru, 'Notes on the Young Turks and the Freemasons', *Middle Eastern Studies*, 25/2 (1989)

Hawgood, John A., *Modern Constitutions since 1787*, Macmillan, 1939

Herold, J. Christopher, *Bonaparte in Egypt*, Hamish Hamilton, 1962

Heyd, Uriel, *Foundations of Turkish Nationalism: The Life and Teachings of Ziya Gokalp*, Luzac and Co. and the Harvill Press, 1950

Heyworth-Dunne, J., *An Introduction to the History of Education in Modern Egypt*, Frank Cass & Co., 1968

Hillenbrand, Robert, *Islamic Art and Architecture*, Thames and Hudson, 1999

Hourani, Albert, *Arabic Thought in the Liberal Age*, Oxford University Press, 1970

Hussein, Taha, *The Days*, translated by E. H. Paxton, Hilary Wayment and Kenneth Cragg, The American University in Cairo Press, 1997

Irwin, Robert, *For Lust of Knowing: The Orientalists and their Enemies*, Allen Lane, 2006

Issawi, Charles, *An Economic History of the Middle East and North Africa*, Methuen, 1982

Juchereau de Saint-Denys, A. de, *Révolutions de Constantinople en 1807 et 1808*, Librairie de Brissot-Thivars, 1819

Kadri, Sadakat, *Heaven on Earth: A Journey through Sharia Law*, Bodley Head, 2011

Jouannin, J. M. et Gaver, Jules van, *Turquie*, Paris, 1840

Kasravi, Ahmad, *History of the Iranian Constitutional Revolution*, vol. 1, trans. Evan Siegel, Mazda, 2006

Kasravi, Ahmad, *Tarikh-e Mashrouteh-e Iran*, Amir Kabir, n.d.

Katouzian, Homa, 'Sayyed Hassan Taqizadeh: Three Lives in a Lifetime', *Comparative Studies of South Asia, Africa and the Middle East*, 32/1 (2012)

Keddie, Nikki R., *Religion and Rebellion in Iran: The Tobacco Protest of 1891–1892*, Frank Cass, 1966

Keddie, Nikki R., *Sayyid Jamal ad-Din 'al-Afghani': A Political Biography*, University of California Press, 1972

Kedourie, Elie, *Afghani and Abduh: An Essay on Religious Unbelief and Political Activism in Modern Islam*, Frank Cass, 1966

Kelly, Laurence, *Diplomacy and Murder in Tehran: Alexander Griboyedov and Imperial Russia's Mission to the Shah of Persia*, IB Tauris, 2002

Ker Porter, Sir Robert, *Travels in Georgia, Persia, Armenia, Ancient Babylonia, &c*, Longman, Hurst, Rees, Orme and Brown, 1821

Kuntay, Mithat Cemal, *Namik Kemal*, Istanbul Universitesi Edebiyat Fakultesi Yayinlari, 1944

Kyle, Keith, *Suez: Britain's End of Empire in the Middle East*, Weidenfeld & Nicolson, 1972

Lane, Edward William, *An Account of the Manners and Customs of the Modern Egyptians*, Knight and Co., 1836

Lane-Poole, Stanley, *Life of Edward William Lane*, Williams and Norgate, 1877

Langles, L. (ed.), *Diatribe de l'ingénieur Séid Moustapha sur l'état actuel de l'art militaire, du génie et des sciences à Constantinople*, Ferra, 1810

Laurens, Henry, *L'Expédition d'Egypte*, Armand Colin, 1989

Lewis, Bernard (ed.), *Islam from the Prophet Muhammad to the Capture of Constantinople*, Oxford University Press, 1987

Lewis, Bernard, *The Muslim Discovery of Europe*, Weidenfeld and Nicolson, 1982

Lewis, Bernard, *The Emergence of Modern Turkey*, Oxford University Press, 1961

Lewis, Bernard, *What Went Wrong? The Clash between Islam and Modernity in the Middle East*, Weidenfeld and Nicolson, London, 2002

Livingston, J. W., 'Shaykhs Jabarti and Attar: Islamic Reaction and Response to Western Science in Egypt', *Der Islam*, 74 (1997), pp. 92–106

Lyons, Jonathan, *The House of Wisdom: How the Arabs Transformed Western Civilization*, Bloomsbury, 2009

MacFarlane, Charles, *Constantinople in 1828; a Residence of Sixteen Months in the Turkish Capital and Provinces*, Saunders and Otley, 1829

MacFarlane, Charles, *Turkey and its Destiny*, John Murray, 1850

Mahmoudi, Abdelrashid, *Taha Husain's Education: From the Azhar to the Sorbonne*, Curzon, 1998

Manafzadeh, Alireza, *Ahmad Kasravi: L'homme qui voulait sortir l'Iran de l'obscurantisme*, l'Harmattan, 2004

Mango, Andrew, *Atatürk*, John Murray, 1999

Mansel, Philip, *Constantinople: City of the World's Desire, 1453–1924*, John Murray, 1995

Mansel, Philip, *Levant: Splendour and Catastrophe on the Mediterranean*, John Murray, 2010

Mardin, Serif, *The Genesis of Young Ottoman Thought*, Princeton University Press, 1962

Marozzi, Justin, *Baghdad: City of Peace, City of Blood*, Allen Lane, 2014

Marsot, Afaf Lutfi al-Sayyid, *Egypt in the Reign of Muhammad Ali*, Cambridge University Press, 1984

Marsot, Afaf Lutfi al-Sayyid, 'Modernization among the Rectors of al-Azhar, 1798–1879', in William R. Polk and Richard L. Chambers, *Beginnings of Modernization in the Middle East*, University of Chicago, 1968

Marsot, Afaf Lutfi al-Sayyid, A Comparative Study of 'Abd al-Rahman al-Jabarti and Niqula al-Turk', in Daniel Crecelius (ed.), *Eighteenth Century Egypt: The Arabic Manuscript Sources*, Regina, 1990

Massie, Robert K., *Peter the Great*, Victor Gollancz, 1981

Mazower, Mark, *Salonica, City of Ghosts: Christians, Muslims and Jews, 1430–1950*, Harper Perennial, 2004

McCullagh, Francis, *The Fall of Abd-ul-Hamid*, Methuen and Co., 1910

McMeekin, Sean, *The Ottoman Endgame: War, Revolution and the Making of the Modern Middle East, 1908–1923*, Allen Lane, 2015

Midhat, Ali Haydar, *The Life of Midhat Pasha*, John Murray, 1903

Mishra, Pankaj, *From the Ruins of Empire: The Revolt against the West and the Remaking of Asia*, Allen Lane, 2012

Mitchell, Richard P., *The Society of Muslim Brothers*, Oxford University Press, 1969

Montana, Ismael M., *The Abolition of Slavery in Ottoman Tunisia*, University Press of Florida, 2013

Montgomery Watt, W., *Islamic Philosophy and Theology*, Edinburgh University Press, 1985

Morier, James, *A Second Journey through Persia, Armenia and Asia Minor, to Constantinople*, Longman, Hurst, Ress, Orme and Brown, 1818

Mottahedeh, Negar, 'Ruptured Spaces and Effective Histories: The Unveiling of the Babi Poet Qurrat-al-Ayn-Tahirih in the Gardens of Badasht', *UCLA Historical Journal*, 17 (1997)

Mottahedeh, Roy, *The Mantle of the Prophet*, Oneworld, 2000

Mowafi, Reda, *Slavery, Slave Trade and Abolition Attempts in Egypt and the Sudan, 1820–1882*, Scandinavian University Books, 1981

Nabil Zarandi, Sheikh Muhammad, trans. and ed. Shoghi Effendi, *The Dawn-Breakers: Nabil's Narrative of the Early Days of the Baha'i Revelation*, Baha'i Publishing Trust, 1953

Nazem al-Islam Kermani, Mirza K., *Tarikh-e Bidari-ye Iranian*, Chapkhaneh-e Majles, 1945–46

Nisbet, Robert, *History of the Idea of Progress*, Heinemann, 1980

Okay, M. Orhan, *Besir Fuad: Ilk Turk Pozitivist ve Naturalisti*, Hareket Yayinlari, 1969

Otte, T. G., 'A Course of Unceasing Remonstrance': British Diplomacy and the Suppression of the Slave Trade in the East, 1852–1898', in Keith Hamilton and Patrick Salmon, *Slavery, Diplomacy and Empire: Britain and the Suppression of the Slave Trade, 1807–1975*, Sussex Academic Press, 2009

Ouseley, William, *Travels in Various Countries of the East, more particularly, Persia*, Rodwell and Martin, 1823

Pamuk, Sevket, *The Ottoman Empire and European Capitalism, 1820–1913*, Cambridge University Press, 1987

Panzac, Daniel, *La Peste dans l'empire ottoman, 1700–1850*, Editions Peeters, 1985

Parker, John W., 'Kaghaz-e Akhbar', *Journal of the Royal Asiatic Society*, V (1839)

Paton, A. A., *History of the Egyptian Revolution, from the Period of the Mamelukes to the Death of Mohammed Ali*, Trubner and Co., 1870

Pedersen, Susan, *The Guardians: The League of Nations and the Crisis of Empire*, Oxford, 2015

Perkins, Kenneth J., *History of Modern Tunisia*, Cambridge University Press, 2014

Qutb, Sayyid, *A Child from the Village*, Syracuse University Press, 2004

Rahnama, Ali, *An Islamic Utopian: A Political Biography of Ali Shariati*, IB Tauris, 2014

Rapport, Mike, *1848: Year of Revolution*, Little, Brown, 2008.

Raymond, André, *Artisans at Commerçants au Caire au XVIIIe siècle*, Institut français d'archéologie orientale, Cairo, 1999

Richard, Yann, *L'Iran: naissance d'une république islamique*, Editions de la Martinière, 2006

Roberts, Andrew, *Napoleon the Great*, Allen Lane, 2014

Rodenbeck, Max, *Cairo: The City Victorious*, Picador, 1998

Rodenbeck, Max, 'Islam Confronts its Demons', *New York Review of Books*, 29 April 2004

Rodenbeck, Max, 'The Father of Violent Islamism', *New York Review of Books*, 9 May 2013

Rogan, Eugene, *The Arabs: A history*, Basic Books, 2009

Rogan, Eugene, *The Fall of the Ottomans; The Great War in the Middle East, 1914–1920*, Allen Lane, 2015

Ruthven, Malise, *Islam in the World*, Penguin, 1984

Saleh Shirazi, Muhammad Mirza, *Majmueyi Safarnamehha*, Negar Muasser, 2008–9

Scholch, Alexander, *Egypt for the Egyptians!: The Socio-Political Crisis in Egypt 1878–1882*, Ithaca, 1981

Sedgwick, Mark, *Muhammad Abduh*, Oneworld, 2010

Shaarawi, Huda, *Harem Years: The Memoirs of an Egyptian Feminist*, trans. Margo Badran, Virago, 1986

Sheil, Mary (Lady), *Glimpses of Life and Manners in Persia*, John Murray, 1856

Shlaim, Avi, *War and Peace in the Middle East*, Penguin, 1995

Shushtari, Abdullatif, 'Tuhfat al-alam va Zayl al-Tuhfah', *Ketabkhane-ye Tahouri*, 1363 (1984/85)

Shuster, Morgan, *The Strangling of Persia*, T. Fisher Unwin, 1912

Silvera, Alain, 'The First Egyptian Student Mission to France under Muhammad Ali', *Middle East Studies*, XVI/2 1980, pp 1–22

Sinasi, Ibrahim, *Makaleler*, ed. Fevziye Abdullah Tansel, Dun-Bugun Yayinevi, 1960

Siviloglu, Murat Remzi, 'The Emergence of Public Opinion in the Ottoman Empire, 1826–1876', doctoral dissertation, Cambridge University, 2014

Sohrabi, Nader, *Revolution and Constitutionalism in the Ottoman Empire and Iran*, Cambridge University Press, 2011

Steegmuller, Francis, *Flaubert in Egypt*, Michael Haag, 1983

Stone, Norman, *Turkey: A Short History*, Thames and Hudson, 2010

Sykes, Ella C., *Persia and its People*, Methuen and Co., 1910

Sykes, Ella C., *Through Persia on a Side-Saddle*, John MacQueen, 1901

Sykes, Percy, *A History of Persia*, Macmillan, 1958

Tabatabai, Seyed Javad, *Dibachei dar Nazariyeh-ye Enhetat-e Iran*, Negah-e Moasser, 2010–11

Tanpinar, Ahmet Hamdi, *19. Asir Türk Edebiyati Tarihi*, Cagalayan Kitabevi, 1967

Taqizadeh, Hassan, *Zendegi Tufani*, ed. Iraj Afshar, Elmi, 1979–80

Temperley, Harold, *England and the Near East: The Crimea*, Longmans, Green and Co., 1936

Thompson, Elizabeth F., *Justice Interrupted: TheStruggle for Constitutional Government in the Middle East*, Harvard University Press, 2013

Toledano, Ehud R., *The Ottoman Slave Trade and its Suppression, 1840–1890*, Princeton University Press, 1982

Toledano, Ehud R., *Slavery and Abolition in the Ottoman Middle East*, University of Washington Press, 1998

Tucker, Judith E., *Women in Nineteenth-Century Egypt*, Cambridge University Press, 1985

Vatikiotis, P. J., *The History of Modern Egypt: From Muhammad Ali to Mubarak*, Weidenfeld and Nicolson, 1991

von Kotzebue, Moritz, *Narrative of Journey into Persia*, Longman, Hurst, Rees, Orme and Brown, 1819

Walsh, R., *A Residence at Constantinople*, Frederick Westley and A. H. Davis, 1836

White, Charles, *Three Years in Constantinople*, London, Henry Colburn, 1846

Wright, Denis, *The English among the Persians: Imperial Lives in Nineteenth-Century Iran*, IB Tauris, 2001

Wright, Denis, *The Persians among the English: Episodes in Anglo-Persian History*, IB Tauris, 1986

Wright, William, *A Tidy Little War*, Spellmount, 2009

Index